*Anarchist
Thinkers
and Thought*

Anarchist Thinkers and Thought

An Annotated Bibliography

Compiled and Edited by
Paul Nursey-Bray

with the assistance of
Jim Jose *and* Robyn Williams

*Bibliographies and Indexes in Law
and Political Science, Number 17*

Greenwood Press
New York • Westport, Connecticut • London

Library of Congress Cataloging-in-Publication Data

Nursey-Bray, Paul F.
    Anarchist thinkers and thought : an annotated bibliography /
compiled and edited by Paul Nursey-Bray with the assistance of Jim
Jose and Robyn Williams.
        p.   cm.—(Bibliographies and indexes in law and political
science, ISSN 0882-7052 ; no. 17)
    Includes index.
    ISBN 0-313-27592-0 (alk. paper)
    1. Anarchists—Bibliography. 2. Anarchism—Bibliography.
I. Jose, Jim, 1952- . II. Williams, Robyn. III. Title.
IV. Series.
Z7164.A52N87   1992
[HX833]
016.335′83′0922—dc20   91-33407

British Library Cataloguing in Publication Data is available.

Library of Congress Catalog Card Number: 91-33407
ISBN: 0-313-27592-0
ISSN: 0882-7052

First published in 1992

Greenwood Press, 88 Post Road West, Westport, CT 06881
An imprint of Greenwood Publishing Group, Inc.

Printed in the United States of America

(∞)™

The paper used in this book complies with the
Permanent Paper Standard issued by the National
Information Standards Organization (Z39.48-1984).

10 9 8 7 6 5 4 3 2 1

For Rosie

Contents

Preface

The bibliography was begun in 1983 as an extended reading list for a course that I was preparing on anarchist political theory. It gradually assumed a shape and size that suggested the idea of turning it into a full-scale annotated bibliography The present volume is the result. As it has been in preparation there has been a growing interest in anarchist theory and history, manifest in the ever increasing body of relevant literature. It is hoped that the present volume does justice both to that literature and to the interest.

The University of Adelaide has provided a number of grants that have enabled research assistance to be organized for the pursuance of the project. I would like to record my gratitude. I also wish to thank the Barr Smith Library at the University of Adelaide, with particular thanks to Les Howard and Teresa Atkinson.

The secretarial staff of the Politics Department have worked long and hard on a number of versions of the bibliography. I would like to thank Christine Hill, Ruth Ellickson, and Tina Esca for the enthusiasm they have shown for the project, and their help in negotiating tight corners!

I would like to record my appreciation of the efforts of other members of the team that compiled and annotated the bibliography, Jim Jose and Robyn Williams. With myself they share the collective responsibility for the final product.

Lastly, on a personal note I would like to thank Ron Sampson, who first inspired in me an interest in anarchist ideas, and Rosie and my children, Melissa, Joanna, Mark and Sarah, for their continuing support.

Paul Nursey-Bray

Introduction

Among the great traditions of political thought Anarchism is the poor relation. While the historical impact of anarchist movements has been acknowledged, the theories that animated, inspired and set in train such movements, have, in general, been accorded far less respect. Rejected by both Marxists and liberals alike, although for quite different reasons, anarchism has been popularly dismissed, somewhat paradoxically, as both utopian and nihilistic. But it is the latter characterization that is dominant. It is a regrettable fact that the wing of the anarchist movement that argues for the limited programme of *le propagande par le fait* has secured an almost exclusive hold on the popular imagination. The cloaked, mustachioed figure, with the smoking bomb, has cast a long shadow, diminishing the anarchist espousal of individual autonomy and equality, and obscuring the anarchist vision of a community of free individuals harmoniously regulating their own affairs. Moreover, this identification of anarchism with nihilist violence completely ignores the fervent rejection of violence by pacifist anarchists like Tolstoy, undervalues the reformist anarchism of Godwin and Goodman, and places in a false light the utilitarian espousal of violence by revolutionary anarchism which it shares with other contemporary radical traditions.

The misunderstandings that have bedevilled anarchism have proceeded partly from ignorance. But it is also true that competing schools of thought, not least the Marxist, have contributed to deliberate misinterpretations. Whatever the cause of the problem, however, it is clear that, as a corrective, more knowledge regarding anarchism needs to be disseminated. It is hoped that the present bibliography will be serviceable in this cause. It is not, of course, intended as a complete compilation of all sources. Rather it is offered as a basis on which others may be encouraged to build.

What is Anarchism ?

In seeking to answer any such question of definition there is bound to be contention. It is not claimed that a complete answer is provided. However, in introducing a collection of works about anarchism, there must be some discussion of what the term was taken to mean, so that the process of thought underlying the selection can be understood.

On the face of it the question is easily answered. Yet anarchist theory is more diverse than it appears to be at first glance. This is not only true of the wide variety of approaches to the issue of how an anarchist society is to be brought into being, that range from education through passive resistance to violent insurrection. It is also true of the views regarding the actual form of the anarchist society that is to be created.

The belief in the autonomy of the individual and the consequent opposition to authority, vested in institutions like states, was used as a basic criterion. All anarchists, it was assumed, eschew the state, or any central form of organized authority, as violations of the individual's right to self-direction and self-regulation. In their place most anarchists would create decentralized, small, self-regulating communities linked to each other federally for purposes of co-ordination and the pursuance of large-scale projects. While there are variations as to the extent and complexity of the federal organization envisaged, and while, for egoistic anarchists like Stirner the vision of cooperation without central authority is bleak, nonetheless, broadly speaking, the criterion can be applied effectively.

On this basis it is clear where anarchism departs from liberalism, as Godwin departed from Paine, on the question of state authority. It must not be merely diminished. For true individual autonomy to thrive it must be abolished. In this vision of a stateless, self-regulating society of autonomous individuals, the anarchist tradition, in political terms at least, precedes the Marxist.

It is the question of property that provides the major source of division regarding an anarchist vision of the future, with societies based both on communal and private ownership being advocated. The dominant view of property relations is that associated with the main stream of the revolutionary tradition of anarchist communism in Europe and America, community ownership. It is this view to which Bakunin, Kropotkin, Malatesta, Berkman, Goldman and many others subscribe. It was described by Kropotkin in the terms similar to those used by Marx to describe the final stage of communism, a situation where "everybody, contributing for the common well-being to the full extent of his capacities, shall enjoy also from the common stock of society to the fullest possible extent of his needs." (*Revolutionary Pamphlets*, op.cit., entry 538, p.59). This approach to property highlights what must be seen as another crucial distinguishing characteristic of the anarchist tradition, the adherence to the principle of equality. It is a principle of equality that, for communist anarchists, demands not simply equal rights for individuals entering society, but the enjoyment of a continuous operative equality in the social relationships of a society based on communal ownership.

The acceptance of private property by various anarchists places their concern for equality and liberty in a number of different settings. For William Godwin the right to control the product of one's own labor was intrinsic to the right to private judgement that, for him, was the essence of liberty. But this private ownership of the product of one's own labor was radically tempered by his notion of altruistic distribution. By freely distributing the fruits of production, in accordance with a utility principle that specified that one should keep only that which by its retention will not diminish the general good, Godwin's citizenry could achieve a community of property that could coexist with individual ownership of production.

For Proudhon, while the appropriation of collective labor by an employer is a species of theft, individual ownership of labor power and its products is the basis for the system of communal exchange that he termed Mutualism. Proudhon's belief was in economic systems based on free, mutual agreements, between communities of workers, to exchange the products of their labor on the basis of the value of labor power. While distribution was to labor value rather than to need, nevertheless Proudhon envisaged an essentially egalitarian society the social relations of which would be based on justice. Free credit, giving everyone the opportunity to borrow money without interest, would, Proudhon believed, tend to reduce profits to a minimum and diminish, if not remove, riches as well as poverty. The source of economic inequality, monopoly, would be denied an existence. Speculation and unearned wealth would disappear. The Mutualist system of Proudhon envisaged a community, or federated communities, wherein the system of production and exchange based on labor value is exclusive of monopoly and central authority, and maintains that level of equality necessary for mutual exchange to work.

It was Robert Owen's ideas on cooperation that initially inspired the American tradition of individualist anarchism, although the ideas of Fourier and Proudhon were also significant for its development. Josiah Warren, the originator, and most important theorist, of individualist anarchism, advocated stateless, cooperative, voluntary associations of sovereign individuals. Property, essential to individual sovereignty, would be privately owned, but there would be equitable exchange on the basis of the cost of labor and mutual agreement. Warren's "Time Store," the site for the free exchange of products on the basis of labor time, the work of greatest repugnance securing the highest remuneration, epitomizes his ideas. While strict equality was not a goal, economic justice and equity for members of the voluntary community was essential. Cost was to be the limit of price, most importantly of labor power. Profiteering and speculation would cease and banking and the credit system would be replaced by exchange on the basis of labor cost. With labor justly rewarded, all would work. Monopoly would vanish with the abolition of the state authority that protected it. The ideas of Warren, and of disciples like

Stephen Pearl Andrews and William B. Greene, were synthesized and transmitted by Benjamin Tucker in his journal *Liberty*. Tucker extended the attack on Monopoly with his stigmatization of the four monopolies, of land, of credit, of tariffs and of patents and copyrights, all created and backed by the state and all sources of evil in society.

Linking all of these approaches, the communist, the Godwinian, the mutualist, the individualist anarchist, despite the dissimilarity of the ideas on the ownership of property, is not just the belief in individual liberty and its corollary, the opposition to central or state authority, but also a belief in community, and an equality of community members. This community ideal underlies the classic anarchist strategy of decentralization of the social order. Of course, the concept of community is at best elusive. It has beguiled political thinkers from the time that the *polis* was first conjectured as community. Nevertheless, for anarchists, the desired level of liberty and equality is only to be found in a small community that must, by definition, have achieved a remarkable degree of unity and self-regulation. If the ideal liberal community can be seen as one where high levels of consensus and individual responsibility have made an intrusive state unnecessary, as it is undesirable, the anarchist community can be seen as one where the level of consensus and self-regulation is such as to make the state redundant.

In a sense we have closed the circle, since we have returned to the first criterion. The criterion of individual autonomy and statelessness demands a more perfect community, involving self-regulation and a voluntary adherence to the community will or counsel, however formed and expressed. This more perfect community must demand a harmony among its members that should, in theory, set limits to inequality and division of wealth and interest, regardless of the strict form of ownership. As with Rousseau, it is the continuing consensus that is of the essence.

The division over forms of property, while clearly of great significance, should not be allowed to obscure the commonality of the idea of the free community of self-regulating individuals. Communist anarchists will continue to decry mutualists and individualist anarchists as naive in their belief that the inequalities and divisions fostered by private ownership can be constrained by mutual agreement and political community. In their turn, communist anarchists will continue to be criticized as ingenuous in believing that communal systems of ownership can be organized without central authority. But there are meeting points in the crucial ideas of individual autonomy and community that suggest, at the least, a basis for the discussion of equality and property relations.

Scope

The bibliography focuses on the nature and development of anarchism as a tradition of political thought. Accordingly, prime emphasis has been placed on anarchist thinkers, those works in which they develop their ideas and commentaries on those ideas. However, anarchist movements have not been neglected. The section entitled "The Anarchist Experience" provides a number of readings listed by country.

While an effort has been made to include as many thinkers as possible in the separate listings of the first section, limitations on space, and on the availability of material, have meant that some thinkers have had to be omitted. Thus, while the majority of the major anarchist communist thinkers are covered, some important individuals like Luigi Fabbri, Carlo Cafiero and Paul Brousse have not been accorded a distinct status. While key representative figures have been singled out from the individualist anarchist tradition, others like Henry Bool, Joshua Ingalls, William B. Greene, E. C. Walker and Ezra Heywood have not been so distinguished. Information on all such individuals can be found in the section on general theory and history, or in the section on the appropriate country in the discussion of the anarchist experience.

The omission of Gandhi from the first section also needs a word of explanation. Gandhi's philosophy certainly raises issues of relevance and importance to anarchism. Although *Satyagraha* is more a philosophy of moral action than a designation of any particular societal form, Gandhi's views on village communities have resonances with key anarchist themes. However, the treatment of community theory on which they are based has important reference points outside the Western tradition. To include Gandhi in a major way would be to raise questions about the inclusion of ideas on the African traditional community, African socialism etc. The decision was made, therefore, to provide only a representative selection of work, by, or on Gandhi, in the sub-section on India.

As with any tradition of political theory there are, on the margin, areas of definitional difficulty. In the case of anarchism these areas exist where the concerns of the tradition intersect with those of socialism and of liberalism. These areas have been dealt with by the inclusion of two sections explicitly concerned with marginal cases, the first concerned with the theorists Ivan Illich, William Morris and Murray Rothbard, the second with contemporary debates within liberal theory that raise issues pertinent to anarchism.

The theses that have been cited have been those that have a clear and obvious anarchist content. Theses of marginal relevance were not included. Every effort has been made to check the existence and verify the addresses of the contemporary journals cited. Since they are, by the nature of the thing, frequently ephemeral, some errors may exist. It was felt that the list should be kept as full as possible to maximize its utility as a resource.

A decision was also made to limit the selection to works in English, except where, in the case of major thinkers, works do not exist in translation. Where there are several publications the latest and/or most easily available is cited. However, where other editions are distinguished by their introductions, they too are cited. The existence of such introductions is commented on in the annotation of the works in question. American editions of volumes published in England, and vice versa, have also been included. Throughout all sections works are listed alphabetically. Articles in anarchist journals have been cited where they are written by a major anarchist thinker, or where they bear on a specific issue in anarchist theory or history. Other articles in such journals have not been included in order to prevent the bibliography from becoming unwieldy. Reference can be made to the journals themselves which are listed in the appropriate section.

Generally the work is fully annotated, although there are a small number of entries where an annotation does not exist. Either the work was newly published and had not found its way to Adelaide at the time of publication, or it was a newly found citation that had to be checked outside Australia, which was not possible in the time available. Where such entries appeared important they were inserted without annotation.

Sources

Four main methods were used to compile the lists of entries and to annotate them; computer searches, inter-library loans, consultation of reference works, and research trips to libraries in Australia and in Europe.

Initially material was gathered by bibliographic computer searches, using in particular the Australian Bibliographic Network and the Dialog Information Retrieval Service. The *Social Science Index* on CD(ROM) was another useful computer generated resource.

The Inter-Library Loan system was used to get copies of books and photocopies of articles from other libraries in Australia, New Zealand, the United States, Canada and the United Kingdom.

The reference works that were consulted included : (1) Current Publication Information: *Books in Print; Ulrich's International Periodicals Directory; Whitaker's Books in Print; Willings Press Guide;* (2) Abstracts and Indexes: *Economic Abstracts; The Education Index; Environment Index; History Abstracts; International Political Science Abstracts; Journal of Economic Literature; The Philosopher's Index; Social Science Citation Index; Social Sciences Index; Sociological Abstracts; Women Studies Abstracts;* (3) Library Catalogs: *British Library Catalogue; Library of Congress Catalog;* (4) Book Reviews: *Book Review Digest; Book Review Index; An Index to Book Reviews in the Humanities;* (5) Periodical Lists: *British Union Catalogue of Periodicals; Catalog Collectif des Périodiques; New Serial Titles; Union List of Serials;* (6) Dissertation List: *American Doctoral Dissertations; The BRITS Index; Comprehensive Dissertation Index; Dissertation Abstracts; Theses in Australian Universities; Theses in Canadian Political Studies.*

Finally, research was undertaken in various libraries using their collections. The most important libraries in this respect were the Barr-Smith Library, University of Adelaide; the Australian National Library,

Canberra; the British Library, London; the British Library of Economic and Political Science, London School of Economics; the Library of the University of London; British Library Newspaper Collection, Colindale, London; Biblioteca Nazionale, Florence.

Paul Nursey-Bray,
Department of Politics,
University of Adelaide.

Anarchist Philosophers
and Thinkers

GUY ALDRED (1886-1963)

Works by Aldred :

1. *Bakunin.* 'The Word' Library. Second series, no. 1. Glasgow: Strickland Pr., 1940. Useful discussion of Bakunin, particularly of his relationship with Marx and Marxism.

2. *The Chicago Martyrs.* With portraits of the comrades who were tried. London: Freedom Pr., 1912. A discussion and description of the Haymarket Meeting with excerpts from the trial speeches.

3. *Pioneers of Anti-Parliamentarism.* Glasgow: The Strickland Pr., 1940. A selection of short essays written as a tribute to the pioneers of anti-parliamentarianism. Discusses the lives and activities of Bakunin, Morris, Most and Malatesta, with personal reminiscences of them. Aldred asserts an uncompromising faith in true proletarian socialism and opposition to the parliamentary socialism of Labor leaders, whom, he argues, have betrayed the working class.

4. *The Possibility and Philosophy of Anarchist Communism.* London: Bakunin Pr., 1907. A pamphlet that argues for anarchism as the correct anticipation of the future state of society.

5. *Studies in Communism.* Glasgow: The Strickland Pr., 1946. Contains several essays by Aldred including "The Case for Anarchism," 5-11, previously published as *The Possibility and Philosophy of Anarchist Communism,* op.cit., entry 4.

Works about Aldred :

6. Caldwell, J. T. *Come Dungeons Dark: The Life and Times of Guy Aldred, Glasgow Anarchist*. Barr, Ayrshire: Luath Pr., 1988. A biography of one of the leading propagandists of the British anarchist movement. Aldred was an active proponent of anti-parliamentary socialism who believed in the non-violent creation of communes. He founded the Strickland Press in 1939. Includes bibliography.

7. Jones, R. W. "Anti-Parliamentarism and Communism in Britain 1917-1921" *The Raven* 3,3 (July/Sept. 1990): 245-62. There is some consideration of Guy Aldred's activities in a discussion of the British anti-parliamentary movement in the period preceding the formation of the Anti-Parliamentary Communist Federation in 1921.

8. Walter, N. "Guy A. Aldred 1886-1986." *The Raven* 1,1 (1986): 77-92. A discussion of the life and ideas of Guy Aldred on the centenary of his birth. Walter describes him as "one of the most energetic and eccentric figures ever involved in the British anarchist movement."

STEPHEN PEARL ANDREWS (1812-1886)

Works by Andrews :

9. *Love, Marriage and Divorce, and the Sovereignty of the Individual: A Discussion Between Henry James, Horace Greeley and Stephen Pearl Adams*. Boston: 1889. A collection of the pieces written in the course of a controversy that raged in the columns of the New York *Tribune* in April 1853 following a reply by Andrews to a review of Josiah Warren's *Equitable Commerce*. Andrews defends Warren's principles vigorously.

10. *The Science of Society*. Edited by Charles Shively. Weston, Mass.: M & S Pr., 1970. Andrews was an individualist anarchist who was influenced by Josiah Warren and elaborated upon his ideas. *The Science of Society* was published in New York in 1852 in two parts. This version contains both the first part, "True Constitution of Government in the Sovereignty of the Individual as the Final Development of Protestantism, Democracy and Socialism," and the second, "Cost the Limit of Price: Scientific Measure and Honesty in Trade as one of the Fundamental Principles of the Solutions of the Social Problem." It was regarded by contemporaries as a first class statement of Warren's philosophy. Argues for the need to establish scientific laws for the true constitution of human government on the basis of the sovereignty of the individual. Concludes that people need not govern each other if they each govern themselves.

11. *The Sovereignty of the Individual*. Berkeley Hts., N.J.: Freeman Pr., 1938. Andrews collaborated with Josiah Warren and was involved with utopian

experiments such as "Modern Times." This is a reprint of the first part of *The Science of Society*, op.cit., entry 10.

Works about Andrews :

12. Hall, B. N. "The Economic Theories of Stephen Pearl Andrews: Neglected Utopian Writer." *South African Journal of Economics* 43,1 (March 1975): 45-55. Reviews Andrews' ideas regarding a labor theory of value and his use of the value of labor as the basis for currency, exchange and remuneration.

13. Wish, H. "Stephen Pearl Andrews, American Pioneer Sociologist." *Social Forces* 19 (May 1941): 477-82.

14. Martin, J. J. *Men Against the State: The Expositors of Individualist Anarchism in America, 1827-1908.* Colorado Springs: Ralph Myles, 1970. First published Dekalb, Ill: Adrian Allen, 1953. Contains a discussion of the ideas of Andrews, of his association with Josiah Warren. See entry 1838.

15. Dorfman, J. "The Philosophical Anarchists: Josiah Warren, Stephen Pearl Andrews." In *The Economic Mind in American Civilization*. Vol. 2, 671-78. New York: Viking Pr., 1944. A discussion of the economic and social ideas of the two individual anarchist proponents of equitable commerce.

16. Stern, M. B. *The Pantarch: A Biography of Stephen Pearl Andrews.* Austin: Univ. of Texas Pr., 1971. A biography that discusses the various roles played by Andrews; an American reformer, advocate of civil rights, supporter of reformed spelling and author of pioneering work on sociology. It also considers his dubious status as a crank.

17. Rocker, R. *Pioneers of American Freedom.* Los Angeles, Rocker Pubns. Comm., 1949. A discussion of the origins of liberal and radical individualist thought in America with a consideration of Stephen Pearl Andrews, 70-85.

ÉMILE ARMAND (ERNST LUCIEN JUIN) (1872-1962)

Works by Armand :

18. *Anarchism and Individualism: Three Essays.* London: S. E. Parker, 1962. Armand, who was influenced by Tolstoy, was a Christian anarchist. This short collection of pieces emphasizes the value of autonomy and of the free individual.

19. "Life as Experience." & "Life and Society." In *Man! An Anthology of Anarchist Ideas, Essays, Poetry and Commentaries*, 4-9. Op.cit., entry 1389. Two essays that deal with the development of the individual and the relation of the individual to society in individualist anarchism.

MIKHAIL BAKUNIN (1814-1876)

Works by Bakunin :

20. *A mes amis Russes et Polonais*. Traduit du Russe. Leipzig: 1862.

21. "Bourgeois Socialism." *Freedom* 24,310 (Feb. 1915). A letter from Bakunin to the Press Committee of the journal *Égalité* in Geneva, offering several articles on the difference between True Socialism and the "ridiculous socialism" of the bourgeoisie.

22. "Catéchisme révolutionnaire". In *Ni Dieu Ni maître*, edited by Daniel Guérin. Paris: Éditions de Delphes, 1965. Written while Bakunin's association with Nechayev was at its closest his contribution to the authorship of this pamphlet, outlining the duties of a revolutionary dedicated to violence, is the subject of great controversy. See entries 52, 57, 63, 97, 104, 111, 112.

23. *The Confession of Mikhail Bakunin*. With the marginal comments of Tsar Nicholas I. Translated by Robert C. Howes. Notes by Lawrence D. Orton. Ithica, New York: Cornell Univ. Pr., 1977. Written in 1851 to Tsar Nicholas, it was not published in Bakunin's lifetime. Excerpts were published in 1919 and it was published in full, in Russian, in 1921. It covers the period 1840-49, from Bakunin's arrival in Berlin to his arrest and eventual deportation to Russia, charting his philosophical shift away from German idealism.

24. *A Criticism of State Socialism*. With an afterword on modern state socialism. London: Coptic P. on behalf of Cuddon's Cosmopolitan Review, 1968. Extracted from Bakunin's writings the essay sets out his position on authority, and on revolution, and details his critical attitude to Marx.

25. *A Critique of State Socialism*. With drawings by Richard Warren. Sanday, Orkney: Cienfuegos Pr., 1981. A cartoon with Bakunin's arguments against state socialism expressed in dialogue.

26. *Fédéralisme, socialisme, antithéologisme*. Proposition motivé au comitée centrale de la ligue de la paix et de la liberté. Lausanne: Éditions l'Age d'Homme, 1971. Also published in *Oeuvres 1*. Paris: 1895. See entry 28.

27. *God and the State*. With a preface by Carlo Cafiero and Elisée Reclus. Reprint of the 1916 edition. New York: Books for Libraries Pr., Freeport, 1971. Written in February-March 1871 the first part was published in July 1871 as *L'empire knouto-Germanique*. The second part was published posthumously in 1908. In 1882 Reclus and Cafiero published an extract from the manuscript under the title *Dieu et l'état*. The first correct text in French is in Vol. III of *Oeuvres*. Paris: 1908. The first correct English edition

published London: Freedom Pr., 1910, a translation based on that made by Tucker and published in Boston: 1883. Bakunin's classic attack on state authority and the role of religion in its maintenance. Paraphrasing Voltaire he declares that, "if God really existed, it would be necessary to abolish him."

28. *Oeuvres*. Vol. 1 edited by Max Nettlau; vols. 2-6 edited by James Guillame, Paris: 1895-1913; Paris: Stock, 1972-.

29. *The Organisation of the International, 1814-1876*. Translated by Freda Cohen. London: Bakunin Pr., 1919. First published 1872 in *Almanach du Peuple*. Also appears in *Mikail Bakunin: From out of the Dustbin*, op. cit., entry 43. Asserts that the power of mass organization, combined with science, can accomplish the goals of the people. As well as a statement of grievances, it is a call for unity of purpose and method.

30. *The Paris Commune and the Idea of the State*. London: Centre International de Récherche sur l'Anarchisme, 1971. Bakunin's essay on the Paris Commune written during June 1871 and found among his papers at his death. Intended by Bakunin as a preamble to the second part of *The Knouto-Germanic Empire*, it first appeared, in part, in *Le Travailleur* 2,4 (April/May 1878), published by Elisée Reclus. The essay as a whole was first published by Bernard Lazare in *Entretiens Politiques et Littéraires*, 5,29 (1892), and as a separate pamphlet, with a preface by Kropotkin, in 1899.

31. *The Policy of the International*. First instalment appeared in *L'Égalité* 29,7 (Aug. 1869). London: Bakunin Pr., 1919. It also appears in *Mikail Bakunin: From out of the Dustbin*, op. cit., entry 43. Argues that the policy of the International must ignore religious beliefs and political affiliations when considering membership, since to focus on such issues is to destroy unity between workers. The aim of the International, it is asserted, must be economic emancipation through practical action, and under no circumstance should an alliance with the bourgeoisie be considered.

32. *La révolution sociale ou la dictature militaire,*. Présentation par André Prudhommeaux. Paris: 1946.

33. "The State and German Social Democracy." *Freedom* 28,303 (July 1914): 50. A discussion of the German social-democratic party written at Locarno, 3-9 September, 1870.

34. *Statism and Anarchy*. Translated by C. H. Plummer. Edited by J. F. Harrison. New York: Revisionist Pr., 1976. Bakunin's definitive critique of the State, in particular the Marxist theory of the State. It contains some key ideas regarding intellectuals.

35. *La théologie politique de Mazzini et l'Internationale*. Neuchatel: 1871. Infuriated by Mazzini's condemnation of the Communards Bakunin wrote this pamphlet criticizing him.

36. "An Unpublished Letter: Bakunin and Nechayev." *Encounter* 39,182 (1972): 80-91 & 85-93. Written in 1870, this very long letter was only recently discovered. It reveals a great deal about the Russian underground movement as well as the nature of Bakunin's differences with Nechayev including his conditions for a reconciliation.

Anthologies:

37. *Bakunin on Anarchy: Selected Works by the Activist-Founder of World Anarchism*. Edited with introduction by Sam Dolgoff. Preface by Paul Avrich. New York: Knopf, 1972. Also with introduction by Paul Avrich. New York: Dover Publications, 1970. An excellent anthology of Bakunin's ideas, drawing on excerpts and selections from his letters, speeches, essays etc. It is, in fact, the most useful of the anthologies of Bakunin's work, setting out his writings in a chronological order that makes sense of the somewhat disparate nature of his *oeuvre*.

38. *Correspondence de Michel Bakounine: Lettres à Herzen et à Ogareff, 1860-1874*. Publiées avec préface et annotations par M. Dragomanov. Paris: Perrin et Cie, 1896. Letters written to Alexander Herzen and Nicholas Ogarez.

39. *De la guerre à la Commune*. Textes de 1870-1871 établis sur les manuscrits originaux et presentés par Fernand Rude. Paris: Editions Anthropos, 1972.

40. *Bakunin's Writings*. Edited Guy A. Aldred. New York: Kraus Reprint, 1972. Originally published Indore City: Modern Pubs., 1947. Contains some important texts but these are often presented in a rather fragmented manner.

41. *Marxism, Freedom and the State*. Translated and edited with a biographical sketch by K. J. Kenafick. London: Freedom Pr., 1950. A brief compilation of some of Bakunin's key views on freedom and the state.

42. *Michel Bakounine et ses relations slaves, 1870-1875*. Textes, établis et annotés par Arthur Lehning. Leiden: E.J. Brill, 1974.

43. *Michel Bakounine sur la guerre Franco-Allemande et la révolution sociale en France: 1870-1871*. Écrits et materiaux, textes établis et annotés par Arthur Lehning. Leiden: E.J. Brill, 1977.

44. *Mikhail Bakunin: From out of the Dustbin-Bakunin's Basic Writings 1869-1871*. Translated and edited R. M. Cutler. Ann Arbor: Ardis Publishing, 1985. A collection of Bakunin's writings and speeches on revolutionary socialism, setting out his views on the International. Includes an introductory essay by the editor. Also includes annotated bibliography, index and chronology.

45. *The Political Philosophy of Bakunin: Scientific Anarchism.* Preface by Bert F. Hoselitz. Introduction by Rudolf Rocker. Biographical sketch of Bakunin by Max Nettlau. Edited G. P. Maximoff (Maksimov). New York: Free Pr., 1964. A comprehensive collection of Bakunin's writings by a Russian anarchist who worked as the co-editor of *Golos Truda* (Voice of Labor) and its successor, *Novy Golos Truda*, during the heady days of 1917. The collection is organized thematically with notes, and covers Bakunin's views on anarchism, the state, the individual, science, authority, and revolutionary strategy. This has the virtue of making his writings appear more coherent than they are, but with some loss of historical perspective.

46. *Selected Writings [of] Michael Bakunin.* Edited by Arthur Lehning. Translation from the French by Steven Cox. Translation from the Russian by Olive Stevens. London: Cape, 1973. A selection of important essays covering Bakunin's theories of state and society, dictatorship, centralization and federalism, Marx and Marxism, socialism, and freedom.

Works about Bakunin :

47. Aldred, G. A. *Bakunin.* 'The Word' Library. Second series, no. 1. Glasgow: Strickland Pr., 1940. See entry 1.

48. Avrich, P. "Anarchism and Anti-Intellectualism in Russia." *Journal of The History of Ideas* 27,3 (1966): 381-90. Suggests that the deep seated mistrust of intellectuals in the Russian Anarchist movement in the early twentieth century stemmed primarily from Bakunin's ideas. Also notes, however, the influence of the Marxist idea that workers should be liberated through their own efforts.

49. Avrich, P. "Bakunin and his Writings." *Canadian American Slavic Studies* 10,4 (1976): 591-97. Very useful bibliographic overview of editions/commentaries of Bakunin's works.

50. Avrich, P. "Bakunin and the United States." *International Review of Social History* 24,3 (1979): 320-40. Discusses Bakunin's impressions of the United States during his visit in 1861, and evaluates his subsequent influence on its anarchist movement.

51. Avrich, P. "The Legacy of Bakunin." *Russian Review* 29,2 (1970): 129-42. A discussion of Bakunin's influence on several 20th century writers (Fanon, Debray, Marcuse, Cohn-Bendit). Also covers his dispute with Marx and points to the relevance of his ideas for Third World revolutions.

52. Avrich, P. "The Legacy of Bakunin," "Bakunin and the United States." and "Bakunin and Nechaev." In *Anarchist Portraits,* 5-15/16-31/32-52. Op.cit., entry 1303. A discussion of various aspects of Bakunin's life and ideas comprising Chapters 1-3 of the book, and containing material previously published. See entries 49 and 50. Some new perspectives are developed particularly with respect to the United States.

53. Benés, V. L. "Bakunin and Palacky's Concept of Austroslavism." *Indiana Slavic Studies* 2 (1958): 79-113. Comparative analysis of Bakunin's Panslavism and Palacky's Austroslavism which draws heavily on Bakunin's *Confession*.

54. Berlin, I. "Herzen and Bakunin on Individual Liberty." In *Russian Thinkers*, 82-113. Op. cit., entry 1317. Focuses mainly on Herzen. Bakunin's ideas are used to cast Herzen's views on liberty in a favorable light.

55. Bienek, H. *Bakunin, an Invention*. Translated from the German by Ralph R. Read. London: Gollancz, 1977. An awkward book which attempts to demonstrate the painful process of researching a book, in this instance on Bakunin.

56. Bowlt, J. E. "A Monument To Bakunin: Morolev's Cubo-Futurist Statue Of 1919." *Canadian American Slavic Studies* 10,4 (1976): 577-91. One of the results of Lenin's programme of dismantling monuments to Tzarist heroes and erecting statues of progressive figures was Korolev's statue of Bakunin. Popular outrage forced its dismantling even before it was formally unveiled.

57. Carr, E. H. *The Romantic Exiles: A Nineteenth Century Portrait Gallery*. Harmondsworth: Penguin Bks., 1933. Chapters 10, 11 and 14 discuss Bakunin, in particular his relationship with Nechayev.

58. Carr, E. H. *Michael Bakunin*. London: Macmillan, 1937. Standard English-language biography which, though a bit dated, still remains very useful. Excellent historical detail.

59. Chadwick, W. "The Mailed Fist vs. the Invisible Hand." *Reason* 10,5 (1978): 18-23. Compares the positions of Proudhon, Bakunin and Kropotkin on state power and individual autonomy.

60. Chastain, J. G. "Bakunin as a French Secret Agent in 1848." *History Today* 31 (Aug. 1981): 5-9. Argues that Bakunin was an agent of the French government in 1848.

61. Cipko, S. "Mikhail Bakunin and the National Question." *The Raven* 3,1 (Jan. 1990): 3-14. Discusses Bakunin's views on national liberation movements, contrasting them with those of Marx and Mazzini.

62. Clark, J. "Marx, Bakunin and the Problem of Social Transformation." *Telos* 42 (Winter 1979-80): 80-97. Useful comparative analysis sympathetic to Bakunin's advocacy of stringent critiques of science and bureaucracy.

63. Cochrane, S. T. *The Collaboration of Nechaev, Ogarev, and Bakunin in 1869: Nechaev's Early Years*. Glessen: W. Schmitz, 1977. An analysis of Bakunin's contribution to Nechayev's early years is given in Chapter 3.

64. Confino, M., ed. *Daughter of a Revolutionary: Natalie Herzen and the Bakunin-Nechayev Circle.* Translated from the Russian by Hilary Sternberg and Lydia Bott. London: Alcove Pr., 1974. A collection of correspondence, diaries and documents. Includes a useful introduction and a glossary of names.

65. Cranston, M. "A Dialogue on Anarchy: An Imaginary Conversation Between Karl Marx and Michael Bakunin." In *Political Dialogues,* 116-38. London: British Broadcasting Commission, 1968. Originally a radio broadcast. Published in *Anarchy* 22 (Dec. 1962). One of a series of imaginary conversations that Cranston uses very effectively to elucidate the viewpoints of the protagonists.

66. Dellijudice, M. "Bakunin's 'Preface' to Hegel's 'Gymnasium Lectures': The Problem of Alienation and the Reconciliation with Reality." *Canadian American Slavic Studies* 16,2 (1982): 161-89. Argues that, contrary to accepted views, Bakunin regarded education as an important means to unite theory and practice. Draws on Bakunin's early manuscripts, Hegel's published works and some secondary sources.

67. Dunn, P. P. "Belinski and Bakunin: A Psychoanalytic Study of Adolescence in Nineteenth Century Russia." *Psychohistory Review* 4 (1979). A brief psychoanalytic look at Belinski and Bakunin in which the latter is treated as an overgrown adolescent.

68. Eaton, H. "Marx and the Russians." *Journal of the History of Ideas* 41,1 (Jan.-March 1980): 89-112. The first half of the essay deals with Bakunin.

69. Fattal, D. "Three Russian Revolutionaries on War." *New Review* 11,2-4 (1971). Argues for a connection between the views of Bakunin, Tkachev, and Kropotkin on the state and on war.

70. Fischer, G. "'The State Begins To Wither Away...': Notes on the Interpretation of the Paris Commune by Bakunin, Engels and Lenin." *Australian Journal of Politics and History* 25,1 (1979): 29-38. Argues that Bakunin's views on smashing the state apparatus are closer to those of Marx and Engels than to those of Lenin. The writings of Marx and Engels on the Paris Commune form the basis of the argument.

71. Guérin, D. "From Proudhon to Bakunin." *Our Generation* 17,2 (Spring/Summer 1986): 232-4. Discusses the relationship between Proudhon and Bakunin, their friendship in Paris in the years 1845-47, and the degree of interchange between their ideas.

72. Halbrook, S. P. "Bakunin and Marx on Nationalism." *Anarchy* Second series, 1,4 (197?): 20-4. Discusses nationalism as a fundamental point of divergence between Marx and Bakunin.

73. Halbrook, S. P. "Lenin's Bakuninism." *International Review of History and Political Science* 8 (Feb.1971). A Bakuninist side to Lenin is suggested.

74. Hall, B. "Another View of Marx: A Closer Look at Bakuninism." *New Politics* 7,1 (1968): 78-85. A brief overview of Bakunin's attacks on Marxism.

75. Hardy, D. "Consciousness and Spontaneity, 1875: The Peasant Revolution seen by Tkachev, Lavróv and Bakunin." *Canadian Slavic Studies* 4 (Winter 1970): 699-720. Relies heavily on *Statism and Anarchy* for Bakunin's views.

76. Harrison, F. "Bakunin's Theory of Revolution." *Our Generation* 11,4 (Winter 1976): 27-37. Argues that Bakunin's anarchism, reflecting the preoccupations of Russian populism, brought to the European socialist movement the orientation and goals of a pre-industrial society.

77. Hodges, D. C. "Bakunin's Controversy with Marx: An Analysis of Tensions within Modern Socialism." *American Journal of Economics and Sociology* 19 (April 1960): 259-74. Looks at the legacy of the Bakunin/Marx dispute and its influence on the views of twentieth century exponents of revolutionary theory and practice.

78. Jakobsh, F. K. "Gunter Eich: Homage To Bakunin." *Germano-Slavica* 3 (Spring 1974): 37-46. Looks at Bakunin's influence on Eich's poetry.

79. Jourdain, M. "Mikhail Bakunin." *Open Court* 34 (Oct. 1920). Brief biographical outline with some commentary on Bakunin's ideas.

80. Kelly, A. *Michael Bakunin: A Study of the Psychology and Politics of Utopianism.* New Haven & London: Yale Univ. Pr., 1987. First published New York: Oxford Univ. Pr., 1982. Unsympathetic but detailed treatment of Bakunin as a millenarian.

81. Kenafick, K. J. *Michael Bakunin and Karl Marx.* London: Freedom Pr., 1949. Discusses their relationship with the emphasis on Bakunin.

82. Kennard, M. P. "A Russian Anarchist Visits Boston in 1861: Text of an Account Written Some Twenty Years After." *New England Quarterly* 15 (March 1942): 104-9. Edited by O. Handlin. A contemporary, anecdotal account of Bakunin's visit to the United States.

83. Kofman, M. "The Reaction of Two Anarchists to Nationalism: Proudhon and Bakunin on the Polish Question." *Labour History* 14 (May 1968): 34-6. Contrasts their respective understandings of the Polish question and their analyses of the social conditions of Eastern Europe.

84. Kostka, E. "Schiller's Impact on Bakunin." *Monatshefte* 54 (Jan. 1962): 109-16. Discusses Bakunin's reactions to Schiller's prose and its possible influence on him, in the context of a discussion of the Stankevich Circle, especially in the years 1838-40.

85. Kun, M. "Bakunin and Hungary, 1848-1865." *Canadian American Slavic Studies* 10,4 (1976): 503-35. Draws on unpublished archival material to discuss an area of Bakunin's life that is rarely addressed in English works.

86. Lampert, E. *Studies in Rebellion: Belinsky, Bakunin and Herzen.* London: Routledge & Kegan Paul, 1957. Very good on Bakunin's ideas but not much attention is given to the historical circumstances that helped form them.

87. Lavrin, J. "Bakunin the Slav and Rebel." *Russian Review* 25,2 (1966): 135-149. Focuses on the years 1848-49 to evaluate the Slavic theme in his revolutionary theories. Bakunin's anarchism is rarely mentioned.

88. Lehning, A. "Bakunin's Conceptions of Revolutionary Organizations and their Role: A Study of his 'Secret Societies'." In *Essays in Honor of E.H. Carr*, edited by C. Abramsky and Beryl L. Williams, 57-81. Hampden, Conn.; Archon Bks., 1974. A sympathetic overview of Bakunin's theory and practice of revolution drawing on published and unpublished manuscripts.

89. Malatesta, E. "Anarchist Schools of Thought." In *Errico Malatesta: His Life and Ideas*, edited Vernon Richards, 29-33. London: Freedom Pr., 1977. Bakunin is characterized as a collectivist.

90. Marx, K. "Conspectus of Bakunin's *Statism and Anarchy*," in *Karl Marx: The First International and After: Political Writings*, edited by David Fernbach, 333-38. Harmondsworth: Penguin Bks., 1974. Extracts from Marx's critical notes on key passages of Bakunin's *Statism And Anarchy*.

91. Masters, A. *Bakunin: The Father of Anarchism.* London: Sidgwick & Jackson, 1974. Very readable and sympathetic account of Bakunin's ideas, if somewhat simplistic in places.

92. Mendel, A. "Bakunin: A View from within." *Canadian American Slavic Studies* 10,4 (1976): 466-89. A psychoanalytic assessment concluding that Bakunin's life and actions indicate an unresolved Oedipal complex.

93. Mendel, A. P. *Michael Bakunin: Roots of Apocalypse.* New York: Praeger, 1981. A patchy psycho-biography, but of some use in explaining Bakunin's early philosophical development. Bibliography and index.

94. Molnar, M. "Bakunin and Marx." *The Review: A Quarterly of Pluralist Socialism* 5,3 (1963). Looks at the International in 1871-72 and argues that it was structurally ill-equipped to reconcile the divergent aspirations of different spokespeople from widely different regions.

95. Nettlau, M. "Bakunin's So-Called 'Confession' of 1851." *Freedom* 35 (Dec. 1921): 75-6. A discussion of Bakunin's motives in writing his "Confession," and a rebuttal of contemporary attacks.

96. Nettlau, M. "Bakunin's 'Confession' to Tsar Nicholas I (1851)." *Freedom* 36 (May 1922): 28-9. Brief discussion of the circumstances surrounding the writing of the "Confession."

97. Nettlau, M. "Bakunin's 'Revolutionary Catechism'." *Freedom* 38,418 (June 1924): 30. Argues that Bakunin's authorship of the controversial "Revolutionary Catechism" is proved and that Nechayev, while he may have influenced it, did not write it.

98. Nettlau, M. "Elisée Reclus and Michael Bakunin." In *Elisée and Elie Reclus: In Memoriam*, edited by Joseph Ishill. Woodcuts by Louis Moreau. Berkeley Heights, N.J.: Oriole Pr., 1927. A discussion of their friendship. A rare book printed by Ishill's private press.

99. Nettlau, M. "An English Life of Bakunin." *Spain and the World* 2,27/28/29/30 (5 Jan., 21 Jan., 2 Feb., 18 Feb. 1938). A very strident critique of E. H. Carr's biography of Bakunin.

100. Nettlau, M. "A Last Word on Bakunin's 'Confession'." *Freedom* 29 (Sept. 1925): 42-3. A review of a Russian work on Bakunin's middle years.

101. Nettlau, M. "New Bakunin Documents." *Freedom* 28 (March-April 1924): 18-19. A review of a collection of Russian documents concerning Bakunin taken from the archives of the Tsarist police and published.

102. Nomad, M. "Marx and Bakunin." *Hound and Horn* 6 (April-June 1933): 381-418. Concentrates on their dispute within the International.

103. Nomad, M. "Michael Bakunin, 'Apostle of Pan-Destruction'." In *Apostles of Revolution*, 151-213. New York: Collier Bks., 1961. A study of the life and career of Bakunin focussing on his role as a militant organizer of revolution. Charts his dispute with Marx.

104. Nomad, M. "Sergei Nechayev 'The Possessed'." In *Apostles of Revolution*, 214-56. New York: Collier Bks., 1961. A discussion of the career of Nechayev that examines his relationship with Bakunin and the writing of the *Revolutionary Catechism*. See entry 22.

105. Odlozilik, O. "The Slavic Congress of 1848." *Polish Review* 4,4 (Autumn 1959): 3-15. Review of a volume of sources relating to the Prague Congress of 1848 with a discussion of Bakunin's participation in the Congress.

106. Orton, L. D. "Bakunin's Plan for Slav Federation." *Canadian American Slavic Studies* 8,1 (1974): 107-116. Translation, with introductions, of the three speeches made by Bakunin at the Prague Congress.

107. Orton, L. D. "The Echo of Bakunin's *Appeal to the Slavs*." *Canadian American Slavic Studies* 10,4 (1976): 489-503. A study of the influence of Bakunin's pamphlet, with a discussion of the period.

108. Palmieri, F. A. "A Theorist of the Russian Revolution." *Catholic World* 110 (Dec. 1919). Argues that the Bolsheviks' anti-religious practices were the outcome of the atheist views of Bakunin, the roots of which can be found in Feuerbach and the early Hegel.

109. Peterson, A. and Johnson, O. M. *The Virus of Anarchy: Bakuninism vs. Marxism.* New York: New York Labor News Co., 1932. An anti-anarchist pamphlet defending Marxism against the claims of Anarcho-Communism.

110. Pirumova, N. "Bakunin and Herzen: An Analysis of their Ideological Disagreements at the End of the 1860's." *Canadian American Slavic Studies* 10,4 (1976): 552-70. A patchy assessment of the two thinkers.

111. Pomper, P. "Bakunin, Nechaev and the 'Catechism of a Revolutionary': The Case for Joint Authorship." *Canadian American Slavic Studies* 10,4 (1976): 535-52. Bases his conclusion for joint authorship on a close textual analysis of the documents.

112. Pomper, P. *Sergei Nechaev.* New Brunswick, N.J.: Rutgers Univ. Pr., 1979. Tells the story of Nechayev's short but extraordinary life, detailing his activities as a violent revolutionary, including his association with Bakunin. His ideas are condemned unreservedly as dangerous and insane, and the hope is expressed that readers will recognize in Nechayev the threat posed by all radical movements. Includes bibliography and index.

113. Prawdin, M. *The Unmentionable Nechaev: A Key to Bolshevism.* London: Allen and Unwin, 1961. There is some mention of Nechayev's relationship with Bakunin, but the main thrust of the work is aimed at demonstrating links between Nechayev's ideas and those of the Nihilists, and establishing them as the main source of Leninism.

114. Pyziur, E. *The Doctrine of Anarchism of Michael A. Bakunin.* 2nd. edition. Chicago: Henry Regnery, 1968. A useful exposition of Bakunin's ideas which are set out thematically with a consideration of Bakunin's contribution to anarchist doctrine.

115. Ravindranathan, T. R. "Bakunin in Naples: An Assessment." *Journal of Modern History* 53,2 (1981): 189-212. Drawing on archival and published primary sources, the article argues that Bakunin's impact on the emergence and growth of early Italian socialism was substantial.

116. Ravindranathan, T. R. *Bakunin and the Italians.* Kingston/Montréal: McGill-Queen's Univ Pr., 1988. A detailed historical discussion of the important influence of Bakunin on the development of Italian anarchism, focusing on the 1860s and 1870s.

117. Reichert, W. O. "Art, Nature and Revolution." (Aesthetics of Bakunin, Kropotkin and Proudhon). *Arts in Society* 9,3 (1972): 409-30. A brief exposition of an anarchist theory of aesthetics which draws on the works of Bakunin, Proudhon, and Kropotkin. Argues that social progress stems from

the creative spirit of the people and that it is within aesthetics, not political ideology, that revolutions are created.

118. Reszler, A. "Bakunin, Marx and the Aesthetic Heritage of Socialism." *Yearbook of Comparative and General Literature,* 22 (1973): 42-50. A brief analysis of the relationship of revolution to art and creativity.

119. Rezneck, S. "Political and Social Theory of Michael Bakunin." *American Political Science Review* 21 (May 1927): 270-96.

120. Richards, V. "Some Notes on Malatesta and Bakunin." *The Raven* 1,1 (1986): 38-45. Discusses the relationship between the ideas of the two theorists.

121. Russell, B. "Bakunin and Anarchism." In *Proposed Roads to Freedom: Socialism, Anarchism and Syndicalism,* 32-55. London: Allen & Unwin, 1918. In an examination of the historical genesis of the three traditions, Bakunin figures as the exemplar of anarchism.

122. Saltman, R. B. *The Social and Political Thought of Michael Bakunin.* Westport, Conn.: Greenwood Pr., 1983. Draws heavily on Bakunin's first-draft manuscripts to argue that Bakunin's anarchist theories were predicated on a concept of natural authority. Focuses mainly on the 1866-74 period, and arranges Bakunin's ideas so that they emerge in a systematic fashion.

123. Senese, D. L. "Bakunin's Last Disciple: Sergei Kravchinskii." *Canadian American Slavic Studies* 10,4 (1976): 570-77. Traces Bakunin's influence on the views of Kravchinskii.

124. Silberner, E. "Two Studies of Modern Anti-Semitism." *Historia Judaica* 14 (Oct. 1952). Argues that Bakunin and Marx were anti-Semites and attempts to trace the origin and development of this (alleged) aspect of their philosophies.

125. Svoboda, G. J. "Anarchism in Bohemia: The Prague Anti-Habsburg Revolutionary Society (1868-1872)." *East European Quarterly* 11,3 (1977): 267-91. Based on research on archival material in Prague it confirms the existence of an anarchist movement which operated along Bakuninist lines.

126. Venturi, F. "Bakunin" and "Bakunin and Lavróv." In *Roots of Revolution: The History of Populist and Socialist Movements in Nineteenth Century Russia,* 36-62/429-468. Translated Francis Haskell. Introduction by Isaiah Berlin. London: Weidenfeld & Nicholson, 1960. The first piece is an appreciation of Bakunin's ideas and a discussion of his career up to 1850. The second piece discusses the creation of the Russian Brotherhood in 1872 in Zurich, and the disputes that broke out with Petr Lavrovich Lavróv, populist and socialist, over revolutionary tactics.

127. Voegelin, E. "Bakunin's 'Confession'" *Journal of Politics* 8 (Feb. 1946): 24-43. Summary of the Confession with an appraisal of Bakunin's motives for writing it.

128. Voegelin, E. "Bakunin: The Anarchist." In *From Enlightenment to Revolution.* edited John H. Hallowell, 217-39. Durham, N.C.: Duke Univ. Pr., 1975. Surveys the post-Bakunin meaning of 'anarchism' and then evaluates his post-1861 activities and some of his writings. Portrays Bakunin in very negative terms.

129. Voegelin, E. "Revolutionary Existence." In *From Enlightenment to Revolution,* edited by John H. Hallowell, 195-216. Durham, N.C.: Duke Univ. Pr., 1975. Analyzes Bakunin's decision to become a revolutionary activist, and offers a close examination of his metaphysical ideas, commenting on their relation to Marx's philosophy.

130. Walicki, A. "Hegel, Feuerbach and the Russian 'Philosophical Left', 1836-1848." *Annali Dell'Instituto Giangiacomo Feltrinelli* 6 (1963): 105-136. Briefly discusses Bakunin's encounter with the works of Fichte and Hegel.

131. Weintraub, W. "Mickiewicz and Bakunin." *Slavonic and East European Review* 28 (Nov. 1949): 72-83. Assesses the significance of their meeting in the light of the Polish question; mainly concerned with Mickiewicz.

132. Wilson, E. "Historical Actors: Bakunin." In *To the Finland Station*, 260-87. New York: Harcourt, Brace, 1940. A lively account of Bakunin in the 1860s and 1870s, his confrontation with Marx and his relationship with Nechayev.

133. Woodcock, G. "Bakunin: The Destructive Urge." *History Today* 11 (July 1961): 469-78. A general discussion of Bakunin's life and revolutionary activities.

134. Wright, C. H. "Bakounine." *Fortnightly Review* 115 (May 1921): 759-71. A biographical discussion with some attention to Bakunin's ideas.

ALEXANDER BERKMAN (1870-1936)

Works by Berkman :

135. *A.B.C. of Anarchism.* London: Freedom Pr., 1971. Originally published in 1929 under the title *Now and After: The ABC of Communist Anarchism?* New York: Vanguard Press of the Jewish Anarchist Federation, 1929, and London: Freedom Pr., 1929. Also published with an introduction by Paul Avrich, as *What is Communist Anarchism?* New York: Dover Publications, 1972. Berkman's classic text outlining the principles of

communist anarchism, held by many to be the best available statement of the principles involved. It is clear, succinct and forceful.

136. *The Bolshevik Myth*. Introduction by Nicolas Walter. London: Pluto Pr., 1989. Originally published New York & London: 1925. The chapters in this book were compiled from the diary Berkman kept while he was in Russia. In it he aims to discuss the inner life of the Revolution revealed in the people, rather than concentrating on its external forms. Records his meeting with Kropotkin and the latter's death.

137. "How to End War." *Freedom* 23 (March 1932): 2. A reprint, by request, of a short piece by Berkman which argues that to abolish war we must abolish exploitation and authority.

138. "Kronstadt - The Paris Commune of Russia." *Freedom* 36,393 (March 1922): 18. An account of the Kronstadt Revolt noting the irony that, on March 18, 1921, the Bolsheviks celebrated the Paris Commune as they celebrated their victory at Kronstadt.

139. "The Kronstadt Rebellion." In *The Russian Tragedy*. Op.cit., entry 145. Published as a separate pamphlet. Berlin: Der Syndikalist, 1922. An account of the anarchists' uprising in Kronstadt and the crushing of it by the Bolsheviks.

140. "The Paris Commune 1871 and Kronstadt 1921." *Freedom* 35/36/37 (March, April, May 1933): 3/4/3. A comparison of the two events noting their historic and revolutionary significance.

141. *Prison Memoirs of an Anarchist*. Originally published in 1912 with an introduction by Hutchins Hapgood. New York: Schocken Bks., 1970. Introduction by Paul Goodman. A diary written during Berkman's fourteen years of imprisonment in the United States. Regarded as a classic in the *genre* of prison memoirs, it presents an anarchist critique of the institution of prisons, and provides important insights into Berkman's political and social theories.

142. "The Russian Revolution and the Communist Party." In *The Russian Tragedy*. Op.cit., entry 145. Published as a separate pamphlet. Berlin: Der Syndikalist, 1922. Argues in the strongest possible terms for an anarchist solution in Russia, insisting that it is the Communist Party itself which most effectively hinders the revolution through its "bureaucratization of every sphere of human activity and effort."

143. "The Russian Tragedy." In *The Russian Tragedy*. Op.cit., entry 145. Published as a separate pamphlet. Berlin: Der Syndikalist, 1922. Argues passionately that the great lesson of the Russian Revolution for the workers is that government is inherently destructive of social revolution. Only through their own direct efforts can workers achieve emancipation.

144. "Some Bolshevik Lies about Russian Anarchists." *Freedom* 36,394 (April 1922): 24-6. A discussion of Bolshevik dealings with Russian anarchists concentrating on the perfidy of the treatment of Makhno.

145. *The Russian Tragedy*. Edited by William G. Nowlin Jr. Sanday, Orkney: Cienfuegos Pr., 1976. An edited collection of Berkman's most important pamphlets on the Russian experience of 1917 and after. See entries 139, 142 and 143.

Works about Berkman :

146. Avrich, P. "Alexander Berkman: A Sketch." In *Anarchist Portraits*, 200-7. Op.cit., entry 1303. A short appreciation of the life and ideas of Berkman.

147. Detelbaum, W. "Epistolary Politics: The Correspondence of Emma Goldman and Alexander Berkman." *Prose Studies* 8,1 (1986): 30-46. A brief description of the events immediately following the expulsion of Goldman and Berkman from the United States and the anarchist content of their correspondence between 1929 and 1936.

148. Goldberg, H. J. "Goldman and Berkman View the Bolshevik Régime." *Slavonic and East European Review* 53,131 (1975): 272-6. Explains that until the suppression of the Kronstadt rebellion of 1921 Goldman and Berkman actively supported the Bolsheviks.

149. Graham, M. "Alexander Berkman." In *Man!*, 584-7. Op.cit., entry 1389. A brief appreciation that appeared in the journal *Man!* on the occasion of Berkman's death.

150. Walter, N. "Alexander Berkman's Russian Diary." *The Raven* 1,3 (Nov. 1987): 280-8. Discusses the diary which Berkman kept during his time in Russia and which was only partially reproduced in *The Bolshevik Myth*.

151. Ward, J. W. "Violence, Anarchy and Alexander Berkman." *New York Review of Books* 15 (5 Nov. 1970): 25-30. An extended review of Berkman's *Prison Memoirs of an Anarchist* that discusses his life and ideas while seeking to understand the place of Berkman's anarchism and the politics of violence within the American democratic tradition.

MURRAY BOOKCHIN (1921-)

Works by Bookchin :

152. "Against Meliorism." *Anarchy* 88 (June 1968): 191-2. A polemic in favour of revolutionary anarchism.

153. "Recovering Evolution: A Reply to Eckersley and Fox." *Environmental Ethics* 12,3 (Fall 1990): 253-74. A response to the critiques of Eckersley and Fox, claiming that they are ignoring much of what he has written, and advancing an argument based on dialectical naturalism that places humanity and nature in a complementary and evolutionary relationship.

154. *Crisis in Our Cities.* New York: Prentice-Hall, 1965. Examines the urban environment looking at air and water pollution, congestion, stress, urban sprawl etc. All are in epidemic proportions, it is argued, and can only be managed by revolutionary methods of control.

155. "Desire and Need." *Anarchy* 80 (Oct. 1967): 311-19. A discussion of desire and need in the work of Hegel, Reich and others, concluding that revolutionary libertarianism must not be imprisoned in the realm of Need.

156. "Ecology and Revolutionary Thought." *Antipode* 10/11, 3/1 (1979): 21-32. A reprint in the double issue of *Antipode* on anarchism of part of *Post-Scarcity Anarchism*, op.cit., entry 165, establishing Bookchin's broad argument.

157. *The Ecology of Freedom.* Montréal: Black Rose Bks., 1982. Urges people not to reject but to harness modern technology in order to build an organic society based on individual autonomy and libertarian practices.

158. *The Limits of the City.* Montréal: Black Rose Bks., 1986. A political economy of urban development, arguing that the progressive urban spirit of the medieval period, which reflected and promoted human values, has been removed from the modern cities of consumerist, capitalist society. To overcome the urban crisis a change in the social system that is decentralizing and liberating must occur.

159. "Marxism as Bourgeois Sociology." *Our Generation* 13,3 (Summer 1979): 21-8. Argues that Marx's work, while the most sophisticated critique of capitalism, impedes a revolutionary idea of freedom, since it remains blind to the problem of authority and hierarchy independent of class, and tied to notions of dominating nature.

160. *The Modern Crisis.* Montréal: Black Rose Bks., 1987. Argues that the modern social and ecological crisis is caused by consumerism and the destructive and inhuman nature of market society. The only alternative is a society founded on social ecology, a community of sharing individuals living in harmony with themselves and with the world.

161. "New Social Movements: The Anarchic Dimension." In *For Anarchism: History, Theory and Practice*, 259-74. Op.cit., entry 1385. A review of counter-culture movements since the 1960s, including pacifism, feminism and environmentalism. It concludes that the new social movements have a fundamentally anarchic dimension which, reflecting Kropotkin's ideas, leads towards a totally decentralized society that rejects

capitalism and hierarchy, gender domination and ecological destruction, and embraces social ecology, eco-feminism and a radical civic politic.

162. "An Open Letter to the Ecological Movement." *Our Generation* 14,2 (Summer/Fall 1980): 23-28. A challenging essay arguing that the decade of the 1980s is crucial to the future of the ecology movement and will determine whether a new society will arise based on mutual aid, simple technology, decentralized communities and harmony between humanity and nature.

163. *Our Synthetic Environment.* Published under the name Lewis Herber. Introduction William A. Albrecht. New York: Knopf, 1962. An early attack on the effect of agricultural chemicals, additives, antibiotics, industrial pollutants and radioactive fallout etc. on the human environment.

164. *The Philosophy of Social Ecology.* Montréal: Black Rose Bks., 1990.

165. *Post-Scarcity Anarchism.* Berkeley, Calif.: Ramparts Pr. 1971. Advances a libertarian theory of the potential for social change in America based on technologically created abundance.

166. "Radical Politics in an Era of Advanced Capitalism." *Our Generation.* 21,2 (Summer 1990): 1-12. Argues for direct action, community self-management and the creation of local networks involving the transformation of municipal institutions into agencies of freedom.

167. "Reflections on Spanish Anarchism." *Our Generation* 10,1 (1974): 8-36. An historical analysis that focuses on the role of revolutionary ideas and movements.

168. *Remaking Society.* Montréal: Black Rose Bks., 1989. A book in which Bookchin seeks to summarize his views on the need to remake society from an ecological and anarchist standpoint. The book discusses the emergence of hierarchy and modern capitalism, technology, ideals of freedom and radical alternatives, urbanization and communities and the ethics of social ecology. Argues that what is needed is "a truly libertarian society."

169. *The Rise of Urbanization and the Decline of Citizenship.* New York: Sierra, 1987. An attack on urbanization which Bookchin views as inimical to civic values. Bookchin identifies forces such as nationalism and capitalism as responsible for the process of urbanization and the degeneration of mores, culture and the institutions of civilized, civic life.

170. "Social Ecology versus 'Deep Ecology'. A Challenge for the Ecology Movement." *The Raven* 1,3 (Nov. 1987): 219-50. An extended attack on Deep Ecology as a " 'black hole' of half-digested, ill-formed, and half-baked ideas," and a statement of the ethics and politics of social ecology as the preferable alternatives.

171. *The Spanish Anarchists: The Heroic Years, 1868 - 1936.* New York: Free Life Eds., 1977. A study of Spanish anarchism tracing its history from the early days to the opening of the Civil War in 1936. Includes a detailed bibliographic essay.

172. "Theses on Libertarian Municipalism." *Our Generation* 16, 3&4 (Spring/Summer 1985): 9-22. Advances an argument for libertarian municipalism and a new civic politics following a decentralization of authority and the creation of new confederated communities.

173. "Thinking Ecologically: A Dialectical Approach." *Our Generation* 18,2 (Spring/Summer 1987): 3-40. A critical review of trends within the ecology movement such as 'deep ecology,' Taoism etc.. Bookchin argues that the real issue is to think ecologically rather than feel ecologically, perceiving humanity and nature to be in a dialectical, not an antagonistic, relationship.

174. "Towards a Liberatory Technology." *Our Generation* 7,4 (Sept. 1971): 64-84. Part 1, 8, 182 (Winter/April 1972): 71-90. Part 2. Argues that technology is vital to a dynamic human society but that it must be a technology geared to decentralized community life, scaled to human proportions, and sympathetic to the natural environment.

175. *Towards an Ecological Society.* Montréal: Black Rose Bks., 1980. A collection of essays which begins with the premise that true radicalism and genuine ideals of freedom have been lost. Bookchin argues that it is urgent that they be rediscovered and developed in the light of our current evironmental plight.

Works about Bookchin :

176. Albrecht, G. "Social Ecology and Ecological Ethics." In *Ecopolitics IV,* edited Ken Dyer and John Young, 238-45. Adelaide: Univ. of Adelaide Graduate Centre for Environmental Studies, 1990. An examination of Bookchin's ideas that endorses social ecology as a realistic attempt to solve ecological problems on an objective ethical basis. Deep Ecology is dismissed as mystical and subjective in its orientation.

177. Beresford, M. "Doomsayers and Eco-nuts: A Critique of the Ecology Movement." *Politics* 12,1 (May 1977): 98-106. A Marxist critique that dismisses the ecology movement in general as bourgeois and the Bookchin of *Post-Scarcity Anarchism* as idealist.

178. Borrelli, P. "The Ecophilosophers." *The Amicus Journal* 10,2 (Spring 1988): 30-9. Discusses the work of Bookchin as part of a new wave of radical ecophilosophy.

179. Clark, J. *The Anarchist Moment: Reflections on Culture, Nature and Power.* Montréal: Black Rose Bks., 1984. A critique of classical radical theory

from an anarchist viewpoint. An analysis of the definition of anarchism includes a discussion of Bookchin's ideas on social ecology.

180. Eckersley, R. "Divining Evolution: The Ecological Ethics of Murray Bookchin." *Environmental Ethics* 11,2 (Summer 1989): 99-116. A critique of Bookchin that argues that his claim that his ecological ethics offers the greatest freedom to all lifeforms is invalidated by the manner in which he distinguishes between second nature (humanity) and first nature (non-humanity) to the advantage of the former.

181. "The Ecology Manifesto of the Regroupement Ecologique Québécois, Montréal Region." *Our Generation* 13,4 (Fall 1979): 7-13. Relevant to Bookchin's ideas on social ecology, the manifesto states that to fight pollution the system of capitalist production based on profit must be vanquished and decentralization to free communal living established.

182. Fox, W. "The Deep Ecology-Ecofeminism Debate and its Parallels." *Environmental Ethics* 11,1 (Spring 1989): 5-25. In the course of the discussion Bookchin's attack on Deep Ecology is considered and issue is taken with his interpretation and analysis.

183. Freeman, B. "The Ecology Movement and the Radical Project: Ecology versus Marxism." *Our Generation* 13,4 (Fall 1979): 16-17. Hails the ecology movement as the new radical path while endorsing Bookchin's view of Marxism.

184. Hallam, N. and Potter, D. "Feminism, Anarchism and Ecology and Some Connections." *The Raven* 3,1 (Jan. 1990): 46-55. Some discussion of Bookchin's ideas in a piece that argues for connections between anarchism and the feminist and ecology movements.

185. Harrison, F. "Science and Anarchism: From Bakunin to Bookchin." *Our Generation* 20,2 (Spring 1985): 72-84. Discusses the linkages between anarchist ideas and scientific knowledge.

186. Mellos, K. "Discourses on the Crisis of the Ecology Issue." *Environments* 16,3 (1984): 49-56. An examination of six principal discourses on the eco-crisis covering eco-anarchism and the ideas of Bookchin.

187. Roussopoulos, D. I. "Review of Bookchin's *Limits of the City.*" *Our Generation* 10,3 (Fall 1974): 50-7. A lengthy review that includes discussion of Bookchin's general philosophy.

188. Salzman, L. "Politics as if Evolution Mattered: Some Thoughts on Deep and Social Ecology." In *Ecopolitics IV,* edited by Ken Dyer and John Young 260-270. Adelaide: Univ. of Adelaide Graduate Centre for Environmental Studies, 1990. A review of the debate between deep and social ecology that critically examines the ideas of Bookchin.

189. Watson, R. A. "Review of George Bradford. *How Deep is Deep Ecology?*" (Ojai: Times Change Pr., 1989). *Environmental Ethics* 12 (Winter 1990): 371-4. A review of anarchist Bradford's critique of Deep Ecology which parallels that of Bookchin, with some discussion of Bookchin's ideas.

190. Wiabley, R. B. J. "Neo-Conservatism and Social Ecology: 1960s to 1980s." *Our Generation* 20,2 (Spring 1989): 18-53. Discusses the critique of neo-conservatism by social ecology, with some consideration of the work of Bookchin.

MARTIN BUBER (1878-1965)

Works by Buber :

191. *Paths in Utopia*. London: Routledge & Kegan Paul, 1949. Buber was a German-Jewish religious philosopher who embraced Zionism and founded the journal *Der Jude* in 1916. His religious anarchism stressed dialogue between human beings and between them and God. *Paths in Utopia* is an extended discussion of radical theory and the community with chapters on Proudhon, Kropotkin and Landauer. It concludes with the positive view that the Jewish Village Commune, the Kibbutz, has been a successful experiment in communal living.

Works about Buber :

192. Mendes-Flohr, P. M. "Buber's Reception Among the Jews." *Modern Judaism* 6,2 (1986): 111-26. An account of the reception of the controversial religious, anarchist views of Martin Buber which have divided Jewish opinion.

193. Ramana Murti, V. V. "Buber's Dialogue with Gandhi's *Satyagraha.*" *Journal of the History of Ideas* 29,4 (Oct.-Dec. 1968): 605-13. Discusses the polemical exchange between Gandhi and Buber over the Jewish problem on the eve of World War II. Gandhi, addressing the question of how the persecuted Jews of Europe were to resist persecution, advocated non-violent resistance to Nazism. Buber was critical of the application of *Satyagraha* to Germany, considering it inappropriate.

194. Yassour, A. "Lenin as Seen by Martin Buber." *Studies in Soviet Thought* 35 (May 1988): 271-86. Buber adopted some of Lenin's ideas on the building of a new society in the development of his anarcho-socialist theories set out in *Paths in Utopia*, op.cit., entry 191.

NOAM CHOMSKY (1928-)

Works by Chomsky:

Titles included here are exclusive of Chomsky's work on linguistic philosophy or on American foreign policy except where it is relevant to anarchist themes.

195. *American Power and the New Mandarins.* London: Chatto & Windus, 1969. Published in USA, New York: Pantheon Bks., 1969. A collection of political essays on foreign policy, the responsibility of intellectuals and resistance.

196. *The Culture of Terrorism.* London: Pluto Pr., 1989. A discussion of United States foreign policy that raises the question of the maintenance of the 'culture of terrorism' by an ideological, elitist control. See Chapter 15, "Standards for Ourselves," 255-9.

197. *For Reasons of State.* London: Collins, 1973. A collection of political essays and lectures, already published separately, which covers the role of force in international affairs, Indochina, civil disobedience, the function of the university, psychology and ideology, language and freedom and anarchism.

198. "His Right to Say It: The Faurisson Affair." *Social Alternatives* 2,3 (1982): 45-8. Reprinted from *The Nation*, February 28 1981. Chomsky discusses his defense of Prof. Faurisson's right to express his view that the holocaust did not happen.

199. *'Human Rights' and American Foreign Policy.* Nottingham: Spokesman Bks., 1978. Essays that discuss the way propaganda systems in advanced industrial countries recruit the intelligensia into systems of indoctrination, legitimization and power to serve the interests of the dominant elite.

200. "Ideological Conformity in America." *The Nation* 228,3 (27 Jan. 1979): 77-81. Chomsky laments the lack of a socialist voice in the American mass media, claiming that ideological conformity makes the USA a "mirror image" of the Soviet Union.

201. "Intellectuals and the State." In *Towards a New Cold War: Essays on the Current Crisis and How We Got There*, 60-85. New York: Pantheon Bks., 1982. Examines the role of intellectuals in modern industrial societies, particularly the United States, and their willingness to serve the state in the creation of moral and ideological frameworks.

202. "The Intelligensia and the State." In *After the Cataclysm. Postwar Indochina and the Reconstruction of Imperial Ideology.* Vol. 2 of *The Political Economy of Human Rights*, 23-31. Co-author E. S. Herman. Boston:

South End Pr., 1975. Discusses the way influential elements in the intelligensia have in the past responded to abuses of state power.

203. *Language and Responsibility.* New York: Pantheon Bks., 1979. Based on conversations with Mitson Ronat, in which, while Chomsky speaks of his linguistic theories in the main, there is some discussion of the sources and nature of his political ideas.

204. "The Manufacture of Consent." *Our Generation* 17,1 (Fall/Winter 1985-6): 85-106. A essay in which Chomsky reflects on the mechanisms for swaying, creating and directing opinion in a modern democracy. Asserts that techniques beyond the dreams of Orwell are used to create a consensual basis for authority in a manner that undermines freedom.

205. *Manufacturing Consent: The Political Economy of the Mass Media.* Co-author S. Herman. New York: Pantheon Bks., 1988. Argues that the mass media in America mobilize support for the special interests of either private capital or the state. Discusses how legitimacy and consent are manufactured to support a hierarchical system of power, authority and wealth.

206. *Necessary Illusions: Thought Control in Democratic Societies.* London: Pluto Pr., 1989. Based on the 1988 Massey lectures, Chomsky examines the role of the media in liberal democratic capitalist societies, arguing that in practice it serves the special interests of the state or large corporations. To secure freedom of thought and speech necessitates a continuing struggle.

207. "Notes on Anarchism." *Anarchy* 116 (Oct. 1970): 309-21. Reprinted from the *New York Review of Books,* 21 May 1970, this revised version of the introduction to Daniel Guérin's *Anarchism: From Theory to Practice* op.cit., entry 457, was also collected in *For Reasons of State,* op.cit., entry 197, 151-166. It is a general discussion of the importance of anarchism and libertarian socialism, which will remain relevant, Chomsky believes, so long as economic exploitation and political enslavement are with us.

208. "Objectivity and Liberal Scholarship." In *American Power and the New Mandarins,* 23-129. Op.cit., entry 195. A critical analysis of the various ways in which intellectuals and academics, the "new Mandarins," subordinate their talents to the service of the State for counter-revolutionary ends. Draws on examples arising from the Vietnamese struggle for national self-determination and the Spanish Civil War.

209. "Philosophers and Public Philosophy." *Ethics* 79,1 (Oct. 1968): 1-9. Chomsky expresses his views on the professional responsibilities of philosophers towards political morality and political power. For responses see entries 221 and 223.

210. *Pirates and Emperors: International Terrorism in the Real World.* New York: Claremont Research and Pubns., 1986. Chomsky argues that the attention paid to individual acts of terrorism obscures the terror committed by the United States and its client states which in turn reflects the

bankruptcy of the system. His argument raises the question of the state use of force as against the use of force by private individuals or agencies.

211. *Problems of Knowledge and Freedom. The Russell Lectures.* New York: Pantheon Bks., 1972. The second lecture takes, as a point of departure, Russell's discussion of social problems and develops into a discussion of Chomsky's own political philosophy.

212. "The Responsibility of Intellectuals." In *The Dissenting Academy*, edited by Theodore Roszak, 227-64. Harmondsworth: Penguin, 1969. First published in the *New York Review of Books*, 23 February 1967, this piece analyzes and discusses the particular responsibilities of intellectuals in Western society with respect to speaking out in defense of the truth, and exposing the lies of governments These are responsibilities often shirked, in Chomsky's view, by modern intellectuals.

213. "Some Thoughts on Intellectuals and the Schools." In *American Power and the New Mandarins*, 247-55. Op.cit., entry 195. Chomsky argues that schools must encourage more critical thought on national policy given the abdication of intellectuals from their role as objective critics.

214. "The Soviet Union versus Socialism." *Our Generation* 17,2 (Spring/Summer 1986): 47-52. Argues that the society created by Lenin, Stalin and their successors is the contradiction of libertarian socialism.

215. "What Is Anarchism?" *Our Generation* 8,2 (Winter/April 1972): 58-70. Provides an interesting insight into Chomsky's political philosophy. For him anarchism is libertarian socialism, an amalgam, he notes citing Rocker, of the two great traditions that since 1789 have informed the intellectual life of Europe, socialism and liberalism.

Anthologies :

216. *The Chomsky Reader*, edited by J. Peck. New York: Pantheon Bks., 1987. A collection of essays focussing on the role of intellectuals, and various political issues which are, in the main, involved with American foreign policy.

217. *Language and Politics* edited by Carol P. Otero. Montréal: Black Rose Bks., 1988.

218. *Radical Priorities*, edited by C. P. Otero. Montréal: Black Rose Bks., 1981. A useful collection of Chomsky's writings on U.S. foreign policy, state power, and the contemporary role and influence of intellectuals. In "The Relevance of Anarcho-Syndicalism" there is a brief account of modes of libertarian organization appropriate to advanced industrial countries, while in "Some Tasks for the Left" it is argued that self-management and co-operation should be recognized as essential human rights.

Works about Chomsky :

219. Coker, C. "The Mandarin and the Commissar: The Political Thought of Noam Chomsky." In *Noam Chomsky: Consensus and Controversy*, edited by Sohan Modgil and Celia Modgil, 269-78. Lewes, East Sussex and New York: Falmer Pr., 1987. A general survey of Chomsky's political philosophy.

220. D'Agostino, F. *Chomsky's System of Ideas*. Oxford: Clarendon Pr., 1986. A section entitled "Chomsky's Libertarianism," 206-14, suggests that Chomsky's libertarian socialism and his views on the nature of an ideal society can be derived from his account of linguistic phenomena. Bibliography.

221. Earle, W. "The Political Responsibilities of Philosophers." *Ethics* 79,1 (Oct. 1968): 10-13. A discussion with reference to Chomsky's piece, entry 209, in the same issue, of the professional and political responsibilities of philosophers.

222. Leiber, J. *Noam Chomsky: A Philosophic Overview*. Boston: Twayne Pubs., 1975. Mainly concerned with Chomsky's work on language the work does contain a short appreciation of his political philosophy, 178-83.

223. Silber, J. R. "Soul Politics and Political Morality." *Ethics* 79,1 (Oct. 1968): 14-23. A critical discussion of Chomsky's view, expressed in an article in the same issue of the journal of intellectuals and their ability to influence power. See entry 209.

224. Woodcock, G. "Chomsky's Anarchism." *Freedom* 16 (Nov. 1974): 4-5. Published in the *New York Review of Books*, 21 June 1970, *Anarchy* 116 (Oct. 1970), *Our Generation* 8,2 (Winter 1971). A critique of Chomsky's views as expressed in his introduction to Daniel Guerin's *Anarchism*, New York: Monthly Review Pr., 1970.

VOLTAIRINE DE CLEYRE (1866-1912)

Works by De Cleyre :

225. *Anarchism and American Tradition*. Chicago: Free Society Group, 1932. An interesting pamphlet that links the ideals of anarchism with the revolutionary doctrines of eighteenth century America.

226. "Anarchism." In *Man!*, 30-4. Op.cit., entry 1389. A short piece by De Cleyre, collected by Graham in the anthology of pieces from the journal *Man!* that discusses systems of property and communal organization.

227. *Crime and Punishment*. Philadelphia: Social Science Club, 1903. Lecture delivered before the Social Science Club of Philadelphia, 15 March 1903.

228. *Direct Action*. New York: Mother Earth Pubg. Assn., 1912. A lecture delivered in Chicago, 21 January 1912 on anarchism, trade unionism and the need for direct action.

229. *The Dominant Idea*. New York: Mother Earth Pubg. Assn., 1910.

230. *The Gods and the People*. San Francisco: Free Society, 189-?

231. *The Haymarket Speeches, 1895-1910*. Edited with introduction and notes by Paul Avrich. Sanday, Orkney: Cienfuegos Pr., 1980. Voltairine de Cleyre, moved by the fate of the Haymarket anarchists, gave a memorial oration for them nearly every November from 1895 onwards. Most of the speeches were delivered in Chicago, although some were given in Boston, New York and Philadelphia. Avrich has brought those extant together in a valuable collection.

232. "In Defense of Emma Goldman". In *Selected Works of Voltairine de Cleyre*, edited Alexander Berkman, 205-19. Op.cit., entry 235. Originally published in Philadelphia in 1894, this is a piece written on the occasion of Emma Goldman's arrest in that city in 1893, prior to the delivery of a speech to the unemployed. Goldman had already given a speech to a large crowd in Union Square, New York, in which, it was alleged, she had called for the immediate appropriation of property. Voltairine de Cleyre asserts that the authorities did not fear what Goldman was but what she might become.

233. *Sex Slavery*. Valley Falls, Kan.: Lucifer Pubg. Co., n.d. Voltairine de Cleyre denounced not just conventional marriage and the nuclear family, but any long term relationship as tending to create emotional enslavement.

234. *The Worm Turns*. Philadelphia: Innes and Sons, 1900. A collection of Voltairine de Cleyre's poetry.

Anthologies :

235. *Selected Works of Voltairine de Cleyre*. Edited by Alexander Berkman. New York: Mother Earth Pubg. Assn., 1914. A collection of the prose and verse of Voltairine de Cleyre published after her death. It contains a biographical sketch by Hippolyte Havel. Issued as a photocopy, Ann Arbor, Michigan: Univ. Microfilms, 1967.

Works about de Cleyre :

236. Avrich, P. *An American Anarchist: The Life of Voltairine de Cleyre*. Princeton N.J.: Princeton Univ. Pr., 1978. A look at the anarchism of Voltairine de Cleyre through letters, memoirs, journals and oral testimonies.

237. Goldman, E. *Voltairine de Cleyre*. Berkeley Hts. N.J.: Oriole Pr., 1932. A biographical sketch of Goldman's anarchist contemporary with whom she was in political accord, but who viewed Goldman's romantic adventures with some measure of disapproval.

238. March, M. "Voltairine de Cleyre." In *Anarchist Women, 1870-1920*, 122-50. Philadelphia: Temple Univ. Pr., 1987. A discussion of the life and work of Voltairine de Cleyre, who, named after Voltaire by her French socialist father, became an anarchist after the Haymarket trial. At first drawn to the American individualist anarchist tradition, with its defense of the rights of private property, she was later to adopt the communist anarchism of Kropotkin.

LUIGI GALLEANI (1861-1931)

Works by Galleani :

239. *The End of Anarchism?* Sanday, Orkney: Cienfuegos Pr., 1982. Luigi Galleani and Saverio Merlino were militant anarchists working together in the 1880's. When Merlino later declared himself to be a "libertarian socialist," and in an interview expressed his belief that anarchism as a force was at an end, Galleani responded with this series of articles in which he turned the statement into a question. Includes an introduction which locates the debate historically and reproduces the original interview with Merlino. Merlino, at this later stage in his career, also debated with Malatesta on the question of the utility of elections. See: Malatesta, *Gli Anarchici e la Questione Elettorale: Un Dibattito*, op.cit., entry 617.

WILLIAM GODWIN (1756-1836)

Works by Godwin : Philosophy :

240. *Considerations on Lord Greville's and Mr. Pitts' Bills Concerning Treasonable and Seditious Practices, and Unlawful Assemblies. By a Lover of Order*. London: J. Johnson, November, 1795. In *Uncollected Writings, 1785-1822*, op.cit., entry 260. Godwin's attack on the Bills was based on the belief that the government was forcing people to surrender important rights and freedoms.

241. *Cursory Strictures on Lord Chief Justice Eyre's Charge to the Grand Jury, October 2, 1794*. London: D. I. Eaton, 1794. In *Uncollected Writings, 1785-1822*, op.cit., entry 260. Shows that Godwin applied his political principles in practice. He attacked the government's attempt to change the legal definition of treason, and influenced public opinion in favour of the prisoners on trial for treasonable writings. The result of the trial was the

establishment of the important principle in English law that one cannot be convicted of treason on the basis of what one speaks or writes.

242. *The Enquirer: Reflections on Education, Manners and Literature.* Facsimile of the original London edition of 1797. New York: A. M. Kelly, 1965. A series of essays in which Godwin addresses such topics as education (which he believes is the basis of freedom) and morality, as well as economic and social questions. The arguments continue and extend those of *Political Justice.*

243. *An Enquiry Concerning Political Justice, and its Influence on General Virtue and Happiness.* Edited and abridged by Raymond A. Preston. Reproduction of 1st edition of 1793. New York: A. Knopf, 1926. Godwin's definitive work on anarchism set in the form of an enquiry into the philosophical basis of all government. This edition is abridged and the reproduction makes difficult reading.

244. *Enquiry Concerning Political Justice and its Influence on Morals and Happiness.* 3rd Edition. Corrected and edited, with variant readings of the 1st and 2nd editions. With a critical introduction and notes by F. E. L. Priestley. Toronto: Univ. of Toronto Pr., 1946. Reprinted 1962, 1969. In three volumes, the first two being facsimile reproductions of Godwin's work and the third a thorough-going attempt to locate Godwin in the eighteenth century philosophical tradition, assessing the influences on him and his aims in writing *Political Justice.* This facsimile reproduction makes very difficult reading.

245. *An Enquiry Concerning Political Justice.* Edited by Isaac Kramnick. Harmondsworth: Penguin, 1976. This unabridged version has a useful introduction which gives a detailed assessment of Godwin's anarchism as a philosophy of individual moral autonomy.

246. *Essay on Sepulchres: or, A Proposal for Erecting Some Memorial of the Illustrious Dead in All Ages on the Spot Where Their Remains Have Been Interred.* London: W. Miller, 1809. Written and published at his own expense it called for greater reverence for noble ancestors. Godwin also addresses a wider range of philosophical questions.

247. *Essays... Never Before Published.* Facsimile of the original London edition of 1873. New York: Folcroft Library Editions, 1976. Essays written in the last years of his life. Although entrusted to his daughter, Mrs. Shelley, she was unable, for a number of reasons, to get them published, and they did not appear until 1873. The content is largely concerned with moral and theological issues.

248. *Four Early Pamphlets, 1783-84.* Facsimile reproductions with an introduction by Burton R. Pollin. Gainesville, Florida: Scholar's Facsimiles and Reprints, 1966. (i) *An Account of the Seminary;* (ii) *A Defence of the Rockingham Party;* (iii) *Instructions to a Statesman;* (iv) *The Herald of*

Literature (Literary satire). Offers an insight into Godwin's interests and ideas a decade before his major works began to appear.

249. *History of the Commonwealth of England. From its Commencement, to the Restoration of Charles the Second.* 4 vols. London: Colburn, 1824-28. Based on extensive research of primary sources it is a large work in which Godwin not only narrates the main events but attempts to assign motives, and discuss causation. The fourth volume, devoted to Cromwell, is the first history of the period written from a republican perspective.

250. *The History of the Life of William Pitt, Earl of Chatham.* 2nd edition. London: G. Kearsley, 1783. Although not highly regarded as a biography of Pitt, it provides a glimpse of the early Godwin. He discusses Pitt's first Tory administration and his opposition to American Independence.

251. *Letters of Verax, to the Editor of the Morning Chronicle, on the Question of a War to be Commenced for the Purpose of Putting an End to the Supreme Power in France of Napoleon Bonaparte.* London: R. & A. Taylor, 1815. In *Uncollected Writings, 1785-1822*, op.cit., entry 260. An anti-war polemic inspired by events after the return of Napoleon from Elba.

252. *Life of Geoffrey Chaucer, the Early English Poet, including Memoirs of his Near Friend and Kinsman, John of Gaunt, Duke of Lancaster: With Sketches of the Manners, Opinions, Arts and Literature of England in the Fourteenth Century.* 2 vols. London: R. Phillips, 1803. As well as a history and criticism of all of Chaucer's works it contains details of life in fourteenth century England.

253. *Lives of Edward and John Phillips, Nephews and Pupils of Milton. Including Various Particulars of the Literary and Political History of Their Times.* London: Longman, Hurst, Rees, Orme & Brown, 1815. Of more interest than the lives and works of the subjects of the essay are Godwin's political and literary observations.

254. *The Lives of the Necromancers: or, An Account of the Most Eminent Persons in Successive Ages, Who Have Claimed for Themselves, or to Whom Has Been Imputed by Others, the Exercises of Magical Power.* London: F. J. Mason, 1834. Looks at the conflict between reason and the irrational forces at work in people, concluding that it is not to the supernatural but to themselves that people must look for guidance in how they must behave.

255. *Memoirs of the Author of a Vindication of the Rights of Woman.* Facsimile of the 1798 first edition. Introduction by Gina Luria. New York: Garland Publishing, 1974. The frankness of these memoirs, written following his wife's death, provoked some controversy. They show enormous love and respect for her.

256. *Of Population: An Enquiry Concerning the Power of Increase in the Numbers of Mankind, Being an Answer to Mr. Malthus's Essay on That*

Subject. Facsimile of the original London edition of 1820. New York: A. M. Kelly, 1964. A comprehensive refutation of Malthus whose theories seriously challenged Godwin's doctrine of perfectability.

257. *Sketches of History: In Six Sermons*. London: T. Cadell, 1784. Brings together sermons delivered when he was a dissenting minister from 1779-1783, one of which includes the famous sentence "God himself has not a right to be a tyrant."

258. *Thoughts Occasioned by the Perusal of Dr. Parr's Spital Sermon... Being a Reply to the Attacks of Dr. Parr, Mr. Mackintosh, the Author of an Essay on Population [i.e. T.R. Malthus] and Others*. London: G. G. & J. Robinson, June 12 1801. In *Uncollected Writings, 1785-1822*, op.cit., entry 260. In defending the principles of *Political Justice* from attack Godwin disavows the French Revolution and makes a plea for gradual change on the basis of reason. But, improvement in the human condition, he insists against Malthus, is possible.

259. *Thoughts on Man, His Nature, Productions and Discoveries. Interspersed with Some Particulars respecting the Author*. Fascimile of the original London edition of 1831. New York: A. M. Kelly, 1969. A series of essays which are the product of mature reflection and contain a reaffirmation of Godwin's faith in the perfectability of human beings. Significantly, Godwin's views on familial relations and sociability temper his earlier, and bleaker, view of individual autonomy.

260. *Uncollected Writings, 1785-1822*. Facsimile reproductions with introductions by J. W. Marken and B. R. Pollin. Gainesville, Florida: Scholar's Facsimiles and Reprints, 1968. Contains articles from periodicals and six pamphlets with brief but essential notes which locate the pieces in their historical contexts. In addition to the major pieces cited above numerous letters and newspaper articles are reprinted.

Works by Godwin : Novels and Letters :

261. *Antonio: A Tragedy in Five Acts*. London: G. G. & J. Robinson, 1800. A melodrama which failed miserably. Godwin regarded it as an unjustly condemned masterpiece.

262. *Cloudesley. A Tale*. 3 vols. London: Colburn & Bentley, 1830. A sentimental story of family intrigue.

263. *Damon and Delia*. London: T. Hookham, 1783. To be republished by the British Library. Godwin's first novel, it was short and well received. Its theme is that of ill-fated love and he employs a popular mixture of satire and sentimentality to make broad, sweeping social comments.

264. *Deloraine*. 3 vols. London: R. Bentley, 1833. His last novel, it deals with Godwin's continuing theme of the individual at odds with society. The character of Emilia was his last portrait of Mary Wollstonecraft.

265. *The Elopement of Percy Bysshe Shelley and Mary Wollstonecraft Godwin. As Narrated in a Letter of 27th August, 1814, to John Taylor.* Commentary by H. Buxton Foreman. Boston?: Privately printed, 1911.

266. *Faulkener: A Tragedy*. London: R. Phillips, 1807. A play on a theme adapted from the life of Richard Savage.

267. *Fleetwood; or, The New Man of Feeling*. 3 vols. London: R. Phillips, 1805. 2nd. edition, R. Bentley, 1832. Intended as a condemnation of libertines and jealousy.

268. *Imogen: A Pastoral Romance from the Ancient British*. London: W. Lane, 1784. Edited with an introduction by J. W. Marken and a critical discussion by M. W. England *et al*. New York: New York Public Library, 1963. The latter edition contains a helpful introduction to the book which portrays an ideal druidical society isolated from modern evils. In the introduction it is suggested that it may make a useful complement to his later major works of *Political Justice* and *Caleb Williams*.

269. *Italian Letters; or, The History of the Count De St. Julian*. 2 vols. London: G. Robinson, 1784. Edited with introduction by Burton R. Pollin. Lincoln: Univ. of Nebraska Pr., 1965. Of Godwin's nine novels this was the only one to use the epistolary form popular at the time. Its theme is seduction and betrayal, while it also aims to demonstrate the importance of education.

270. *Mandeville. A Tale of the Seventeenth Century in England*. 3 vols. Edinburgh & London: A. Constable & Co. & Longman, Hurst, Rees, Orme & Brown, 1817. Depicts the conflict between society and the individual but argues for forbearance rather than hatred. An early study of madness and moral conflict.

271. *St. Leon: A Tale of the Sixteenth Century*. 3 vols. London: 1799. A reproduction of the 1831 edition, with a foreword by Devenora P. Varma and an introduction by Juliet Beckett. New York: Arno Pr., 1972. A Gothic romance which is also concerned with moral philosophy.

272. *Things as They Are; or, The Adventures of Caleb Williams*. 3 vols. London: G. G. & J. Robinson, 1794. With an introduction by Ernest A. Baker, London: Four Square Bks., 1966. Edited with an introduction by D. McCracken, London: Oxford Univ. Pr., 1970. Generally seen as a fictional version of *Political Justice*, it eschews false ideals of honor and condemns existing institutions by which "man becomes the destroyer of man." As the title suggests the intention is to attack "things as they are."

273. "Letters of Godwin and Mary Wollstonecraft." In *Godwin and Mary*, edited Ralph M. Wardle. Lawrence: Univ. of Kansas Pr., 1966. Gives some insight into how they were both enriched by their association.

Works by Godwin under Pseudonyms:

274. Under pseudonym of Edward Baldwin. *Fables, Ancient and Modern. Adapted for the Use of Children*. 2 vols. London: T. Hodgkins, 1805. Godwin adapted some of the best known fables for very young children and contrived happy endings. He combined natural history and moral enlightenment in the belief that children are keen learners if their interests and sympathies are excited.

275. Under pseudonym of Edward Baldwin. *The History of England. For the Use of Schools and Young Persons*. London: T. Hodgkins, 1806. Traces the great landmarks of English history in which he welcomes the Commonwealth, the Glorious Revolution and the American War of Independence, and defends the French Revolution. It was used as a text in schools.

276. Under pseudonym of Edward Baldwin. *The History of Rome: From the Building of the City to the Ruin of the Republic*. London: M. J. Godwin & Co., 1809. Less concerned with historical accuracy than moral education, Godwin explores the reasons behind the rise and fall of Rome making obvious his attitudes to property, wealth and power. Aimed at young readers.

277. Under pseudonym of Edward Baldwin. *The History of Greece*. London: M. J. Godwin & Co., 1811. The last book written for the Juvenile Library it was intended as a replacement for an earlier school text. Godwin displays great admiration for the achievements of the Greeks and devotes considerable time to praising Spartan institutions.

278. Under pseudonym of Theophilus Marcliffe. *The Life of Lady Jane Grey, and of Guildford Dudley, Her Husband*. London: T. Hodgkins, 1806. Aimed at young readers it tells a tragic story which concludes with a plea for religious toleration.

279. Under pseudonym of Theophilus Marcliffe. *The Looking Glass: A True History of the Early Years of an Artist*. London: T. Hodgkins, 1805. Written with the aim of encouraging young people to emulate people who have achieved excellence, especially in the cultivation of the fine arts.

280. Under pseudonym of Edward Baldwin. *Mylius's School Dictionary of the English Language. To Which Is Prefixed "A New Guide to the English Tongue."* London: M. J. Godwin & Co., 1809. An extensive revision of Mylius's dictionary. Godwin aimed at improving the efficiency with which language and grammar was learnt. His definitions of words like "politics," "anarchy," "Pope," "God" and "novel" make an interesting study.

281. Under pseudonym of Edward Baldwin. *The Pantheon, or Ancient History of the Gods of Greece and Rome.* London: T. Hodgkins, 1806. A study of ancient mythology which was intended to elucidate the works of the poets and awaken the imagination. The tales and engravings, having been stripped of their "licentious coloring," were widely used as a basic text in schools.

Works about Godwin :

282. Barrell, J. *Shelley and the Thought of his Time: A Study in the History of Ideas.* New Haven: Yale Univ. Pr., 1947. Examines the importance of the influence of romantic radicalism and romantic Hellenism on Shelley's work and credits Godwin with having had a significant impact in the first area.

283. Brailsford, H. N. *Shelley, Godwin, and their Circle.* London: Williams & Norgate, 1913. Offers a brief discussion of Godwin's ideas and his influence on Shelley. An excellent short introduction to Godwin and the period.

284. Brown, F. K. *The Life of William Godwin.* London: Dent, 1926. While in many ways a useful biography it lacks any systematic discussion of Godwin's ideas. It is more useful in sketching the contemporary background of his life and times.

285. Claeys, G. "The Concept of 'Political Justice' in Godwin's *Political Justice:* A Reconsideration." *Political Theory* 11,4 (Nov. 1983): 565-84. Argues that Godwin's notion of political justice was an attempt to create a moral norm based on Christian maxims that was to be practiced by the individuals of the future, rather than, as in the past, being enforced by the state.

286. Claeys, G. "The Effect of Property on Godwin's Theory of Justice." *Journal of the History of Philosophy* 22,1 (Jan. 1984): 81-101. Surveys Godwin's views on property as they unfold in *Political Justice.* Suggests that Godwin accepted the idea of a right to private property and that the only basis in justice for unequal property rights lay in the use of property in the realization of the social good.

287. Clark, J. P. "On Anarchism in an Unreal World: Kramnick's View of Godwin and the Anarchists." *American Political Science Review* 69,1 (1975): 162-7. A defense of Godwin and his anarchism in response to Kramnick, entry 302. Clark argues that anarchism is not elitist.

288. Clark, J. P. *The Philosophical Anarchism of William Godwin.* Princeton, N.J.: Princeton Univ. Pr., 1977. A comprehensive analysis of Godwin's philosophy and its application to social and political issues.

289. Clark, J. P. "Rejoinder to "Comment" by Isaac Kramnick." *American Political Science Review* 69,1 (1975): 169-70. A final response in the Kramnick/Clark debate. See entries 287, 300 and 302.

290. Fearn, M. "William Godwin and the 'Wilds Of Literature'." *British Journal of Educational Studies* 29,3 (Oct. 1981): 247-57. Suggests that Godwin's concern for the proper education of the young naturally led to his career in the writing and publishing of books for children.

291. Fleisher, D. *William Godwin: A Study in Liberalism.* London: Allen & Unwin, 1951. An analysis of Godwin's *Political Justice* against the background of the development of English liberalism with some comments on his views on religion.

292. Furbank, P. N. "Godwin's Novels." *Essays in Criticism* 5,3 (July 1955): 214-28. With particular reference to *Caleb Williams* it argues that Godwin's novels complement and illuminate his political writings, especially *Political Justice*. Likens Godwin to Dostoevsky, calling them "historians of conscience."

293. Garrett, R. W. "Anarchism or Political Democracy: The Case of William Godwin." *Social Theory and Practice* 1 (Spring 1971): 111-20. Analyzes Godwin's arguments against national legislatures etc. and, although critical of Godwin's reasoning, finds that Godwin's arguments are valuable for demonstrating the restrictiveness of some democratic institutions.

294. Grylls, R. G. *William Godwin and his Work.* London: Odhams Pr., 1953. A patchy account of Godwin's ideas, life and times, covering the period 1794 to 1836.

295. Hazlitt, W. "William Godwin." In *The Spirit of the Age,* edited by E.D. Mackerness, 19-38. London: Collins 1969. Contains a contemporary essay on Godwin's ideas and influence, which applauds Godwin's philosophy while satirizing his person.

296. Hodgart, M. "Radical Prose in the Eighteenth Century." In *The English Mind: Studies in The English Moralists,* (Presented to Basil Willey), edited by Hugh Sykes Davies and George Watson, 146-52. Cambridge: Cambridge Univ. Pr., 1964. Deals with the connections between the political thought and literary styles of Thomas Paine in *The Rights of Man* and William Godwin in *Political Justice.* It is generally critical of Godwin's literary skills and describes him as a metaphysical revolutionary.

297. James, C. L. *Anarchism and Malthus.* New York: Mother Earth Pubg. Assoc., 1910. Discusses the debate between Malthus and Godwin, noting the ultimate triumph of Malthus's views, and arguing that, in order to defeat Malthus, an anarchism that embraces the emancipation of women is needed.

298. Jenkins, P. "Varieties of Enlightenment Criminology: Beccaria, Godwin, De Sade." *British Journal of Criminology* 24,2 (1984): 112-30. Suggests that Beccaria's ideas on the nature of crime were in fact deeply conservative. The work of de Sade and Godwin are cited as representative of the radicalism which condemned society before the criminal.

299. Kirschner, J. "Civic Education and the Anarchist Critique of William Godwin." *Proceedings of the Annual Meeting of the Philosophy of Education Society* 32 (1976): 221-31. Discusses Godwin's attitude to education in relation to his belief that the unfettered mind can discern truth and justice, and that, in consequence, reason is the necessary basis of a society.

300. Kramnick, I. "Comment on Clark's 'On Anarchism in an Unreal World'." *American Political Science Review* 69,1 (1975): 168-69. A very brief reply which concedes little. See entries 287, 289 and 302.

301. Kramnick, I. "The Left and Edmund Burke." *Political Theory* 11,2 (1983): 189-214. Suggests that Godwin found some of Burke's views relevant for his own theories.

302. Kramnick, I. "On Anarchism and the Real World: William Godwin and Radical England." *American Political Science Review* 66,1 (1972): 114-28. Points out what are seen as problems in Godwin's anarchist philosophy by giving an outline of it in the context of his debate with Thelwall. It is suggested that Godwin was less than enthusiastic about some reform measures, and was guilty of elitism. While advocating radicalism in theory he was conservative in practice. See entries 287, 289 and 300.

303. Locke, D. *A Fantasy of Reason: Life and Thought of William Godwin.* London: Routledge & Kegan Paul, 1980. A detailed study of Godwin's life and works set in the context of his times which seeks both to account for Godwin's relative obscurity and to discuss and analyze his philosophy.

304. Luria, G. "Mary Hays's Letters and Manuscripts." *Signs: Journal of Women in Culture and Society* 3,2 (1977): 524-30. A discussion of the work of Mary Hays as a dissenting radical and aspiring novelist. Adopted by Godwin as a pupil, he became her "tutelary genius." Her novel *Memoirs of Emma Courtney*, 1796, had an early and strong feminist element. A fragment of correspondence between Hays and Godwin is included. Also see A. F. Wedd, ed. *The Love Letters of Mary Hays, 1779-1780.* London: Methuen, 1925.

305. Marshall, P. H. *William Godwin: Philosopher, Novelist, Revolutionary.* New Haven: Yale Univ. Pr., 1984. A detailed look at the life and writings of Godwin which disputes the image of him as the naive, abstract philosopher. Argues that a depiction of him as a complete man must include consideration of Godwin the revolutionary. Excellent bibliography, index.

306. McCracken, D. "Godwin's Literary Theory: The Alliance between Fiction and Political Philosophy." *Philological Quarterly* 49 (Jan. 1970): 113-33. Argues that Godwin's two styles of writing showed great versatility but should be understood as part of one single vocation in which he demonstrated that reason and imagination were complementary.

307. Monro, D. H. "Archbishop Fénelon versus My Mother." *Australasian Journal of Philosophy* 28,3 (Dec. 1950): 154-73. An analysis of the debate generated by Godwin's concern with the justification for moral choices in the elucidation of his principle of justice.

308. Monro, D. H. "Godwin, Oakeshott and Mrs. Bloomer." *Journal of the History of Ideas* 35,4 (1974): 611-24. Discusses Godwin's and Oakeshott's divergent views on whether it is possible or desirable to disregard tradition. It concludes that Oakeshott's argument fails to undermine Godwin's rationalist position that tradition can be disregarded.

309. Monro, D. H. *Godwin's Moral Philosophy: An Interpretation of William Godwin*, London: Oxford Univ. Pr., 1953. Analyzes many of the conventional criticisms of Godwin and dismisses them as facile, but goes on to suggest that his philosophy is still deeply flawed. Godwin's ideas are explored within the context of English utilitarianism.

310. Murry, J. M. *Heaven and Earth*. London: Jonathan Cape, 1938. From a profoundly Christian perspective this book looks at the growth of the modern world through the minds of some of its great thinkers, a category in which Godwin is included.

311. Ousby, I. "'My Servant Caleb': Godwin's Caleb Williams and the Political Trials of the 1790's." *University of Toronto Quarterly* 44,1 (1974): 47-55. Suggests a new dimension to Godwin's criticism of Caleb's conduct as a detective or spy, arguing that Godwin disliked spies (largely because of their role in the political trials of the time). Concludes that Falkland's tyrannical behavior in the latter half of the book and Caleb's earlier rashness and deceit are both condemned.

312. Paul, C. K. *William Godwin: His Friends and Contemporaries*. 2 vols. London: H. S. King, 1876. One of the best sources for biographical research, containing a great amount of Godwin's correspondence, extracts from his journals and other writings. There is narrative and commentary to link Godwin's writings.

313. Pollin, B. R. *Godwin Criticism: A Synoptic Bibliography*. Toronto: Univ. of Toronto Pr., 1967. Includes articles from British, French, German and American periodicals. Over 2,000 entries.

314. Pollin, B. R. "Godwin's 'Letters of Verax'." *Journal of the History of Ideas* 25,3 (1964): 253-73. A review of a very rare pamphlet of 1815 in which Godwin engages in anti-war polemics on the subject of the struggle against Bonaparte. See entry 251.

315. Preu, J. A. *The Dean and the Anarchist*. Tallahasse: Florida State University Studies 33 (1959). Examines Johnathon Swift's influence on Godwin.

316. Preu, J. "Swift's Influence on Godwin's Doctrine of Anarchism." *Journal of the History of Ideas* 15,3 (June 1954): 371-83. Suggests that Swift's *A Voyage To The Houyhnhnms* influenced Godwin's work but that his admiration for Swift was based on a misunderstanding and a distortion of Swift's intention.

317. Priestman, D. G. "Godwin, Schiller and the Polemics of Coleridge's *Osorio.*" *Bulletin of Research in the Humanities* 82,2 (Summer 1979): 236-49. Discusses *Osorio* as a critical response to Godwin's *Political Justice*.

318. Ritter, A. "Godwin, Proudhon and the Anarchist Justification of Punishment." *Political Theory* 3,1 (1975): 68-87. Argues that anarchists do not have to eschew punishment if it is non-legal, and compares Godwin's utilitarian rationale with Proudhon's view that it may be necessary on deontological grounds. It is argued that both agreed that reparation was preferable to punishment.

319. Rodway, A. E. *Godwin and the Age of Transition*. London: Harrap, 1952. A selection of articles by people like Burke, Wordsworth, Hazlitt, Shelley, Paine and Priestley intended to reflect the times in which Godwin wrote and the people he influenced. Includes a select bibliography and chronological table.

320. Rosen, F. "The Principle of Population as Political Theory: Godwin's *Of Population* and the Malthusian Controversy." *Journal of the History of Ideas* 31,1 (1970): 33-48. Argues that Godwin regarded himself as the first to respond to all the implications of Malthus' theory, not just the moral implications alone, by appealing to earlier theories of population and using them against Malthus.

321. Scrivener, M. H. "Godwin's Philosophy: A Revaluation." *Journal of the History of Ideas* 39,4 (1978): 615-26. Outlines Godwin's gradualist position which in essence asserts that the elevation of consciousness is the revolution.

322. Sherburn, G. "Godwin's Later Novels." *Studies in Romanticism* 1 (Winter 1962): 65-82. Comments at length on evidence in Godwin's later novels, such as *Fleetwood* and *Mandeville*, which suggests an obsession with guilt arising from misanthropy.

323. Smith, E. E. and Smith, E. G. *William Godwin*. New York: Twayne Publishers, 1965. An attempt to address all facets of Godwin's work and assess his influence on other thinkers. It is sympathetic but critical. Concludes that it is in his conception of evil that his greatest strengths and weaknesses as a philosopher are manifest. Includes a chronology, bibliography and index.

324. St Clair, W. *The Godwins and the Shelleys: The Biography of a Family.* London: Faber and Faber, 1989. A well-reviewed, detailed biographical work that focuses on Godwin, but with his familial relations in high relief.

325. Stafford, W. "Dissenting Religion Translated into Politics: Godwin's Political Justice." *History of Political Thought* 1,2 (1980): 279-301. Suggests that argument pursued by Godwin in *Political Justice* should be seen as influenced by the debate between the Sandemanians and Methodists. Dissenting culture is an important ingredient of Godwin's philosophy.

326. Tysdahl, B. J. *William Godwin as a Novelist.* London: Athlone Pr., 1981. A discussion of Godwin's fiction in relation to his works of political philosophy.

327. Williams, D. A. "William Godwin's Problem of Autonomy, 1790-1800." In *The Consortium on Revolutionary Europe*, edited by L. Kennett. Gainesville: U. of Florida Pr., 1973. Suggests that both Godwin's political philosophy and his novels must be studied in concert to create a comprehensive understanding of his thought. Such a study reveals a person whose insistence on the value of personal autonomy jarred with his aspirations to found a new social order.

328. Woodcock, G. *William Godwin: A Biographical Study.* Originally published London: Porcupine Pr., 1946, with a foreword by Herbert Read. Montréal: Black Rose Bks., 1989 A useful critical study of Godwin's life and political philosophy, that considers his influence in his lifetime and the relevance of his ideas to the present.

EMMA GOLDMAN (1869-1940)

Works by Goldman:

329. *Anarchism and Other Essays.* Introduction by Richard Drinnon. New York: Dover Pubns., 1969. Originally published in 1911 this contains some important essays. Also contains a biographical sketch by Hippolyte Havel. Includes the classic essays "Anarchism," "The Traffic in Women," "Woman Suffrage", "The Tragedy of Woman's Emancipation," "Anarchism: What It Really Stands for", "The Psychology of Political Violence" and "Prisons: A Social Crime and Failure."

330. *Anarchism: What It really Stands For.* New York: Mother Earth Pubg. Assn., 1914. Goldman's definitive analysis of anarchist principles and practices. Reprinted in several anthologies. See *Red Emma Speaks*, 47-63. Op.cit., entry 360. Originally published in *Anarchism and Other Essays*, 47-67. Op.cit., entry 329.

331. *Anarchism on Trial.* New York: Mother Earth Pubg. Assn., 1917. The speeches by Goldman and Alexander Berkman during their trial, in the U.S.

District Court, New York, in July 1917, for their public advocacy of opposition to conscription in the 1914-18 war. Reprinted in *Red Emma Speaks*, 311-27. Op.cit., entry 360.

332. *The Crushing of the Russian Revolution*. London: Freedom Pr., 1922. An analysis of the Revolution based on her two years in Russia. Includes details about the lives of the people and special characters such as Kropotkin. The experience confirmed her belief that "all government...is a dead weight that paralyses the free spirit and activities of the masses." The piece ends optimistically, however, with the suggestion that the people are disillusioned with political processes and will attempt more direct action in the future.

333. *Deportation, its Meaning and Menace; Last Message to the People of America*. With Alexander Berkman. New York: E. M. Fitzgerald, 1919. Written on the occasion of the deportation of Goldman and Berkman from the United States, after two years in jail for obstructing the military draft.

334. *Living my Life*. Edited by Richard and Anna Maria Drinnon. New York: New American Library, 1977. Abridged version of Goldman's autobiography till 1924 which was originally published in two volumes by Alfred A. Knopf in 1931, and reprinted unabridged New York: Dover Pr., 1970 and Salt Lake City: Peregrine Smith, 1982, with an introduction by Candice Falk. Gives details of her time in Russia, including her impressions of Kropotkin.

335. *Marriage and Love*. New York: Mother Earth Pubg. Assn., 1911. A critique of the institution of marriage, arguing that marriage is primarily an economic arrangement with no necessary connection to love, since the latter presupposes a relationship between free and equal human beings. Reprinted in several anthologies.

336. *My Disillusionment in Russia*. With a biographical sketch by Frank Harris, and an introduction by Rebecca West. New York: Crowell, 1970. An analysis of the Russian Revolution and the statist policies pursued by the Bolsheviks, based on her own experiences in Russia from 1919-1921. This work was originally titled *My Two Years in Russia* but was changed, without Goldman's permission, by the publisher.

337. *My Further Disillusionment in Russia*. New York: Doubleday, Page & Co., 1924. When Goldman wrote *My Two Years in Russia* it was published as *My Disillusionment in Russia* with the last twelve chapters missing. These were later published in a separate volume entitled *My Further Disillusionment in Russia* which included her "Afterword" on the forces behind the Russian Revolution. She reiterated her views on the Revolution in "There Is No Communism in Russia." *American Mercury* 34 (April 1935).

338. *Nowhere at Home: Letters from Exile of Emma Goldman and Alexander Berkman*. Edited by Richard and Anna Maria Drinnon. New

York: Schocken Bks., 1975. A wide selection of the letters of Goldman and Berkman, to each other and to their comrades, covering the post 1919 period. Arranged chronologically within five broad thematic areas. Useful introduction by the editors.

339. *Patriotism: A Menace to Liberty.* New York: Mother Earth Pubg. Assn., 1908? An early critique of patriotism in which its causes are held to be rooted in the need to harness popular support for military protection of commercial activities. Reprinted in *Anarchism and Other Essays.* Op.cit., entry 329.

340. *Philosophy of Atheism and the Failure of Christianity.* New York: Mother Earth Pubg. Assn., 1916. Originally delivered as separate lectures, "Philosophy of Atheism," February 1916 and "The Failure of Christianity," April 1913. In the "Philosophy of Atheism" Goldman argues that such a philosophy has its roots in the material world, does not presuppose the prior or concurrent existence of a divine regulator, and hence affirms the responsibility of human beings for their own lives. Reprinted in *Red Emma Speaks*, 186-202. Op.cit., entry 360.

341. *The Place of the Individual in Society.* Chicago: The Free Society Forum, 193-. Argues that there is no legitimate authority outside the individual, but tempers this with a strong defense of collectivism. Reprinted as "The Individual, Society and the State" in *Red Emma Speaks*, 86-100. Op.cit., entry 360.

342. *Preparedness, the Road to Universal Slaughter.* New York: Mother Earth Pubg. Assn., 1917. A strong critique of rationalizations for the arms race, the justifications then being used for U.S. entry into the 1914-1918 war, and the institution of militarism. Reprinted in *Red Emma Speaks*, 301-10. Op.cit., entry 360.

343. *The Psychology of Political Violence.* New York: Gordon Pr., 1974. Provides a sharp analysis of the causation of terrorist acts, arguing that such acts must be seen in the context of the material conditions that engender them. Reprinted in several anthologies.

344. *The Social Significance of the Modern Drama.* Boston: Badger, 1914. Goldman examines the radical potential of modern literature and drama, examining the work of, among others, Hauptmann, Wedekind, Ibsen and Shaw. Reprinted in *Anarchims and Other Essays*, 241-71. Op.cit., entry 329.

345. "The Story of Bolshevik Tyranny." *Freedom* 36,396/397/398 (June/July/Aug. 1922): 37-41/47-51/54-5. A discussion of the events in Russia arguing that the Bolshevik's attempt to create communism has been a failure. Includes an account of a visit to Kropotkin.

346. *Syndicalism: The Modern Menace to Capitalism.* New York: Mother Earth Pubg. Assn., 1913. A discussion of syndicalism noting with approval the advocacy of direct action and its agreement with anarchism on the need

to base social organization on voluntary associations. Reprinted as "Syndicalism: Its Theory and Practice" in *Red Emma Speaks*, 64-77. Op.cit., entry 360.

347. *The Tragedy of Woman's Emancipation*. New York: Mother Earth Pubg. Assn., 1910. Argues that women's servitude is created by the nature of the social order. An emancipation movement limited only to gaining the vote for women is a betrayal of the movement for emancipation in its fullest sense. Reprinted in several anthologies. See *Red Emma Speaks*, 133-42. Op.cit., entry 360.

348. *Trotsky Protests Too Much*. Glasgow: Anarchist-Communist Fedn., 1938. A pamphlet that grew out of an article for the New York anarchist monthly, *Vanguard*, July 1938, in which she criticizes Trotsky's attempts to distance himself from the suppression of the Kronstadt uprising and blame it on Stalin. Argues that Trotsky was also responsible and is now falsifying the facts.

349. *The Truth about the Bolsheviks*. New York: Mother Earth Pubg. Assn, 1918. An early defense of the Russian Revolution and the Bolshevik regime.

350. "An Unpublished Letter." *Anarchy* 114 (Aug. 1970): 245-6. A letter to Vernon Richards, 10 September 1938.

351. *Victims of Morality and the Failure of Christianity*. New York: Mother Earth Pubg. Assn., 1913. Originally presented as two separate lectures - "Victims of Morality", March 1913, and "The Failure of Christianity", April 1913. The former looks at the effects and the hypocrisy of the imposition of prevailing moral standards on women. The latter essay examines the slave-mentality of Christianity, arguing that its shortcomings are part of its very being and concluding that it is "the conspiracy of ignorance against reason" and hence incapable of providing a way out of the poverty produced by exploitation. Reprinted separately in *Red Emma Speaks*, 126-32 and 186-94. Op.cit., entry 36.

352. "Vladimir Ilyich Lenin." *Freedom* 38,416 (March-April 1924): 14-15. Goldman takes issue with eulogies that have appeared following Lenin's death. She brands him as great in the sense that Torquemada was great - unscrupulous and Jesuitical.

353. *Voltairine de Cleyre*. Berkeley Heights, N.J.: Oriole Pr., 1932. Biographical sketch of a leading American radical, a contemporary of Goldman.

354. *What I Believe*. New York: Mother Earth Pubg. Assn., 1908. A brief summary of her beliefs, concerning property, government, militarism, freedom, the Church, marriage and love, and violence, as part of her public defense of anarchism following the assassination, by a self-proclaimed

follower of Goldman, of President McKinley. Reprinted in *Red Emma Speaks*, 34-46. Op.cit., entry 360.

355. "Was My Life Worth Living?" *Harper's Magazine* 170 (Dec. 1934). Reprinted in *Red Emma Speaks*, 386-98. Op.cit., entry 360. A retrospect in which Goldman unrepentedly reaffirms her faith in anarchism.

356. *The White Slave Traffic*. New York: Mother Earth Pubg. Assn., 1909. A short, eight page, pamphlet in which Goldman looks at the social causation of prostitution, sexual ignorance and the sexual oppression of women, while linking the eradication of prostitution to the abolition of industrial slavery.

357. *A Woman without a Country*. Sanday, Orkney: Cienfuegos Pr., 1979. A pamphlet in which Goldman describes the bankruptcy of the notion of citizenship since World War I, describing how governments, in particular that of the U.S., justified the exile and deportation of thousands of people as undesirable aliens.

358. "Women of the Russian Revolution." *Freedom* 39,427 (June 1925): 34-5. An account of the revolutionary careers of leading women activists and anarchists in the Russian Revolution and of their persecution by the Bolsheviks.

Anthologies :

359. *Glimpses of Emma Goldman*. Compiled and edited by Lydia Gans. Pasadena, Calif.: Tabula Rasa, 1978. Edition of 300 copies only. A beautifully presented series of quotes from Goldman's work under headings, for example "On Women, Children and Education." More a keepsake than a text.

360. *Red Emma Speaks: Selected Writings and Speeches*. Compiled by Alix Kates Shulman. New York: Random Hse., 1972. An excellent collection of Goldman's essays and speeches that demonstrate her wide-ranging interests and ability to analyze critically social institutions. Includes essays published in *Mother Earth* like "The Child and its Enemies" and "Intellectual Proletarians," as well as previously unpublished lectures such as "Socialism: Caught in the Political Trap." See entries 340, 341, 342, 351 and 355.

361. *The Traffic in Women and other Essays on Feminism*. With a biography by Alix Kates Shulman. Washington: Times Change Pr., 1970. Contains the three essays "The Traffic In Women," "Marriage And Love" and "Woman Suffrage" and a useful introductory biographical sketch which together constitute a good statement of Goldman's feminism.

362. *Visions on Fire: Emma Goldman on the Spanish Revolution*. Edited by David Porter. New York: Commonground Pr. 1983. Detailed excerpts from

Goldman's letters dealing with various aspects of the Spanish Revolution. There is a scholarly commentary and introductory passages by the editor. Excellent notes and references.

Works about Goldman :

363. Anderson, M. "The Challenge of Emma Goldman." *The Little Review* 1 (May 1914): 5-9. Written by a person who attended Goldman's lectures and admired her courage and commitment, this article condemns those who criticize Goldman without ever having read or heard her. Concludes that even if her practical goals are never achieved the challenge with which she confronts people remains enormously valuable.

364. Barko, N. "The Emma Goldman You'll Never See in the Movies." *MS* (March 1982): 27-31. A brief summary of Goldman's life and ideas.

365. Chalberg, J. *Emma Goldman: American Individualist.* New York: Harper/Collins, 1991.

366. Cook, B. W. "Female Support Networks and Political Activism: Lillian Wald, Crystal Eastman, Emma Goldman" 412-44. In *A Heritage of Our Own*, edited with an introduction by Nancy F. Cox and H. Pleck, 412-44. New York: Simon & Schuster, 1979. A revised version of an essay published in *Chrysalis* 3 (1977): 43-61. Discusses the problems faced by women activists and the extent to which they can draw on female support networks.

367. Dell, F. *Women as World Builders.* Westport, Conn.: Hyperion Pr., 1976. Reprint of an account by one of Goldman's contemporaries in which her politics are somewhat uncritically assessed.

368. Detelbaum, W. "Epistolary Politics: The Correspondence of Emma Goldman and Alexander Berkman." *Prose Studies* 9,1 (1986) 30-46. Brief description of the events immediately following the expulsion of Goldman and Berkman from the United States and the anarchist content of their correspondence between 1929 and 1936.

369. Drinnon, R. "Emma Goldman, Alexander Berkman and the Dream We Hark back To" and "Back to the Future." *Anarchy* 114, (Aug. 1970) 229-246. A discussion of the lives and work of Goldman and Berkman which emphasizes the continuing relevance of their ideas.

370. Drinnon, R. *Rebel in Paradise: A Biography of Emma Goldman.* Chicago: Univ. of Chicago Pr., 1961. Definitive biography of Goldman which includes a comprehensive guide to sources and bibliographic information.

371. Falk, C. *Love, Anarchy and Emma Goldman.* New York: Holt & Rinehart, 1984. Focuses almost exclusively on Goldman's ten year relationship with Ben Reitman and explores the public/personal dichotomy

as revealed in the Goldman/Reitman correspondence. Deals with her anarchist ideas and activities only briefly.

372. Frank, W. "Elegy for Anarchism." *New Republic* 30 (Dec. 1931): 193-4. Primarily a review of Goldman's *Living my Life* but draws some interesting conclusions about anarchism after the experience of the Russian revolution.

373. Frazer, W. L. *E.G. and E.G.O.: Emma Goldman and "The Iceman Cometh."* Gainesville: Univ. of Florida Pr., 1974. Examines the influence of Emma Goldman on the playwright Eugene Gladstone O'Neill.

374. Ganguli, B. *Emma Goldman: Portrait of a Rebel Woman.* New Delhi: Allied Pubs., 1979. Based on lectures delivered at the Centre for the Study of Developing Societies, Delhi, Ganguli presents a short account of the main features of Goldman's life and thought, with consideration given to the connections between the latter and the thought of Gandhi.

375. Goldberg, H. J. "Goldman and Berkman View the Bolshevik Régime." *Slavonic and East European Review* 53,131 (1975): 272-6. Claims that Goldman and Berkman were actually very slow to condemn the Bolsheviks and were prepared to excuse many of the defects of the regime right up until the crushing of the Kronstadt Uprising in 1921.

376. Goldsmith, M. *Seven Women against the World.* London: Methuen, 1935; 153-82. A chapter on Goldman provides a brief biographical sketch of her anarchism.

377. Harris, F. "Emma Goldman, the Famous Anarchist." In *Contemporary Portraits,* 4th Series, 222-49. London: Grant Richards, 1924. Harris describes Goldman as the greatest woman he has ever met and condemns as despotic the Wilson government which abused and deported her. He quotes Goldman at length.

378. Havel, H. "Emma Goldman: A Biographic Sketch." In *Anarchism and Other Essays,* 1-40. Op.cit, entry 329. An early biography written in December 1910 by a fellow anarchist.

379. Hewitt, M. "Emma Goldman: The Case for Anarcho-Feminism." *Our Generation* 17,1 (Fall-Winter, 1985-86) 167-77. Asserts the importance of the link between sexual liberation and human liberation which, for Goldman, was of paramount importance. Concludes that it is the task of anarcho-feminists to develop this analysis.

380. Ishill, J. *Emma Goldman: A Challenging Rebel.* Berkeley Heights, N.J.: Oriole Pr., 1957. Originally published in *Freie Arbeiter Stimme* in 1944, this study pays close attention to Goldman's participation in cultural debates.

381. Kern, R. W. "Anarchist Principles and Spanish Reality: Emma Goldman as a Participant in the Civil War 1936-1939." *Journal of*

Contemporary History 11,2-3 (1976) 237-261. Negative assessment of Goldman's analysis of, and contribution to, the Spanish Revolution.

382. Kirchwey, F. "Emma Goldman." *The Nation* 2 (Dec. 1931): 612-13. A review of Goldman's *Living my Life* full of praise for her passion and commitment.

383. Madison, C. "Emma Goldman, Anarchist Rebel." In *Critics and Crusaders*. New York: Holt, 1947. A sympathetic sketch of Goldman's life and activities, characterizing her as an idealist who nonetheless appreciated that ideals usually fall dismally short of reality.

384. Reifen, G. "Emma Goldman." In *Women Who Fought: An American History*, edited by E. M. Dermody, 171-9. Norwalk, Calif.: Cerritos College, 1978. A brief biographical sketch.

385. Rosenberg, K. "An 'Autumnal Love' of Emma Goldman." *Dissent* (Summer 1983): 380-3. An attempt to explain Goldman's apparently contradictory attitudes to love and sex by an examination of the personal relationships of her later years.

386. Rosenberg, K. "The 'Autumnal Love' of Red Emma." *Harvard Magazine* (Jan-Feb. 1984): 52-6. Based on some unpublished letters, the article examines the sometimes strained relationship between Goldman's politics and passions, with particular reference to her relationship with Leon Malmed.

387. Shulman, A. K. "Dancing in the Revolution: Emma Goldman's Feminism." *Socialist Review* 12,2 (March-April 1982): 3-6. An analysis of Goldman's feminist views and their relevance to the various strands of feminist thought in the contemporary era of "second wave" feminism.

388. Shulman, A. K. "Emma Goldman, Anarchist and Feminist." *Women: A Journal of Liberation* 7,2 (Spring 1980). A brief, introductory biographical sketch focussing on Goldman's feminism. Reprinted in *The Traffic in Women*, op.cit., entry 362.

389. Shulman, A. K. "Emma Goldman 'Anarchist Queen'." In *Feminist Theorists: Three Centuries of Women's Traditions*, edited Dale Spender, 218-228. London: Women's Pr., 1983. An abridged version of "Dancing in the Revolution," op.cit., entry 387.

390. Shulman, A. K. *To the Barricades: The Anarchist Life of Emma Goldman*. New York: Harper & Row, 1971. Very readable account of Goldman's life and achievements, but with no detailed analysis of her ideas.

391. Solomon, M. *Emma Goldman*. Boston: Twayne Pubs., 1987. Acknowledges the work of Drinnon, Falk and Wexler and asserts that the aim is not to compete with them but to extend the overall picture we have

of Goldman by focussing on her writing and speaking as a propagandist for anarchism. Includes a very good bibliography.

392. Spacks, P. M. "Selves in Hiding." In *Womens' Autobiography*, edited E. C. Jelinek, 112-32. Bloomington: Indiana Univ. Pr., 1980. Focuses on the problem of reconciling one's private and public life by looking at Goldman's autobiography.

393. Waldstreicher, D. *Emma Goldman: Political Activist*. New York: Chelsea Hse., 1990.

394. Walter, N. "Emma Goldman's Disillusionment in Russia." *The Raven* 2,3 (July 1989): 232-42. Examines the background and the significance of the publication of Goldman's writings on Russia.

395. Wexler, A. "The Early Life of Emma Goldman." *Psychohistory Review* 8,4 (1980): 7-21. A detailed examination of the powerful influences in Goldman's early life which may have determined her later attitudes and activities, based on the argument that her commitment to anarchism was the beginning of her intellectual development, not its end result.

396. Wexler, A. "Emma Goldman on Mary Wollstonecraft." *Feminist Studies* 7,1 (1981): 113-34. Examines briefly Goldman's comparisons of herself with Wollstonecraft and then analyzes Goldman's own life in the light of that comparison.

397. Wexler, A. "Emma Goldman in Love." *Raritan: A Quarterly Review* (Summer 1982): 116-45. An intimate account of Goldman's relationship with Ben Lewis Reitman during the period 1908-18, with photographs and extracts from personal letters.

398. Wexler, A. *Emma Goldman: An Intimate Life*. London: Virago Pr., 1984. A detailed account of Goldman's life and work up to her deportation in 1919. Provides an informative account of both the public and private Goldman by exploring the various tensions arising from her desire to live out her anarchist principles.

399. Wexler, A. "Emma Goldman and Women." *Our Generation* 17,1 (Fall-Winter 1985-6): 151-67. Explores Goldman's relations with men and her difficulties identifying with women. See entry 400 for sequel.

400. Wexler, A. *Emma Goldman in Exile: From the Russian Revolution to the Spanish Civil War*. Boston: Beacon Pr., 1989. The second part of Wexler's excellent biographical study. A sensitive, but critical analysis of Goldman's dedication to anarchist ideals and their dissemination.

PAUL GOODMAN (1911-1972)

Works by Goodman :

This selection from Goodman's wide range of publications focuses on his anarchism and related themes.

401. "Anarchism and Revolution." In *Great Ideas Today*. Chicago: Encyclopaedia Britannica, 1970. Republished in *Drawing the Line*, 215-32. Op.cit., entry 421. A definition of anarchism and its relationship to revolution. Goodman takes up the issue of the youth revolt, identifying it as anarchist, and repeating material from "The Black Flag of Anarchism."

402. "The Black Flag of Anarchism." In *Drawing the Line*, 203-14. Op.cit., entry 421. Published in the *New York Times Magazine*, 14 July 1968. One of Goodman's best known arguments regarding decentralizing principles. Asserts that the student revolt is based on anarchist principles of decentralization, anti-police, anti-party, anti-bureaucracy, pro-spontaneity and voluntary organization, direct action etc. Criticism is made of neo-Leninist elements of the student alliance.

403. *Communitas*. Co-author Percival Goodman. New York: Alfred Knopf, 1947. Written with his architect brother, this early work is hailed by many as perhaps Goodman's most important work. Exploring ideas on the planning of cities, while embracing rather than eschewing utopianism, it is a book that examines the first principles underlying the formation of human communities. Further it seeks to develop a framework for the creation of communities that can provide for all human needs, the spiritual and the aesthetic as well as the material.

404. *The Community of Scholars*. New York: Random Hse., 1962. Discusses the 1,900 American Colleges and Universities as the only important remaining, self-governing communities. Goodman described this work as "an anarchist critique of the the colleges," where "I show how certain centers of learning were doing beautifully before they officially 'existed' at all." (*Seeds of Liberation*, 439. Op.cit., entry 417). Goodman discusses the tensions that can exist between the goals of these communities and the goals of the society in which they exist. He argues that scholars must not conform to outside pressures for performance, and that the community of scholars must be prepared to confront society.

405. *Compulsory Mis-education*. New York: Alfred Knopf, 1962. A libertarian argument against compulsory education, advocating decentralization, voluntary learning and a focus on the individual worth of each student. The philosophy of A. S. Neill provides a reference point, for the assertion that the aim must be to encourage understanding rather than simply a knowledge of facts.

406. "Confusion and Order." In *Drawing the Line*, 233-45. Op.cit., entry 421. Discusses the problems of modern society; crowding, urbanization,

pollution, technological domination and the attendant dehumanization, and the break-down of the social order. Concludes that it is promising, from the viewpoint of an anarchist and a psychologist, when things fall apart that have been too tightly and artificially held together.

407. "The Empty Society." *Commentary* 42,5 (Nov. 1966): 53-60. A criticism of American society as an empty system based on empty institutions, a corporate and bureaucratic society that has lost its common sense. The only hope lies in American traditions of populism, democracy, individualism and liberty. In a revised form this essay forms Chapter VI, "Is American Democracy Viable?" of *Like a Conquered Province*, 353-70. Op.cit., entry 411.

408. "The Formal Content of Democracy." In *Drawing the Line*, 178-84. Op.cit., entry 421. A draft of Chapter 2 of *People and Personnel*. Also published in *Liberation* (June-July 1964). Charts the movement from the individualist anarchism of the Frontier to the institutionalized, corporate democracy of modern society.

409. "Freedom and Learning: The Need for Choice." *Anarchy* 94 (Dec.1968): 372-4. An account of Goodman's views on the need for free, that is liberated, education and education for freedom.

410. "Kropotkin at this Moment." *Anarchy* 98 (April 1969): 124-8. Discusses the renewal of interest in the ideas of Kropotkin. Written as a preface to the Horizon Press Edition of Kropotkin's *Memoirs of a Revolutionist*, op.cit., entry 506.

411. *Like a Conquered Province: The Moral Ambiguity of America.* New York: Vintage Bks., 1968. Published in a double volume with *People or Personnel*, entry 414, it argues that the vital conflict today is between a global, dehumanized system and human decency. It is a struggle for the survival of human values. This double edition also contains seven essays previously unpublished in book form.

412. *New Reformation: Notes of a Neolithic Conservative.* New York: Random Hse., 1970. Calls for a complete restructuring of American society to make it ecologically aware and organizationally decentralized. In the section "Legitimacy" Goodman describes his theory of anarchy, emphasizing decentralization and participatory democracy. In "Notes of a Neolithic Conservative" Goodman embraces a gradualism that makes of anarchism a process of changing consciousness towards freedom.

413. "Notes on Decentralization." In *Drawing the Line*, 185-202. Op.cit., entry 421. Notes towards *People or Personnel* published in *Dissent* (Autumn 1964). A critique of centralized systems, including the school system, monolithic communication systems and transport systems. Advocates mixed systems, with decentralization allowing for autonomous activity.

414. *People or Personnel: Decentralizing and the Mixed System*. New York: Vintage Bks., 1968. Published in a double volume with *Like a Conquered Province*, this is a critique of American society and its military-industrial complex that deplores the way in which people have become dehumanized, 'personnel' within over-centralized and over-organized industrial and urban structures. Decentralization is advocated as a remedy to this denial, by modern society, of human worth and meaning, and to the concomitant stultification of social progress.

415. "The Present Moment in Education." *Anarchy* 107 (Jan. 1970): 1-17. Reprinted from the *New York Review of Books*, 10 April, 1969, the article sets out Goodman's educational philosophy and its implications for social theory.

416. "Reflections on the Anarchist Principle." *Anarchy* 62 (April 1962). Republished in *Drawing the Line*, 176-7. Op.cit., entry 421. Argues that anarchism represents a continual vigilance to protect freedom from encroachment.

417. *Seeds of Liberation*. Edited Goodman. New York: Braziller, 1964. A collection of essays and poems giving first hand accounts of human rights activism. Mainly reprinted from the journal *Liberation*, the volume also contains some new essays. Includes work by Martin Luther King, Lewis Mumford, Gene Hoffman, Aldous Huxley, Dave Dellinger and Goodman himself. In "Getting Into Power," 433-44, Goodman reviews the Senate campaign of a pacifist, discusses conventional systems of power, and concludes that a radical pacifism must be in agreement with anarchism on the need to diminish abstract authority and decentralize power.

418. *The Society I Live in Is Mine*. New York: Horizon Pr., 1963. A collection of Goodman's letters published in his neighborhood newspaper, speeches book reviews etc.. The purpose of the collection is to urge, by example, that people become more concerned, involved and, thereby, authentic citizens.

419. *Utopian Essays and Practical Proposals*. New York: Vintage Bks., 1964. A collection of essays in which Goodman argues that the chief social problem facing Americans is the drive for greater and greater technological domination with a concomitant dehumanization of human beings who, increasingly, feel impoverished and powerless.

420. "Utopian Means They Don't Want To Do It." *Anarchy* 85 (March 1968): 87-9. A rejection of the terms "utopian"and a call for positive action for reform.

Anthologies :

421. *Drawing the Line: Political Essays*. Edited by Taylor Stoehr. New York: Free Life Editions, 1977. A selection of Goodman's political essays covering the period from the early 1940s to 1972. Section 4, entitled "The Black Flag of

Anarchism" includes essays on revolution, decentralization, democracy and anarchism. This edition also includes his last public speech before his death in 1972. See entries 401, 402, 406, 408, 413 and 416.

Works about Goodman :

The selection focuses on his anarchism and related social comment.

422. Chappell, R. H. "Anarchy Revisited: An Inquiry into the Public Education Dilemma." *Journal of Libertarian Studies* 2,4 (Winter 1978): 357-72. Primarily concerned with the identification and documentation of educational viewpoints espoused by nineteenth century anarchists, there is discussion of the views of Goodman and Illich.

423. Ellerby, J. "The World of Paul Goodman." *Anarchy* 11 (Jan. 1962): 1-19. A discussion of Goodman's anarchist approach to education with reviews of his major works on the subject.

424. Epstein, J. "Paul Goodman in Retrospect." *Commentary* 65,2 (Feb. 1978): 70-3. A rather negative retrospective view of Goodman's work that concludes, somewhat surprisingly, that, since many of the things he asked for "have come about," he now seems a voice "overvalued in his own lifetime."

425. Greene, M. "Paul Goodman and Anarchistic Education." In *Social Forces and Schooling*, edited N. K. Shimahara and Adam Scrupski, 313-16. New York: McKay & Co., 1975. A critical examination of the character of Goodman's anarchist position in general, with special attention paid to education and the continuing relevance of Goodman's ideas.

426. Hannam, C. and Stephenson, N. "Celebrator of Youth." *Times Educational Supplement* 3434 (23 April 1982): 19. Argues that Goodman's ideas on decentralization, on the free individual, and on the capacity of people to determine their own lives, have acquired a new urgency in the 1980s.

427. Harrington, M. "On Paul Goodman." *The Atlantic Monthly* 216 (Aug. 1965): 88-91. A critical discussion of *People and Personnel*, entry 414, concluding that, while its proposals are admirable, it is out of touch with the political exigencies of radical politics in the mid-60s.

428. Hentoff, N. "Citizen Va-r-ooooooom! In Memory of Paul Goodman." *Harvard Educational Review* 43,1 (Feb. 1973): 1-4. An appreciation of Goodman the man and thinker.

429. King, R. "Paul Goodman." In *The Party of Eros: Radical Social Thought and the Realm of Freedom*, 78-115. Chapel Hill, N.C.: Univ. of North Carolina Pr., 1972. A discussion of Goodman's social thought in the context of Freud and post-Freudians like Reich and Marcuse.

430. Molnar, G. "Meliorism." *Anarchy*, 8 (March 1968): 76-83. This is an anarchist critique of Goodman's ideas, with a reply in the same edition by Ross Poole, 83-7.

431. Petry, W. "Review of Paul Goodman: *Drawing the Line: The Political Essays: Creator Spirit Come: The Literary Essays: Nature Heals: The Psychology Essays.*" *Our Generation* 13,2 (Spring 1979): 61-5. A discussion and critical review of Goodman's work from an anarchist viewpoint.

432. Roszak, T. "Exploring Utopia: The Visionary Sociology of Paul Goodman." In *The Making of a Counter-Culture*, 178-204. New York: Doubleday, 1969. A discussion of Goodman's social thought in all its aspects, emphasizing the importance of his vision of decentralized community, and concluding that his "communitarianism" has been his greatest contribution to the youth culture.

433. Roszak, T. "The Future as Community." *The Nation* 20,16 (15 April 1968): 497-503. An earlier version of the essay on Goodman that appeared in *The Making of the Counter-Culture*, op.cit., entry 1849, but with some differences that perhaps make it worth consulting.

434. Smith, M. P. *The Libertarians and Education*. London: Allen & Unwin, 1984. Goodman's ideas are considered as part of a discussion of anarchism and education.

435. Steiner, G. "On Paul Goodman." *Commentary* 36 (Aug. 1963): 158-63. A comparative analysis of Goodman's social and political theory that involves a discussion of what is called "positive regional anarchism."

436. Stoehr, T. "The Attitude of Anarchism." *The Nation* 224,14 (9 April 1977): 437-40. The first part of a two-part treatment of Goodman's life and ideas. This is a useful introduction to Goodman detailing the development of his main lines of thought and focussing attention on his anarchism of decentralization.

437. Stoehr, T. "Cunning, Fraud or Flight." *The Nation* 224,12 (26 March 1977): 373-6. The second part of Stoehr's appreciation of Goodman's life and ideas.

438. Stoehr, T. "Growing-Up Absurd Again: Re-Reading Paul Goodman in the Nineties." *Dissent* 37 (Fall 1990): 486-94. On the thirtieth anniversary of the publication of *Growing Up Absurd* Stoehr discusses the revelatory impact of the work when first published, reflecting that many of the ideas it contains, which were always common sense, have now become part of common knowledge and experience.

439. Ward, C. "Communitas Revisited." *Liberation* 7 (June 1962): 11-6. A retrospective of the work and ideas of Goodman.

440. Ward, C. "Paul Goodman's Legacy." *Times Educational Supplement* 30,14 (2 March 1973): 19. An obituary that discusses the importance of Goodman's social theory. Ward concludes that Goodman was the most original and creative anarchist thinker of his generation. It is interesting to compare his earlier appreciation of Goodman in "Communitas Revisited," op.cit., entry 439.

441. Widmer, K. "American Conservative Anarchism." *Anarchy* 1,4 (Second Series 1975?): 14-19. Second Series; A review of Goodman's *New Reformation: Notes of a Neolithic Conservative*, op.cit., entry 412, discussing Goodman's critique of American society coupled, in this work, with a demand for humane but gradual responses to problems. Goodman describes himself here as a "conservative anarchist."

442. Widmer, K. "The Conservative Anarchist of 'Politics Within Limits'." *The Nation* 216,1 (1Jan. 1973): 21-3. A review of *New Reformation*, op.cit., entry 412, that contains some reflections on his social theory.

443. Widmer, K. *The End of Culture*. San Diego: San Diego State Univ. Pr., 1975. Continues the broad discussion of Goodman that was begun in *The Literary Rebel*, op.cit., entry 444.

444. Widmer, K. *The Literary Rebel*. Carbondale: Univ. of S. Illinois Pr., 1975. Chapter 12, "Several American Perplexes," examines Goodman's communitarianism in relation to his role as a literary rebel.

445. Widmer, K. *Paul Goodman*. Boston: Twayne Pubs., 1980. A discussion and analysis of various aspects of Goodman's thought. Chapter 2, "The Conservative Anarchist," and Chapter 5, "Conclusion: The Libertarian Legacy," directly considers his relationship to the anarchist tradition. Widmer concludes that Goodman was not a major anarchist thinker, lacking theoretical originality and rigor. Rather he was an important post-War libertarian social critic.

446. Woodcock, G. "Paul Goodman: The Anarchist as Conservator," in *The Anarchist Papers*, 55. Op.cit, entry 1514. A discussion of the conservative anarchism of the later Goodman. The changeover to a free society will not be brought about by sudden revolution Goodman believes. Rather gradualism has to be accepted for change to occur. Anarchism is an attitude that resists changes that make society less human while promoting changes that foster freedom.

JEAN GRAVE (1854-1939)

Works by Grave:

447. *Anarchy on Trial*. Freedom Pamphlet No.9. Co-authors G. Etievant and S. Caserio. London: Freedom Office, 1901. The speeches of the authors at

their trials. Etievant, charged with the theft of dynamite received five years; Grave was sentenced to two and a half years for publishing *La Societé Mourante et L'Anarchie*; Caserio killed President Carnot in 1894.

448. "Du révolté aux temps nouveaux." *Les Temps Nouveaux*. 45,47,48(5-11 March/19-25 March/26 March-1 April 1904).

449. *Moribund Society and Anarchy*. Translated by Voltairine de Cleyre. San Francisco: A. Isaak, 1899. Publication in English of *La societé mourante et L'anarchie*, op.cit., entry 450. A discussion of contemporary problems from an anarchist viewpoint, focussing on patriotism, colonialism, militarism, the family, property and human nature.

450. *Le mouvement libertaire sous la Troisième République*. Paris: Les Oeuvres Représentatives, 1930.

451. *Quarante ans de propagande anarchiste*. Par préface de Jean Maitron. Présenté et annoté Mireille Delfau. Paris: Flammarion, 1973.

452. *La société future*. Paris: Stock, 1895.

453. *La société mourante et l'anarchie*. Paris: Tresse et Stock, 1893.

454. "Ought Anarchists To Take Part in the War?" *Freedom* 28,307 (November 1914): 84-5. Grave's contribution to a symposium on the war in which he justifies participation in the war on the grounds that the oppression of foreign conquerors is infinitely worse than the oppression of their masters at home, and in the hope that it will be the war to end all wars. Grave's position was criticized by Malatesta, as was the pro-war stance of Kropotkin. See entries 471 and 620.

455. "What We Want." *Freedom* 28,304 (Aug. & Sept. 1914): 62-70. A list of anarchist goals with a discussion of the dangers of syndicalism.

Works about Grave :

456. Patsouras, L. *Jean Grave and French Anarchism*. Dubuque, Iowa: Kendall/Hunt Pub. Co., 1978. A biography of Grave which discusses his involvement in the journals *Le Révolté*, *La Révolte* and *Les Temps Nouveaux*, his responses to the 1914-18 war, the Russian Revolution and syndicalism in France.

DANIEL GUÉRIN (1904-)

Works by Guérin :

457. *Anarchism: From Theory to Practice*. Translated by Mary Klopper. Introduced by Noam Chomsky. New York: Monthly Review Pr., 1970. One of the best short introductions to the ideas of anarchism with an emphasis on attempts at the implementation of these ideas. Contrasts authoritarian socialism with libertarian socialism.

458. *Anarchism and Marxism*. From a paper given in New York on 6 November 1973. Introduction by the author. Sanday, Orkney: Cienfuegos Pr., 1981. Equates orthodox Marxism with authoritarianism and argues for a synthesis of libertarianism and communism adapted to the needs of workers in a technologically advanced society. Republished in a revised and extended version, as "Marxism and Anarchism." In *For Anarchism: History, Theory and Practice*; 109-26. Op.cit., entry 1385.

459. "From Proudhon to Bakunin." *Our Generation* 17,2 (Spring-Summer 1986): 23-34. Discusses the relationship between Proudhon and Bakunin, their friendship in Paris in the period 1845-47 and connections between their ideas.

AMON HENNACY (1893-1970)

Works by Hennacy :

460. *Autobiography of a Catholic Anarchist*. New York: Catholic Worker Bks., 1954. An autobiography of a Christian anarchist which includes an account of his refusal, on Tolstoyan pacifist grounds, to pay income tax during the Second World War.

PETER ALEKSEEVICH KROPOTKIN (1842-1921)

Works by Kropotkin :

461. "1848-1871." *Freedom* 12,125 (April 1898): 17-8. A speech at the Commune celebration 1898 in which Kropotkin contrasts the Commune with Jacobinist centralism and asserts that the social revolution must begin by organizing consumption not production.

462. *Act for Yourselves*. Compiled and edited N. Walter and H. Becker. London: Freedom Pr., 1988. Like the articles that were collected for *The Conquest of Bread*, a similar series of articles was written for *Freedom* from October 1886 until 1890. But these articles were not collected at the time,

although Kropotkin wanted to see them in book form. This volume represents the publication of this collection and covers a gap in the *ouevre* of Kropotkin. "The Coming Revolution" opens the series, arguing that an international, proletarian revolution was imminent and would spread to Britain. "What Revolution Means" asserts the need for far-reaching political and economic structural change, while "Act for Yourselves" argues that the revolution should involve direct action and expropriation. In "Parliamentary Rule" a case is made against parliamentary democracy. Elsewhere direct action is urged ("Local Action") and a revolutionary approach to land reform ("The End Set Before Us"), the expropriation of property and the creation of communism ("The Necessity of Communism"). "Practical Questions" looks at post-revolution issues, while other essays deal with the supply of food ("Revolution and Famine"), human nature and utopianism ("Are We Good Enough?") and the abolition of the wage system ("Communism and the Wage System").

463. *"Advice to Those About to Emigrate."* Freedom 7,74 (March 1893): 13-14. A discussion of migration to Australia which recommends *inter alia* intensive agriculture and no government.

464. *"Anarchism."* In *Encyclopaedia Britannica*. 11th Edition. 1910. Included in *Revolutionary Pamphlets*, 83-300. Op.cit., entry 53. Also *The Essential Kropotkin*, 108-20. Op.cit., entry 537. This is a dispassionate summary of the meaning and history of anarchism, significant partly because it is atypical of Kropotkin's style and contrasts interestingly with the rest of his work.

465. *Anarchism: Its Philosophy and Ideal.* London: Freedom Office/J. Turner, 1897. Included in *Revolutionary Pamphlets*, 114-44. Op.cit., entry 538. Discusses the philosophy of anarchism, emphasizing freedom and opposition to authority and private appropriation. Distinguishes free communism from collectivism, and creative from selfish individualism as the basis of self-development.

466. *Anarchist Communism: Its Basis and Principles.* London: Freedom Office/J. Turner, 1905. Originally written in the form of two articles for *The Nineteenth Century*, 1887. Included in *Revolutionary Pamphlets*, 44-78. Op.cit., entry 538. Kropotkin sets out the principles of communist anarchism, asserting the vital differences between free anarchism and state orientated socialism. Criticizing private appropriation, he extolls the virtues of co-operative production in a free, stateless society, while seeking, in the second part, to answer familiar objections to this idea.

467. *"The Anarchist Ideal from the Viewpoint of Its Practical Realization."* Freedom 28,6 (25 Feb. 1967). Translated from *Le Révolté* 1, (1879), by Nicolas Walter. Published as a pamphlet Geneva: 1879. Described by Nettlau as Kropotkin's first statement of anarchist communist ideas, it represents a report given to a meeting of the Jura Federation at La Chaux-de-Fonds, 12 October, 1879.

468. *Anarchist Morality*. Freedom Pamphlets No.6. London: Freedom Office, 1896? Originally published in *La Révolte* in March/April 1890. A discussion of morals setting out ideas developed later in his *Ethics*. While asserting the principle of equality as, in essence, the Golden Rule - do unto others as you would be done by - it is stressed that the morality of equality must be allied to the full and free liberty of each individual, which cannot be sacrificed to some ideal of equality. In *Revolutionary Pamphlets*, 79-113. Op.cit., entry 538.

469. "Anarchists and the French Revolution." *Freedom* 17, 183 (Dec. 1904): 1/18,184 (Jan. 1904): 1-2. Kropotkin takes issue with Brissot's attack on "Anarchists" in the French Revolution in his *Brissot to his Constituents*, 23 May, 1793.

470. "Anarchists and Trade Unions." *Freedom* 21,218 (June 1907): 33-34. Part of a debate conducted in the pages of *Les Temps Nouveaux*. Kropotkin defends himself against a charge that he is opposed to trade unions and affirms his faith in revolutionary syndicalism and direct action.

471. "Anti-Militarism: Was It Properly Understood?" *Freedom*. 28,307 (Nov. 1914): 82-83. Argues that in a war of invasion everyone is bound to take sides against the invader. Part of a symposium with Grave and Malatesta. See entries 454 and 620.

472. *An Appeal to the Young*. New York: C. H. Kerr, 1984. Originally published London: The Modern Pr., 1885. Translated H. M. Hyndman. Also published London: Lighthouse Pubns., 1976. An appeal to young men and women, particularly young professionals such as lawyers, doctors, scientists etc., to use their skills in the cause of and on behalf of a workers' revolution. In *Revolutionary Pamphlets*. 260-82. Op.cit., entry 53. Also *The Essential Kropotkin*; 10-26. Op.cit., entry 537.

473. "Caesarism." *Freedom* 13,137 (April 1899): 25-6/13,138 (May 1899): 28-9. A discussion of Caesarism and militarism in France set against the backdrop of the Dreyfus Affair.

474. *The Coming Revival of Socialism*. Freedom Pamphlet No.15. London: Freedom Office/J. Turner, 1903. Argues for the revival, in England, not of social-democracy, since social-democrats have ceased to be socialist, but of true socialism. The last phase of socialism was dominated by German social-democracy; the time is now ripe for the English labor movement to forge a new path to true socialism.

475. *The Commune of Paris*. Freedom Pamphlet No.2. London: Freedom Office/J. Turner, 1895. First appeared in *Le Révolte* 20 March, 1880. A discussion of the experience of the Commune, arguing that it is a model for direct revolutionary action to break down the state, abolish private property and create free federation and free production.

476. "Communism and Anarchy." *Freedom* 15,158 (July 1901): 30-1/15,159 (Aug. 1901): 38-9. A report from the Paris Congress of 1900 that discusses various approaches to communism and concludes that it becomes possible in association with anarchy.

477. *The Conquest of Bread.* Introduction by George Woodcock. Montréal: Black Rose Bks., 1989. Originally published as *La Conquête du Pain*, Paris: Stock, 1892. Published in English, London: Chapman and Hall, 1906. Reissued with introduction by Paul Avrich, London: Allen Lane, 1972; with introduction by Alfredo M. Bonnano, London: Elephant, 1985. A collection of articles which appeared in *Le Révolté* and *La Révolte* between 1886 and 1896, which were expressly designed as a series for collection, although a number were issued as separate pamphlets. Together they form one of Kropotkin's most visionary works. The book details the philosophy and practice of an ideal anarchist communist society, discussing the mechanisms for its creation and continuance. Issues like food, dwellings and clothing are discussed and the broad features sketched of the political economy of anarchism, including the use of needs to integrate production and consumption, the end of the division of labor, the decentralization of industry and the use of intensive methods of agriculture.

478. "The Constitutional Agitation in Russia." *The Nineteenth Century and After* 57,335 (Jan. 1905): 27-45. Discusses the meeting of the Zemstov delegates at St. Petersburg, the decisions of which were expressed in eleven resolutions which became the programme for agitation all over Russia. Warns that whether or not the autocracy yields, the movement cannot now be stopped.

479. "Conversation with Lenin." In *Selected Writings on Anarchism and Revolution*, 325-32. Op.cit., entry 539. Originally published in *Zveda* 4 (1930), and translated by Miller. Records a meeting between Kropotkin and Lenin at which there was broad agreement over shared goals, but sharp differences over methods of achieving them. While Kropotkin emphasized co-operation, Lenin spoke portentously of a possible 'terror'.

480. "Co-operation: A Reply to Herbert Spencer." *Freedom* 10,111 (Dec. 1896): 117-18/11,112 (Jan. 1897): 1-2. Takes issue with Herbert Spencer's views regarding industrial production and co-operation in the last volume of *Principles of Sociology*.

481. "The Development of Trade Unionism." *Freedom* 12,124 (March 1898): 9-10. Lecture delivered at Memorial Hall, 24 January 1898, urging trade unionists to take more militant action aimed at workers' emancipation.

482. "Elisée Reclus." *Freedom* 14,199 (Aug. 1905): 21/23-4. An obituary of Reclus celebrating his work as, like Kropotkin himself, both a scientist and an anarchist.

483. "Enough of Illusions." *Freedom* 21,220 (Aug. 1907): 45-6. Argues that the dissolution of the Second Duma marked the close of the first period of

revolution in Russia - the period of illusion. The second period should involve the seizure of production by the people.

484. "The Ethical Needs of the Present Day." *The Nineteenth Century and After* 330 (Aug. 1904): 207-26. A republishing of Chapters 1 and 2 of *Ethics*. Examines the relationship between ethics and nature with a discussion of Darwin, mutual aid and progressive evolution that affirms the existence of moral progress.

485. *Ethics: Origin and Development.* Petrograd-Moscow, *Golos Truda*, 1922. New York: McVeagh, 1924. Also New York: Tudor, 1947. Articles collected after the death of Kropotkin some of which were published separately between 1904 and 1906. Contains an historical overview of ethical principles and theories from earliest times to the nineteenth century with discussions on the concepts of justice, socialist ethics and like matters. Denies any connection between morality and religious metaphysics and bases ethics on the principle of mutual aid between equals, the only basis, he asserts, for morality.

486. *Expropriation: An Anarchistic Essay.* London: International Pubg. Co., 1886. Freedom Pamphlet No.7. Translated by H. Glasse from *Le Révolté*, 25 November 1882, it also appeared as an essay in *The Conquest of Bread*, op.cit., entry 447. Included in *Selected Writings on Anarchism and Revolution*, 162-209. Op.cit., entry 539. Discusses how the social revolution will expropriate the property owners, abolish rents and establish free production. Money will be replaced by an exchange of products and productivity will flourish.

487. "The Expropriation of Dwellings." *Anarchy* 102 (Aug. 1969): 244-50. Kropotkin's essay on the expropriation of housing in the revolution was written for *Le Révolté* and later reprinted in both *Paroles d'un Revolté* and *The Conquest of Bread*.

488. "A Few Thoughts About the Essence of Anarchism." *Freedom* 28,297 (Jan. 1914): 4-5. A letter by Kropotkin to the French Anarchist Congress, Paris 1913, on anarchist strategy for the future.

489. *Fields, Factories and Workshops Tomorrow.* Edited and introduced by Colin Ward, with additional material. London: Freedom Pr., 1985. Originally published London: Hutchinson and Co., 1899. This edition is a repeat of London: Allen and Unwin, 1974. Also published New York: Left Bank, 1985. Beginning from the premise that industrial production would become global Kropotkin argues that small-scale production for a local market would be a better alternative than trying for overseas markets. By combining industry and agriculture on an intensive small-scale basis, with an education system geared to the unity of mental and manual labor, and with the economy under the immediate control of the direct producers, the material needs of people could be amply satisfied. Useful introduction and commentary provided by the editor.

490. "Foreword," to Thomas Smith, *French Gardening*. London: Joseph Fels/Utopia Pr., 1909, v-x. A short foreword in which Kropotkin extolls the virtues of intensive horticulture, that is French market-gardening, which, in the market-gardens of Paris, Rouen and other cities, achieved astonishing levels of productivity by the use of frames, cloches and liberal doses of manure.

491. "The Geneva Tragedy." *Freedom* 12,131 (Oct. 1898): 68-9. A letter from Kropotkin to Georg Brandes, the eminent Danish critic, on the subject of the assassination of the Empress of Austria in Geneva, after criticism of himself.

492. "Glimpses into the Labour Movement in this Country." *Freedom* 21,222 (Oct. 1907): 57-8. A discussion of the labor movement in Britain from the perspective of the files of *Freedom*. Kropotkin looks at the divisions of the past, and forward to anarchist communism as opposed to collectivist state socialism.

493. "The Great French Revolution and its Lessons." *The Nineteenth Century* 25,148 (June 1889): 838-51. Written on the occasion of the centenary of the French Revolution. Kropotkin draws parallels with the situation in Russia and urges those in power to take notice of the lessons it has to offer.

494. *The Great French Revolution*. New introduction by George Woodcock. Montréal: Black Rose Bks., 1989. Translated from the French by N. F. Dryhurst, London: Heinemann, 1909. Reprinted New York: Schocken Bks., 1971; London: Elephant Bks., 1986. A work in which Kropotkin argues that previous historians had neglected the two most important factors of the revolution - namely the role of the intellectuals who gave it a theoretical basis, and of the ordinary people themselves who gave it its force and momentum. This edition was released as part of the 200th Anniversary of the French Revolution.

495. "Herbert Spencer." *Freedom* 18,185,187,188,190,191 (Feb.-Sept. 1904): 7-8/15/23/31/35. A sympathetic discussion of Spencer's life and work following the latter's death in December 1903.

496. *Ideals and Realities in Russian Literature.* Westport, Conn.: Greenwood Pr., 1970. Originally published New York: 1905, as *Russian Literature*. Published with present title, New York, A. A. Knopf, 1915. This is a work on Russian literature that also contains some discussion of Kropotkin's political views and statements of his social theory.

497. "In Memory of William Morris." *Freedom* 10,110 (Nov. 1896): 109-10. A tribute to William Morris and to *News from Nowhere*, hailed as "the most thoroughly and deeply Anarchistic conception of future society that has ever been written."

498. *In Russian and French Prisons.* New York: Schocken Bks., 1971. Originally published London: Ward and Downey, 1887. A partly autobiographical discussion of the prison systems of Russia, including exile in Siberia or Sakhalin, and France. Examining penal theory, Kropotkin concludes that prisons have a deleterious influence, morally and practically. Since crime is a product of social conditions, prisons should be replaced by fraternal care in a free society.

499. "Integral Education." *Freedom* 15,160 (Sept. 1901): 49. A discussion of educational curricula that argues the case for the inclusion of more science.

500. *Kropotkin Escapes: His Own Account of His Escape to England from a Russian Prison Hospital in 1876.* London: World's End Pr., 1988. The title speaks for itself.

501. "Kropotkin's Letter." *Freedom* 15,160 (Sept. 1901): 50. A letter to a meeting at the South Place Institute, 21 June, 1901, on the occasion of a visit by French trade union delegates, that urges the formation of an International Federation of all trade unions.

502. "Kropotkin's Speech to the Moscow National Conference, 28 August, 1917." In *The Birth of Russian Democracy*, by A. J. Sack, 466. New York: Russian Information Bureau, 1918. Kropotkin, making an anarchist contribution to the debate about the progress of revolution in Russia in the interlude between March and October 1917, spoke immediately preceding Plekhanov. They were both introduced by the leader of the Provisional Government, A. P. Kerensky.

503. *Law and Authority.* London: International Pubg. Co., 1886. A chapter in *Paroles d'un Révolté.* This argues that while law is, on the one hand, usage and custom, it is also the way in which the ruling class gives itself title to its advantages. There is, Kropotkin insists, no need for law in a free society, since crime is produced by inequality, authority and property. In *Revolutionary Pamphlets*, 195-218. Op.cit., entry 538. Also *The Essential Kropotkin*, 27-43. Op.cit., entry 539.

504. "Letter to Gustav Steffen." *Freedom* 28,306 (Oct. 1914): 76-7. Included in *Selected Writings on Anarchism and Revolution*, op.cit., entry 539. A letter on the issues raised by the 1914-18 war. Kropotkin affirms his belief that the German invasion must be repulsed.

505. "Letter to the Workers of Western Europe" and "What to Do?" in *Revolutionary Pamphlets*, 251-9. Op.cit., entry 538. Written as a public statement on the Soviet Government for the British Labor Mission of 1920 the *Letter* was sent to the Danish critic Georg Brandes in early 1919. The memorandum, "What to Do?" is uncompleted and dates from 1921.

506. *Memoirs of a Revolutionist.* Introduction George Woodcock. Montréal, Black Rose Bks., 1989. Originally published Boston: Houghton, Mifflin. 1899, with an introduction by Georg Brandes. Reprinted with a new foreword by

Barnett Newman and a preface by Paul Goodman, New York: Horizon Pr., 1968. Also introduced by Colin Ward, London: Folio Society, 1978. Reprinted with extensive notes by Nicolas Walter, New York: Dover Pubs., 1971. Kropotkin's own account of his transition from sceptical supporter of the Russian aristocracy, into which he was born, to a dedicated revolutionary. It provides a brilliant portrait of the Russia of his youth.

507. *Modern Science and Anarchism.* London: Freedom Pr., 1912. Published Paris: Stock, 1913 as *La Science Moderne et L'Anarchie*, a volume that also contained the essays on anarchist communism and the state. Included in *Revolutionary Pamphlets*, 145-94. Op.cit., entry 538. Also *The Essential Kropotkin*, 57-83. Op.cit., entry 537. Kropotkin discusses the application of the inductive-deductive method to the development of human institutions and concludes that the inevitable progressive movement of the natural sciences leads to anarchism.

508. "The Modern State." *Freedom* 27/28,295-300 (Nov. 1913-April 1914): 86-7/94-5/2-3/10-11/18/26-7. Discusses the character of the modern state, looking at monopoly, wealth, education and taxation.

509. "Modern Wars and Capitalism." *Freedom* 27,289-292 (May-Aug. 1913): 35/46-7/54-5/62-3. An interesting pre-conflict piece that argues that the basis of modern war is competition between capitalist powers and that great industrial crises anticipate great wars. The monopolistic state, involved in maintaining the power of the rich, subverts normal economic forces and produces conflict.

510. "The Morality of Nature." *The Nineteenth Century and After* 57,337 (March 1905): 407-26. A republishing of Chapter 3 of *Ethics*, op.cit., entry 485. A discussion of Darwin's ethics, asserting that social instinct is, in his view, the basis of all morality.

511. "Must We Occupy Ourselves with an Examination of the Ideal of a Future System?" in *Selected Writings on Anarchism and Revolution*, 49-116. Op.cit., entry 539. Composed for consideration by the Chaikovsky Circle, a leading revolutionary group in St. Petersburg to which Kropotkin belonged in the early 1870s, it was published in abbreviated form in the Russian journal *Byloe* 17 (1921). Significant in terms of the Russian revolutionary movement, then divided between gradualist followers of Peter Lavróv and revolutionaries who followed Bakunin, Kropotkin's argument favoured the Bakuninists' position.

512. *Mutual Aid: A Factor of Evolution.* Introduction by George Woodcock. Montréal: Black Rose Bks., 1988. Published as a series of articles in *The Nineteenth Century* from Sept. 1890 to June 1896 and collected as a book, London: Heinemann 1902. Also Boston: Extending Horizons Bks., 1955 ; London: Allen Lane, the Penguin Pr., 1972; London: Freedom Pr., 1987. Written as a direct rebuttal of the Huxley interpretation of Darwinism, that is "the survival of the fittest," the central tenet of this work is the principle

of mutual cooperation within species as the key to survival and progress. As such, it provides a philosophical basis for Kropotkin's anarchism.

513. "Organised Vengeance Called 'Justice.'" *Freedom* 15,161 (Oct. 1901): 58-9. A critique of conventional views of justice and punishment, arguing that we can do without judges in a free society just as we can do without bosses in production.

514. *Paroles d'un Revolté.* Paris: Flammarion, 1885. A collection, selected by Elisée Reclus, of articles which appeared in *Le Révolté* between 1879 and 1882, when Kropotkin was arrested. A number of the chapters were translated into English and appeared as pamphlets: *Appeal to the Young, War, Expropriation, Revolutionary Government, Law and Authority* and *The Commune of Paris.*

515. "Past and Future." *Freedom* 3,29 (April 1889): 17-78. A speech at South Place Chapel commemorating the eighteenth anniversary of the Paris Commune in which he looks towards the next revolutionary commune.

516. *The Place of Anarchism in Socialistic Evolution.* New York: Gordon Pr., 1974. First published London: International Pub. Co., 1886. Kropotkin argues that the underlying tendency in the social movement is not towards authoritarian communism but towards freedom, that is anarchist communism, which is an amalgam of all that is beautiful and most durable in human progress.

517. "Preface," to *How Shall We Bring About the Revolution: Syndicalism and the Co-operative Commonwealth.* E. Pataud and E. Pouget, vii-xiii. (New preface by Geoff Brown). London and Winchester, Mass.: Pluto Pr., 1989. Originally published as *Syndicalism and the Co-operative Commonwealth* Oxford: New International Pubg., 1913. In his preface Kropotkin seeks to establish links between the revolutionary syndicalist utopia put forward by Pataud and Pouget and the anarchist idea of decentralized production in a stateless society.

518. "The Present Condition of Russia." *The Nineteenth Century* 38,223 (Sept. 1895): 519-35. Discusses the need for fundamental change in Russia, examining the history of its social and political problems. The growing awareness of the people will Kropotkin asserts, be the basis for change.

519. "The Present Crisis in Russia." *North American Review* 172 (May 1901): 711-23. Comments on the repression of students in Russia and the curtailment of education by the Russian Ministry due to the fear of revolution. Making military service a punishment for rebellious students has provoked existing riots and disturbances. It can all be taken as a sign that autocracy in Russia is finished.

520. "Prisons and Their Moral Influence on Prisoners." In *Revolutionary Pamphlets,* 219-35. Op.cit., entry 538. Also appears in *The Essential Kropotkin;* 45-56. Op.cit., entry 537. The edited text of a speech delivered in

Paris, 20 December, 1877. Kropotkin attacks the evils of the prison system and looks forward to the free society of anarchism where they will be unnecessary. Community and modern science will together vanquish anti-social conduct.

521. "Recent Science." *The Nineteenth Century* 43,258 (Aug. 1898): 255-80. Discussion of recent discoveries relating to the transmission of power, with a focus on electricity.

522. "Representative Government." *Commonweal* 7, 312-21 (7 May-9 July 1892). A discussion of the representative system, admitting its useful role at a particular point in history, but arguing that popular control is more or less fictional and that the system now stands in the way of progress.

523. "The Revolution in Russia," in *Selected Writings on Anarchism and Revolution*, 267-90. Op.cit., 539. Originally published in *The Nineteenth Century and After*, 335 (Jan. 1905). Analyzes the events of 1905, commenting on the role of labor and proclaiming that Russia has begun her great revolution.

524. *Revolutionary Government.* London: Freedom Pr., 1943. First published 1880 in *Le Révolté*, appearing in English in *Commonweal* 7 (Aug. 1892). Included in *Revolutionary Pamphlets*, 237-50. Op.cit., entry 538. An attack on the idea of 'revolutionary government' as a term that is self-contradictory. Governments, by definition, cannot be revolutionary.

525. "Revolutionary Studies." *Commonweal* 7, 294-300 (July 10-Nov. 7, 1891). A series of seven pieces on questions raised by a consideration of revolution and anarchism. Attributed to Kropotkin the articles are, in fact, signed "La Révolte."

526. "The Russian Revolutionary Party," in *Selected Writings on Anarchism and Revolution*, 135-58. Op.cit., entry 539. First appeared in the journal *Fortnightly Review*, 31 (1882). A defense of Russian revolutionaries against charges of nihilism and terrorism, arguing that their demands are reasonable ones in favour of democratic reform and that violence has been precipitated by Tsarist absolutism.

527. "Russian Schools and the Holy Synod." *North American Review* 174 (April 1902): 518-27. Joins debate with the Procurator of the Holy Synod who had written a rejoinder to Kropotkin's "The Present Crisis in Russia," op.cit., entry 519.

528. *Socialism and Politics.* Freedom Pamphlet No.14. London: Freedom Office/J. Turner, 1903. A criticism of the uses of the term "socialism" which, rather than indicating a social movement, has come to be identified with political parties and forms of central state control. Social-democrats have thus robbed the term of its meaning.

529. "Some of the Resources of Canada." *The Nineteenth Century* 43, 253 (March 1898): 494-514. Notes geographical similarities between Canada and parts of Russia. Concludes that it is social conditions which drive people to emigrate from Russia to Canada and remarks on the excellent progress made in Canada where the government does not crush the people with taxes. Warns however that bad decisions by the Canadian government may adversely affect the future.

530. "The Spirit of Revolt." In *Revolutionary Pamphlets*, 34-43. Op.cit., entry 538. Originally published in *Le Révolté* in 1880, the piece appeared in English in *Commonweal* in 1892. Also collected in *The Essential Kropotkin*, 3-9. Op.cit., entry 537. Arguing that at certain points in history revolution is inevitable, this is a call for the minority, that is anarchist activists, to take action to help develop the spirit of revolt in the mass of the people in order to bring into being a free society based on communal property.

531. *The State: Its Historic Role*. Translated by Vernon Richards. London: Freedom Pr., 1987. Originally published in *Les Temps Nouveaux*, 19 December, 1896, and London: 1898. An analysis of the modern state that distinguishes it from government and traces its origins and development. Presaging the discussion in *Mutual Aid*, Kropotkin celebrates the free towns and communes of the medieval period, associating the rise of the centralized state, and its fetishized authority, with the decline of communalism and the federalist tradition.

532. *The Terror in Russia*. London: Methuen & Co., 1909. Written following the 1905 revolutionary push in Russia for the British Parliamentary Russian Committee, it is a report on the Tzarist régime's terror tactics against its political opponents.

533. "The Theory of Evolution and Mutual Aid." *The Nineteenth Century and After* 395 (Jan. 1910): 86-107. A discussion of what were, given the tension between the idea of sociability and the Malthusian notion of struggle, Darwin's views on competition as a factor in evolution.

534. *The Wage System*. Freedom Pamphlet No.1. London: Freedom Office/C. M. Wilson, 1894. Included in *The Essential Kropotkin*, 94-107. Op.cit., entry 537. A discussion focussing on the advantages of distribution according to needs compared to the collectivist system of distribution according to deeds.

535. *War!* London: William Reeves, 1872. Originally written for *Le Révolté* in 1882, this is an attack on war as only a means by which competition between national financial oligarchies is pursued. Only social revolution, it is argued, can end war by removing its bases. A interesting piece considering Kropotkin's later position on the 1914-18 war.

536. "What Geography Ought To Be." *The Nineteenth Century* 104 (Dec. 1885): 940-56. Republished *Antipode*, 10/11, 3/1, (1979). An interesting discussion of Geography as a subject for study, emphasizing that it can, in

particular, teach children that they are all members of a human community.

Anthologies :

537. *The Essential Kropotkin.* Editors Emile Capouya and Keith Tomkins. London: Macmillan, 1976. A general selection from the writings of Kropotkin in two parts. Part 1 collects a number of key essays, "The Spirit of Revolt," "An Appeal to the Young," "Law and Authority," "Prisons and Their Moral Influence on Prisoners," "Modern Science and Anarchism" and "The Wage System" and the article on anarchism written for the *Encyclopaedia Britannica.* Part 2 contains selections from his major books.

538. *Revolutionary Pamphlets: A Collection of Writings by Peter Kropotkin.* Edited Roger N. Baldwin. New York: Dover Publications, 1970. Introduction and biographical sketch by Roger N. Baldwin. A good cross-section of Kropotkin's political and social writings covering such areas as anarchism and its practice, the relationship between science and anarchism, law and authority, prisons and revolution. Useful bibliographic material and notes.

539. *Selected Writings on Anarchism and Revolution.* Martin M. Miller. Edited with introduction. Cambridge, Mass.: M.I.T. Pr., 1976. A very useful collection of pieces by Kropotkin that have become hard to obtain. The selection is directed towards Kropotkin's interpretation of the role of anarchism, modern history, his critique of capitalism and his conception of revolution. It includes his essays: "The State: Its Historic Role," "The Revolution in Russia," "The Commune of Paris" and his "Conversation with Lenin." There are also interesting letters to Lenin, Steffen and Brandes.

540. *Selections from his Writings.* Edited with introduction by Herbert Read. London: Freedom Pr., 1942. Selections from Kropotkin's work arranged thematically in four sections: Autobiographical, Historical, Economic and Political, Philosophical. Includes select bibliography.

Works about Kropotkin :

541. Avrich, P. "Kropotkin's Ethical Anarchism" and "Kropotkin in America," in *Anarchist Portraits*, 53-78/79-106. Op.cit., entry 1303. Two useful discussions of Kropotkin's life and ideas. The first features a discussion of his moral vision in the context of nineteenth century anarchism, while the second contains some interesting details of his time in America.

542. Bax, E. B. *Reminiscences and Reflections of a Mid and Late Victorian.* London: Allen & Unwin, 1918. These recollections give some feel for the period but are only of very limited use with respect to Kropotkin.

543. Becker, H. "Kropotkin as Historian of the French Revolution." *The Raven* 2,3 (July 1989): 225-31. Discusses Kropotkin's *The Great French Revolution, 1789-1793* as an example of anarchist historiography.

544. Berkman, A. *The Bolshevik Myth.* Introduction by Nicolas Walter. London & Winchester, Mass.: Pluto Pr., 1989. Based on his Russian Diary this is Berkman's account of his time in Russia. Chapter 10, "A Visit to Peter Kropotkin" and Chapter 37, "Early Days of 1921," deal with his meeting with Kropotkin and the latter's death.

545. Berkman, A. "Reminiscences of Kropotkin." *Freedom* 36,393 (March 1922): 14-15. Translation of an article prepared for *Freie Arbeiter Stimme*. Berkman reports on meetings with Kropotkin in Moscow, speaking of the latter's irrevocable opposition to Bolshevism and his anguish at the character and conduct of the Revolution.

546. Berneri, C. *Peter Kropotkin: His Federalist Ideas.* London: Simian, 1977. Originally published in Italian in 1922. Published in English, London: Freedom Pr., 1943. A succinct analysis of Kropotkin's federalism by an Italian anarchist.

547. Breitbart, M. M. "Impressions of an Anarchist Landscape." *Antipode* 7,2 (Sept. 1975): 44-9. Discusses the ideas of Proudhon and Kropotkin, with a focus on decentralization, federalism and regional self-sufficiency.

548. Brocher, G. "Kropotkin: The Great Rebel and Savant," in *The Oriole Press-A Bibliography*, 89-91. Op.cit., entry 1420. A reprint of a brief reflection on Kropotkin's life and work written in January 1924.

549. Cahm, C. "Kropotkin and Law." In *Law and Anarchism*, 106-21. Op.cit., entry 1413. Kropotkin's approach to law is discussed as part of a series of essays on the anarchist theory of law, the state, rules etc. .

550. Cahm, C. *Kropotkin and the Rise of Revolutionary Anarchism, 1872-1886.* Cambridge: Cambridge Univ. Pr., 1989. Analyzes Kropotkin's role in the transformation of the work of Bakunin and offers some new suggestions about his views on the revolutionary task of the labor movement.

551. Chadwick, W. "The Mailed Fist vs. the Invisible Hand". *Reason* 10,5 (1978): 18-23. See entry 59.

552. De Haan, R. "Kropotkin, Marx and Dewey." *Anarchy* 5,9 (Sept. 1965): 271-84. A discussion of Kropotkin's philosophy, with some partial treatment of Dewey, emphasizing its adaptability to modern society.

553. Dugger, U. M. "Veblen and Kropotkin on Human Evolution." *Journal of Economic Issues* 18,4 (1984): 971-85. Examines the progressive theory of evolution as put forward by Veblen and Kropotkin as an antidote to the Social Darwinist theories supporting the status quo. Compares Kropotkin's

views on mutual aid with Veblen's notion of the group-orientated traits of workmanship, parentship etc. that became part of human nature during an extended period of primitive life.

554. Eltzbacher, P. *Anarchism: Exponents of the Anarchist Philosophy.* Translated Steven T. Byington. Edited James J. Martin. Op.cit., entry 1365. Consisting largely of quotations from anarchists, it includes a section on Kropotkin, who recommended the book.

555. Evers, W. M. "Kropotkin's Ethics and the Public Good." *Journal of Libertarian Studies* 2,3 (Fall 1978): 225-41. A discussion of Kropotkin's ethics in the context of the contemporary libertarian debate, making reference to Machan and Rothbard, regarding the tension between the public good and individual autonomy and initiative. Concludes that reconciliation is possible.

556. Fattal, D. "Three Russian Revolutionaries on War." *New Review* 11,2-4 (1971). A study of Bakunin, Tkachev and Kropotkin as representatives of the Russian revolutionary movement. Concerned with political as well as social and economic issues.

557. Galois, B. "Ideology and the State of Nature: The Case of Peter Kropotkin." *Antipode* 8,3 (1976): 1-16. Discusses Kropotkin's use of nature in developing an ethic of co-operation, placing it in the context of sociobiology and the search for altruism.

558. Goldman, E. *My Further Disillusionment in Russia.* New York: Doubleday, 1924. A continuation of Goldman's *My Disillusionment in Russia.* Chapter 5 deals with the death and funeral of Peter Kropotkin; Chapter 7 with the persecution of the anarchists.

559. Goodman, P. "Kropotkin at this Moment." *Dissent* 15,6 (1968): 519-22. Also published in *Anarchy* 98 (April 1969): 124-8. Discussing the renewal of interest in Kropotkin this was written as a preface to the Horizon Press edition of his *Memoirs of a Revolutionist.* Suggests that the main lesson to be learned from a re-examination of Kropotkin is how an authentic professional becomes a revolutionary.

560. Gould, N. "Peter Kropotkin: The Anarchist Prince." *The Ecologist* 4 (1974): 261-4. A discussion of the significance of Kropotkin's ideas to ecology, focussing on his advocacy of small-scale decentralized communities.

561. Hare, R. *Portraits of Russian Personalities.* Oxford: Oxford Univ. Pr., 1959. Discusses the life and work of a number of anarchists including Bakunin, Tolstoy and, in Chapter 10, Kropotkin.

562. Hewetson, J. "Mutual Aid and Social Evolution." *Anarchy* 5,9 (Sept. 1965): 257-70. Published as a pamphlet in 1946. A discussion of Kropotkin's ideas on mutual aid, their relation to the theories of Darwin, and their political and social implications.

563. Horner, G. M. "Kropotkin and the City: The Socialist Ideal in Urbanism." *Antipode* 10,3 (1978): 33-58. Explores the linkage between the ideas of Kropotkin and contemporary anarchist thinkers, exploring the conception of the city as a socialist ideal.

564. Hulse, J. J. *Revolutionists in London: A Study of Five Unorthodox Socialists.* Oxford: Oxford Univ. Pr., 1970. A series of loosely connected studies of five radicals resident in London at various times. Chapter 3 looks at Kropotkin and his work from his arrival in London in 1886 to the end of the 1890s. Chapter 7 examines the period from his American tour in 1897 to his death in 1921. Bibliography.

565. Hyndman, H. M. *The Record of an Adventurous Life.* London: Macmillan, 1911. This autobiography by the founder of British Marxism includes reminiscences of old comrades and combatants, including Kropotkin, 261-7.

566. Kelly, A. "Lessons of Kropotkin." *New York Review of Books* 23,17 (28 Oct. 1976): 40-4. A review of Martin M. Miller, *Kropotkin,* op.cit., entry 578, and Capouya & Tomkins, edited, *The Essential Kroptkin,* op.cit., entry 537. Kropotkin is characterized as a visionary idealist whose rejection of coercion diminished the revolutionary potential of his ideas compared to, say, Bakunin. He is criticized for believing in a static utopia, rejecting the concept of a tension between the individual and the social environment.

567. Kennan, G. "The Escape of Prince Krapotkin (sic)." *The Century Magazine* 62 (New Series 1912): 246-53. Celebrates, in a popular American journal, the escape of Kropotkin from the prison of the Nikolaievsk Hospital in St. Petersburg in 1876.

568. Lansbury, G. *What I Saw in Russia.* London: Leonard Parsons, 1920. Lansbury's account of his visit to Russia with some discussion in Chapter 2 of his meeting with Kropotkin, and of the latter's criticism of the Soviet government and its methods.

569. MacLaughlin, J. "State-Centred Social Science and the Anarchist Critique - Ideology in Political Geography." *Antipode* 18,1 (1986): 11-38. Argues for Kropotkin's idea of a radical geography which would focus on the unity of humanity as opposed to the inherently divisive, nationalistic geography of the capitalist state.

570. Maisky, I. *Journey into the Past.* London: Hutchinson, 1962. Written by someone who was Soviet Ambassador to the United Kingdom from 1932 to 1943, the memoir covers Russian political emigrés in London in the early part of the century. Chapter 12 looks at Kropotkin.

571. Malatesta, E. "Peter Kropotkin: Recollections and Criticisms of an old Friend." In *Errico Malatesta: His Life and Ideas,* 257-68. Op.cit., entry 630. Written just before his death Malatesta shows great affection and respect for

his friend but criticizes his commitment to the Great War and his "mechanistic fatalism."

572. Masaryk, T. G. *The Spirit of Russia.* 2 vols. Translated by Eden and Cedar Paul. London: Allen & Unwin, 1919-37. A general history of Russia that, in Volume 2, Chapter 19, contains a discussion of Kropotkin and his "modern anarchism," contrasting it with Marxism and socialism.

573. Mavor, J. *My Windows on the Street.* London & Toronto: J. M. Dent, 1923. A semi-autobiographical and anecdotal account of aspects of world history. Chapter 30 is devoted to Kropotkin.

574. McCulloch, C. "The Problems of Fellowship in Communitarian Theory: William Morris and Peter Kropotkin." *Political Studies* 32,3 (Sept. 1984): 437-50. Discusses the nature and implications of fellowship, its alleged dual nature, the tension arising between its psycho-social and moral elements, and offers a resolution.

575. Miller, D. "The Neglected Kropotkin." *Government and Opposition* 18,3 (Summer 1983): 319-38. Brief synopsis of Kropotkin's political views on revolution and anarcho-communist society within the framework of the theory of mutual aid, arguing that this framework is inadequate for the realities of modern industrial society.

576. Miller, D. *Social Justice.* Oxford: Clarendon Pr., 1976. A detailed analysis of the concept of social justice. Chapter 7 deals with Kropotkin's theory of justice.

577. Miller, M. M. "Ideological Conflicts in Russian Populism: The Revolutionary Manifestoes of the Chaikovsky Circle, 1869-1874." *Slavic Review* 29,1 (1970): 604-14. An account of the workings of the Chaikovsky Circle between 1869 and 1874, whose disputes mirrored the shifts in revolutionary thought and showed the influence of Nechayev, Bakunin and Kropotkin, who was a member of the Petersburg group from 1872. He was the author of the most detailed programme of the period and the final manifesto produced for the Chaikovsky Circle in 1873.

578. Miller, M. A. *Kropotkin.* Chicago: Univ. of Chicago Pr., 1976. A detailed biographical study of the life and work of Kropotkin focussing on both his development as an anarchist intellectual and his theory of revolutionary social change. Contains some unpublished notes by Kropotkin on revolution and violence and a section quaintly entitled "Kropotkiniana."

579. Osofsky, S. *Peter Kropotkin.* Boston: Twayne Publishers, 1979. A comprehensive analysis of Kropotkin's social and political theories which aims to show that Kropotkin's theories remain relevant for the present era since their challenge has yet to be answered effectively.

580. Peet, R. "For Kropotkin." *Antipode* 7,2 (Sept. 1975): 42-3. A short appreciation of Kropotkin's ideas.

581. Peet, R. "The Geography of Human Liberation." *Antipode* 10/11,3/1 (Double issue 1979): 119-34. Discusses ideas on human liberation through a contrast between Kropotkin and Marx, with a focus on anarchist ideas of decentralization.

582. Punzo, V. "The Modern State and the Search for Community: The Anarchist Critique of Kropotkin." *International Philosophical Quarterly* 16 (1976). A critical exposition of Kropotkin's critique of the state which focuses on three key areas, his methodology, the communitarian basis of his critique, and his appeal to communitarian ethics.

583. Reichert, W. O. "Anarchism, Freedom and Power." *Ethics* 79 (Jan. 1969): 139-49. Elucidates the important distinction between social and political power for anarchist theory, focussing on the rejection of authority espoused by Proudhon and Kropotkin. Calls for a profound psychological transformation of a society where people have been conditioned to look to political leaders for guidance.

584. Reichert, W. O. "Art, Nature and Revolution." (Aesthetics of Bakunin, Kropotkin and Proudhon) *Arts in Society* 9,3 (1972): 409-30. See entry 117.

585. Reichert, W. O. "Proudhon and Kropotkin on Church and State." *Journal of Church and State* 9,1 (Winter 1967): 87-100. Argues, on the basis of the work of Proudhon and Kropotkin, that, while anarchism generally rejects religion as normally defined and practiced, it nonetheless represents a highly developed moral view.

586. Reszler, A. "Peter Kropotkin and His Vision of Anarchist Aesthetics." *Diogenes* 78 (1972): 52-63. Argues for the importance of the arts in politics citing Kropotkin's position.

587. Rocker, R. *The London Years.* Chapter 12. London: R. Anscombe, 1956. Rocker's recollections of his time in London containing reminiscences of old comrades such as Kropotkin. There are some interesting comments on the latter's pro-war stance.

588. Sack, A. J. *The Birth of Russian Democracy.* New York: Russian Information Bureau, 1918. A history of revolutionary movements in Russia beginning with the Decembrists. Part 2, Chapter 3 comprises a discussion, mainly biographical, of Kropotkin. The book contains a lot of useful documentation including Kropotkin's speech to the Moscow National Conference 28 August, 1917. Photographs.

589. Sellers, E. "Our Most Distinguished Refugee." *The Contemporary Review* 66 (Oct. 1894): 537-49. A somewhat condescending account of Kropotkin's life and activities in exile.

590. Shpayer-Makov, H. "The Reception of Peter Kropotkin in Britain, 1886-1917." *Albion* 19,3 (1987): 373-90. Based on contemporary newspaper

accounts and Kropotkin's memoirs, this is an assessment of the balance between the public bias against anarchism and Kropotkin's personal appeal.

591. Shub, D. "Kropotkin and Lenin." *The Russian Review* 12,4 (Oct. 1953) 227-34. Argues that although Bolsheviks and Anarchists appeared to have many shared goals in the early stages of the revolution, Kropotkin disputed Lenin's program from the outset. Very sympathetic to Kropotkin.

592. Smith, M. "Kropotkin and Technical Education." In *For Anarchism: History, Theory and Practice*; 217-34. Op.cit., entry 1385. Examines Kropotkin's contribution to the British debate of the 1880s about vocational education.

593. Startt, J. D. "The Evolution of an Anarchist: An Autobiographical Statement by Varlaan Tcherkesoff, 1846-1925." *Biography* 10,2 (1987): 142-50. Tcherkesoff was a close friend of Kropotkin and had a similar background.

594. Stepniak, S. (pseud. Sergey Mikhailovich Kravchinsky). *Underground Russia: Revolutionary Profiles and Sketches from Life*. Preface by P. Lavroff. Stepniak, an ex-member of the Chaikovsky Circle, and author of the novel *The Career of a Nihilist*, wrote this while in exile in London. Peter Krapotkine (sic) is discussed, 90-101, and the claim made that, while he was at the time of writing a notable and influential emigré, he had no influence, during his time in Russia, over revolutionary movements.

595. Swan, T. "Modern Influences. XXI. Prince Kropotkin." *The Millgate Monthly* 11,21 (June 1907). A short, popular and sympathetic account of Kropotkin's ideas. Good, late photograph included of Kropotkin at work in his study.

596. Tcherkesoff, F. "Peter Kropotkin as I Knew Him." *Freedom* 32-35 (New Series Dec. 1932-March 1933): 3/3/3/6. Reminiscences about Kropotkin the man and his family life.

597. Thompson, J. L. "Mutual Aid and Selfish Genes." *Metaphilosophy* 15,3/4 (July-Oct. 1984): 270-81. Examines two opposing views about the foundations of human nature.

598. Van Duyn, R. *Message of A Wise Kabouter*. Translated by Hubert Hoskins. Foreword by Charles Bloomberg. London: Gerald Duckworth & Co., 1962. Originally published in Holland in 1969, this is an attempt to develop and articulate an anarchist philosophy through a study of the philosophy of Peter Kropotkin. Van Duyn was the founder of the Dutch anarchist journal *Provo*, from which the movement took its name He uses the idea of the "kabouter", the gnome or pixie at the bottom of the garden that can talk to animals and plants, to express ideas on co-operation and mutual aid, and to demand recognition for a necessary interaction between humanity and nature.

599. Walter, N. "Kropotkin and his Memoirs." *Anarchy* 109 (March 1970): 84-94. Reflections on Kropotkin's *Memoirs*.

600. Woodcock, G. "Kropotkin's *The Great French Revolution." Our Generation.* 20,2 (Spring 1989): 1-19. Discusses the background of personal and international events to the writing of the volume in question, Kropotkin's longest book.

601. Woodcock, G. "The Scientific Contribution of Peter Kropotkin." In *The Writer and Politics*, 80-110. London: Porcupine Pr., 1948. Part of a collection of essays looking at the relationship of the writer to society with particular emphasis on movements for social reform or revolution.

602. Woodcock, G. and Avakumovic, I. *The Anarchist Prince: A Biographical Study of Peter Kropotkin.* London: T.V. Boardman & Co., 1950. Reissued as *Prince Kropotkin: From Prince to Rebel*, Montréal: Black Rose Bks., 1988. A long and detailed study of Kropotkin combining biographical details with an analysis and assessment of his important ideas and their influence on the anarchist tradition.

JOSEPH LABADIE (1850-1933)

Works by J. Labadie :

603. *Anarchism: Genuine and Asinine.* New York: Revisionist Pr., 1976. Seeks to distance anarchism from violence and authoritarian socialism, focussing on freedom and freedom of association.

604. *The Red Flag and Other Verses.* Detroit: Labadie, 1910. A publication by Labadie of his own verses on subjects that include "The Anarchistic View," "Fair Play" and "Plea for Freedom."

Works about J. Labadie :

605. Martin, J. J., *Men against the State.* Colorado Springs: Ralph Myles, 1970. Some limited discussion of Labadies's work with Tucker on the journal *Liberty*, 243-5. See entry 1838.

LAURENCE LABADIE (1896-1975)

Works by L. Labadie :

606. *Selected Essays.* With an introduction and appendices by James J. Martin. Colorado Springs: Ralph Myles, 1978. A collection of essays by Labadie, put together after his death in 1975 at the age of 78. Labadie, who

knew Tucker in earlier years, was part of the American mutualist tradition which blended the ideas of Owen and Proudon. Includes a useful biographic and critical introduction to the essays.

607. *The Writings of Laurance Labadie: Individualist, Anarchist, and Mutualist.* New York: Revisionist Pr., 1976. A useful collection of work by Labadie in the individualist anarchist tradition.

GUSTAV LANDAUER (1870-1919)

Works by Landauer:

608. *For Socialism.* Translated by David J. Parent. Introduction by Russell Berman and Tim Luke. St. Louis, Miss.: Telos Pr., 1978. In *For Socialism*, Landauer, while criticizing modern science and the forces of advanced capitalism, also attacks the Second International, orthodox Marxism and centralized state socialism. In their stead he advocates a stateless, free society based on the tradition of the organic community. Socialism is involved, for Landauer, with the moral regeneration of the individual and the development of free individual activity within a spiritual community.

Works about Landauer:

609. Avrich, P. "The Martyrdom of Gustav Landauer." In *Anarchist Portraits*, 247-54. Op.cit., entry 1303. A brief appreciation of Landauer's life and work.

610. Berman, R. and Luke, T. "On Gustav Landauer." *Our Generation* 17,2 (Spring/Summer 1986): 97-114. A examination of the life, ideas and legacy of Landauer.

611. Link-Salinger [Hyman]. R. *Gustav Landauer: Philosopher of Utopia.* Indianapolis: Hacket, 1977. A carefully researched piece which assesses the impact of Landauer's work both during his own lifetime and on present day radical thought and movements. Includes an extensive bibliography the first section of which lists everything written by Landauer. Index.

612. Lunn, E. *Prophet of Community. The Romantic Socialism of Gustav Landauer.* Berkeley: Univ. of Calif. Pr., 1973. A detailed and complete analysis based on archival research that examines Landauer's philosophical and intellectual development while giving an account of his personal history. There is discussion of Landauer's proposed communities based on equality and participatory democracy.

613. Maurer, C. B. *Call to Revolution: The Mystical Anarchism of Gustav Landauer.* Detroit: Wayne State Univ. Pr., 1971. A biography of the German anarcho-socialist, set against the historical background of Imperial

Germany. Landauer believed in individual freedom coupled with responsibility to society. He was a Minister in the short-lived Bavarian Soviet Republic of 1919 and was executed by the military.

JOSEPH LANE (1851-1920)

Works by Lane :

614. *An Anti-Statist Communist Manifesto.* Sanday, Orkney: Cienfuegos Pr., 1978. Originally published London: J. Lane, 1887. A defense of liberty, equality and solidarity as part of what Lane called libertarian socialism. Lane was one of the founders of the libertarian socialist/anarchist movement in Britain.

Works about Lane :

615. Oliver, H. *The International Anarchist Movement in Late Victorian London.* London: Croom Helm, 1983. A useful discussion of anarchist groups and activities in late nineteenth century London that covers the career of Joseph Lane.

ERRICO MALATESTA (1853-1932)

Works by Malatesta :

616. *Al caffè: Conversazioni sull anarchismo.* Torino: Edizioni del CDA-La Fiaccola, 1978. Collected Bologna: 1922. Reprinted, Torino: Sargref, 1961. This is a collection of seventeen dialogues on anarchism that ranks with *Fra Contadini* and *L'Anarchia* in demonstrating Malatesta's genius for presenting complex arguments in a manner that makes them easily understandable. The dialogues, presumed to take place in a café, involve a variety of protagonists, a bourgeois, a shopkeeper, a student and an anarchist. They were produced over a number of years. The first ten were written in 1897 and appeared in *L'Agitazione* (Ancona). In 1913 Malatesta republished them, with the addition of four new dialogues, in the journal *Volontà* which he was editing at the time.The last three dialogues were written in 1922 for the first edition of the collected dialogues, which appeared in that year under the title *Al Caffè.*

617. *Gli anarchici e la questione elettorale: Un dibattito.* With Francesco Saverio Merlino, *Il Messaggero*, 29 Jan. 1897-13 Jan. 1898. Rome: Savelli, 1976. A debate between Malatesta and Merlino, representing, respectively, the anarchist and social democratic positions on the use of the electoral process. Malatesta invited Merlino to debate the question in a letter to *Il*

Messaggero on 29 January 1887. The debate continued in the pages of the journal for almost a year. See also entry 239.

618. *Gli anarchici in tribunale. Autodifesa di Errico Malatesta.* Edited F. Serantoni. Rome/Florence: 1905. This is Malatesta's speech in his own defense during his trial in Ancona in April 1898. He had been arrested for alleged involvement in the bread riots of January 1898.

619. "Anarchism and Syndicalism." *Freedom* 21,223 (Nov. 1907): 65-6. Argues that anarchists should not identify themselves completely with syndicalism. It should be seen as only one of a number of forms of propagandist action that can be directed to anarchist goals.

620. "Anarchist Have Forgotten their Principles." *Freedom* 28,307 (Nov. 1914): 86. Part of a symposium on war in which Grave and Kropotkin took part, this is Malatesta's strong anti-war statement. See entries 454 and 471.

621. *Anarchy.* London: Freedom Pr., 1974. A translation by Vernon Richards, from the Italian original *L'Anarchia*, London: 1891. The first English translation appeared in serial form in the journal *Freedom* from September 1891 to June 1892. The work has since been issued as a pamphlet by Freedom Press on numerous occasions. Perhaps the best known of Malatesta's pamphlets it develops a strong argument about the origins and bases of government and authority. In places it moves close to a Marxist position on social class, while skilfully delineating a distinct anarchist position. Malatesta is alleged to have said in 1920 that he considered *Anarchy* to be the best piece he had written.

622. *Le due vie. The Two Roads.* Milano: 1920. This discussion of the two roads or paths, contrasts reform with revolution. While rejecting social democracy in favour of revolution, Malatesta is severely critical of the path of the Bolshevik revolution in Russia.

623 *Fra contadini.* Publicazione del giornalo *La Questione Sociale*, Firenze: 1884. English translation by Jean Weir; Italian title retained. Port Glasgow: Bratach Dubh Pubns., 1981. In 1884 Malatesta founded the weekly *La Questione Sociale*, the first serious, propagandist, anarchist paper to be published in Italy. *Fra Contadini*, one of Malatesta's most popular and widely read pamphlets, appeared that year. It depicts a conversation - a form that Malatesta frequently adopted - between peasants (fra contadini) in which the nature of work, the ownership of wealth and land and the existence of the bourgeois/landlord class are all examined. The virtues of communist anarchism are lauded as an answer to these problems.

624. "Peter Kropotkin - Recollections and Criticisms of an Old Friend." *Studii Sociali* (15 April, 1931). Contained in *Errico Malatesta: His Life and Ideas*, 257-68. Op.cit., entry 630. Written just before his own death Malatesta shows great affection and respect for his friend but criticizes his commitment to the Great War and his "mechanistic fatalism."

625. *La politica parlamentare nel movimento socialista.* London: 1890. Reprinted as *Il movimento operaio e la tattica elettorale.* Forlì: L'Aurora, 1948.

626. "Pro-Government Anarchists." *Freedom* (April 1916). Contained in *Errico Malatesta: His Life and Ideas,* 248-51. Op.cit., entry 630. Urges anarchists not to compromise with governments and reminds them that real peace can only be achieved through revolution.

627. *Il programma anarchico.* Catania: Edigraf, 1969. Originally published as *Il nostro programma,* Bologna: 1920. A programme presented by Malatesta to the Congress of the Union of Italian Anarchists on 1 July, 1920. It was not entirely new at that time, being based on a programme published in Paterson, N.J., in 1899, and on various ideas published in *La Questione Sociale,* Firenze: 1884-.

628. *Verso l'anarchia.* Orvieto: 1921.

629. *Vote - What For?* London: Freedom Pr., 1945. A translation freely adapted from the original *In Tempo di Elezioni: Dialogo.* London: 1890. A critique of the "ballot-box swindle." An argument for local control and direct action in place of parliamentarianism.

Anthologies :

630. *Errico Malatesta: His Life and Ideas.* Compiled and edited by Vernon Richards. London: Freedom Pr., 1965. A compilation in three parts; selections from Malatesta's writings; notes for a biography; an assessment of Malatesta's ideas and tactics and their contemporary relevance.

631. *Errico Malatesta: Pagine di lotta quotidiana.* 2 vols. Presentazione di Gino Cerrito. Carrara: Movimento Anarchico Italiano/Il Seme, 1975. A collection of Malatesta's writings in *Umanità Nova* in the period 1920-22, with other writings from the period 1919-23 in the second volume, including *Il programma anarchico* of 1920. Originally published in Geneva: Edizione del "Risveglio" 1935, entitled *Scritti: Volume I & II.*

632. *Pensiero e Volontà e ultimi scritti 1924-32.* Presentazione di Gino Cerrito. Carrara: Movimento Anarchico Italiano/Il Seme, 1975. Malatesta's writings in *Pensiero e Volontà,* 1924-26, plus other work from the period 1926-32, the year of Malatesta's death. Originally published, with a preface by Luigi Fabbri, Geneva: Edizione del "Risveglio," 1936, as *Scritti: Volume III.*

633. *Scritti antimilitaristi dal 1912 al 1916.* Con Appendice di Max Nettlau, "Malatesta e la Guerra." Milano: Cooperativa Segno Libero, 1982. Antimilitarist and anti-war writings from 1912-16.

634. *Scritti scelti.* Saggio introduttivo a cura di Gino Cerrito. Roma: La Nuova Sinistra, 1973. Selected writings.

Works about Malatesta:

635. Aldred, G. "Malatesta." In *Pioneers of Anti-Parliamentarianism*, 25-36. Glasgow: The Strickland Pr., 1940. Useful, short introduction to Malatesta's life and ideas.

636. Carey, G. W. "The Vessel, the Deed and the Idea: Anarchists in Paterson, 1895-1908." *Antipode.* 10/11,3/1 (1979): 46-58. Discusses the way in which silk-workers, involved in the anarchist movement in Italy, spread anarchist ideas in Paterson, New Jersey, after migrating. Contains some useful material on Malatesta, *La Questione Sociale* and anarchist activities in Italy.

637. Levy, C. "Italian Anarchism, 1970-1926." In *Anarchism: History, Theory and Practice*, 25-78. Op.cit., entry 1385. Malatesta's career is covered in a broad discussion of Italian anarchism during its formative period.

638. Levy, C. "Malatesta in Exile." *Ann. della Fondazione Luigi Einaudi* 15 (1981): 245-80. Drawing on primary resources in the Central State Archive in Rome the piece discusses Malatesta's exile and his influence on international anarchism.

639. Nettlau, M. *Errico Malatesta.* New York: Jewish Anarchist Federation, 1922? A brief and sometimes confusing biography. It is a condensed sketch from a book that no longer appears to be available. It concludes in 1922.

640. Nomad, M. *Dreamers, Dynamiters, and Demagogues.* New York: Waldon Pr., 1964. A personal memoir by a disillusioned ex-anarchist (in his nineties) recalling events and acquaintances within the anarchist movement. There are a number of reminiscences of Malatesta whom Nomad knew and admired.

641. Nomad, M. *Rebels and Renegades.* New York: Macmillan, 1932. Errico Malatesta is the subject of the first chapter, subtitled "The Romance of Anarchism." Nomad, who knew Malatesta personally, regarded him as the only other anarchist who could be placed on the same level as Peter Kropotkin.

642. Richards, V. "Malatesta's Relevance for Anarchists Today. An Assessment." In *Errico Malatesta: Life and Ideas*, 271-309. Op.cit., entry 630. A discussion of the relevance of Malatesta's ideas that focuses attention on the issue of the General Strike.

643. Richards, V. "Notes for a Biography." In *Errico Malatesta: His Life and Ideas;* 201-42. Op.cit., entry 630. A somewhat limited and spasmodic biography but still the best available in English.

644. Richards, V. "Some Notes on Malatesta and Bakunin." *The Raven* 1,1 (1986): 38-45. Discusses the relationship between the ideas of the two theorists.

645. Wieck, D. "About Malatesta." *Anarchy* 1,8 (Second Series 197?): 25-31. A discussion of Malatesta's ideas with consideration of their contemporary relevance.

LOUISE MICHEL (1830-1905)

Works by Michel :

646. *La Commune.* Paris: 1898. Trained as a teacher, Michel became a revolutionary while teaching in Montmartre. An enthusiastic supporter of the Paris Commune she fought in its defense against the Versailles troops. Afterwards she was imprisoned, spending the years 1873-80 in the penal colony of New Caledonia.

647. *Legendes et chantes de gestes canaques: Avec dessins et vocabulaires.* Noumea: Hachette Caledonia, 1980. A collection of local folk tales etc. put together while Michel was in exile in the penal settlement in New Caledonia.

648. *The Red Virgin: The Memoirs of Louise Michel.* Edited and translated Elizabeth Gunter and Bullitt Lowry. Huntsville, Al.: Univ. of Alabama Pr., 1981. A translation from *Souvenirs* that, in its comments, takes a somewhat eulogistic approach to this heroine of the French left, best known for her role in the Paris Commune of 1871. The introduction provides useful background information.

649. *Souvenirs et aventures de ma vie.* Édition établie par Daniel Armogathe. Paris: La Découverte/Maspero, 1983. A memoir of her life and work published originally in three parts: *Les journées rouges de la Commune; Les jours noirs de l'exil; Le triste exode anarchiste.* Finished in 1904, just before her death at age 72, the memoir was published in *La Vie Populaire* in sixty parts between 1905 and 1908 ; altogether 1200 pages of text. The present edition arranges the memoirs in four parts: "Les journées rouges de la Commune;" "Dans les prisons de France;" "Londres;" "Le retour en France."

Works about Michel :

650. Leighton, M. "Anarcho-Feminism and Louise Michel." *Our Generation* 21,2 (Summer 1990): 22-9. An account of Michel's career and ideas as representative of a female radical consciousness.

651. Thomas, E. *Louise Michel.* Buffalo, N.Y.: Univ. of Toronto Pr., 1981. A biography of the anarchist writer, poet, feminist and revolutionary who fought on the barricades of the Paris Commune. The work discusses her revolutionary activities, her subsequent trial before the Council of France, her deportation and the continuation of her political activity on her return.

WILLIAM OWEN (1854-1929)

Works by Owen :

652. *Anarchy versus Socialism*. London: Freedom Pr., 1922. Pamphlet originally published New York: Mother Earth, 1908. Also extracted in M. Graham, ed. *Man!*, 79-87. Op. cit., entry 1389. Discusses the nature of anarchism and its advantages over socialism, which reduces the individual to a cipher for the sake of the collectivity and establishes forms of central authority and control.

653. "The Coming Solidarity." In *The Soul of Man Under Socialism*, by Oscar Wilde, 39-48. New York: Humboldt Pub. Co., 1892. Reflecting on the division between Marx and Bakunin Owen looks forward to reunion and solidarity based on a new socialist vision of human beings possessed of infinite capabilities. Discussion follows of socialism and the church and Herbert Spencer. The piece only occurs in this particular edition of Wilde's work.

654. *England Monopolised or England Free?* London: Freedom Office, 1920. In this pamphlet Owen argues that, in the aftermath of the First World War, the monopolization of property, the class system and imperialism cause people to be economically dependent and helpless. Anarchist freedom means becoming one's own economic master.

655. *Set My People Free*. London: Commonwealth Land Party, 1925. A pamphlet written in support of the Commonwealth Land Party which asserts that the existing economic order is insane, "a continuous looting of the helpless by those who have reduced them to helplessness." Supports the CLP's contention that, since each person has an inalienable right to the Earth and its products, everything should be held in common.

Works about Owen :

656. Oliver, H. *The International Anarchist Movement in Late Victorian London*. London: Croom Helm, 1983. Provides some useful historical background to Owen's life and ideas.

ALBERT R. PARSONS (1848-1887)

Works by A. R. Parsons :

657. *Anarchism: Its Philosophy and Scientific Basis, as Defined by Some of Its Apostles*. Edited Lucy E. Parsons. Westport, Conn.: Greenwood Pr., 1970. Originally published Chicago: Mrs. A. R. Parsons, 1889. Prepared during Albert Parsons' eighteen month imprisonment for alleged involvement in

the Haymarket bombing, the work covers the development of capitalism in the United States and Europe, the speeches of the eight condemned anarchists, and excerpts from various journals on the subject of anarchy.

658. *Appeal to the People of America.* Chicago: Lucy Parsons, 1887. A broadsheet published by Lucy Parsons after her husband's conviction for the Haymarket massacre. Albert Parsons pleads his innocence and asserts that, since the act of murder was unproved, he has been tried and convicted for his anarchism.

Works about A. R. Parsons :

659. Calmer, A. *Labor Agitator: The Story of Albert R. Parsons.* New York: International Pubns., 1937. Foreword by Lucy E. Parsons. Appearing on the eve of the fiftieth anniversary of the death of the Haymarket martyrs, 11 November 1887, it presents an account of the life and work of Albert R. Parsons and of the frame-up that ended both.

660. Parsons, L. E. *Life of Albert Parsons, with a Brief History of the Labor Movement in America.* Chicago: L. E. Parsons, 1889. A biography, written and published by his wife, presenting evidence to show that Parsons, although an anarchist, was innocent of any crime and the victim of a furore created by the authorities. Contains Parsons' Haymarket speech and his speech in court. The labor movement is covered in the preface. Ports.

LUCY E. PARSONS (1853-1924)

Works by L. E. Parsons :

661. *Life of Albert Parsons, with a Brief History of the Labor Movement in America.* Chicago: L. E. Parsons, 1889. See 660.

Works about L. E. Parsons :

662. Ashbaugh, C. *Lucy Parsons: American Revolutionary.* Chicago: Charles H. Kerr Pub. Co., 1976. Biographical study of the life and work of Lucy Parsons who was a central figure in the Haymarket affair in Chicago and active thereafter as a radical advocate of women's rights. She spoke on the subject of women at the Founding Convention of the IWW in 1905.

663. Davis, A. Y. "Lucy Parsons." In *Women, Race and Class,* 152-5. New York: Random Hse., 1981. A brief discussion of the life and ideas of Lucy Parsons as an early revolutionary anarchist and feminist.

664. Meyers, A. "The Haymarket Affair and Lucy Parsons: 100th Anniversary." *Our Generation* 17,2 (Spring/Summer 1986): 35-46. A

description of the role of Lucy Parsons in the events of 1886 and of her subsequent life.

PIERRE-JOSEPH PROUDHON (1809-1865)

Works by Proudhon :

665. *Les confessions d'un révolutionnaire.* Paris: Au bureau du journal *La Voix du Peuple,* 1849.

666. *Contradictions politiques. Théorie du mouvement constitutionnel au XIXe siècle.* Paris: Saint Germain, 1870.

667. *Correspondence de P.-J. Proudhon.* Précédée d'un notice sur P.-J. Proudhon par J. A. Langlois. Genève: Slatkine, 1971. Reprint of Paris edition, 1875.

668. *De la capacité politique des classes ouvrières.* Edited by Gustave Chaudey. Paris: Librarie internationale, 1865.

669. *De la célébration du dimanche, considérée sous les rapports de l'hygiène publique, de la morale, des relations de famille et de cité.* Paris: Prévot, 1845.

670. *De la concurrence entre les chemins de fer et les voies navigables.* Paris: Garnier, 1848. Originally published Paris: 1845.

671. *De la création de l'ordre dans l'humanité, ou principes d'organisation politique.* Paris: Prévot, 1843.

672. *Le droit au travail et le droit de propriété.* Paris: Garnier, 1848.

673. *De la justice dans la révolution et dans l'église: Nouveaux principes de philosophie pratique adressés à son eminence Monseigneur Mathieu.* Originally published Paris: Flammarian, n.d. Paris: Garnier, 1858.

674. *Les démocrates assermentés et les réfractaires.* Paris: E. Dentu, 1863.

675. *Du principe de l'art et de sa destination sociale.* Edited by J. A. Langlois and others. Paris: Garnier, 1865.

676. *La fédération et l'unité en Italie.* Paris: E. Dantu, 1862.

677. *France et Rhin.* Edited by Gustave Chaudey. Paris: A. Lacroix 1867.

678. *General Idea of the Revolution in the Nineteenth Century.* (*Idée générale de la révolution au XIXe siècle.*) New York: Itaskell, 1970. Originally published Paris: 1863. A reprint of the 1923 Freedom Press

edition. A collection of essays addressing the issues of progress and revolution during the nineteenth century while proposing solutions for the future. It is addressed to the bourgeoisie whom Proudhon accuses of being reactionary and brutal in their treatment of the poor and laboring classes. The latter, despite their support for the bourgeoisie in their struggle against the ancien régime, are, it is argued, always betrayed.

679. *La guerre et la paix: Récherches sur le principe au droit des gens.* Bruxelles: E. Dentu, 1861.

680. *Idées révolutionnaires.* Avec une préface par Alfred Darimon. Paris: Garnier, 1849.

681. *La justice poursuivie par l'église.* Bruxelles: Librairie de l'office de publicité, 1858.

682. *Les majorats littéraires.* Paris: E. Dentu, 1863.

683. *The Malthusians.* (Les malthusiens). Translated by B.R. Tucker. Berkeley Hts., N.J.: The Freeman Pr., 1938. Originally published in Paris: Boulé, 1848. London: International Publishing Co., 1886. A pamphlet containing an essay reprinted from *The Anarchist* in which Proudhon accuses Malthus of political murder for legitimizing the excesses of capitalism.

684. *Manuel du speculateur à la bourse.* 3rd edition. Paris: Garnier, 1856. Written as a handbook at the request of the publisher the first two editions were published anonymously.

685. *Le miserère ou la pénitence d'un roi: Lettre à R. P. Lacordaire sur son carême de 1845.* Paris: 1849. See also *Lettres de Pierre Joseph Proudhon, choisies et annotées.* Preface de Sainte-Beuve. Paris: B. Grasset, 1929.

686. *Nouvelles observations sur l'unité Italienne.* Paris: E. Dentu, 1865.

687. *Oeuvres complètes.* Vols. 1-13 Publiées avec des notes et des documents inédits sous la direction de C. Hougte et H. Moysset. Paris: Rivière, 1923-26. Imperfect, wanting vol. 14, 15. A further seven volumes projected but not published.

688. *Organisation du crédit et de la circulation et solution du problème social, sans impôt, sans emprint, sans numéraire, sans papier-monnaie, etc.* Paris: Garnier, 1848.

689. *Philosophie du progrès.* Bruxelles: A. Lebègue, 1853.

690. *La pornocratie, ou les femmes dans les temps modernes.* Paris: A. Lacroix, 1875.

691. *The Principle of Federation.* (*Du principe fédératif et de la nécessité de reconstituer le parti de la révolution*). Translated with introduction by Richard Vernon. Toronto: Univ. of Toronto Pr., 1979. Originally published Paris: E. Dentu, 1863, it establishes the historical and philosophical foundations of the principles of federation and concludes that it is the only political form adequate to human progress. The introduction is detailed.

692. *Proposition relative à l'impôt sur le revenue, présentée le 11 juillet 1848, par le citoyen Proudhon; suivie du discours qu'il a prononcé à l'Assemblée nationale, le 31 Juillet 1848.* Paris: Garnier, 1848.

693. *Proudhon's Solution of the Social Problem.* (*Solution du problème social.*) Including commentary by Charles A. Dana and William B. Greene. Edited by Henry Cohen. New York: Vanguard Pr., 1927. Originally published in Paris: Guillaumin, 1848. A collection of writings on mutualism, with a focus on mutual banking, a project close to the heart of Proudhon.

694. *Résumé de la question sociale, banque d'échange.* Paris: Garnier, 1848.

695. *La révolution sociale démonstrée par le coup d'etat du 2 décembre.* Paris: Garnier, 1852.

696. *Si les traités de 1815 ont cessé d'exister?* Paris: E. Dentu, 1863.

697. *System of Economic Contradictions: Or, the Philosophy of Poverty* (*Système des contradictions économique : Ou philosophie de la misère.*) Translated by Benjamin Tucker. Boston: 1888. Originally published in Paris: Guillaumin 1846 this was the work that angered Marx. Proudhon argued that since economic contradictions between capital and labor were inescapable, the principle of justice must be applied to bring about mutual agreement. To Marx any suggestion that economic contradictions must be accepted was anathema. Moreover, any principle of justice tended to divert attention from problems of production to issues of distribution. It must be dismissed as counter-revolutionary. Marx's attack on Proudhon was made in the deliberately entitled *The Poverty of Philosophy*.

698. *Théorie de la propriété.* Paris: A. Lacroix, 1866.

699. *What is Property?* (*Qu'est ce que la propriété ?*) Translated by Benjamin Tucker. Princeton: 1876. Republished New York: Howard Fertig, 1966. Originally published Paris: Brocard, 1840 Proudhon's swingeing attack on the property relations of his day answered the question posed by the title with a simple one-word answer, "Theft!" The employment of a number of laborers as a collective labor force produces values and benefits in excess of those that would be produced if the efforts of the individual laborers were employed in isolated activities. Yet, notwithstanding the extra value produced by collective labor power, the workers are paid as if employed as individuals doing separate tasks. It is in this way that a hidden value is aggrandized by the employer and "theft" takes place.

700. *The Works of P.-J. Proudhon in English.* Trans. and published by Benjamin R. Tucker. Princeton, N.J.: 1876. Vol. 1, *What Is Property?* republished New York: Howard Fertig, 1966. Vol. 4, *System Of Economical Contradictions or the Philosophy of Poverty,* republished Boston: B.R. Tucker, 1888.

Anthologies :

701. *Selected Writings of Pierre-Joseph Proudhon.* Edited with an introduction by Stewart Edwards. Translated from the French by Elizabeth Fraser. London: Macmillan, 1970. A brief anthology which is inclined to emphasize a conservative tendency in Proudhon's later writings at the expense of his influence on the labor movement and his radical contemporaries.

Works about Proudhon :

702. Allen, M. B. "P.-J. Proudhon in the Revolution of 1848." *Journal of Modern History* 24,1 (March 1952): 1-15. Discusses Proudhon's argument that revolution must be generated from below and not imposed from above.

703. Bowle, J. "Proudhon's Attack on the State." In *Politics and Opinion in the Nineteenth Century,* 152-67. New York: Jonathon Cape, 1954. Argues that Proudhon's deepest roots were in peasant life and that all his ideas relate to a concept of social justice based on the dignity of man.

704. Brogan, D. W. *Proudhon.* London: Hamilton, 1934. A short biographical study that is more of an introduction than a detailed analysis.

705. Butchart, M. "Marx and Proudhon." *The Criterion* 17,68 (April 1938): 445-57. Compares and contrasts their economic analyses and concludes that, in the light of events, Proudhon's analysis was arguably more realistic.

706. Carr, E. H. "Proudhon: Robinson Crusoe of Socialism." In his *Studies in Revolution,* 38-55. New York: Macmillan, 1964. Outlines Proudhon's rejection of the State and his advocacy of federalism, but is unsympathetic to Proudhon and anarchism in general, focussing mainly on Proudhon's inconsistencies. While not denying his sincerity, Carr concludes that both Proudhon and anarchism share a common nobility and futility.

707. Chadwick, W. "The Mailed Fist vs. the Invisible Hand." *Reason* 10,5 (1978): 18-23. See entry 59.

708. Chiaromonte, N. "P.-J. Proudhon: An Uncomfortable Thinker." *Politics* 3 (Jan. 1946): 27-9. A critique of J. S. Schapiro's "P.-J. Proudhon, Harbinger of Fascism," *American Historical Review* (July 1945), entry 748.

709. Condit, S. *Proudhonist Materialism and Revolutionary Doctrine.* Sanday, Orkney: Cienfuegos, Pr., 1982. Beginning with a discussion of Proudhon's materialism this short work proceeds to analyze to good effect his approach to property, distinguishing between property and possession.

710. Crapo, P. B. "The Anarchist as Critic: Pierre-Joseph Proudhon's Criticism of Literature and Art." *Michigan Academician* 13,4 (1981): 459-73. Discusses the many disparaging criticisms of Proudhon's ability as an art critic, suggesting that, while his philosophy of the arts is a contentious, he was, in fact, reasonably competent to work in this field.

711. Crapo, P. B. "Proudhon's Conspiratorial View of Society." *Journal of European Studies* 11,3 (1981): 184-95. Argues that commentators and analysts have neglected Proudhon's overly dramatic and conspiratorial view of the workings of the State.

712. Dillard, D. "Keynes and Proudhon." *Journal of Economic History* 2,1 (1942): 63-77. Demonstrates that major similarities exist between their works even though their theories were worked out in very different circumstances and with different aims. The more common comparison of the ideas of Marx and Keynes is used in the discussion.

713. Du Lubac, H. *The Un-Marxian Socialist: A Study of Proudhon.* Translated by R. E. Scantlebury. London: Sheed & Ward, 1948. Originally published in 1945 as *Proudhon et le Christianisme*, it discusses Proudhon's ideas in relation to Christianity.

714. Hall, C. M. *The Sociology of P.-J. Proudhon, 1809-1863.* New York: Philosophical Library, 1971. Aims to outline Proudhon's major sociological theories and evaluate his contribution to the history of sociology. There is an examination of his concept of society and justice, his sociology of religion and his theories of social change and social stratification.

715. Hamerton, P. G. "Proudhon as a Writer on Art." *Fortnightly Review* 4,19 (15 Feb. 1886): 142-62. Concentrates on Proudhon's weaknesses as an art critic rather than addressing his major theme in *Du principe de l'art et de sa destination sociale*, that of the role of Courbet and modern art as a force for change in society.

716. Harbold, W. H. "Justice in the Thought of Pierre-Joseph Proudhon." *Western Political Quarterly* 22,4 (Dec. 1969): 723-41. Argues that Proudhon considered justice to be the principle of social order immanent in historical experience.

717. Harbold, W. H. "Progressive Humanity in the Philosophy of Pierre-Joseph Proudhon." *Review of Politics* 31,1 (1969): 3-47. Traces the development of Proudhon's ideas on progress.

718. Harley, J. H. "Proudhon and the Labor Movement." *Socialist Review* 3 (1909): 273-83. Written on the occasion of Proudhon's centenary it compares

Marx and Proudhon, emphasizing Proudhon's socialist ideas rather than his anarchism.

719. Hoffman, R. "Marx and Proudhon: A Reappraisal of Their Relationship" *The Historian*. 29,3 (May 1967): 409-30. Argues that Marx and Proudhon, in spite of their common concerns with socialism and the philosophy of Hegel, shared no real common ground.

720. Hoffman, R. L. *Revolutionary Justice: The Social and Political Theory of P.-J. Proudhon*. Chicago: Univ. of Illinois Pr., 1972. A comprehensive study of Proudhon's ideas, incorporating biographical information, that draws out the philosophy of Proudhon with sympathy and clarity. Bibliography.

721. Hyams, E. *Pierre-Joseph Proudhon: His Revolutionary Life, Mind and Works*. London: J. Murray, 1979. An assessment of Proudhon's ideas which are categorized as being those of libertarian socialism. The author argues that existing socialism is, in general, split into two, Marxism and trade unionism, each having its own social vision and strategy for social change. Proudhon's libertarian socialism offers a way out of the dilemma created by this division.

722. Jackson, J. J. *Marx, Proudhon and European Socialism*. London: English Universities Pr., 1958. Through studies of the two thinkers the work argues for two distinct strands of European socialism, the one authoritarian, the other anarchist. Much more sympathetic to Proudhon than Marx.

723. Jackson, J. J. "Proudhon: A Prophet in Our Time." *Contemporary Review*. 165, 939 (March 1944): 156-9. Also in *Why?* 3,4 (Sept.-Oct. 1944). Written during World War II it addresses the threat of totalitarianism and looks to anarchism as an alternative. Proudhon is identified as the tradition's founder. The misunderstanding of Proudhon's ideas was due, it is argued, to Marx's jealousy and invective. In fact, Proudhon's ideas may have a future relevance.

724. Jackson, J. J. "The Relevance of Proudhon." *Politics* 2 (Oct. 1945): 297-9. Traces Proudhon's life and influence as well as popular misconceptions about him, predicting that people reacting against increasing authoritarianism may rediscover Proudhon in their search for an alternative.

725. King, P. T. *Fear of Power: An Analysis of Anti-Statism in Three French Writers*. London: Cass, 1967. A critical analysis of the ideas of Proudhon, Sorel and Tocqueville which concludes that power is inherently neither good nor evil; whatever social good is achieved comes through good government.

726. Lewis, W. "Proudhon and Rousseau". In *The Art of Being Ruled*, 333-75. New York and London: Chatto and Windus, 1926. An extended

discussion that compares various aspects of the thought of Proudhon and Rousseau.

727. Lu, S. Y. *The Political Theories of P.-J. Proudhon*. New York: M. R. Gray, 1922. A study of the ideas of Proudhon who is treated as the father of anarchism. There is an extensive discussion of Proudhon's economics and his ideas on anarchy, the state and federalism.

728. Marx, K. "Political Indifferentism." *Bulletin of the Society for the Study of Labour History* 20 (1970) 19-23. A direct attack on Proudhon and, by implication, Bakunin.

729. Marx, K. *The Poverty of Philosophy*. Moscow: Progress Pubs., 1963. Marx's definitive critique of Proudhon's social philosophy and political economy, the title a deliberate inversion of Proudhon's *The Philosophy of Poverty*, op.cit., entry 696.

730. Nelson, R. "The Federal Idea in French Political Thought." *Publius*. 5,3 (1975): 7-63. Through an examination of a range of thinkers, including Proudhon, it is argued that ideas about social and political alternatives develop dialectically.

731. Noland, A. "History and Humanity: The Proudhonian Version." In *The Uses of History*, edited by Hayden V. White, 59-106. Detroit: Wayne State Univ. Pr., 1968. Examines Proudhon's historical thought and work within the context of the general preoccupation with history in the nineteenth century. Argues that Proudhon believed that no new order had been properly established after the French Revolution had removed the old, and so sought to discover the organizing principle on which the new society might be based.

732. Noland, A. "Pierre-Joseph Proudhon as a Social Scientist." *American Journal of Economics and Sociology* 26,3 (1967): 313-28. Concludes that for Proudhon the true science of society consisted in the study of the behavior of collective forces.

733. Noland, A. "Proudhon and Rousseau." *Journal of the History of Ideas* 28,1 (1967): 33-54. Examines the often striking parallels between the ideas of the two thinkers and suggests that Rousseau should be regarded as one of the "masters" of Proudhon.

734. Noland, A. "Proudhon's Sociology of War." *American Journal of Economics and Sociology* 29,3 (July 1970): 289-304. Outlines Proudhon's theory of war, noting its stark contrast with the anti-war views of his socialist contemporaries.

735. Osgood, H. L. "Scientific Anarchism." *Political Science Quarterly* 4,1(March 1889): 1-36. An analysis of anarchism which, focussing on the ideas of Proudhon, contrasts its individualistic and communistic forms. Examines public responses in America to the perceived threat of anarchism

and concludes that no system of government is of itself good or evil, rather it is the character of those who govern that is crucial.

736. Pickles, W. "Marx and Proudhon." *Politica* 3,13 (1938): 236-60. Regrets the bitterness of the struggle between the respective doctrines of Marx and Proudhon, suggesting that they are, in fact, to a large extent complementary.

737. Prélot, M. "Pierre-Joseph Proudhon." In the *International Encyclopedia of the Social Sciences*, 604-6. New York: Macmillan & The Free Pr., 1968. An introductory outline of Proudhon's life, ideas, activities and influence.

738. Rathore, L. S. "Pierre-Joseph Proudhon: Mutualism and Federative Anarchist Society." *Indian Journal of Political Studies* 8 (July 1984). Argues that Proudhon was a brilliant thinker who succeeded in bridging the gap between agrarian populism and urban syndicalism.

739. Reichert, W. O. "Art, Nature and Revolution." (The aesthetics of Proudhon, Kropotkin and Bakunin). *Arts in Society*. 9,3 (1972): 409-30. See entry 117.

740. Reichert, W. O. "Pierre-Joseph Proudhon: One of the Fathers of Philosophical Anarchism." *Journal of Human Relations* 13,1 (1965): 81-92. Aims to rescue the Proudhonian tradition from ideas of terrorism and nihilism, claiming that to adopt his position is to reject the violent overthrow of the State and to advocate non-violent persuasion aimed at the highest moral ends.

741. Reichert, W. O. "Natural Right in the Political Philosophy of Pierre-Joseph Proudhon." *Journal of Libertarian Studies* 4,1 (Winter 1980): 77-91. Argues that Proudhon had a highly developed philosophy of law. His idea of 'Justice' presupposed a free social order where individuals, unaided by governments, would arrive at agreements as to what constitutes 'natural right'. Reprinted in *Law and Anarchism*, 122-40. Op.cit., entry 1413.

742. Rieff, P. "A Jesuit looks at Proudhon: Competition in Damnation." *Modern Review*. 3,2 (Jan. 1950). A review article of Henri du Lubac, *The Un-Marxian Socialist* op. cit., entry 713.

743. Ritter, A. "Godwin, Proudhon and the Anarchist Justification of Punishment." *Political Theory*. 3,1 (1975): 68-87. See entry 318.

744. Ritter, A. *The Political Thought of Pierre-Joseph Proudhon*. Princeton, New Jersey: Princeton Univ. Pr., 1969. A thorough and scholarly work which looks at Proudhon in terms of issues current in the United States during the late 1960s.

745. Ritter, A. "Proudhon and the Problem of Community." *Review of Politics* 29,4 (1967): 457-77. Examines Proudhon's theory of community as an attempt to reconcile individual freedom with social peace. His perspective, it is suggested, is, while radical, realistic.

746. Rogers, J. A. "Proudhon and the Transformation of Russian 'Nihilism'." *Cahiers du Monde Russe et Soviétique* 13,4 (1972): 514-23. Argues that Proudhon's theories had a significant influence in Russia in the 1860's, leading directly to the rise of the school of Russian "subjective sociology."

747. Rubin, J. H. *Realism and Social Vision in Courbet and Proudhon.* Princeton *Essays on the Arts* No. 10. Princeton, N.J.: Princeton Univ. Pr., 1981. Argues that Courbet's work represented a profound opposition to the ruling classes of the Second Empire. Thus Courbet's painting and Proudhon's social theory must be seen as inseparable, representing a confluence of romanticism and positive consciousness that led to modern art. Includes a select bibliography.

748. Schapiro, S. J. "Pierre-Joseph Proudhon, Harbinger of Fascism." *American Historical Review* 50,4 (July 1945): 714-37. Denies that Proudhon was an anarchist because he believed in the principle of private enterprise. Yet, at the same time, he opposed profit and interest. Proudhon's repudiation of democracy and large-scale capitalism, Schapiro argues, mean that the fascists can justifiably claim him as a precursor.

749. Silvera, A. *Daniel Halévy and his Times.* Ithaca: Cornell Univ. Pr., 1966. Though not directly about Proudhon, this work discusses his influence on *fin de siècle* intellectuals.

750. Simon, Y. R. "A Note on Proudhon's Federalism." *Publius: Journal of Federalism* 3,1 (1973): 19-31. Suggests that in writing *The Federal Principle* Proudhon offered his finished conception of an anarchist society and its political organisation.

751. Simon, Y. R. "The Problem of Transcendence and Proudhon's Challenge." *Thought* 54 (June 1979): 176-85. An attack on those of Proudhon's arguments which center on the existence and role of God in human affairs. Makes particular reference to *De la justice dans la révolution et dans l'église.*

752. Spear, L. "Pierre-Joseph Proudhon and the Myth of Universal Suffrage." *Canadian Journal of History* 10,3 (1975): 295-306. Argues that Proudhon did not oppose authentic universal suffrage, but denied that its existence as myth offered any long term social solution.

753. Vincent, S. K. *Pierre-Joseph Proudhon and the Rise of French Socialism.* New York: Oxford Univ. Pr., 1984. Argues for Proudhon's significance as a pioneer of reformist socialism through an analysis of his activities in the republican movements that emerged under the July monarchy. The work challenges, however, Proudhon's place within anarchism, arguing that morally he was religious, politically republican, and in economics, a socialist.

754. Watkins, F. M. "Proudhon and the Theory of Modern Liberalism." *Canadian Journal of Economics and Political Science* 13,3 (Aug. 1947): 429-35. Suggests that Proudhon's political thought is better adapted to the practice of modern parliamentarianism than are orthodox liberal theories.

755. Woodcock, G. "Proudhon and his Mutualist Theories." In *The Writer and Politics*, 42-55. London: Porcupine Pr., 1948. A discussion of Proudhon in the context of a study of the relationship between the writer and society, in particular social movements for reform or revolution.

756. Woodcock, G. "Proudhon, an Appreciation." *Dissent* 2,4 (Autumn 1955): 394-405. Suggests that Marx and Marxist political economy in general owe a great deal more to the work of Proudhon than is generally recognized. Particular reference is made to *What is Property?*, op.cit., entry 698.

757. Woodcock, G. "The Solitary Revolutionary. Proudhon's Notebooks." *Encounter* 33,192 (1969): 46-55. Woodcock discovered the whereabouts of the 11 notebooks in 1951. He quotes several passages from them to demonstrate their value as biographical raw material giving intimate insights into Proudhon's character and thoughts.

758. Woodcock, G. *Pierre-Joseph Proudhon: A Biography.* London: Routledge & Paul, 1956. A biographical study with a close analysis of his key ideas and principles.

HERBERT READ (1893-1968)

Works by Read :

The selection is limited to his anarchism or to anarchist themes in his work.

759. *Anarchy and Order: Essays in Politics.* Introduction by Howard Zinn. London: Souvenir Pr., 1974. Also Boston: Beacon Pr., 1971. Assembles all the essays he wrote specifically on anarchism. His work is based on faith in the fundamental goodness of people. He stresses the creative possibilities while accepting the vulnerability of social organization based on anarchist principles.

760. *Art and Industry.* New York: Horizon Pr., 1961. The book that had a vital influence on the development of the principles underlying industrial design. It relates to anarchist theory through its discussion of the connection between the uniqueness of individual products of art and industrial standardization. Implicit is Read's conception that the fully integrated human personality must have fully developed aesthetic dimensions.

761. *The Cult of Sincerity*. London: Faber & Faber, 1968. A collection of essays set out in two parts. The first part contains essays in which Read expresses his personal philosophy. In the title essay, for example, he discusses selfhood, freedom and authenticity. The second part contains critical sketches of important contemporaries, including T. S. Eliot, Jung, Russell and D. H. Lawrence.

762. *Education through Art*. London: Faber & Faber, 1942? A discussion of education and art that stresses the importance of developing aesthetic sensibility. The broad purpose of education, Read argues, is to encourage both the development of individual human uniqueness and potential and the social consciousness of each individual as a member of a community.

763. *Essential Communism*. London: S. Nott, 1935. Argues that the most difficult step in social reform lies not with the will for change, but in people's reluctance to implement a rational plan because of a fear of sacrificing individuality to the community. Nevertheless the pamphlet looks towards a society without poverty or social injustice, where order and beauty will be the outer manifestations of a free, vital and romantic spirit.

764. *Existentialism, Marxism and Anarchism and Chains of Freedom*. London: Freedom Pr., 1949. Two essays in the one volume. The first is a discussion of existentialism and its concern for freedom, noting the Marxist position, and arguing that the only political philosophy that combines a revolutionary and contingent attitude with a philosophy of freedom is anarchism. The second piece consists of stray notes and ideas towards a philosophy of freedom.

765. *The Forms of Things Unknown: Essays towards an Aesthetic Philosophy*. London: Faber & Faber, 1960. A discussion of the nature of the creative mind, the uniqueness and independence of which Read feels is threatened by automation, technological culture, urbanization etc. Part 4 discusses humanism, individuality, love and force with some examination of the ideas of Stirner and Tolstoy.

766. *Freedom, Is It a Crime? The Strange Case of the Three Anarchists Jailed at the Old Bailey, April 1945: Two Speeches*. Foreword by E. Silverman. London: Freedom Pr. Defence Committee, 1945. While specifically addressing the jailing of certain anarchists for articles they had written, these speeches, one before and one after the trial, also highlight the many encroachments on human liberty imposed in wartime. Concern is expressed that they might remain in place after the war.

767. *Icon and Idea: The Function of Art in the Development of Human Consciousness*. London: Faber & Faber, 1955. Reed argues that art is "the essential instrument in the development of human consciousness." It demonstrates why the aesthetic sense is so vital to his concept of the human in politics.

768. *The Philosophy of Anarchism.* New York: Distributed by the Libertarian League, 1947. Aims to restate the fundamental principles of anarchism in the belief that millions of people instinctively hold these beliefs already. Examines notions of human progress, the role of materialism and religion, and the potential of strikes as a basis for action.

769. *Poetry and Anarchism.* Philadelphia: R. West, 1978. Originally published London: Faber & Faber, 1938. Written out of a despair regarding the problems of contemporary society. Espouses a broadly anarchist solution yet concludes that the only refuge for people is within themselves - a sort of private anarchism. Reviewing a new edition in 1948 George Woodcock called it "one of the most valuable and best written books on libertarian thought in the English language." *Freedom* (7 Feb. 1948).

770. *The Politics of the Unpolitical.* London: Routledge, 1943. This collection of essays is a discussion of democracy which focuses on the problems of the artist, someone who both stands apart and mediates, in a community of supposed equals. At the same time, it is asserted that each individual is potentially an artist.

771. "Pragmatic Anarchism." *Encounter* 30 (Jan. 1968): 54-61. Some reflections and suggestions occasioned by the release of the book *Patterns of Anarchy*, edited Krimerman and Perry, op.cit., entry 1436. Read insists that anarchists are pragmatists, not idealists, and that true freedom consists in free action not indifference.

772. *The Redemption of the Robot: My Encounter with Education through Art.* London: Faber & Faber, 1970. A book that, while focussing on the processes of education, sets out a number of Read's key political beliefs, including the uniqueness and worth of the individual, free education and the fostering of individual development, the need for decentralization, the role of art and aesthetics, and the dangers of technology, centralization, urbanization and bureaucracy.

773. *To Hell with Culture and Other Essays.* London: Routledge & Kegan Paul, 1963. Several essays are reprinted from *The Politics of the Unpolitical*, op.cit., entry 770. The independence and individuality of the creative mind is emphasized within the context of a discussion of culture, democracy, revolution and art. Art, it is asserted is independent of politics, having little concern with any political system. It is an unpolitical manifestation of the autonomous and creative human spirit.

Works about Read :

The selection focuses on Read's social theory, although some discussions of his ideas on aesthetics and literature are obviously relevant.

774. De Fennaro, A. A. "Benedetto Croce and Herbert Read." *Journal of Aesthetics and Art Criticism* 26,3 (Spring 1968) 307-10. Explores the

influence of Croce's philosophy on Read's ideas while acknowledging that Read's position remained distinctly his own.

775. Fouche, J. F. "The Contrary Experience: Herbert Read's Educational Philosophy." In *Critical Issues in Philosophy of Education*, edited by C. Peden. Washington D. C.: Univ. Pr. of America, 1979. Looks at Read's ideas in *Education Through Art*, op.cit., entry 762, in which he argues that in our efforts to industrialize and modernize we have created a barren culture that is reflected in our schooling. Suggests that although Read's criticisms are not original, repeating as they do those of Rousseau and others, his solution is unique.

776. Harder, W. T. *A Certain Order: The Development of Herbert Read's Theory*. The Hague: Mouton, 1971. Discusses Read's theory of poetry in which he grounded modern poetry in the tradition of English romanticism. Contains a chapter "Anarchy and Superreality" in which the author explains how for Read what in art is a romantic principle becomes in life an anarchic principle. Bibliography and index.

777. Hodin, J. P. "Herbert Read - The Man and his Work: A Tribute on his Seventieth Birthday." *Journal of Aesthetics and Art Criticism* 23,2 (Winter 1964): 169-72. A very short article which attempts to assess Read's significance as an aesthetic conscience in the modern world. The major emphasis is on art rather than anarchism.

778. Meeson, P. "Herbert Read's Definition of Art in Education through Art." *Journal of Aesthetic Education* 8 (July 1974): 5-18. A critical analysis of Read's definition of art which questions the adequacy of his philosophy of art education.

779. Parsons, M. J. "Herbert Read on Education." *Journal of Aesthetic Education* 3,4 (Oct. 1969): 27-45. There is only a fleeting reference to *Anarchy and Order*, op.cit., entry 759, in an article concerned with education theory.

780. Reichert, W. "The Relevance of Anarchism: An Introduction to the Social Theory of Herbert Read." *Educational Theory* 17 (1967): 147-57. Supports Read's belief that the abolition of the State is not a political act but a teleological process inherent in people's own aesthetic faculty. The issue of education is crucial to this process.

781. Skelton, R., ed. *Herbert Read: A Memorial Symposium*. London: Methuen, 1969. A collection of essays mainly dealing with Read's contributions to art and culture. Included is an essay by George Woodcock on Read's political philosophy.

782. Thistlewood, D. "Creativity and Political Identification in the Work of Herbert Read." *British Journal of Aesthetics* 26,4 (Autumn 1986): 345-56. Assesses the impact of Read's early membership of a Guild Socialist cell on his mature philosophical anarchism and educational theory.

783. Thistlewood, D. *Herbert Read: Formlessness and Form.* Boston: Routledge & Kegan Paul, 1984. Provides an analysis of Read's aesthetic philosophy and argues that Read was both eclectic and original.

784. Walsh, D. "The Real and the Realized." *Review of Metaphysics* 10,3 (March 1957): 474-81. A sympathetic but critical analysis of Read's *Icon and Idea*, op.cit., entry 767.

785. Wasson, R. "Herbert Read: A Salutation to Eros." *Journal of Aesthetic Education* 3,4 (Oct. 1969): 11-25. Reviews Read's leading role in the changing attitudes to culture that developed through the 1960's.

786. Wieder, C. G. "Herbert Read on Education, Art, and Individual Liberty." *Journal of Aesthetic Education* 17,3 (Fall 1983): 85-93. Examines Read's views on the education process and the cultivation of each student's individuality.

787. Woodcock, G. *Herbert Read: The Stream and the Source.* London: Faber & Faber, 1972. A brief intellectual biography which focuses on his works, his ideas, and his contribution to the anarchist tradition.

ELISÉE RECLUS (1830-1905)

Works by Reclus :

788. *À mon frère, le paysan.* Geneva: 1893.

789. "An Anarchist on Anarchy." *Commonweal* 7,284 (10 Oct. 1891): 126-7. A criticism of modern civilization that argues for the necessity of anarchism as a cure for the ills of society.

790. *Correspondence.* 3 vols. Paris: 1911-25.

791. "De la mutalité, P.-J. Proudhon, travail et capital: formule de conciliation." *L'Association* 8 (1865).

792. *Evolution and Revolution.* London: International Pubg. Co., 1885. Asserts that the opposition between evolution and revolution used by conservatives is misleading. Evolutionary forces exist that will produce inevitable progress in human liberation by means of a revolution. Also published in *Commonweal* 7,268/269/270), (June-July 1891): 61-2/65-6/70-1.

793. *Free Vistas: An Anthology of Life and Letters.* Edited Joseph Ishill. Berkeley Hts., N.J.: Oriole Pr.,1933. A beautifully presented collection of poems, extracts and illustrations from Ishill's private press that contains translations of pieces by Reclus.

794. *L'homme et la terre.* 6 vols. Paris: 1905-8.

795. *The Ideal and Youth.* London: James Tochatti, "Liberty" Pr., 1895. A short pamphlet making an appeal to youth to abandon conservatism, crass materialism and self-indulgence, and to dedicate itself to a future of solidarity and altruism.

796. *The Oriole Press - A Bibliography.* Edited Joseph Ishill. Berkeley Hts., N.J.: Oriole Pr., 1953. Contains short pieces by Elisée and Elie Reclus. See entry 1420.

797. "Pourquoi nous sommes anarchistes!" *La Societé Nouvelle* 31 (Aug. 1889).

Works about Reclus :

798. Dunbar, G. S. "Elisée Reclus and the Great Globe." *Scottish Geographical Magazine* 90,1 (1974): 57-64. This article discusses Reclus' plans to build a massive relief globe for the Paris Exposition of 1900 which would be both scientifically accurate and a symbol of world unity.

799. Dunbar, G. S. "Elisée Reclus in Louisiana." *Louisianna History* 23,4 (1982): 341-52. Recounts Reclus' experiences in Louisianna between 1853 and 1855, arguing that this period was of major significance in the formulation of his thought.

800. Dunbar, G. "Elisée Reclus: Geographer and Anarchist." *Antipode* 10/11,3/1 (1979): 16-21. A brief discussion, in a special double issue of *Antipode* on anarchism, of the relationship between Reclus' geography and his anarchist philosophy.

801. Fleming, M. *The Anarchist Way to Socialism: Elisée Reclus and Nineteenth-Century European Anarchism.* London: Croom Helm, 1979. A useful analysis of the life and ideas of Reclus which characterizes him as a socialist, arguing that, while he was anarchist in his anti-statism, his economic ideas were influenced by Marxism. The relationship between his anarchist and socialist ideals, it is argued, is the key to his thought.

802. Fleming, M. "Elisée Reclus: Between Religion and Science." *Our Generation* 20,1 (Fall 1988): 54-70. Argues that, in his efforts to legitimate anarchism through science, Reclus was led to identify anarchism with science.

803. Fleming, M. *The Geography of Freedom: The Odyssey of Elisée Reclus.* Montréal: Black Rose Bks., 1988. Looks at the contribution Reclus made in his own time as well as examining the relevance of his ideas to the present. Photographs and index.

804. Ishill, J., ed. *Elisée and Elie Reclus: In Memoriam.* Woodcuts by Louis Moreau. Berkeley Heights, N.J.: Oriole Pr., 1927. A rare book printed by

Ishill's own press. Excellently presented memorial volume, with superb woodcuts.

805. Kropotkin, P. "Elisée Reclus." *Freedom* 19,199 (Aug. 1905) 21/23-4. An obituary of Reclus celebrating his work both as a scientist and an anarchist.

806. Nettlau, M. "Elisée and Elie Reclus as Seen by Their Friends." In *The Oriole Press - A Bibliography*, edited by Joseph Ishill, 19-35. Op.cit., entry 1420. A short personal memoir.

807. Owen, W. C. "Elisée and Elie Reclus." In *The Oriole Press - A Bibliography*, 83-8. Op.cit., entry 1420. A short memoir by an English anarchist who was a contemporary of Reclus. The piece first appeared in *Freedom* (Nov. 1927).

808. Sanborn, A. F. *Paris and the Social Revolution: A Study of the Revolutionary Elements in the Various Classes of Parisian Society.* London: Hutchinson, 1905. A detailed study of French anarchism at the turn of the last century with some discussion of Jean Grave, Peter Kropotkin and Elisée Reclus. There is an analysis of the philosophy of anarchism and of *le propagande par le fait.*

RUDOLF ROCKER (1873-1958)

Works by Rocker:

809. *Anarchism and Anarcho-Syndicalism.* London: Freedom Pr., 1973. An abridged version of *Anarcho-Syndicalism*, 1938, which first appeared in Feliks Gross, *European* Ideologies. New York: 1948. Also appears as an appended essay in P. Eltzbacher, *Anarchism.* Op.cit., entry 1365. About one third of the original this nevertheless gives a very clear exposition of the history and aims of anarchism and anarcho-syndicalism.

810. *Anarcho-Syndicalism: Theory and Practice.* New York: Gordon Pr., 1972. Originally published in 1938 Rocker states the case for anarcho-syndicalism, a subject on which the Spanish War had focussed attention. After first giving an excellent overview of anarchist principles, he proceeds to give an historical analysis of the development of anarcho-syndicalism.

811. *The London Years.* Translated by Joseph Leftwich. London: R. Anscombe for the Rudolf Rocker Book Committee, 1956. A memoir covering the period Rocker spent in London with sketches of comrades such as Kropotkin and Malatesta.

812. *Milly Witkop-Rocker.* Sanday, Orkney: Cienfuegos Pr., 1981. A reproduction of Rocker's short memorial biographical essay on his wife, born 1 March, 1877 and died 23 November, 1955. Originally produced in

June 1956 by Joseph Ishill's Oriole Press as a private edition for Rudolf Rocker.

813. *Nationalism and Culture.* Los Angeles: Rocker Pubs. Comm., 1947. One of Rocker's most significant works. A broad-ranging and scholarly discussion that provides a penetrating analysis of culture, and of nationalism and its historical genesis. Rocker believed that a general decline in civilization had produced the Second World War and that a solution could only be found in community and confederation. He sets out what he believes to be the necessary conditions for a free society to come into being and sustain itself.

814. *Pioneers of American Freedom: Origin of Liberal and Radical Thought in America.* Los Angeles: Rocker Pubs. Comm., 1949. A very useful survey of the leading exponents of American radical and liberal theory. Part One looks at the liberal tradition with chapters on Paine, Jefferson and Lincoln. Part Two discusses the individualist anarchists with chapters on Josiah Warren, Stephen Pearl Andrews, Lysander Spooner, William B. Greene and Benjamin Tucker. Contains a brief biographical outline and succinct exposition of the ideas of each thinker. Bibliography and index.

815. *Socialism and State.* With short biography of Rocker. Indore City: Modern Pubns., 1946.

816. *The Tragedy in Spain.* New York: Freie Arbeiter Stimme, 1937. An account of events in Spain focussing on the work and sacrifice of the members of the CNT and the FAI. Argues that the campaign waged against them, and the POUM, by Moscow and the communists, produced a Stalin inspired break-down of the anti-Fascist front.

817. *The Truth about Spain.* New York: Freie Arbeiter Stimme, 1936. See entry 1795.

Works about Rocker :

818. Fishman, W. J. *East End Jewish Radicals, 1875-1914.* London: Duckworth, 1975. Includes an account of the life and work of Rudolf Rocker, the best known representative of the Jewish anarchism that flourished in the old East End.

819. Read, H., Ishill, J. et al. *Testimonial to Rudolf Rocker.* Los Angeles: Rocker Pubns. Committee, 1944. A series of short essays by various authors on the life and work of Rocker, published to mark his seventieth birthday. The volume celebrates his anarchist contribution to humanism and culture. Articles on pages 1-40 appeared in the magazine *The Roman Forum.*

820. Vallance, M. "Rudolf Rocker - A Biographical Sketch." *Journal of Contemporary History* 8,3 (1973): 75-95. Written 15 years after his death it is

more concerned with Rocker's life and the influences on him than with his philosophy.

821. Walter, N. "Rudolf Rocker's *Anarcho-Syndicalism.*" *The Raven* 1,4 (March 1988): 351-360. An historical account of Rocker and the background to the writing of *Anarcho-Syndicalism.*

AUGUST SPIES (1855-1887)

Works by Spies:

822. *August Spies' Auto-biography: His Speech in Court, and General Notes.* Chicago: Nina Van Zandt, 1887. The speeches of August Spies, Michael Schwab, Oscar Neebe, Adolph Fischer, Louis Lingg, George Engel, Samuel Fieldon and Albert R. Parsons, prior to the death sentence being handed down for their alleged part in the Haymarket bombing. Also published by Lucy Parsons as *The Famous Speeches of the Eight Chicago Anarchists in Court, 7, 8, 9, October 1886,* Chicago: 1910.

823. "Socialism and Anarchism." *Commonweal* 7,304 (2 March, 1892). Argues that Anarchism or Socialism means the peaceful reconstruction of society on the basis of equality.

LYSANDER SPOONER (1808-1887)

Works by Spooner:

824. *Collected Works.* Weston, Mass.: M & S Pr., 1971.

825. *An Essay on Trial by Jury.* New York: Da Capo Pr., 1971. Originally published Boston: J. P. Jewett & Co.,1852. A discussion of common law trial by jury, tracing its history from Magna Carta, while asserting that there are no legal juries in the United States since principles like the eligibility of all freeman for jury service have been breached.

826. *A Letter to Grover Cleveland on His False Inaugural Address, the Usurpations and Crimes of Lawmakers and Judges, and the Consequent Poverty, Ignorance, and Servitude of the People.* Boston: B. R. Tucker, 1886. Takes issue with Cleveland's promise to administer law "justly". Government is not concerned with justice but the protection of selfish interests. The Legislature is really four hundred "champion robbers." There must be a destruction of money-monopoly and the restoration of free labor and free money.

827. "No Treason I." In *Individual Anarchist Pamphlets.* New York: Arno Pr., 1972. The collection is subtitled "The Right Wing Individualist Tradition in America." The pamphlets are reproduced as they were

originally printed with individual page numbering. This piece by Spooner, originally published by Spooner himself, Boston: 1867, was written to address issues raised by a consideration of government by consent. The Constitution of the United States, Spooner argues, stresses consent, and implies the separate consent of every individual required to pay taxes or to provide personal service to the support of the government. The Civil War demonstrates the reality of rule by the strongest party.

828. "No Treason II." In *Individual Anarchist Pamphlets*. New York: Arno Pr., 1972. Originally published by Spooner himself, Boston: 1867, this is another pamphlet addressing issues of consent raised by the Civil War. Spooner argues that since the Constitution of the United States rests on the principle of continuous consent, withdrawal of that consent, that is secession, is not treason. But since force has overtaken consent both North and South are in error, since both assume allegiance and consent where none exists. The result is a war between chattel slavery and political slavery with true freedom existing on neither side.

829. "No Treason VI." In *American Issues*. Vol. 1. *The Social Record*, edited Willard Thorp, Merle Curtis and Carlos Baker, 569-74. Chicago/Philadelphia: J. B. Lippincott & Co., 1944. The third of Spooner's extant pamphlets in the series. Despite the numbering there appears to be no record of others. In this, the most radical of the pamphlets, Spooner raises the question of who has robbed humanity of property and restrained liberty. He concludes that since, in modern society, money is power, it is the power of rich capitalism that lies behind government and has, thus, abrogated those liberties guaranteed by the Constitution.

830. *Poverty: Its Illegal Causes and Legal Cure*. Boston: 1846. A discussion of debt and credit advocating Warren's principles of equitable commerce as a solution to the problem of poverty. Poverty occurs because of a violation of the economic principles of natural law which, *inter alia*, include the right of every man to the fruits of his own labor, the right of every man to be his own employer and the right of every man to have capital for his labor to work on.

831. *The Unconstitutionality of Slavery*. New York: Burt Franklin, 1966. Originally published in 1852, and in an expanded form in 1857, this is a reprint of the 1860 edition published in Boston. It argues, from interpretations of law and the Constitution of the United States, that slavery is not constitutional since all men are presumed to be free. There is, therefore, no legal basis for slavery.

Works about Spooner :

832. Alexander, J. A. "The Ideas of Lysander Spooner." *New England Quarterly* 23 (June 1950): 200-17. A discussion that touches on Spooner's anarchism in reference to his economic principles and views on poverty.

833. Kline, W. G. *The Individualist Anarchists*. Boston & London: Univ. of America Pr., 1987. A discussion of the origins and development of the individualist anarchist tradition in America, in which Chapter Two is devoted to a discussion of the ideas of Spooner, pages 35-45.

834. Martin, J. J. *Men against the State*. Dekalb, Ill.: Adrian Allen, 1953. A treatment of individualist anarchism in America which deals with Spooner in Chapter VII, "Lysander Spooner, Dissident Among Dissidents," pages 168-201. See entry 1838.

835. Rocker, R. *Pioneers of American Freedom*. Los Angeles: Rocker Pubns. Comm., 1949. A discussion of the origins of liberal and radical individualist thought in America with a consideration of the life and ideas of Spooner, pages 86-96.

MAX STIRNER (1806-1856)

Works by Stirner :

836. *The Ego and His Own*. New York: Libertarian Book Club, 1963. Translated Steven T. Byington. Edited and introduced by John Carroll. London: Jonathan Cape, 1971. Originally published 1845; translated 1907. The most controversial and extreme statement of egoistic anarchism. Stirner has been identified as a major precursor of political and philosophical movements of both the Left and the Right, although he did not seek to initiate such movements. He asserts an uncompromising rejection of all authority beyond the reach of the individual, arguing that Ego antecedes essence, and that each individual must pursue his or her own freedom with egoism as the only law. Not only the state, but society itself is condemned as a fetter on liberty. A union of egoists is the only possible social order.

Works about Stirner :

837. Bauer, E. "On Stirner and Szeliga, 1882." *Phililosophical Forum* 8 (1978): 167-72. First English translation and publication, with a commentary by Hans-Martin Hass, of a letter from Bauer to Max Hildebrandt. It contains some useful anecdotes concerning Stirner and the writing of *The Ego and His Own*.

838. Bergner, J. T. "Stirner, Nietzsche and the Critique of Truth." *Journal of the History of Philosophy* 11,4 (1973): 523-34. Discusses Stirner's critique of truth, particularly in relation to the ideas of Nietzsche, arguing that Stirner's views have been constantly misinterpreted.

839. Brazill, W. J. *The Young Hegelians*. New Haven: Yale Univ. Pr, 1970. A comprehensive intellectual history of the philosophical ideas of the Young Hegelians. Chapter 6 deals specifically with Stirner.

840. Carroll, J. B. *Break-out from the Crystal Palace: The Anarcho-Psychological Critique: Stirner, Nietzsche, Dostoevsky*. London: Routledge & Kegan Paul, 1974. A comparative study of the ideas of Stirner, Nietzsche and Dostoevsky in which they are identified as representatives of the anarcho-psychological tradition that both paved the way for Freud and was influential in the emergence of existentialist thought in the 20th century.

841. Clark, J. P. *Max Stirner's Egoism*. London: Freedom Pr., 1976. A study of Stirner's thought from the perspective of social anarchism. Chapter 6 concentrates on Stirner and anarchism.

842. Ferguson, K. E. "Saint Max Revisited: A Reconsideration of Max Stirner." *Idealistic Studies* 12 (Sept. 1982): 276-92. Argues that many critics of Stirner have failed to deal adequately with the ontological and axiological questions raised by Stirner, particularly his radical view on moral choice and his process theory of the self. The latter, while failing to deal adequately with human sociability nevertheless usefully sets out a basis for the demystification of authority.

843. Feuerbach, L. "*The Essence of Christianity* in relation to *The Ego And His Own*." *Philosophical Forum* 8,2/3/4 (1978): 81-91. Translation of the German text in Feuerbach's *Sämtliche Werke*, Vol. 7, edited by Wilhelm Bolin & Friedrich Jodl. Stuttgart-Bad: Cannstatt,1960.

844. Gordon, F. M. "The Debate between Feuerbach and Stirner: An Introduction." *Philosophical Forum* 8 (1978): 52-65. Discusses *The Ego and His Own* as a decisive critique of the Young Hegelian movement, in particular of Feuerbach.

845. Lobkowicz, N. "Karl Marx and Max Stirner." *Boston College Studies in Philosophy* 2 (1969): 64-95. A lengthy and complex article which suggests that Stirner's book *The Ego and His Own* played a significant role in prompting the first version of Marx's mature historical materialism in *The German Ideology*. Contains a summary of the contents of *The Ego and His Own* as well as expositions of the Hegelian and Marxian positions.

846. Marx, K. and Engels, F. *The Holy Family: Or Critique of Critical Criticism, against Bruno Bauer and Company*. Moscow: Progress Publishers, 1956. Though not dealing directly with Stirner, the work marks the formalizing of Marx's and Engel's dissatisfaction with the ideas and

programmes of Bruno Bauer and other members of the Young Hegelian movement like Stirner.

847. Marx, K. and Engels, F. *The German Ideology.* Moscow: Progress Publishers, 1964. Marx and Engels' critique of German idealism, with a very long section devoted to Stirner. This work effectively completed their break with the Young Hegelian movement.

848. McLellan, D. *The Young Hegelians and Karl Marx.* London: Macmillan, 1969. An intellectual history of Hegel's disciples with a full chapter devoted to Stirner, pages 117-36.

849. Paterson, R. W. K. *The Nihilistic Egoist, Max Stirner.* London: Oxford Univ. Pr., 1971. A detailed study of Stirner's life and philosophy, his relationship to Marxism and later philosophical traditions, especially existentialism, and his place in the history of ideas.

850. Sass, H. "Bruno Bauer's Critical Theory." *Philosophical Forum* 8 (1978): 92-120. Argues that Bauer's treatment of dialectics foreshadows the interpretations of modern critical theorists and demonstrates that Bauer exercised an important, but little appreciated, influence on Stirner.

851. Stepelevitch, L. S. "Max Stirner as Hegelian." *Journal of the History of Ideas* 46,4 (1985): 597-614. Reviews a wide range of interpretations of Stirner's ideas and goes on to explore the historical relationship between Hegel and Stirner. Concludes that Stirner completes Hegel's philosophy and in that sense truly is "the last of the Hegelians."

852. Stepelevitch, L. S. "The First Hegelians: An Introduction." *Philosophical Forum* 8 (1978): 6-20. Offers an historical overview of the ideas of the Young Hegelians, including Stirner, in the period 1828-48 with the aim of establishing their claim to be legitimate Hegelians.

853. Stepelevitch, L. S. "Hegel and Stirner: Thesis and Antithesis." *Idealistic Studies* 6 (Summer 1976): 263-78. A comparison of Hegel's and Stirner's respective philosophies which aims to prove that Stirner's position became the antithesis of Hegel's.

854. Stepelevitch, L. S. "Max Stirner and Ludwig Feuerbach." *Journal of the History of Ideas* 39,3 (July-Sept. 1978): 451-63. Examines the relationships between Stirner and Feuerbach and argues that Feuerbach's career as a theorist came to an end when he was unable to refute Stirner's critique as presented in *The Ego and His Own.*

855. Stepelevitch, L. S. "The Revival of Max Stirner." *Journal of the History of Ideas* 35,2 (April-June 1974): 323-28. Suggests that the revival of interest in Stirner was concurrent with the revival of interest in the philosophy of Nietzsche. Nevertheless his thought has its own intrinsic value as a completely radical defense of atheism.

856. Thomas, P. "Karl Marx and Max Stirner." *Political Theory* 3,2 (May 1975): 159-79. Argues that Marx's critique of Stirner answers the key issues raised by Stirner regarding revolutionary ideals and individuality.

FRANCIS DASHWOOD TANDY (1867-?)

Works by Tandy :

857. *Modern Socialistic Tendencies*. Columbus Junc., Ia.: E. H. Fulton, 1897. A lecture delivered to the Unity Club in Unity Church, Denver, March 28 1897.

858. *Voluntary Socialism: A Sketch*. New York: Revisionist Pr., 1977. Reprint of the 1896 edition published in Denver. An anarchist (voluntary socialism) text that advocates, in the tradition of Proudhon, Warren and Tucker, the end of the state and of monopoly of wealth. In their place the work argues for the organization of society on the foundation of freedom, natural association and mutual exchange. While advocating the establishment of banks on the basis of labor values, there is a constant opposition to what is described as state socialism.

LEV NIKOLAEVICH TOLSTOY (1828-1910)

Works by Tolstoy :

Selection has been limited to works bearing on Tolstoy's social theory.

859. *Christianity and Patriotism*. Translated by Constance Garnett. Introduction by Edward Garnett. London: J. Cape, 1922. First published in 1894, this is an extensive essay in which Tolstoy demonstrates how governments whip up nationalistic fervor to wage war for their own ends. He argues that patriotism runs counter to love, the law of God.

860. *Essays and Letters*. Translated Aylmer Maude. London: Oxford Univ. Pr., 1911. A collection of essays and letters written between 1884 and 1903, and published that year by World's Classics, in which Tolstoy's maturer views on religion are expressed.

861. *Essays from Tula*. Introduction Nicolas Berdyaev. London: Sheppard Pr., 1948. A series of late essays from the period 1902-09. Includes "The Slavery of Our Times," "Bethink Yourselves," "Thou Shalt Kill No One," and "The End of the Age."

862. *The Kingdom of God and the Peace Essays*. London: Oxford Univ. Pr., 1951. Tolstoy's definitive statement of his pacifist anarchism, published in 1893, proceeds from a profoundly Christian perspective. He rejects any

authority, be it of State or Church, which would coerce him to act against his Christian conscience, while, at the same time, refusing to respond violently to any such coercion.

863. *The Law of Love and the Law of Violence.* Translated by M. K. Tolstoy. Foreword by B. Budberg. London: Anthony Blond, 1970. A useful exposition of Tolstoy's anarchism and pacifism written in 1908, and first published in a censored form in the *Kiev Bulletin* in the same year. Published in full in England in 1909. Note that Tolstoy's original title was *The Law of Violence and the Law of Love.*

864. *Letters on War.* Maldon, Essex: Free Age Pr., 1900. In this pamphlet of collected letters Tolstoy cites the causes of war as first the unequal distribution of property, second the existence of a military class, and third fraudulent religious teaching. He urges people to obey their consciences and God's will by refusing to fight and ceasing to oppress the weak.

865. *My Confession.* London: Bradde Bks., 1963. Originally published 1882. A short and sincere work which outlines the events leading to the deepening of Tolstoy's spiritual anxiety, the eventual crisis and his religious conversion.

866. *On Life and Essays on Religion.* Translated with introduction by Aylmer Maude. London: Oxford Univ. Pr., 1934. *On Life*, 1887, is Tolstoy's statement of the conclusions he reached after ten years devoted to the study of religion. The other essays were written between 1894 and 1909. Index.

867. *On Socialism.* London: Hogarth, 1936. Published Glasgow: Strickland Pr., 1940. In this critique of the aims of socialism Tolstoy attacks the idea of liberation through political rights, opposes centralization, planned social schemes and predicted outcomes, placing his faith instead in a change of consciousness regarding moral law. This was Tolstoy's last essay.

868. *The Only Commandment.* London: Unicorn Pr., 1962. In this late work of 1909 Tolstoy asserts that, as revealed in the Gospels, God is love and that God commands us to love one another. All other commandments derive from this simple law. Only the fulfillment of this commandment can afford us complete happiness.

869. *Resurrection.* Moscow: Foreign Languages Pub. Hse., 1958. Originally published in 1899 this was Tolstoy's last great novel. It is generally regarded as inferior to his earlier works because of its didacticism, although recently this judgement has been the subject of re-evaluation. It makes sweeping indictments of the Church and government and sets out the basic elements of his pacifist/anarchist position.

870. *The Russian Revolution etc..* Translated by Aylmer Maude and others. London: Everett & Co., 1907. A collection of pieces by Tolstoy on the theme of Russia and revolution. Contains "The Meaning of the Russian Revolution," "An Appeal to Russians" and "What's To Be Done?"

Expresses a confidence in change in Russia but also a concern that the revolutionary movements show only a dim recognition of the unreasonableness of violence. He urges that one power not be replaced by another. Rather violence and government should be rejected and a society created where human authority is replaced by divine authority and moral law.

871. *The Slavery of Our Times.* Translated with introduction by Aylmer Maude. New York: Edwin C. Walker, 1900. A discussion of the economic subordination of working people that relates their exploitation to systems of authority, hierarchy and force. These are maintained because people acquiesce in their existence. Economic liberation can only follow liberation from violence, which will in turn produce liberation from governments, laws and organized systems of servitude.

872. *Social Evils and Their Remedy.* Edited by Helen C. Matheson. London: Methuen, 1915. A collection of essays in which Tolstoy spells out more clearly than elsewhere his political position on a number of topics. The need to liberate land from property holders and to end the factory system is discussed. Government and centralized socialism are attacked and, in a discussion of anarchism, Tolstoy asserts that the anarchists are "right in everything" except their ideas on revolution. There are interesting excerpts from Tolstoy's letters and diaries which comment on sexual relations.

873. *Some Social Remedies: Socialism, Anarchism etc..* Christchurch, Hants.: Free Age Pr., 1900. A discussion on reform suggesting that the end of state authority is of the essence, but that it must be brought about non-violently. Includes two letters on Henry George and the land question.

874. *The Teaching of Jesus.* Translated by Aylmer Maude. London: Harper, 1909. Adds little that is new to his attack on the Church in other major works such as *Confession* or his unfinished *Christian Teaching*.

875. "Thou Shalt Not Kill." *Freedom* 14,153 (Dec. 1900): 4-5. A succinct statement of Tolstoy's position on non-violence.

876. *To the Working People.* Translated by V. Tchertoft & I. F. Mayo. London: International Pubn. Co., 1900. Advocates non-compliance with authority and the peaceful occupation of the land, endorsing Henry George's Single-Tax system.

877. *What I Believe.* Also called *My Religion.* London: Allen & Unwin, 1966. Originally published in 1884 the work outlines why he regards as erroneous the doctrine of the Christian Church, arguing that the failure to acknowledge the law of non-resistance to evil is the ultimate perversion of the teaching of Christ. Although suppressed by Russian censorship, the manuscript was circulated both in Russia and abroad and brought an enormous response. It was largely as a result of the fresh insights which the ensuing correspondence gave him that he wrote *The Kingdom of God is within You,* op.cit., entry 862.

878. *What Is Art?* Translated by Aylmer Maude. London: Oxford Univ. Pr., 1946. Tolstoy's critique of contemporary art of 1898 based on his 'new' religious and moral convictions. Concludes that art infects people with the worst feelings of superstition, patriotism and sensualism.

879. *What then Must We Do?* Translated by Aylmer Maude. London: Oxford Univ. Pr., 1942. Published in 1886, it was written as a result of Tolstoy's experience with the poor in Moscow. Dealing with economic and social problems, a plea is made for all to share in manual labor and the struggle for existence.

Works about Tolstoy:

Selection omits literary criticism except where it bears on his social theory.

880. Anschuetz, C. "The Young Tolstoi and Rousseau's *Discourse On Inequality.*" *Russian Review* 39,4 (1980): 401-25. Assesses the relative importance of literary forms and social ideas as influences on the works of Rousseau and Tolstoy and examines the affinity between their philosophies.

881. Archambault, R. D. "Tolstoy on Education." *Midway* 8,1 (1967): 57-68. Writes in praise of Tolstoy's commonsensical, pragmatic and ad hoc approach to the education of children, drawing comparisons with problems encountered in education today, where, he argues, there is too much theory and verbiage and too little intuitive wisdom. Concludes that Tolstoy might be seen as a precursor of A.S. Neill.

882. Archer, D. J. "Tolstoy's *God Sees the Truth, but Waits*: A Reflection." *Religious Studies* 21,1 (March 1985): 75-89. Maintains that, despite what Tolstoy says in his *Confession* about when his soul-searching began, he had in fact, some years earlier, questioned the meaning of life and suggested how an answer might be worked out at an individual level in *God Sees the Truth, but Waits*, the story written as part of a Primer for peasant children in preparation during the years 1871-72.

883. Arthos, J. "Ruskin and Tolstoy: 'The Dignity of Man'." *Dalhousie Review* 43,1 (Spring 1963): 5-15. Explores the extent to which Tolstoy might have been a disciple of Ruskin in his attitude to the importance of enrichment through work. It is critical of Tolstoy.

884. Berlin, I. *The Hedgehog and the Fox.* New York: Mentor, 1957. Basing his argument on Tolstoy's philosophy of history in *War and Peace*, Berlin analyzes the conflict between what Tolstoy was and what he believed. With respect to the line from the ancient Greek poem "The fox knows many things, but the hedgehog knows one big thing," Berlin concludes that Tolstoy was by nature a fox who believed in being a hedgehog. Also in *Russian Thinkers*, 22-81. Op.cit., entry 1317.

885. Berlin, I. "Tolstoy and Enlightenment." In *Russian Thinkers*, 238-60. Op.cit., entry 1317. Discusses the affinity between the ideas of Tolstoy and Rousseau, noting their common rejection of original sin and their common belief in innocence and in the ruinous effect of bad institutions. They both held that formal education is undesirable and that the child and peasant are closer to truth and harmony. Thus, reliance on intuitive innocence and goodness and the contrast between nature and artifice are central themes in Tolstoy's work.

886. Birukov, P. I. *Life of Tolstoy*. Translated from Russian. London: Cassell, 1911. Written by Tolstoy's Russian biographer. The two were very close friends and Tolstoy actually collaborated with him in the selection and arrangement of this work. It is chiefly biographical but also aims at achieving some insights into Tolstoy's thought. Contains an index and a list of Tolstoy's works.

887. Brock, P. "Tolstoyism and the Hungarian Peasant." *Slavonic and East European Review* 58,3 (1980): 345-69. Focuses on the 19th Century experiments in Christian communalism.

888. Donskov, A. "The Peasant in Tolstoi's Thought and Writings." *Canadian Slavonic Papers* 21,2 (1979): 183-96. Traces the development of the image of the peasant in Russian literature and then assesses its place within Tolstoi's work. Argues that the peasant became progressively more important in his work, representing the essence of simplicity and the intuitive ability to converse with God.

889. Egan, D. R. and Egan, M. A. *Leo Tolstoy*. Metuchen, N. J. & London: Scarecrow Pr., 1979. An annotated bibliography of English language sources to 1978.

890. Fausset, H. *Tolstoy: The Inner Drama*. London: Cape, 1927. Not a literary study as such but an attempt to explore Tolstoy's personality through his works, before examining his doctrines in the light of that character study.

891. Flew, A. "Tolstoi and the Meaning of Life." *Ethics* 73,2 (Jan. 1963): 110-47. Using Tolstoi's *Confession* as a case study of an investigation of the meaning of life, Flew explores Tolstoy's ideas and discusses both the sense of free will and the sense of dependence which people experience.

892. Fryde, R. "Tolstoy writes to Gandhi in South Africa." *Quarterly Bulletin of the South African Library* 33,4 (1979): 112-17. Gives the history of the last of the three letters which Tolstoy wrote to Gandhi in South Africa. Includes a translation of the letter which is effectively a statement of Tolstoy's position on non-violent resistance.

893. Gallie, W. B. *Philosophers of Peace and War: Kant, Clausewitz, Marx, Engels and Tolstoy*. Cambridge: Cambridge Univ. Pr., 1978. A concise analysis of the theories of each thinker on this subject. Raises the general

question of the role of force in any society. Includes an anarchist bibliography.

894. Gifford, H. *Tolstoy.* Past Masters Series. New York: Oxford Univ. Pr., 1983. A brief introduction to Tolstoy's life and times which seeks to link his pre-conversion and post-conversion thought.

895. Goscilo-Kostin, H. "Tolstoyan Fare: Credo à la Carte." *Slavonic and East European Review* 62,4 (1984): 481-95. Argues that Tolstoy used the symbolism of food and eating as motifs for his political judgements in the novels *War and Peace* and *Anna Karenina.* With his later works a progressively more puritanical element emerges undermining the effectiveness of the motif.

896. Green, M. *Tolstoy and Gandhi, Men of Peace: A Biography.* New York: Basic Bks., 1983. Compares their public and private lives and the events that shaped their respective world views.

897. Heller, O. *Prophets of Dissent: Essays on Maeterlinck, Strindberg, Neitzsche and Tolstoi.* Port Washington, N.Y.: Kennikat Pr., 1968. Originally published by Alfred A. Knopf, 1918. Presents four radical thinkers the scope of whose ideas, it is argued, represents the full spectrum of contemporary moral philosophy. Suggests that fundamental similarities exist despite their all too obvious differences.

898. Holman, M. J. De K. "The Purleigh Colony: Tolstoyan Togetherness in the Late 1890s." In *New Essays on Tolstoy,* edited by Malcolm Jones, 194-222. Cambridge: Cambridge Univ. Pr., 1978. A discussion of an interesting community experiment based on Tolstoyan principles. There is also a useful bibliographical survey by Garth M. Terry on pages 223-46.

899. Jones, P. *Philosophy and the Novel.* Oxford: Clarendon Pr., 1975. Essays on four novels; *Middlemarch, Anna Karenina, The Brothers Karamazov* and *A la Récherche du Temps Perdu,* with detailed textual annotations. and a consideration of the philosophy of the authors.

900. Kiros, T. "Alienation and Aesthetics in Marx and Tolstoy: A Comparative Analysis." *Man and World* 18 (1985): 171-84. Compares Marx's theory of aesthetic alienation and Tolstoy's views on the role and nature of art in society, addressing the questions of how alienation affects art in general and how alienation applies to Marx's discussion of the human senses. Outlines their specific differences but concludes with an emphasis on the similarities in their arguments.

901. Kuzminskay, T. A. *Tolstoy as I knew Him; My Life at Home and at Yasnaya Polyana.* Translated by Nora Sigerist. Introduction by Ernest J. Simmons. New York: Macmillan, 1948. Primarily of interest for those concerned with details surrounding the writing of *War and Peace,* as her memoirs deal mainly with that period of Tolstoy's life. It also gives a detailed picture of Russian life of the period.

902. Lampert, E. "On Tolstoi, Prophet and Teacher." *Slavic Review* 25,4 (1966): 604-14. Explores the tensions between Tolstoy's teachings and his life, concluding an inner struggle produced the depth and ferocity of his condemnation of hedonism.

903. Lasserre, H. *The Communities of Tolstoyans.* Toronto: Rural Co-op. Comm. Council & Canadian Fellowship for Co-op. Comm., Discusses the creation of Tolstoyan communities in various countries; USA, UK, Canada, Switzerland, Austria, Germany, Poland, Bulgaria. Concentrates on efforts to clarify and define the movement in Canada.

904. Lavrin, J. *Tolstoi: An Approach.* New York: Russell & Russell, 1908. Attempts to interpret Tolstoy's ideas in the light of present day needs and problems.

905. Levitsky, I. "The Tolstoy Gospel in the Light of the Jefferson Bible." *Canadian Slavonic Papers* 21,3 (1979): 347-55. Both Tolstoy and Jefferson claimed to have derived their faith from the teachings of Jesus of Nazareth. Compares Tolstoy's *Christ's Christianity,* and Jefferson's *The Life And Morals of Jesus of Nazareth,* both of which argue that the distilled wisdom of Christianity is to be found in the gospels.

906. Lloyd, J. A. T. *Two Russian Reformers: Ivan Turgenev, Leo Tolstoy.* London: Paul, 1910. Two separate biographies, with Turgenev taking up two thirds of the book. Some comparative analysis is undertaken.

907. Matual, D. "Tolstoi's Gospel as a Polemic with Scientists, Politicians and Churchmen." *Greek Orthodox Theological Review* 25,1 (1980): 49-62. A detailed criticism of Tolstoy's interpretation of the Scriptures.

908. Maude, A. *Life of Tolstoy.* London: Oxford Univ. Pr., 1953. Written by the acknowledged English expert on Tolstoy. Maude knew Tolstoy and worked with him. Index, bibliography, chronology.

909. Maude, A. *Tolstoy and His Problems.* London: G. Richards, 1901. A collection of essays which aims to set out Tolstoy's ideas for the English reading public, which, at the time, had considerable difficulty in getting access to his works.

910. Mayer, F. "Tolstoy as World Citizen." *Personalist* 28 (Autumn 1947): 357-69. Begins with a character analysis which argues that Tolstoy exhibited typical Russian traits. While critical of the perpetual conflict between his ideals and way of life, it concludes that his general message is both timeless and universally applicable.

911. Mikoyan, S. A. "Leo Tolstoy and Mahatma Gandhi." *Indo-Asian Culture* 18,4 (1969): 44-8. Examines the links between Tolstoy and Gandhi, while assessing the impact they had on their respective societies. Concludes that they share similar ends while advocating different means. Draws an

interesting distinction at the end between organized force and mass violence.

912. Perrett, R. W. "Tolstoy, Death and the Meaning of Life." *Philosophy* 60,232 (April 1985). 231-45. Analyzes Tolstoy's *A Confession* and *The Death Of Ivan Illich* to draw out philosophical questions about death and the meaning of life.

913. Perris, G. H. *The Life and Teaching of Leo Tolstoy: A Book of Extracts.* London: Grant Richards, 1907. A useful collection with material on Tolstoy's approach to the state on pages 96-139.

914. Redpath, T. *Tolstoy.* London: Bowes, 1960. A short biography with a good bibliography. Asserts that in Russia politics and literature are inseparable and, therefore, that the dichotomy between thinker and artist in Tolstoy is a false one. Discusses his anarchism in a section on politics and social ethics, pages 23-32.

915. Robinson, J. *Leo Tolstoy: His Life and Work.* London: Freedom Pr., 1968. A short pamphlet study of Tolstoy's life and work that raises the interesting question of whether he can, in the final instance, be called an anarchist.

916. Sampson, R. V. *Tolstoy and the Discovery of Peace.* London: Heinemann, 1973. Written by a convinced pacifist follower of Tolstoy, the work expresses an unbounded admiration for him while examining anarchist pacifist theory and the causes of war. Contains a plea for active civil disobedience in the cause of world peace.

917. Schefski, H. K. "Tolstoi and the Jews." *Russian Review* 41,1 (1982): 1-10. Examines Tolstoy's contradictory and uneven attitude towards the Jews.

918. Simmons, E. J. *Leo Tolstoy.* Boston: Little Brown, 1968. A comprehensive assessment of Tolstoy's life and work which attempts to analyze his literary works and his social, religious and political ideas in an interconnected manner. Excellent bibliography and index.

919. Simmons, E. J. *Introduction to Tolstoy's Writings.* Chicago: Univ. of Chicago Pr., 1968. There is some discussion of Tolstoy's political ideas in Chapter 6, "Religious, Moral and Didactic Writings," pages 94-117.

920. Spence, G. W. *Tolstoy the Ascetic.* London: Oliver & Boyd, 1967. Traces and analyzes the moral and philosophical threads connecting the early and later work of Tolstoy.

921. Tolstaia, A. L. *Tolstoy: A Life of My Father.* Translated by E. R. Hapgood. London: Gollancz, 1953. Written by Tolstoy's youngest daughter who knew him only after the great change in his life. Asserts that it is not through his achievements as a writer but by how he lived that he must be appreciated. Includes several letters from her father written towards the end of his life.

922. Tolstoy, I. *My Father: Reminiscences by Ilya Tolstoy*. Translated by Ann Dunniga. London: P. Owen, 1972. An affectionate recollection of Tolstoy by his second son Ilya.

923. Tolstoy, S. *Tolstoy Remembered by his Son, Sergei Tolstoy*. Translated by M. Budberg. London: Weidenfeld & Nicholson, 1961. A collection of memoirs written when Sergey, Tolstoy's eldest son, was an old man and published after his death. Gives a good impression of life in an aristocratic Russian family at the turn of the century.

924. Troyat, H. *Tolstoy*. Translated Nancy Amphoux. New York: Octagon Bks., 1980. Published in French in Paris: 1965. A biography that in Part 7 considers Tolstoy as an apostle of non-violence. Though not strictly sympathetic, it is a very thorough biography which traces Tolstoy's development. Attempts to reconcile the artist and the preacher.

925. Walicki, A. *A History of Russian Thought: From the Enlightenment to Marxism*. Stanford: Stanford Univ. Pr., 1979. A comprehensive survey of Russian thought which, while concentrating on philosophy, also covers religious, political and economic ideas.

BENJAMIN TUCKER (1854-1939)

Works by Tucker :

926. "The Attitude of Anarchism toward Industrial Combination." In *State Socialism and Anarchism and Other Essays*, 27-34. Op.cit., entry 931. Address delivered Chicago, September 14, 1899. Discusses the anarchist approach to trade unions, setting out Tucker's famous "four monopolies," land monopoly, tariff monopoly, money monopoly and idea monopoly. Issued as a pamphlet, Detroit: 1933, by Laurance Labadie.

927. *Individual Liberty: Selections from the Writings of Benjamin R. Tucker*. New York: Revisionist Pr., 1972. Also published New York: Vanguard Pr., 1926 and New York: Kraus Reprint Co., 1973. Unlike *Instead of a Book*, op.cit., entry 928, this volume contains only Tucker's writings and not those of his correspondents and adversaries. It is a more concise and generally readable account of his individualist anarchism. Index and bibliography.

928. *Instead of a Book, by a Man Too Busy to Write One: A Fragmentary Exposition of Philosophical Anarchism, Culled from the Writings of Benjamin R. Tucker*. New York: Gordon Pr., 1972. Composed of questions and criticisms by Tucker's correspondents, and writers in other periodicals, and the answers provided by Tucker in his journal *Liberty*. Many of the articles deal specifically with local and current events.

929. *State Socialism and Anarchism: How Far They Agree and Wherein They Differ.* London: W. Reeves, 1895. Reprinted in *State Socialism and Anarchism and Other Essays*, 11-25. Op.cit., entry 931. Also see *Patterns of Anarchy*, 61-9. Op.cit., entry 1436. Written in 1886 this essay was not published until March 10, 1888, when in appeared in Tucker's journal *Liberty*. Tucker sought to distinguish between anarchism and state socialism in order to provide a background to the Haymarket trial. He also wished to defend his brand of anarchism, which he traced back to Proudhon and Warren, from accusations of violence.

930. *Why I Am an Anarchist.* New York: Revisionist Pr., 1976. Originally written for Hugh O. Pentecost, editor of the radical weekly, *The Twentieth Century*, in 1892, this is a personal account of his beliefs in an individualist anarchism that he saw as deriving from the Mutualism of Proudhon. Also in *State Socialism and Anarchism and Other Essays*, 35-7. Op.cit., entry 931.

Anthologies:

931. *State Socialism and Anarchism and Other Essays.* Edited by James J. Martin. Colorado Springs: Ralph Myles, 1972. A collection of essays, noted separately, that together express the essence of Tucker's approach to the state and central authority.

Works about Tucker:

932. Avrich, P. "Benjamin Tucker and His Daughter." In *Anarchist Portraits*, 144-52. Op.cit., entry 1303. A record of an interview with Oriole Tucker in June 1974 when she was aged 65.

933. Coughlin, M., Hamilton, C. and Sullivan, M., ed. *Benjamin Tucker and the Champions of Liberty: A Centenary Anthology.* St.Paul, Minn.: M. E. Coughlin, M. Sullivan, 1986. Does not concentrate solely on Tucker, but explore the links between his ideas and those of other writers and thinkers of the same period. It gives a useful general overview.

934. DeLeon, D. *The American as Anarchist: Reflections on Indigenous Anarchism.* Baltimore and London: John Hopkins Univ. Pr., 1978. A discussion of anarchist thought and practice in America, both in its individualist and communist forms. Chapter Five, "Right Libertarianism," pages 61-84, discusses Tucker's ideas. Good bibliography.

935. Ishill, J., ed. *Benjamin R. Tucker: A Bibliography.* Berkeley Hts., N. J.: Oriole Pr., 1959. A bibliography of Tucker's works including his important translations of the work of others such as Proudhon and Tolstoy. There are some useful critical and biographical notes, and an appreciation by George Bernard Shaw, on whom, it is said, Tucker had an early influence.

936. Kline, W. G. *The Individualist Anarchists.* Boston & London: Univ. Pr. of America, 1987. A discussion of the individualist anarchist tradition in America, its origins and development. Chapter Four examines the work of Benjamin Tucker, pages 57-84.

937. Madison, C. A. "Benjamin R. Tucker: Individualist and Anarchist." *New England Quarterly* 16 (Sept. 1943): 444-67. Discusses Tucker as the chief American exponent of individualist anarchism. Partly biographical there is a useful discussion of his ideas in their historical context.

938. Martin, J. J. *Men against the State; the Expositors of Individualist Anarchism in American, 1827-1908.* Dekalb, Ill.: Adrian Allen, 1953. Includes a discussion of Tucker, his life and ideas in Chapters 8 and 9, pages 202-73. See entry 1838.

939. McElroy, W. "The Culture of Individualist Anarchism in Late Nineteenth Century America." *Journal of Libertarian Studies* 5,3 (Summer 1981): 291-304. A discussion of individualist anarchism focussing on Benjamin Tucker's *Liberty* during its 27 year existence from 1881-1908.

940. McElroy, W. *Liberty, 1881-1908: A Comprehensive Index.* St. Paul, Minn.: M. E. Coughlin, c1982.

941. Reichert, W. O. *Partisans of Freedom: A Study in American Anarchism.* Bowling Green, Ohio: Bowling Green Univ. Pop. Pr., 1977. A series of biographical cameos seeking to represent the ideas of anarchists of the individualist tradition. There are some questionable inclusions, like Tom Paine, but also discussion of Benjamin Tucker.

942. Rocker, R. *Pioneers of American Freedom.* Los Angeles: Rocker Pubns. Comm., 1949. A discussion of the origins of liberal and radical theory in America, with a discussion of Tucker's contribution, pages 118-38, and of his collaborators on the journal *Liberty,* pages 139-44.

943. Watner, C. "Benjamin Tucker and his Periodical *Liberty.*" *Journal of Libertarian Studies* 1,4 (Fall 1977): 291-304. Overview of Tucker's main principles, his founding of the periodical *Liberty,* and his influence and significance for anarchist philosophy.

944. Watner, C. "The English Individualists as they appeared in *Liberty.*" *Journal of Libertarian Studies* 6,1 (1982): 59-82. Examines the contributions of Benjamin Tucker, Hiram Levy, and Auberon Herbert to the journal *Liberty.*

COLIN WARD (1924-)

Works by Ward :

945. *The Allotment, Its Landscape and Culture.* Co-author David Crouch. London: Faber & Faber, 1988. A discussion of allotments and the way in which this poorly and spasmodically organized collective activity maintains itself in the face of pressures for development.

946. *Anarchy in Action.* Originally published London: Allen & Unwin, 1973. New York: Harper Torchbook, 1974. An argument concerning the practicality of realizing the anarchist vision of a future society. Covers such topics as planning, housing, family life, education, play, work and the state.

947. *The Child in the City.* New York: Random House, 1987. A study that explores the relationship between children and their urban environment, and investigates how it could be improved.

948. *The Child in the Country.* London: Robert Hale, 1988. A companion to *The Child in the City*, this work looks at the problems of education faced by rural children. It also investigates the paradox produced by the movement of rural poor to the city being paralleled by the movement of the affluent back to the country.

949. *A Decade of Anarchy.* London: Freedom Pr., 1987. Selections from the monthly journal *Anarchy*, during Ward's period as editor, 1961-70, including sections on anarchist thought, work, education and the environment.

950. "A Few Italian Lessons." *The Raven* 2,3 (July 1989): 197-206. Reflections on the success of co-operatives and the small workshop economy in Italy.

951. "Four Easy Pieces and One Hard One." *The Raven* 3,2 (March 1990): 154-85. A review of Michael Smith, *The Libertarians and Education*, op.cit., entry 1541, that develops into a wide-ranging discussion covering, among other topics, education and authority, hierarchy, the Burston school strike, and William Morris as an anarchist educator.

952. *Housing: An Anarchist Approach.* London: Freedom Pr., 1976. A collection of essays and lectures which looks at housing issues in Britain over a period of thirty years. Ward is concerned to suggest constructive and practical solutions to existing problems, arguing that even if these solutions are dependent on the existing structure they are still anarchist solutions. He argues for owner occupation, co-operatives, the relaxation of bureaucratic controls and the provision of incentives to encourage the poor to build their own houses.

953. "Notes of an Anarchist Columnist." *The Raven* 3,4 (Oct.-Dec. 1990): 315-19. Reflections on his activity as an anarchist journalist from *War*

Commentary, through the period of *Anarchy* to his role as columnist for *New Statesman and Society*.

954. "The Path Not Taken." *The Raven* 1,3 (Nov. 1987): 195-200. Reflections on the failure of British socialism to win popular support.

955. "Self-Help in Urban Renewal." *The Raven* 1,2 (Aug. 1987): 115-20. A discussion of urban renewal in the light of Ebenezer Howard's ideas on Garden Cities.

956. *Welcome Thinner City: Urban Survival in the 1990s*. London: Bedford Square Pr., 1989. A discussion of urban planning that argues for dweller control and the essential rights of householders and occupants, while examining self-build housing associations, co-operative workshops, allotments, urban farms and various resident's schemes.

957. *When We Build Again: Let's Have Housing That Works*. London: Pluto Pr., 1985. An attack on postwar housing policies in Britain, characterized as geared to mass public housing schemes that have institutionalized, bureaucratized and dehumanized people.

JOSIAH WARREN (1798-1874)

Works by Warren :

958. *Equitable Commerce: A New Development of Principles as Substitutes for Laws and Governments, for the Harmonious Adjustment and Regulation of the Pecuniary, Intellectual, and Moral Intercourse of Mankind, Proposed as Elements of New Society.* New York: Burt Franklin Reprint, 1967. Originally published New York: Fowlers & Wells, 1852, although a version appeared in 1846, Warren's classic work on individualist anarchism that attempts to design a society aimed at producing individual freedom, coincidence of interests and the proper, legitimate and just reward of labor. Ideally cost should be the limit of price and exchange should be based on labor inputs. Two excerpts, "The Pattern of Life in an Individualist Anarchist Community," and "Equitable Education" appear in *Patterns of Anarchy*, 312-23, 445-8. Op.cit., entry 1436.

959. *True Civilization an Immediate Necessity and the Fast Ground of Hope for Mankind etc.* New York: Burt Franklin Reprint, 1967. Originally published Boston, Mass.: Warren, 1863. Written against the background of the Civil War, this is a defense of individualism and liberty and an attack on the unjust treatment of labor that is held responsible for existing problems in society. Only an equitable exchange of products on the basis of their labor value, it is asserted, will solve these problems, allowing co-operation on the basis of individual sovereignty.

Works about Warren :

960. Arieli, Y. "Individualism Turns Anarchism - Josiah Warren." In *Individualism and Nationalism in American Ideology*, 289-96. Cambridge, Mass.: Harvard Univ. Pr., 1964. A brief discussion of Warren's theory of individualist anarchism.

961. Bailie, W. *Josiah Warren, the First American Anarchist*. New York: Kraus Reprint Co., 1971. Originally published, Boston: Small, Maynard & Co., 1906. An account of the life, thought and social experiments of Josiah Warren, including New Harmony, the "Time Store" which exchanged goods against labor notes, and the Village of Utopia.

962. Barclay, H. "Josiah Warren - The Incomplete Anarchist." *Anarchy* 85 (March 1968): 90-6. A discussion of the ideas of Warren that argues that he is best considered as a democrat who favored decentralization rather than an anarchist.

963. Bestor, A. E. *Backwoods Utopias: The Sectarian and Owenite Phases of Communitarian Socialism in America, 1663-1829*. Philadelphia: Univ. of Philadelphia Pr., 1950. Provides some useful background to Warren's experiments, especially Chapter 7, "The Owenite Legacy."

964. Dorfman, J. "The Philosophical Anarchists: Josiah Warren, Stephen Pearl Andrews." In *The Economic Mind in American Civilization*. Vol. 2, 671-8. New York: Viking Pr., 1944. A discussion of the economic and social ideas of the two individual anarchist proponents of equitable commerce. The discussion of Warren focuses on his ideas about the value of labor and its measurement.

965. Ellis, J. B. *Free Love and Its Votaries or American Socialism Unmasked*. New York: AMS Pr., 1971. A reprint of the original edition, New York: US Pub. Co., 1970. Chapter, 23, "Modern Times," deals with Warren, his scheme of equitable commerce, and the Time Store experiment, as well as discussing his ideas on slavery, marriage and the freedom of women.

966. Fellman, M. "The Substance and Boundaries of Utopian Communitarianism. Albert Brisbane and Josiah Warren." In *The Unbounded Frame*, 3-19. Westport, Conn.: Greenwood Pr., 1973. A comparative analysis that elucidates Warren's views by contrast with those of Brisbane, the American translator of Fourier and advocate of large, structured, authoritarian communities.

967. Hall, B. N. "The Economic Ideas of Josiah Warren, First American Anarchist." *History of Political Economy* 6,1 (1974): 95-108. A discussion of Warren's "equitable system", looking at issues like cost as the limit of price, labor value and wages, exchange and "equivalent labor", and the role of capital, machinery and automation.

968. Kline, W. G. *The Individualist Anarchists*. Boston & London: Univ. Pr. of America, 1987. Warren's contribution to the individualist anarchist tradition is discussed and assessed.

969. Lockwood, G. B. and Prosser, C. *The New Harmony Movement*. New York: Appleton, 1907. There is a discussion of Warren's life and ideas and a chapter on him by William Bailie, pages 294-306.

970. Martin, J. J. *Man against the State: The Expositors of the Individualist Anarchism in America, 1827-1908*. Dekalb, Ill.: Adrian Allen, 1953. There is discussion of the experiences, ideas and history of Josiah Warren, particularly in Chapters 1-3, pages 1-87. See entry 1838.

971. Reichert, W. O. *Partisans of Freedom: A Study in American Anarchism*. Bowling Green, Ohio: Bowling Green Pr., 1977. Contains a discussion of Josiah Warren. See entry 941.

972. Rexroth, K. "Josiah Warren." In *Communalism: From Its Origins to the Twentieth Century*, 235-40. London: Peter Owen, 1975. A brief biographical sketch.

973. Rocker, R. *Pioneers of American Freedom*. Los Angeles: Rocker Pubns. Comm., 1937. Warren's ideas are discussed at some length on pages 49-69. See entry 814.

CHARLOTTE WILSON (1854-1944)

Works by Wilson :

974. *Three Essays on Anarchism*. Sanday, Orkney: Ciefuegos Pr., 1979. Originally published in *Practical Socialist* (Jan. 1886). Three short essays by Charlotte Wilson, who, starting as an active member of the Fabian society, played an important part in the emergence of the British anarchist movement in the 1880s. Influenced by Proudhon, Bakunin and Kropotkin, she was more individualist than the latter. She worked with Kropotkin and was one of the organizing forces behind *Freedom*, which she edited for over ten years at a crucial time for the development of anarchist ideas in Britain.

Works about Wilson :

975. Quail, J. *The Slow Burning Fuse: The Lost History of the British Anarchists*. London: Paladin, 1978. A description of the British anarchist movement from its inception in the 1880s, that includes discussion of the life and work of Charlotte Wilson.

976. Oliver, H. *The International Anarchist Movement in Late Victorian London*. London: Croom Helm, 1983. Charlotte Wilson is discussed in Chapter 2, pages 24-43.

GEORGE WOODCOCK (1912-)

Works by Woodcock :

The selection omits literary and historical work not relevant to anarchism and articles and notes on other anarchists found elsewhere. For an extensive bibliography of works to 1976 see 1013.

977. "Anarchism." In *The New Encyclopaedia Britannica*. 15th edition. Vol. 1, 808-13. Chicago: Britannica, 1974. A survey of anarchist movements, philosophers and ideas, concluding that anarchism is a moral and social doctrine before it is a political one, and that, in its opposition to regimentation and support of local interests, it serves as a touchstone by which to judge the existing society.

978. *Anarchism: A History of Libertarian Ideas and Movements*. Harmondsworth: Penguin, 1963. A comprehensive history, written sympathetically, but critically, which focuses on Godwin, Proudhon, Stirner, Bakunin, Kropotkin and Tolstoy. It also discusses anarchist movements on a country by country basis. Despite criticism regarding inaccuracies, it remains the standard introduction to anarchist history and theory. See entry 1014. Reprinted with a postscript in 1976.

979. *Anarchism and Morality*. London: Freedom Pr., 1945.

980. "Anarchism and Public Opinion." *Freedom* 28 (June 1947): 2. A reply to a point made by George Orwell critical of anarchism in his essay "Politics vs. Literature," *Polemic* 5 (1946).

981. "Anarchism and Violence." *Canadian Forum* (Jan. 1971): 333-5. Reprinted in Abraham Rotstain, ed. *Power Corrupted*, 39-48. A reprint of the January 1971 issue of *Canadian Forum*. Toronto: New Pr., 1971. Written against the background of violence committed by Quebec nationalists the piece argues for relevance for the anarchist ideas on decentralization.

982. "Anarchism Revisited." *Commentary* 46,2 (Aug. 1968): 54-60. Discusses the revival of interest in anarchism in the 1960s, particularly among students. Woodcock concludes that, as a movement for a totally new society, anarchism has failed. What is left is the possibility of using the doctrine to maximize freedom within existing society.

983. *The Anarchist Reader*. Edited by Woodcock. London: Fontana, 1977. The introduction traces the history of anarchism. It includes a bibliographical supplement and brief details of the lives of various authors.

A useful collection of readings covers a wide range of anarchist thought, and includes pieces by Read, Faure, Bookchin, Ward and Goodman, as well as contributions from the classic thinkers.

984. *Anarchy or Chaos?* London: Freedom Pr., 1944. Written in the context of the war against Nazism and Fascism, it contrasts freedom with totalitarian regimes, concluding that anarchism is the form of social organisation best suited to guarantee freedom. A discussion of the history and nature of anarchism follows that clearly prefigures Woodcock's later work. Part of the book later appeared as the essay "The Rejection of Politics," in the book of that name, op.cit., entry 1005.

985. *The Basis of Communal Living.* London: Freedom Pr., 1947. A pamphlet that focuses on the community as an ideal in theory, and as a reality in primitive society, in Spain in the 1930s, in the Jewish kibbutzim and in wartime Britain.

986. *The Centre Cannot Hold.* Routledge New Poets No.10. London: Routledge, 1943. A collection of poems some of which have anarchist subjects and themes.

987. *The Crystal Spirit: A Study of George Orwell.* London: Cape, 1967. Contains observations on Orwell's experiences in Spain, his attitude towards anarchism and its relationship to the major themes of his work.

988. *Dawn and the Darkest Hour.* London: Faber & Faber, 1972. A study of the life and work of Aldous Huxley, that, in part, discusses his search for a moral philosophy and his relationship with radical movements and ideas with which Woodcock was also involved.

989. "The Elizabethan Anarchy." *Freedom* (24 Jan. 1948/7 Feb. 1948): 2/2. A critique of a T. S. Eliot's view that the Elizabethan age was one of anarchism, that is of dissolution and decay.

990. "The Ending Century: Prospect and Retrospect." *The Raven* 3,2 (March 1990): 187-92. Reflections on the career of anarchism in the last half of the twentieth century.

991. *Gandhi.* London: Collins, 1972. A discussion of Gandhi's life and philosophy of *Satyagraha*, concluding that Gandhi was anarchistic rather than anarchist.

992. *Purdy/Woodcock: Selected Correspondence, 1964-1984.* Edited by George Galt. Toronto: ECW Pr., 1988. A collection of letters exchanged between two major literary figures in Canada.

993. *Herbert Read: The Stream and the Source.* London: Faber & Faber, 1972. See entry 787.

994. *Homes or Hovels. The Housing Problem and Its Solution*. London: Freedom Pr., 1944. An essay on slum dwellings and poor housing, arguing that a social revolution is necessary to abolish private property and to vest control of housing in local communities.

995. *A Hundred Years of Revolution: 1848 and After*. Edited by Woodcock. London: Porcupine Pr., 1948. A collection of essays by Woodcock, Max Beloff, Christopher Hollis, Raymond Postgate *et al* on 1848 and its aftermath, written on the centenary of the events in question. There is discussion of the revolutionary roles of Proudhon and Bakunin.

996. *The Anarchist Prince: A Biographical Study of Peter Kropotkin*. Co-author Ivan Avakumovic. London: T.V. Boardman & Co., 1950. See entry 602.

997. *The Doukhobors*. Co-author Ivan Avakumovic. London: Faber, 1968. A study of the Doukhobor community, which fled Russia to settle in Canada, as an example of a self-contained utopian community. Tolstoy's role in their escape from persecution is emphasized. Tolstoy believed the sect to be practicing a form of religious anarchism. Bibliography and index.

998. *Letter to the Past: An Autobiography*. Toronto: Fitzhenry & Whiteside, 1982. The first volume of his autobiography that takes the reader to 1949 when Woodcock returned to Canada from England.

999. "The Manipulators." *Anarchy* 117 (Nov. 1970): 358-62. Essay on drugs and the meaning of liberation.

1000. *New Life to the Land*. London: Freedom Pr., 1942. A discussion of British agricultural policy, advocating local control of production through village syndicates.

1001. "Not Any Power: Reflections on Decentralism." *Anarchy* 104 (Oct. 1969): 305-9. A discussion of decentralization in history. The discussion ranges from ancient communes to Kropotkin and Tolstoy, concluding that there is a continuing need to confront the destructive tendencies of centralism.

1002. *The Paradox of Oscar Wilde*. New York and London: T.V. Boardman & Co., 1949. A study of Wilde's life and work. Chapter 8, "The Social Rebel," considers the close sympathy between Wilde and the anarchists.

1003. *Pierre-Joseph Proudhon: A Biography*. London: Routledge & Kegan Paul, 1956. See entry 758.

1004. *Railways and Society*. London: Freedom Pr., 1943. An argument for a syndicalist, workers' takeover of the railway system to make it function for the benefit of the whole society.

1005. *The Rejection of Politics and Other Essays*. Toronto: New Pr., 1972. A collection of Woodcock's essays and occasional pieces, including a number on anarchism and related issues. Note: Chapter 2, "The Rejection of Politics," which appeared as part of *Anarchy or Chaos?* in 1944, op.cit.; entry 984; Chapter 3 "Anarchism Revisited"; Chapter 5, "Not Any Power: Reflections on Decentralism"; Chapter 9, "Anarchism and Violence."

1006. "Riding with the Hounds." *Anarchy* 114 (Aug. 1970): 258-60. Takes issue with the remarks Richard Drinnon had made on Woodcock's approach to anarchism at the American Historical Association Convention, 1970.

1007. "Tradition and Revolution." *The Raven* 2,2 (Oct. 1988): 103-17. A discussion of the need to consider regional and national specificities when seeking action for the creation of an anarchist society, with extended consideration of Canada.

1008. *William Godwin: A Biographical Study*. Foreword by Herbert Read. London: Athlone Pr., 1981. See entry 328.

1009. *The Writer and Politics*. London: Porcupine Pr., 1948. A collection of essays that examines the relationship between the writer and society, focussing on particular movements for social reform or revolution. There are essays on Kropotkin, Proudhon, Herzen and Orwell.

Works about Woodcock :

1010. Dolgoff, S. "The Relevance of Anarchism to Modern Society." In *Contemporary Anarchism*, 37-50. Op.cit., entry 1495. A discussion of the relevance of anarchism in the contemporary period that attacks the work of Woodcock for seeking to consign anarchism to an historical niche.

1011. Fetherling, D., ed. *A George Woodcock Reader*. Ottawa: Deneau & Greenberg, 1980. A selection from Woodcock's prolific writings, including his political journalism. Includes a previously unpublished letter to Herbert Read.

1012. Hughes, P. *George Woodcock*. Toronto: McClelland & Stewart, 1974. A study of Woodcock's work and ideas, rather than a biography, that discusses his anarchism at length. Select bibliography.

1013. New, W. H. *A Political Art: Essays and Images in Honour of George Woodcock*. Vancouver: Univ. of British Col. Pr., 1978. A collection of essays dealing with all aspects of Woodcock's life and work, that covers both his literary and political output. Note D. S. Savage, "Anarchism," pages 119-47, and Tom Wayman, "The Ghosts of the Anarchists Speak of George Woodcock," pages 162-67. There is an extensive bibliography of Woodcock's works to 1976 by Ivan Avakumovic, on pages 213-49.

1014. Walter, N. "Woodcock Reconsidered." *The Raven* 1,2 (Aug. 1987): 173-84. A review of *Anarchism* and *The Anarchist Reader* that extends to a critical discussion of Woodcock's career and contribution to the anarchist movement.

On the Margins
of Anarchist Theory

IVAN ILLICH (1926-)

The relationship of Illich to anarchism is perplexed. On the one hand his ideas on decentralization, community and conviviality are, in essence, anarchist. On the other hand, he does not eschew the state. Indeed, he asserts that his convivial mode of production "does not of itself mean that one form of government would be more fitting than another, nor does it rule out a world federation, or agreement between nation states, or communes, or many of the most traditional forms of government." (*Tools for Conviviality*, 30. Op.cit., entry 1028.) The selection here is limited to works with a bearing on Illich's social theory.

Works by Illich:

1015. *ABC: The Alphabetization of the Popular Mind.* London: Marion Boyars, 1988. Argues that the relationship that bound speaker to speech and made discourse whole and meaningful has, with the invention of the alphabet, disintegrated. While some unity has been maintained in the past by grammar and vernacular languages, this is now threatened by the swift march of information processing.

1016. "After Deschooling What?" In *After Deschooling What?*, 20. Op.cit., entry 1033. Illich discusses the political revolution associated with deschooling as reasserting the idea of conscious living over the capitalization of manpower.

1017. *Celebration of Awareness.* New York: Doubleday & Co., 1970. A collection of essays in which Illich calls for a cultural revolution that will embrace a celebration of human values, of human needs and of human relationships. Such a recognition of human dignity can be used to confront and challenge bureaucratic, hierarchical, over-tooled and over-schooled contemporary society.

1018. *Deschooling Society.* New York: Harper & Row, 1971. Published in England, Harmondsworth: Penguin, 1973. Illich's famous attack on schooling as a system the chief aim of which is the preservation of the status quo, of systems of hierarchy and authority. Obligatory schooling is, in practice, socially divisive and educationally dysfunctional. Illich calls for a deschooling of the social processes of learning, for the liberation of critical and creative resources, and for the creation of self-motivated activity within learning networks.

1019. *Disabling Professions.* With others. London: Marion Boyars, 1977. A collection of essays, the title essay by Illich, in which a concerted attack is made on the professions in a modern consumer market society. The various professions are characterized as 'disabling' in their pursuit of activities that thwart human creativity and the fulfillment of human need, and support and maintain the barren status quo of technological, consumerist society.

1020. *Energy and Equity.* London, Marian Boyers, 1974. Illich argues that liberated society, participant democracy and productive social relationships go together with low energy technology such as bicycles.

1021. *Imprisoned in the Global Classroom.* Co-author Etienne Verne. New York: Writers & Readers Pub. Inc., 1980.

1022. *Gender.* New York: Pantheon Bks., 1983. Beginning with an account of the position of women Illich proceeds to develop a scheme for examining gender in an historical context. History is depicted as the transition from "gender" to "sex" coinciding with the transition from subsistence to commodity based society. The modern world is one of "sex" relations where men and women, notionally equal but practically disadvantaged, compete for the same goods and services. The break-down of gender was the precondition for capitalism. Self-realization entails, in the view of Illich, the somewhat contentious idea of the reclaiming of gender.

1023. *H2O and the Waters of Forgetfulness: Reflections on the Historicity of "Stuff."* Dallas: Dallas Inst. Pubns., 1985. Published in England, London: Marion Boyars, 1986.

1024. *Medical Nemesis: The Expropriation of Health.* New York: Pantheon Bks., 1976. Published as *Limits to Medicine,* London: Marian Boyars, 1976. A attack on the medical profession as part of a campaign against the "disabling professions" that maintain modern society. Doctors are attacked as a "major threat to health." Their claim to indispensability is dismissed as unfounded, and it is asserted that they create new diseases, dependence and anxiety, while being expensively unnecessary.

1025. *Retooling Society*. Cuernavaca: Centro Intercultural de Documentaçion, 1973. A critical examination of the dimensions of the contemporary crisis, discussing overgrowth, industrialization, over population, pollution and the programming of humanity to fit the demands of an inhuman system. Illich demands the retooling of society to produce a convivial, pluralist mode of production orientated to human values.

1026. *The Right to Useful Employment*. London: Marian Boyars, 1978. An attack on the professions of modern, technocratic society, the engineers, doctors, lawyers and others who, it is argued, thrive on the maintenance of the system and the anti-human values and politics it generates. They are, for Illich, "disabling professions" in their anti-social functions. Illich argues for the Politics of Conviviality which implies a subordination of production to participatory justice, the creation of use values, the protection of equity and the exercise of liberty.

1027. *Shadow Work*. London: Marion Boyars, 1981. Based on a series of lectures delivered at conferences and seminars, this is a discussion of the uncompensated work required by a market economy and consumer society. Shadow work is, for instance, commuting to the office, preparing for an examination or, archetypically, housework.

1028. *Tools for Conviviality*. London: Fontana, 1973. Published in USA, New York: Harper & Row, 1973. Discussing the crisis produced by a dependence on machines and 'schooling', Illich argues for the reconstruction of society to allow the contribution of autonomous individuals within a technology of production designed to satisfy human needs. A convivial tool is one designed for a maximization of use-value in a convivial society where creative relationships exist between free individuals, and between humanity and the natural environment.

1029. *Towards a History of Needs*. New York: Pantheon Bks., 1977. Five essays in which Illich explores familiar themes; the trade-off between commodities and use-values; rich nations and development; the problem of medical care in a commodity-centered culture; the connection between energy use and social values; shared living and free social relationships.

Works about Illich :

1030. Apple, M. W. "Ivan Illich and Deschooling Society: The Politics of Slogan Systems." In *Social Forces and Schooling: An Anthropological and Sociological Perspective*, edited by N. K. Shimarara and Adam Scrupski, 337-60. New York: McKay Co., 1975. A critical discussion of Illich's views, comparing his position to that of Marxism and arguing that his fundamental weakness lies in an inability to deal with the complexity of the problems that he identifies.

1031. Chappell, R. H. "Anarchy Revisited: An Inquiry into the Public Education Dilemma." *Journal of Libertarian Studies* 2,4 (Winter 1978): 357-72. Primarily concerned with the identification and documentation of the educational viewpoints espoused by nineteenth century anarchists, the article also discusses the ideas of Illich and Goodman.

1032. Elias, J. L. *Conscientization and Deschooling: Freire's and Illich's Proposals for Reshaping Society.* Philadelphia: Westminster Pr., 1976. A general discussion of Illich's social theory. The relationship of his ideas to the anarchist tradition is considered, pages 104-7, and his dependence on Rawls' notion of justice and on ideas of socialism is noted.

1033. Gartner, A., *et al. After Deschooling What?* New York: Harper & Row, 1973. Nine critiques and reactions from educators on issues raised by the idea of *Deschoooling Society*, plus the title essay by Illich himself.

1034. Hedman, C. G. "The 'Deschooling' Controversy Revisited: A Defense of Illich's 'Participatory Socialism'." *Educational Theory* 29,2 (Spring 1979): 109-16. Locates the deschooling programme of Ivan Illich within the tradition of Kropotkin and Goldman.

1035. Reagan, T. "The Foundation of Ivan Illich's Social Thought." *Educational Theory* 30,4 (Fall 1980): 293-306. Argues that Illich draws his inspiration not so much from libertarian or radical perspectives, but from the medieval ideal of human society.

1036. Smith, M. *The Libertarians and Education.* London: Allen & Unwin, 1984. Illich's ideas are discussed in the context of a consideration of anarchism and education.

1037. Thomas, K. "Back to Utopia." *New York Review of Books* 30,12 (May, 1983): 6-10. A review of *Gender* that extends to a general discussion of Illich's ideas.

1038. Watt, A. J. "Illich and Anarchism." *Educational Philosophy and Theory* 13, (Oct. 1981): 1-15. Compares Illich's ideas with those of Bakunin and Kropotkin, arguing that as a theorist he has strong affinities with the syndicalist stream of anarchist philosophy.

WILLIAM MORRIS (1834-1896)

The relationship of Morris to anarchism is at best ambiguous. During his lifetime he explicitly rejected the tradition, saying the he would "about as soon join a White Rose society as an Anarchist one; such nonsense as I deem the latter." (A. Clutton-Brock, 165. Op.cit., entry 1057.) Yet he wrote a work, *News from Nowhere*, acclaimed by Kropotkin as one of the best anarchist visions of the future ever written. This selection is limited to those political works of Morris that either have some bearing on his vision

of a future society, or have some connection with the anarchist faction of
The Socialist League.

Works by Morris:

1039. "Art and Socialism." In *The Political Writings of William Morris*,
109-93. Op.cit., entry 1049. Originally delivered as a lecture before the
Leicester Secular Society, 23 January 1884. Published as a pamphlet in 1884.
Collected Works 23, 192-214. Op.cit., entry 1040.

1040. *Collected Works.* 24 vols. Preface by Joseph Riggs Dunlap. Edited May
Morris. New York: Oriole Eds., 1973. Originally published London:
Longmans, Green & Co., 1910-15. Volume 23 contains a number of political
essays issued as pamphlets, including "Communism" (1893) "Lectures on
Socialism" (1894) and "How I Became a Socialist" (1894), in which there is
some discussion of Morris' negative view of anarchism. His animosity
towards anarchism was spurred by what he saw as the politics of the
anarchist faction that had seized control of the Socialist League.

1041. "Communism." In *The Political Writings of William Morris*, 227-46.
Op.cit., entry 1049. Originally a lecture delivered to the Hammersmith
Socialist Society at Kelmscott House on 10 March, 1893. Published as a
Fabian Tract 1903. *Collected Works* 23, 264-76. Op.cit., entry 1040. A
description of the functioning of a communist society noting community
ownership and the minimization of waste.

1042. *A Dream of John Ball.* London: Lawrence & Wishart, 1974. In this
edition published with *News from Nowhere.* Originally published in serial
form in the *The Commonweal.* Published in book form London: Reeves &
Turner, 1896. An imagined meeting with John Ball, one of the leaders of
the Peasants Revolt of 1381, provides Morris with a basis for reflecting on
equality and freedom. The frontispiece by Burne-Jones of Adam and Eve
bears the inscription, attributed to Ball, "When Adam delved and Eve span
who was then the gentleman."

1043. *Socialism, Its Growth and Outcome.* Co-author E. Bax. New York:
Kerr, 1909. More Bax than Morris, the work traces the history of socialism,
discussing the development of society from ancient to modern times.

1044. "How I Became a Socialist." In *The Political Writings of William
Morris*, 241-6. Op.cit., entry 1049. First published *Justice*, (16 June 1894).
Morris's own view of his political and intellectual development.

1045. *News from Nowhere.* London: Routledge & Kegan Paul, 1970. First
published in serial form in *The Commonweal*, 11 January to 4 October 1890.
First published in book form in Boston: Roberts Brothers, 1890, and London:
Reeves and Turner, 1891. The work was partly written as a response to
Edward Bellamy's *Looking Backward*, 1888, which envisaged a centralized,
bureaucratic ideal society of America, 2000 A.D., with humanity dominated

by experts and technology. By contrast, the future England of *News from Nowhere* is a green and unpolluted land that blends Morris' views on community life and art. It is a decentralized society that practices garden agriculture and workshop industry. Goods are produced for use only and are freely exchanged. Wages and money do not have any place. Machines exist only for repetitive tasks, and craft skills and the decorative arts flourish in a a society where work is a pleasure. Women have attained liberation and social relationships are based on equal relations betwen free individuals unconstrained by state authority. Kropotkin described it as "the most thoroughly and deeply Anarchistic conception of future society that has ever been written." *Freedom* 10,110 (November 1896): 109.

1046. "Socialism and Anarchism." In *The Political Writings of William Morris*, 210-14. Op.cit., entry 1049. Morris's letter that appeared in *The Commonweal* on 5 May, 1889 as part of the discussion taking place over the direction of the Socialist League. An interesting discussion in which, in defending authority as "public conscience" in a society of equality and reason, Morris, it can be argued, still leaves his political position open to question.

1047. "The Society of the Future." In *The Political Writings of William Morris*, 188-204. Op.cit., entry 1049. Originally a lecture delivered to the Hammersmith Branch of the Socialist League 13 November, 1887, this is a discussion of aspects of an ideal future society which parallels the society of *News from Nowhere* in its forms of work, education and the distribution of wealth.

1048. *Useless Work versus Useless Toil*. London: Communist Party of Great Britain, 1986. Originally delivered as a lecture before the Hampstead Liberal Club 16 January, 1884. Published as a Socialist League pamphlet in 1885. Collected by Morton, op.cit., entry 1050, pages 88-108. A discussion of the nature of work that examines the question of how work is productive of pleasure.

Anthologies :

1049. *The Political Writings of William Morris*. Edited with introduction A. L. Morton. London: Lawrence & Wishart, 1973. A useful collection of Morris's political writings that includes "The Lesser Arts," "Art Under Plutocracy," "London in a State of Siege," "Under an Elm-Tree," "Where Are We Now?" as well as those important essays and lectures cited separately above.

1050. *Selected Writings and Designs*. Edited Asa Briggs. Harmondsworth: Penguin, 1962. With a supplement by Graeme Shankland on "William Morris, Designer." A useful collection that contains some political work, including writings on socialism.

1051. *William Morris on Art and Socialism.* Edited with introduction by Holbrook Jackson. London: John Lehmann, 1947. Contains important essays and lectures on socialism, collected by a well-known author, anthologist and bibliophile.

Works about Morris :

Selection is limited to works treating of his social theory and of his dealings with anarchists.

1052. Arnot, R. P. *William Morris: The Man and the Myth.* London: Lawrence & Wishart, 1964. A book specifically devoted to Morris's political ideas that is built around 30 newly discovered letters and 20 made available in the 1950s. This represents correspondence between Morris and John Lincoln Mahon, the first secretary of The Socialist League and Dr. John Glasse, a prominent member of the League.

1053. Boos, F., ed. *William Morris's Socialist Diary.* London: Heinemann, 1985. A diary kept by Morris for three months from January 25 1887, which contains comments on the anarchist faction of The Socialist League.

1054. Boos, F. and Boos, W. "The Utopian Communism of William Morris." *History of Political Thought* 7,3 (1986): 489-510. Establishes Morris as a "utopian-communist" and compares him with a range of other writers, including Marx, Kropotkin, Schumacher and Bahro.

1055. Boris, E. *Art and Labor; Ruskin, Morris and the Craftsman Ideal in America.* Philadelphia: Temple Univ. Pr., 1986. Discusses the adaptation of Morris's ideas to America with examination of the crafts movement in late nineteenth century America, utopian colonies and the role of women.

1056. Casement, W. "William Morris on Labor and Pleasure." *Social Theory and Practice* 12 (Fall 1986): 351-82. Discusses Morris's attitude to labor as pleasure in terms of the hope present in labor, identified by Morris as "hope of rest, hope of produce and hope of pleasure in work itself."

1057. Clutton-Brock, A. *William Morris: His Work and Influence.* London: Williams and Norgate, 1914. Contains a useful discussion of the relations between Morris and the anarchists in The Socialist League with some account of his response to their doctrine.

1058. Cole, G. D. H. *Persons and Periods: Studies.* New York: A. M. Kelley, 1969. Contains a discussion of William Morris and the modern world.

1059. Coote, S. *William Morris: His Life and Work.* London: Garamond, 1990.

1060. Eshelman, L. W. *A Victorian Rebel: The Life of William Morris.* New York: Charles Scribner's Sons, 1940. A biography that covers his political life and ideas in Book 4, "The S.D.F. - And Revolution," pages 191-243, Book 5,

"The Socialist League - And Bloodshed," pages 247-307, and Book 6, "The Hammersmith Socialist Society - And Victory," pages 311-47.

1061. Faulkner, P. *Against the Age: An Introduction to William Morris.* London: Allen & Unwin, 1980. A biography that gives a lot of attention to the political ideas and career of Morris, discussing his relationship with the Anarchists. See Chapter 4, "Into Politics, 1877-82," pages 87-110, Chapter 5, "Socialism, 1883-90," pages 111-46, and Chapter 6, "The Last Stage, 1890-6, pages 147-78.

1062. Glasier, J. B. *William Morris and the Early Days of the Socialist Movement.* Preface by May Morris. London: Longmans, Green & Co., 1921. A personal memoir by a friend and comrade of Morris with some observations on The Socialist League and its anarchist wing, especially in Chapter 14.

1063. Henderson, P. *William Morris.* London: Thames & Hudson, 1967. A biography that involves some discussion of Morris's political ideas and career. Chapters 11, 12 and 13 cover the period 1883-1890 and his involvement with The Socialist League; Chapter 14, covers the period 1890-93, examining *News from Nowhere.*

1064. Hulse, J. J. *Revolutionists in London: A Study of Five Unorthodox Socialists.* London: Clarendon Pr., 1970. Includes chapters on Peter Kropotkin and William Morris.

1065. Jones, M. "Humane Socialist." *New Statesman* 107,2766 (23 March 1984): 12-13. On the 150th anniversary of his birth this celebrates the continuing relevance of Morris's ideas.

1066. Kirchoff, F. *William Morris.* London & Boston: Twayne Pubs., 1979. Discusses his political life and ideas in their literary context. In particular see Chapter 5 "'How We Might Live.' Morris as a Socialist," pages 111-136.

1067. Kropotkin, P. "In Memory of William Morris." *Freedom* 10,110 (Nov. 1896): 109-10. A tribute to William Morris and to *News from Nowhere* hailed as "the most thoroughly and deeply Anarchistic conception of future society that has ever been written."

1068. Lindsay, J. *William Morris: His Life and Work.* London: Constable, 1975. Chapters 12-15 discuss Morris as a social theorist and activist.

1069. Lloyd, E. G. *William Morris.* London: Cassell & Co., 1949. There is a discussion in Chapter 7 of anarchism and divisions within The Socialist League.

1070. Lloyd, T. "The Politics of William Morris's *News From Nowhere*." 9,3 (1977): 273-88. Discusses the changes in the text of Morris's *News From Nowhere*, from its serialized form in *Commonweal* to its book form a year later, claiming that Morris moved from a discernibly anarchist position in the earlier version towards parliamentary socialism and trade unionism in the final version.

1071. Mackail, J. W. *The Life of William Morris.* 2 vols. London: Longmans, Green & Co., 1920. The earliest and most extensive biography of Morris. Discusses "The Democratic Federation, 1883-1884," in Chapter 15, and "The Socialist League, 1885-1886," in Chapter 16. *News from Nowhere* is treated as a "slightly constructed and essentially insular romance," page 256.

1072. Marshall, R. *William Morris.* London: Compton Pr., 1979. Discusses Morris's socialism in relation to his aesthetics, his literary work and his approach to moral theory. In particular see "Paradise for All Through 'Aesthetic Socialism' 1882-1890," pages 234-71.

1073. McCulloch, C. "The Problem of Fellowship in Communitarian Theory: William Morris and Peter Kropotkin." *Political Studies* 32, 3 (Sept. 1984): 431-50. Discusses Kropotkin and Morris as theorists of the community, focussing on the problematic nature of fellowship in communities, in particular the tensions betwen its social-psychological and moral aspects.

1074. McKercher, W. R. *Freedom and Authority.* Montréal: Black Rose Bks., 1989. Identifies the major concerns and personalities in libertarian political philosophy in the nineteenth century, with particular emphasis on William Morris, tracing links to modern social movements.

1075. Meier, P. *William Morris. The Marxist Dreamer.* New York: Humanities Pr., 1978. An analysis of Morris's vision of the future, focussing on *News from Nowhere*, which is treated as a realistic prediction of the outcome of scientific socialism.

1076. Morris, M. *William Morris: Artist, Writer, Socialist.* 2 vols. Oxford: Kemp Hall Pr., 1936. Volume Two, with an introduction by Bernard Shaw, discusses Morris's socialism and his activities in The Socialist League. Chapter 12 looks at socialism and anarchism, page 307, and communism and anarchism, page 317. Letters, articles and lectures by William Morris form the basis of the work.

1077. O'Sullivan, P. E. "Environmental Science and Environmental Philosophy: Part 2 Environmental Science and the Coming Social Paradigm." *Journal of Environmental Studies* 28 (1987): 257-67. *News from Nowhere* is discussed as an early contribution to environmentalism.

1078. Shaw, G. B. *William Morris as I Knew Him.* New York: Dodd, 1937. A memoir of Morris, someone Shaw met as a fellow socialist when they were both young men, that deals with his political and social convictions.

1079. Stansky, P. *Redesigning the World: William Morris, the 1880s and the Arts and Crafts.* Princeton, N.J.: Princeton Univ. Pr., 1985. A discussion of the aesthetics of Morris as part of his social and political philosophy. The arts and crafts movement is placed in the social and political context of Victorian England and Morris's attitude to work and to machines is examined.

1080. Stansky, P. *William Morris.* Oxford: Oxford Univ. Pr., 1983. There is a discussion of the politics of Morris in Chapters 5 and 6, pages 60-89.

1081. Thompson, E. P. *William Morris: Romantic to Revolutionary.* London: Lawrence & Wishart, 1955. A study of William Morris that concentrates on his political ideas and career. There is a detailed discussion of the Socialist League, founded by Morris, Eleanor Aveling and Belfort Bax after the split with Hyndman's Social Democratic Federation, and the divisions within it between socialists and anarchists.

1082. Thompson, P. *The Work of William Morris.* London: Heinemann, 1967. Chapters 11-13 examine Morris's socialism, discussing his admiration for Marx, his association with Hyndman and his idea of a future socialist society. He is characterized, somewhat contentiously, as believing in the necessity of a first stage of state socialism before free individualism could flourish under communism.

1083. Vallance, A. *William Morris. His Art, His Works and His Public Life.* London: George Bell & Sons, 1898. Chapter 12, "Socialism," examines the development of his political ideas, discussing the influence of Ruskin, Mill and Marx.

1084. Von Helmholz-Phelan, A. A. *The Social Philosophy of William Morris.* Durham, N.C.: Duke Univ. Pr., 1927. A discussion of Morris's social and political ideas, dealing both with his socialism and the relationship between art and society. There is a useful discussion of "Morris's Conception of a True Society," pages 149-84.

1085. Ward, C. *"Four Easy Pieces and One Hard One." The Raven* 3,2 (March 1990): 154-85. A review of Michael Smith, *The Libertarians and Education,* op.cit., entry 1541, that develops into a wide-ranging discussion covering, among other topics, William Morris as an anarchist educator.

MURRAY ROTHBARD (1926-)

Either the inclusion or the omission of Rothbard as an anarchist is likely, in one quarter or another, to be viewed as contentious. Here, his Anarcho-Capitalism is treated as marginal, since, while there are linkages with the tradition of individualist anarchism, there is a dislocation between the mutualism and communitarianism of that tradition and the free market theory, deriving from Ludwig von Mises and Friedrich von Hayek, that underpins Rothbard's political philosophy, and places him in the modern Libertarian tradition.

Works by Rothbard:

1086. *America's Great Depression.* Princeton, N.J.: Van Nostrand, 1963. An interpretation of the Great Depression based on a Misesian view of the business cycle that questions the conventional wisdom that *laissez-faire* capitalism was at fault.

1087. *Conceived in Liberty.* 5 vols. New Rochelle, N.Y.: Arlington Hse., 1975- Rothbard's mammoth history of America. The central emphasis is on the struggle between liberty and power as a motivating force for American revolutionaries and the American struggle for nationhood. History is seen as a struggle between social power, produced by voluntary actions among human beings, and state power. The American tradition, in Rothbard's account, is individualist, libertarian and anarchic.

1088. *The Ethics of Liberty.* Atlantic Highlands, N.J.: Humanities Pr., 1982. A libertarian argument for liberty and rights in a free market setting advancing the proposition that, in a truly free society where individual rights of person and property are secure, the state would cease to exist. The key to the theory of liberty, it is argued, is the establishment of guaranteed rights of private property.

1089. *For a New Liberty.* New York: Macmillan, 1973. Puts forward the basis of a theory of liberty and defends the theory of anarcho-capitalism. More popular than scholarly, the work concentrates on the application of the libertarian creed to important social and economic problems in American society.

1090. *The Great Depression and New Deal Monetary Policy.* Co-author G. Garett. San Francisco: Cato Inst., 1980. A study of New Deal monetary policy written from a perspective that portrays it as self-serving abuse of privilege and trust that subverted America's fundamental individualist, anarchic tradition.

1091. *Individualism and the Philosophy of the Social Sciences.* San Francisco: Cato Inst., 1979. A discussion of free will and individualism and a critique of collectivist views that seek to subordinate the individual to the primacy of social wholes. A methodological individualism is proposed that is associated with Max Weber, Ludwig von Mises and Friedrich von Hayek.

1092. *Man, Economy and State.* Los Angeles: Nash, 1970. A comprehensive analysis of the free market economy that, while it reaches no direct political conclusions, upholds the view that the free market possesses great virtue. Coercive intervention of any kind is to be eschewed.

1093. "Myth and Truth about Libertarianism." *Modern Age* 24 (Winter 1980): 9-15.

1094. *The Panic of 1819*. Princeton, N.J.: Van Nostrand, 1962. A study of America's first great economic crisis and the various remedies advocated. Links with later protectionism are suggested.

1095. *Power and Market: Government and the Economy*. Menlo Park: Instit. for Humane Studies, 1971. Carries on the analysis of *Man, Economy and the State*, detailing types of government intervention in the free economy, and showing the unfortunate consequences of such intervention. A case is advanced for a totally stateless and therefore free, anarchic market society. Criticisms of the free market are considered and dismissed as lacking meaning and consistency.

1096. "Society without a State." In *Anarchism*. Edited by J. Roland Pennock and John W. Chapman, 191-207. New York: New York Univ. Pr., 1978. A useful discussion of anarchist premises that focuses attention on how an anarchist society would settle disputes over alleged violations of person and property in the absence of a state. Concludes that an anarchist system for settling disputes, once established, could work and continue indefinitely.

1097. *Towards a Reconstruction of Utility and Welfare Economics*. New York: Center for Libertarian Studies, 1977. An argument that the unhampered free market maximizes social utility, and that *laissez-faire* economists were better welfare analysts than they are generally considered.

1098. "The Transformation of the American Right," "The Anatomy of the State" and "Why Be Libertarian?" In *Contemporary Anarchism*, chapters 8, 9, 10, 111-55. Op.cit., entry 1495. Rothbard sets out the parameters of his libertarianism and his attitude to the state.

Works about Rothbard :

1099. Barry, N. P. "Anarcho-Capitalism." In *On Classical Liberalism and Libertarianism*, 161-91. London: Macmillan, 1986. A useful discussion of Rothbard's contribution to right libertarianism and his ideas on a free market, stateless society.

1100. Block, W. "On Robert Nozick's 'On Austrian Methodology'." *Inquiry* 23,4 (1980): 397-444. A critical response to Nozick that involves discussion of Rothbard. See entry 1105.

1101. Block, W. and Rockwell, L. H. J., ed. *Man, Economy and Liberty: Essays in Honor of Murray N. Rothbard*. Auburn, Alabama: Ludwig von Mises Institute, 1988. Essays that examine and discuss Rothbard's work on economics, politics, philosophy and history.

1102. Fielding, K. T. "The Role of Personal Justice in Anarcho-Capitalism." *Journal of Libertarian Studies* 2,3 (Fall 1978): 239-41. A discussion of the issues raised by the notion of free-market courts.

1103. Friedman, D. *The Machinery of Freedom: Guide to a Radical Capitalism.* New York: Harper and Row, 1973. Not directly related to Rothbard, this work is a popular explication of libertarianism with a strong assertion of the value of the free market, liberty and property. It concludes that anarcho-capitalism is the best form of social organization. A radical critique of American universities as unfree agencies of power is followed by a substantial discussion of anarchism.

1104. Horn, W. "Libertarianism and Private Property in Land: The Positions of Rothbard and Nozick, Critically Examined, Are Disputed." *American Journal of Economics and Sociology* 43,3 (1984): 341-56. A critical examination of Rothbard and Nozick. Suggests that both positions are untenable because of their vagueness and ambiguity over the definition of value.

1105. Nozick, R. "On Austrian Methodology." *Synthese* 36, (1977): 353-92. Discusses Rothbard in connection with von Mises, pointing to faults in their methodology. See entry 1101.

1106. Yandle, B. "Property Rights Paradox: George and Rothbard on the Conservation of Environmental Resources." *American Journal of Economics and Sociology* 41,2 (April 1982): 183-95. Notes that Rothbard treats Henry George's recommendation that governments act to affect private land transactions as an assault on property rights. Argues that, while Rothbard's social system has no mechanism to govern tradeable property rights in environmental resources, George's scheme allows for the evolution of new property rights.

On the Margins
of Liberal Theory

THE WOLFF DEBATE

The Text:

1107. *In Defense of Anarchism.* New York: Harper & Row, 1970. Wolff's seminal essay on authority, democracy and the State, in which he investigates the consequences of the conflict between authority and the desire for autonomy on the part of individuals. He argues that, given the incompatibility of authority and autonomy, anarchism must be the logical outcome of the conflict. The weaknesses of the majoritarian model of democracy are considered as part of a discussion of the difficulties of constructing a viable model of an anarchist society.

The Debate:

1108. Bates, S. "Authority and Autonomy." *Journal of Philosophy* 69,7 (6 April 1975): 173-9. Suggests that the concept of a prima facie obligation adequately resolves the supposed conflict between authority and autonomy.

1109. Baugh, G. "The Poverty of Autonomy: The Failure of Wolff's Defence of Anarchism." *Our Generation* 17,1 (Fall-Winter 1985-6): 105-21. An examination of the ethical theory underlying Wolff's work which concludes that his contribution is anything but a defense of anarchism.

1110. Bayles, M. "In Defense of Authority." *Personalist* 52,4 (Autumn 1971): 755-58. Contests Wolff's argument that authority and autonomy are incompatible.

1111. Beauchamp, T. and Witkowski, K. "A Critique of Pure Anarchism." *Canadian Journal of Philosophy* 2,4 (June 1973): 533-39. Criticizes Wolff's inconsistent characterizations of legitimacy as a poor foundation for his defense of anarchism. Briefly sketches non-anarchist alternatives.

1112. Curtler, H. M. "Freedom and Civil Obedience." *Journal of Thought* 14 (April 1979): 153-63. Contests the idea that democracy fosters positive liberty. Rather, it is argued, positive liberty is the outcome of active obedience to law, regardless of the form of government.

1113. Frankfurt, H. G. "The Anarchism of Robert Paul Wolff." *Political Theory* 1,4 (Nov. 1973): 405-14. Argues that Wolff is inconsistent and confused and that it is inappropriate to label him an anarchist.

1114. Kirwan, K. A. "The Poverty of Robert Paul Wolff." *Political Science Review* 5 (Fall 1975): 333-59. Criticizes Wolff's assessment of key concepts and thinkers and expresses concerns about his program for reform in the American political system.

1115. Laszlo, E. "A Moralizing Note to Professor Wolff's Reply." *Journal of Value Inquiry* 7,4 (Winter 1973): 307-8. Argues that the logical extension of Wolff's thesis is the inevitable dissolution of social systems, and condemns Wolff's lack of moral responsibility in expounding such a theory.

1116. Martin, M. W. "Reason and Utopianism in Wolff's Anarchism." *Southern Journal of Philosophy* 18 (Fall 1980). Suggests that Wolff's contention that all political authority is unjustified has little of value to offer.

1117. Martin, R. "Wolff's Defense of Philosophical Anarchism." *Philosophical Quarterly* 24,95 (April 1974): 140-9. Suggests that Wolff's argument against obligation still leaves an opening for political philosophers to develop a doctrine based on de jure political authority.

1118. Menzel, P. T. "Wolff's Critics: Confusing the Confusing." *Personalist* 57,3 (Summer 1976): 308-24. A qualified defense of Wolff's argument which, while pointing out some inadequacies in his conceptual analysis, claims that it has definite applicability in the real world.

1119. Nowell-Smith, P. "What is Authority?" *Philosophic Exchange* 2, (Summer 1976). Based on an examination of the concepts of authority, autonomy, command and obedience the article disputes Wolff's conclusion that there is no such thing as legitimate authority. Suggests that it is possible to submit to authority without sacrificing moral autonomy.

1120. Perkins, L. H. "On Reconciling Autonomy and Authority." *Ethics* 82,2 (Jan. 1972): 114-123. Argues, in opposition to Wolff, that the state can be legitimate and that obligation to the state is a function of the duty to maintain one's autonomy.

1121. Pritchard, M. S. "On Understanding Political Power." *Journal of Value Inquiry* 13,1 (Spring 1979): 21-31. Examines Wolff's analysis of the concept of political power by looking at the theories which link his books *The Poverty of Liberalism* and *In Defense of Anarchism*.

1122. Pritchard, M. S. "Wolff's Anarchism." *Journal of Value Inquiry* 7,4 (Winter 1973): 296-302. Part of a discussion on Wolff in the Winter issue. See entries 1126 and 1131. Asserts that Wolff's argument is superficially persuasive but that he glosses over vital distinctions and ignores awkward questions. He fails, it is argued, to analyze autonomy, authority, legitimacy and consent with the care necessary to allow his use of the concepts to bear the weight of his argument.

1123. Reiman, J. H. "Anarchism and Nominalism: Wolff's Latest Obituary for Political Philosophy." *Ethics* 89,1 (Oct. 1978): 95-110. When, in a later edition of *In Defense of Anarchism*, Wolff replied to Reiman's original critique, op.cit., entry 1124, Reiman made this response in order to address what he perceived to be a major in Wolff's premise regarding the legitimacy of the state.

1124. Reiman, J. H. *In Defense of Political Philosophy*. New York: Harper & Row, 1972. A reply to Robert Paul Wolff's *In Defense of Anarchism*, claiming that Wolff fails to argue in defense of anarchism because he reaches no real conclusions about the possibility of, or rejection of, the state.

1125. Shipka, T. A. "A Critique of Anarchism." *Studies in Soviet Thought* 27,3 (April 1984): 247-61. Reviews the critiques of Wolff's position from a Lockean perspective. Since political authority and personal autonomy are not irreconcilable then citizens are morally bound to uphold legitimate government. Thus, the anarchist aim of a non-coercive substitute for government must fall short of the mark.

1126. Smith, M. B. E. "Wolff's Argument for Anarchism." *Journal of Value Inquiry* 7,4 (Winter 1973): 307-8. Part of a discussion on Wolff in the Winter issue. See entries 1122 and 1131. Wolff is berated for seeking to destroy faith in the legitimacy of the state in what is said to be a cavalier manner.

1127. Sobers, D. "Wolff's Logical Anarchism." *Ethics* 82,2 (Jan. 1972): 173-6. Suggests that the problems Wolff sees as being associated with majority rule are the product of a set of inconsistent premises rather than being inherent in democracy.

1128. Sterba, J. P. "The Decline of Wolff's Anarchism." *Journal of Value Inquiry* 11,3 (Fall 1977): 213-17. Argues that the ethical theory proposed in Wolff's *The Autonomy of Reason*. New York: 1973, provides a weaker basis for anarchist conclusions than the argument in *In Defense of Anarchism*.

1129. Steward, D. "A Pseudo-Anarchist Belatedly Replies to R. P. Wolff." *Journal of Critical Analysis* 4 (July 1972): 51-61. Contends that Wolff's case for moral autonomy as an individual's primary obligation does not lead to anarchism as the only practical outcome.

1130. Wilson, K. D. "Autonomy and Wolff's Defense of Anarchism." *Philosophical Forum* 8,1 (Fall 1976): 108-21. Argues that, despite its apparent simplicity and straightforwardness, Wolff's argument for the irreconcilability of political and moral authority is deceptive, with a weakness grounded in his approach to the concept of autonomy.

1131. Wolff, R. P. "Reply to Professors Pritchard and Smith." *Journal of Value Inquiry* 7,4 (Winter 1973): 303-6. See entries 1122 and 1126. Part of the discussion of Wolff in the Winter issue. Wolff responds and seeks to rebut the critiques.

THE NOZICK DEBATE

The Text :

1132. *Anarchy, State and Utopia*. Oxford: Blackwell, 1975. Also New York: Basic Bks., 1974. Nozick's influential and controversial libertarian treatment of individual rights, the origins of the political state and the source of its legitimacy. The study concludes that a minimal state, providing basic protection against fraud, theft and coercion and establishing a legal framework for the enforcement of contractual obligations, can be justified. A state more broadly empowered, however, would be a violation of the rights of individuals. Nozick seeks to demonstrate that the state is superior even to the "most favored situation of anarchy" where people behave within the limits of moral constraint. Arguing that the state arises naturally from a state of nature, seen as "the best anarchic situation one reasonably could hope for," Nozick concludes that the most desirable utopian model is, in fact, the minimal state.

The Debate :

1133. Allen, B. G. and Patten, S. C. "Getting out of Harm's Way." *Dialogue: Canadian Philosophical Review* 21,2 (June 1982): 293-305. Argues that Nozick's claim for the State arising from an individual's right to punish cannot be sustained. Rather, the right to punish is a right not transferred from its members but a right peculiar to any form of political association.

1134. Altham, J. E. J. "Reflections on the State of Nature." In *Rational Action*, edited by Ross Harrison, 133-46. Cambridge: Cambridge Univ.Pr., 1979.

1135. Altman, A. "Nozick's Theory of Value and its Implications." *Southern Journal of Philosophy* 22,2 (Summer 1984): 139-53. A critical analysis of the implications of Nozick's theory of value. Concludes that it begs the question of how 'value' is to be defined and explained.

1136. Andrew, E. "Inalienable Right, Alienable Property and Freedom of Choice: Locke, Nozick and Marx on the Alienability of Labour." *Canadian Journal of Political Science* 18,3 (1985): 529-50. A critical comparison of the respective approaches to property rights of Locke, Nozick and Marx. The main aim is to distinguish between inalienable and alienable forms of property so that claims to rights can be clarified.

1137. Arneson, R. J. "The Principles of Fairness and Free-Rider Problems." *Ethics* 92,4 (July 1982): 613-33. Argues that Nozick cannot, as he would like, abandon the principle of fairness, because this would entail abandoning the central commitments of his political philosophy. It might be possible, however, for Nozick's egoist principle to be modified to support a revised principle of fairness.

1138. Arrow, K. J. "Nozick's Entitlement Theory of Justice." *Philosophia (Israel)* 7,2 (June 1978): 265-79. A generally sympathetic though critical discussion of Nozick's entitlement theory of justice. Argues that Nozick's case lacks decisive, systematic argument but it nevertheless raises issues usually ignored by the utilitarian tradition. Possible roles for the state are not negated by Nozick's account.

1139. Axinn, S. "The Law of Land Warfare as Minimal Government." *Personalist* 59,4 (Oct. 1978): 374-85. An analysis of international relations which argues for the need to evolve a Nozick-type minimal state on an international scale. See entries 1149, 1152, 1177, 1182, 1196, 1222, 1228, 1237.

1140. Barber, B. "Deconstituting Politics: Robert Nozick and Philosophical Reductionism." *Journal of Politics* 39,10 (Feb. 1977): 2-23. Suggests that it is possible to get beyond anarchism, without violating anarchist premises, to construct a defense of political legitimacy on wholly non-political grounds. Nozick's arguments about freedom, free market relations, entitlement and distributive justice are considered and refuted.

1141. Barnett, R. E. "Whither Anarchy: Has Robert Nozick Justified the State?" *Journal of Libertarian Studies* 1,1 (Winter 1977): 15-21. Argues that Nozick fails to meet his burden of proof and that the state remains unjustified.

1142. Barry, N. P. "Robert Nozick and the Minimal State." In *On Classical Liberalism and Libertarianism*, 132-60. New York: St. Martin's Pr., 1987. A critical analysis of Nozick's ideas within the context of a discussion of modern libertarianism. *Anarchy, State and Utopia* is acclaimed as the "most important book to be published on libertarian political thought since the war."

1143. Becker, L. C. "Against the Supposed Differences between Historical and End-State Theories." *Philosophical Studies* 41,2 (March 1982): 267-72. Argues that the supposed contrast between historical and end-state theories has been overdrawn. Historical theories are as substantive, and constrictive of liberty, as end-state theories.

1144. Bell, N. K. "Nozick and the Principle of Fairness." *Social Theory and Practice* 5,1 (Fall 1978): 65-73. Contends that Nozick, in arguing against the principle of fairness as presented by H. L. A. Hart and John Rawls, misses the point. He is wrong in concluding that he has lessened the force of the fairness principle or demonstrated that certain kinds of obligations do not arise from it.

1145. Berger, F. R. "Mill's Substantive Principle of Justice: A Comparison with Nozick." *American Philosophical Quarterly* 19,4 (Oct. 1982): 373-80. Attempts to draw out the theory of justice used by Mill when discussing the principle of economic rewards being proportional to effort Applied to the issue of taxation on wages and compared with the position taken by Nozick, it is concluded that Mill's view is equally plausible.

1146. Bernick, M. "A Note on Promoting Self-Esteem." *Political Theory* 6,1 (Feb. 1978): 109-18. Criticizes Nozick's view that nothing can be done to promote the self-esteem of individuals within a given society.

1147. Beversluis, E. H. "Benefit Rights in Education: An Entitlement View." *Philosophy of Education Society Proceedings* 40 (1984): 381-90. Distinguishes between "benefit rights" and "liberty rights" and modifies Nozick's view of entitlement so that it accords with a better understanding of people's "liberty rights."

1148. Biesenthal, L. "Natural Rights and Natural Assets." *Philosophy of the Social Sciences* 8,2 (June 1978): 153-71. Suggests that Nozick has only promised rather than argued for a theory of natural rights. Despite his claims, he is closer to Rawls' position on individualism than would at first appear to be the case.

1149. Blackstone, W. T. "The Minimal State: An Assessment of Some of the Philosophical Grounds." *Personalist* 59,4 (Oct. 1978): 333-43. Part of a symposium on the minimal state. See entries 1139, 1152, 1177, 1182, 1196, 1222, 1228, 1237.

1150. Buchanan, A. "Distributive Justice and Legitimate Expectations." *Philosophical Studies* 28,6 (Dec. 1975): 419-25. Argues that Nozick's assumptions about end-state or patterned principles mean that his theory might undermine legitimately generated expectations.

1151. Buchanan, A. "Exploitation, Alienation and Injustice." *Canadian Journal of Philosophy* 9,1 (March 1979): 121-39. Primarily an exposition of Marx's theory of exploitation. Provides a brief but concise critique of Nozick's interpretation of Marx's analysis.

1152. Burrill, D. R. "Distributive Justice and the Minimal State: A Response to Blackstone." *Personalist* 59,4 (Oct. 1978): 394-97. Part of a symposium on the minimal state. See entries 1139, 1149, 1177, 1182, 1196, 1222, 1228, 1237.

1153. Carey, G. W. "The Just and Good State: Rawls and Nozick Read Anew." *Modern Age* 20,4 (Fall 1976): 372-82. Asserts that neither Rawls's *A Theory of Justice*, nor Nozick's *Anarchy, State and Utopia* are deserving of the lavish praise and high reputation they have attracted. To the extent that either book opens up new areas or develops new conceptual approaches to the just or good state, it does so within structures and premises that are extremely limited.

1154. Chapman, B. "Rights as Constraints: Nozick vs. Sen." *Theory and Decision* 15,1 (1983): 1-10. Defends Nozick's views of rights as constraints, against Sen's view that individual rights cannot be adequately met through a preference maximization framework. See entry 1270.

1155. Coburn, R. G. "Distributive Justice and 'the Arbitrariness of Fortune'." *Philosophical Inquiry* 2 (Spring-Summer 1980): 441-57. Argues, against the position developed by Nozick, in support of a "qualified egalitarianism."

1156. Cohen, G. A. "Nozick on Appropriation." *New Left Review* 150 (March-April 1985): 89-105. Argues that even if self-ownership is a good thing, it does not warrant the unequal distribution of resources advocated by Nozick's position. This is particularly true of his theory dealing with the original appropriation of private property.

1157. Cohen, G. A. "Robert Nozick and Walt Chamberlain: How Patterns Preserve Liberty." *Erkenntnis* 11,1 (May 1977): 5-23. Seeks to provide a refutation of Nozick's argument that liberty cannot be achieved in a socialist society. Cohen also argues that the libertarian capitalist society favoured by Nozick is ultimately inimical to liberty. See entries 1193, 1209.

1158. Cohen, G. A. "Self-Ownership, World Ownership, and Equality: Part II." *Social Philosophy and Policy* 3,2 (Spring 1986): 77-96. A continuation of the argument begun in "Nozick on Appropriation." See entry 1156. Concludes that Nozick's claim that freedom and equality are inconsistent cannot be upheld.

1159. Coleman, J. S. "Individual Rights and the State: A Review Essay." *American Journal of Sociology* 82,2 (Sept. 1976): 428-42. An extended review in which Coleman uses a discussion of Nozick's work as a means of putting the discussion of liberty, equality, justice and autonomy back on the agenda of sociology.

1160. Cummiskey, D. "Desert and Entitlement: A Rawlsian Consequentialist Account." *Analysis* 47,1 (Jan. 1987): 15-19. Primarily a defense of Rawls' key position on entitlement in which Cummiskey discusses Nozick's views.

1161. Danielson, P. "Taking Anarchism Seriously." *Philosophy of the Social Sciences* 8,2 (June 1978): 137-52. Criticizes Nozick on his own ground, namely from a natural rights perspective. Argues that Nozick's political theory does not match up to his moral theory of natural rights.

1162. Danley, J. R. "Contracts, Conquerors and Conquests." *South West Journal of Philosophy* 10 (Spring 1979): 171-77. Argues that Nozick's method commits him to placing the interests of aggressors above those of the conquered.

1163. Danley, J. R. "An Examination of the Fundamental Assumptions of Hypothetical Process Arguments." *Philosophical Studies* 34,2 (Aug. 1978): 187-95. Argues that both Nozick and Rawls employ versions of the hypothetical process argument. He suggests that such arguments involve logical anomalies which render them problematic for determining moral obligations in any given society.

1164. Danley, J. R. "Robert Nozick and the Libertarian Paradox." *Mind* 88,351 (July 1979): 419-23. A response to Sampson's critique, entry 1261, of Nozick's attempt to resolve the perceived paradox of liberalism.

1165. Davidson, J. D. "Note on *Anarchy State and Utopia.*" *Journal of Libertarian Studies* 1,4 (Fall 1977): 341-8. A critique of Nozick's "invisible hand" explanation of the origin of the state which, it is argued, fails to provide a satisfactory explanation of its emergence.

1166. Davis, L. "Comments on Nozick's Entitlement Theory." *Journal of Philosophy* 73,2 (Dec. 1976): 836-44. A constructive criticism of Nozick's entitlement theory.

1167. Davis, M. "Necessity and Nozick's Theory of Entitlement." *Political Theory* 5,2 (May 1977): 219-32. Argues that Nozick is successful in refuting anarchism but not in defending libertarianism. The crucial problem for Nozick is the theory of distributive justice.

1168. De Gregori, T. R. "Market Morality: Robert Nozick and the Question of Economic Justice." *American Journal of Economics and Sociology* 38,1 (Jan. 1979): 17-30. Asserts that Nozick's attempts to use normative arguments to justify free markets are inconsistent, illogical and unscientific.

1169. Den Uyl, D. and Rasmussen, D. "Nozick on the Randian Argument." *Personalist* 59,2 (April 1978): 184-205. Nozick is criticized because, it is argued, his analysis of Ayn Rand's argument, that individuals have a natural right to liberty, distorts her position.

1170. Diggs, B. J. "Liberty without Fraternity." *Ethics* 87,2 (Jan. 1977): 97-112. Examines some alleged shortcomings of Nozick's theories with particular reference to entitlement and the 'difference principle'.

1171. Drury, S. B. "Locke and Nozick on Property." *Political Studies* 39,1 (March 1982): 28-41. Seeks to demonstrates that the differences between Locke and Nozick concerning private property are substantial, in that their theories stem from quite different moral and political premises.

1172. Ehman, R. R. "Nozick's Proviso." *Journal of Value Inquiry* 20,1 (1986): 51-6. Draws out the implications of Nozick's theory of property rights, particularly his use of Locke's proviso. Nozick's reworked version of this is argued to be far narrower than he claims.

1173. Exdell, J. "Distributive Justice: Nozick on Property Rights." *Ethics* 87,2 (Jan. 1977): 142-9. Argues that, contrary to Nozick's view, the idea that people may not be used as means is not necessarily incompatible with the notion that certain resources must be managed for the common good.

1174. Exdell, J. "Liberty, Equality and Capitalism." *Canadian Journal of Philosophy* 11,3 (Sept. 1981): 457-72. Argues that Nozick is mistaken in his view that liberty and equality are in moral conflict. The basis for inequality is located in the process of production.

1175. Farrell, D. "Punishment without the State." *Nous* 22,3 (Sept. 1988): 437-53. After showing that punishment was possible within a Lockean state of nature, Farrell goes on to argue that punishment, as a deterrent, need not always violate the Kantian imperative.

1176. Fishkin, J. S. *Tyranny and Legitimacy: A Critique of Political Theories.* Baltimore: Johns Hopkins Pr., 1979. Analyzes various theories of legitimacy in terms of three categories: procedural principles, structural principles, and absolute rights principles. All three of these involve a violation of the condition of non-tyranny, which Fishkin specifies as a necessary condition for any adequate theory of legitimacy. In Nozick's case, the reliance on absolute rights is problematic.

1177. Flower, E. and Edel, A. "What Does Minimal Government Minimize?" *Personalist* 59,4 (Oct. 1978): 386-93. An examination of the problems experienced by theories of minimal government, specifying what such theories seek, but usually fail, to minimize. Part of a symposium. See entries 1139, 1149, 1152, 1182, 1196, 1222, 1228, 1237.

1178. Fowler, M. "Self-ownership, Mutual Aid, and Mutual Respect: Some Counter-Examples to Nozick's Libertarianism." *Social Theory and Practice* 6,2 (Summer 1980): 227-45. Suggests that the strength of Nozick's theory rests on his claim that rival theories are inconsistent with particular moral judgements. Fowler argues that these judgements are open to question. In particular, Nozick's arguments about property rights and self-ownership are not necessarily proven by his use of counter-examples, especially if the notions of "mutual respect" and "mutual aid" are taken seriously.

1179. Fowler, M. "Stability and Utopia: A Critique of Nozick's Framework Argument." *Ethics* 90,4 (July 1980): 550-63. Contends that all of Nozick's innovations within the liberal tradition are quite implausible.

1180. Francis, L. P. and Francis, J. G. "Nozick's Theory of Rights: A Critical Assessment." *Western Political Quarterly* 29,4 (Dec. 1976): 634-44. Argues that Nozick's claims are too strong and are not supported by historical evidence. By drawing on an empirical example the authors seek to demonstrate the inflexibility of Nozick's position on absolute rights with respect to actual historical, technological and social change.

1181. Francis, M. "A Critique of Robert Nozick's *Anarchy, State and Utopia*." *Political Science (N.Z.)* 29,2 (1977): 152-70. Begins by examining Nozick's fundamental explanation of the political realm. Nozick explains politics by referring to Locke's theory of property. But, since Locke does not provide a notion of property which is distinct from politics, it cannot, it is argued, be used in the way Nozick attempts.

1182. Gill, E. R. "Responsibility and Choice in Robert Nozick: Sins of Commission and of Omission." *Personalist* 59,4 (Oct. 1978): 344-57. Argues that Nozick's theory of freedom is one-sided, consisting only in the absence of impediments to individual actions, thus giving positive acts, rather than failures to act, exclusive attention. See entries 1139, 1149, 1152, 1177, 1196, 1222, 1228, 1237.

1183. Goldman, A. H. "The Entitlement Theory of Distributive Justice." *The Journal of Philosophy* 73,21 (2 Dec. 1976): 823-35. Sees Nozick's position as a philosophical extreme and seeks a more rational middle ground between it and egalitarianism.

1184. Goldsmith, M. M. "The Entitlement Theory of Justice Considered." *Political Studies* 27,4 (Dec. 1979): 578-93. Suggests that the three principles underlying Nozick's entitlement theory of justice raise difficulties in application. In particular, Nozick's theory fails to specify what rights may be acquired, transferred or bequeathed.

1185. Goldsworthy, J. D. "Nozick's Libertarianism and the Justification of the State." *Ratio* 29,2 (Dec. 1987): 180-89. Argues that Nozick's attempt to justify the state ultimately fails. Without such a justification libertarianism collapses into anarchism.

1186. Gorr, M. "Nozick and the Opposed Preferences Theory of Exchange." *Theory and Decision* 8,3 (July 1977): 289-92. Points out that Nozick's argument about the ranking of value for exchange purposes is not as strong as he supposes. Preferences for exchange of goods, or services, may well be exercised in terms of some mutually agreed notion of exchangeability rather than in terms of perceived utility.

1187. Gorr, M. "Nozick's Argument against Blackmail." *Personalist* 58,2 (April 1977): 187-91. Claims that Nozick's arguments against blackmail should be rejected.

1188. Grafstein, R. "The Ontological Foundations of Nozick's View of Politics: Robert's Rules of Order." *Philosophical Studies* 44,3 (Nov. 1983): 401-24. Suggests that Nozick's argument lacks a precise justification of the particular rights accruing to individuals. In essence, Nozick posits an individualist ontology that takes priority over the social.

1189. Gransrose, J. T. "*Anarchy, State and Utopia,* by Robert Nozick." *Social Theory and Practice* 3,4 (Fall 1975): 487-96. A critical review suggesting that Nozick's arguments for the minimal state rest on a theory of rights which may not be as absolute as he claims.

1190. Haksar, V. *Equality, Liberty and Perfectionism.* London: Oxford Univ. Pr., 1979. Argues that egalitarianism cannot bypass the notion of perfectionism.

1191. Harris Jr., C. E. "Kant, Nozick and the Minimal State." *South West Journal of Philosophy* 10,1 (Spring 1979): 179-87. Argues that Nozick's use of the Kantian principle that humans are ends not means is misguided. Kant would have accepted that the state could act in a benevolent fashion for the common good.

1192. Harrison, F. "Rights and the Right Wing: Nozick Reconsidered." *Our Generation* 16,2 (Spring 1984): 27-34. Argues that Nozick's views provide a sophisticated but erroneous support for Friedmanism, and defends anarchism and socialism against Nozick's critique.

1193. Harsanyi, J. C. "Liberty under Socialism and the New Socialist Man: Comments on Cohen's Paper." *Erkenntnis* 11,3 (May 1977): 427-28. Suggests that the historical examples of existing socialism do not bear out Cohen's claims about the compatibility of liberty and socialism. See entries 1157, 1209.

1194. Hart, H. L. A. "Between Utility and Rights." *Columbia Law Review* 79,5 (June 1979): 828-46. Argues that while Nozick's critique of utilitarianism offers some useful insights, his argument that morality stems from inviolable individual rights fails to convince.

1195. Held, V. "John Locke on Robert Nozick." *Social Research* 43,1 (Spring 1975): 169-95. Argues that Nozick's framework derives not from John Locke but from Locke's protagonist Robert Filmer.

1196. Held, V. "What is Minimal Government ?" *Personalist* 59,4 (Oct. 1978): 405-9. A definitional discussion forming part of a symposium on the minimal state. See entries 1139, 1149, 1152, 1177, 1182, 1222, 1228, 1237.

1197. Henley, K. "Children and the Individualism of Mill and Nozick." *Personalist* 59,4 (Oct. 1978): 415-19. Discusses the views of Mill and Nozick on the rearing and educating of children. While Nozick notes the problem he does not address it.

1198. Himmelfarb, M. "Liberals and Libertarianism." *Commentary* 59,6 (1975): 65-70. Suggests that Nozick's argument in *Anarchy, State and Utopia* is basically tautological. Contrasts Nozick's position with Jewish philosophy to show that Nozick's atomistic individualism is false.

1199. Hiskes, R. P. *Community without Coercion*. Newark: Univ. of Delaware Pr., 1982. Critically examines the notion of "community" in the work of three individualist thinkers: Robert Nozick, Benjamin Tucker, and Herbert Spencer. Argues that each of them values the notion of community and that each attempts to redefine "community" through a re-evaluation of the notion of "self-interest".

1200. Holmes, R. L. "Nozick on Anarchism." *Political Theory* 5,2 (May 1977): 247-56. Argues that since, in disadvantaging independent agents through a monopoly of force, the movement from the ultraminimal to the minimal state involves a morally impermissible step, the state has not been justified by Nozick's own criteria.

1201. Horn, W. "Libertarianism and Private Property in Land: The Positions of Rothbard and Nozick, Critically Examined, Are Disputed." *American Journal of Economics and Sociology* 43,3 (1984): 341-56. A critical examination of Rothbard and Nozick. Suggests that both of their positions are untenable because of their vagueness and ambiguity over the definition of value.

1202. Hurka, T. "Rights and Capital Punishment." *Dialogue: Canadian Philosophical Review* 21,4 (1982): 647-60. Argues for a new approach to capital punishment based on natural rights principles.

1203. Hustvedt, A. "Robert Nozick's Entitlement Theory of Distributive Justice: An Explication and Critique." *Dialogue* 24 (April 1982): 29-34. Argues that despite his use of Kant's categorical imperative, Nozick fails to prove that his envisaged social system, in which some prosper and others are left in need, does not violate Kant's injunction.

1204. Johnson, K. "Government by Insurance Company: The Anti-Political Philosophy of Robert Nozick." *Western Political Quarterly* 29,2 (June 1976): 177-88. Attempts to draw out the implications of Nozick's views on the state, arguing that his views are anti-political.

1205. Kavka, G. S. "An Internal Critique of Nozick's Entitlement Theory." *Pacific Philosophical Quarterly* 63,4 (Oct. 1982): 371-80. Nozick's entitlement theory suffers, it is argued, because two of his main principles, namely the Lockean proviso and the rectification principle, do not perform the task that he requires of them.

1206. Kelley, D. "Life, Liberty and Property." *Social Philosophy and Policy* 1,2 (Spring 1984): 108-18. A critical examination of three perspectives, including that of Nozick, that attempt to ground the justification for private ownership in a principle of liberty. Argues that such approaches fail because they lack appropriate consideration of the social ends or goals of human activity.

1207. Klosko, G. "Presumptive Benefit, Fairness and Political Obligation." *Philosophy and Public Affairs* 16,3 (1987): 241-59. Examines the ideas of Simmons, Rawls and Nozick, discussing the grounding of general political obligation on the principle of fairness. See entries 1531 and 1537.

1208. Knowles, D. R. "Autonomy, Side-Constraints and Property." *Mind* 88,350 (April 1979): 263-5. Examines the relationship between moral theory, property rights and justice in distribution.

1209. Kolm, S. "Comment on Cohen's Paper." *Erkenntnis* 11,3 (Nov. 1977): 429-30. Suggests that Cohen's approach, entry 1157, to distributional justice is useful when contrasted with the "cut-throat anarchism" of Nozick and others. See also entry 1193.

1210. Kuflik, A. "Process and End-State in the Theory of Economic Justice." *Social Theory and Practice* 8,1 (Spring 1982): 73-94. Analyzes Nozick's claim to have provided a "pure-process" solution to the problem of distribution. Suggests that Nozick's appeal to the Lockean proviso is analogous to Rawls' difference principle, and that their respective solutions to the problem of distribution are similar in form.

1211. Ladenson, R. F. "Does the Deterrence Theory of Punishment Exist? A Response to Nozick." *Philosophy Research Archives* (A Bilingual Microfilm Journal of Philosophy). Fiche 5. 2,1090 (1976): 391-405. Nozick's critique of the utilitarian theory of deterrence is faulty, it is asserted, because he wrongly assumes that knowledge of penalties will be sufficient to deter potential wrongdoers. Ladenson argues that a utilitarian does not need to make any such assumption.

1212. Ladenson, R. F. "Nozick on the Law and the State: A Critique." *Philosophical Studies* 34,4 (Nov. 1978): 437-44. Argues that Nozick's account rest on three false assumptions: first, that a state is defined by its control of territory; second, that his protective associations function as states; third, that there is no necessary correlation between political authority, that is rights of sovereignty, and the duties of subjects.

1213. Lederkramer, D. L. "Quest on the Entitlement Theory." *Analysis* 39,4 (Oct. 1979): 219-22. A response to Quest's critique of Nozick, entry 1251. Argues that Quest's case is not proven because Quest's argument confuses aspects of Nozick's approach.

1214. Lieberman, J. K. "The Relativity of Injury." *Philosophy and Public Affairs* 7,1 (Fall 1977): 60-73. Contends that Nozick's argument for the minimal state has broader reach than he concedes. Suggests that the law derives from an already legitimate state rather than, as Nozick claims, the reverse.

1215. Lind, D. "The Failure of Nozick's Invisible-Hand Justification of the Minimal State." *Auslegung* 15 (Winter 1989): 57-68. Argues that Nozick's justification of a minimal state rests on a flawed conception of the state of nature.

1216. Litan, R. E. "On Rectification in Nozick's Minimal State." *Political Theory* 5,2 (May 1977): 232-46. Suggests that Nozick fails to apply libertarian principles to his theory of rectification, since it can be argued that nothing in Nozick's exposition precludes a strictly egalitarian distribution of entitlements.

1217. Lyons, D. B. "Rights against Humanity." *Philosophical Review* 85,2 (April 1976): 107-21. An examination of Nozick's arguments for the minimal state.

1218. Machan, T. R. "Fishkin on Nozick's Absolute Rights." *Journal of Libertarian Studies* 6,3-4 (Summer-Fall 1982): 317-20. Argues that Fishkin's claims about Nozick's arguments, in his *Tyranny and Legitimacy*, entry 1176, are in error since he does not appreciate Nozick's distinction between political/legal propriety and moral propriety.

1219. Machan, T. R. "Nozick and Rand on Property Rights." *Personalist* 58,2 (April 1977): 192-5. A brief analysis of Nozick's discussion of Ayn Rand. Contends that Nozick has misread Rand and that her argument has more substance than Nozick claims.

1220. Machan, T. R. "Some Recent Work in Human Rights Theory." *American Philosophical Quarterly* 17,2 (April 1980): 103-15. A survey of a number of important and influential philosophers in the field of human rights. Includes Blackstone, Dworkin and Nozick.

1221. Mack, E. "Distributive Justice and the Tensions of Lockeanism." *Social Philosophy and Policy* 1,1 (Autumn 1983): 132-50. While primarily concerned with a critical analysis of the views on property developed by Hillel Steiner, entry 1279, the paper contains an informed discussion of Nozick's theory of property and entitlement. It emphasises the existence and persistence of the Lockean tension between the idea of an individual as "proprietor of his own person" and the claim that God gave nature to humanity in common.

1222. Maneli, M. "Expanding the Functions of the State and the Freedom of the Individual." *Personalist* 59,4 (Oct. 1978): 424-27. Part of a symposium on the minimal state. See entries 1139, 1149, 1152, 1177, 1182, 1196, 1228, 1237.

1223. Margolis, J. "Political Equality and Political Justice." *Social Research* 44,2 (Summer 1977): 308-29. Primarily concerned with an analysis of general theoretical presuppositions for equality and justice. Deals with Nozick towards the end of the analysis only to dismiss his account as tantamount to an apology for acquisitive individualism.

1224. Mayo, B. "Justice, Truth and Nozick." *Analysis* 40,3 (June 1980): 119-23. Argues that Nozick confuses justice with truth While logical modes of inference may be truth preserving, they need not necessarily preserve fairness or justice.

1225. Meyers, D. T. "The Inevitability of the State." *Analysis* 41,1 (Jan. 1981): 46-9. Questions Nozick's assumptions that procedural rights are not a necessary basis for the state's existence.

1226. Miller, D. "Justice and Property." *Ratio* 22,1 (June 1980): 1-14. Argues that theories of property presuppose theories of justice since the Lockean principle of acquisition implies a prior theory of distribution of desert.

1227. Miller, R. W. "Rights and Reality." *Philosophical Review* 90,3 (July 1981): 783-407. A critical comparative analysis of the natural rights arguments of Nozick, Rawls, and Dworkin, arguing that it is not certain that such absolute rights can be defended in the ways that the three theorists intend.

1228. Moffat, R. C. L. "'Minimal government': An Introductory Appraisal." *Personalist* 59,4 Oct. 1978): 321-32. A critical introduction to Nozick's key claims. Suggests that Nozick's account omits any understanding of the dominant power wielded by social and economic institutions. See also entries 1139, 1149, 1152, 1177, 1182, 1196, 1222, 1237.

1229. Morris, C. W. "Human Autonomy and the Natural Right to Be Free." *Journal of Libertarian Studies* 4,4 (Fall 1980): 379-92. Argues that the natural right to be free can be argued for from the premise of autonomy. Reference is made to the work of Rawls and Nozick.

1230. Mulholland, L. A. "Rights and Utilitarianism." *Journal of Philosophy* 83,6 (June 1986): 323-40. A comparison of Nozick, Rawls and Hart. Contends that Nozick's arguments are insufficient to prove the inadequacy of a utilitarian theory of rights.

1231. Mumy, G. E. "What Does Nozick's Minimal State Do?" *Economics and Philosophy* 3,2 (Oct. 1987): 275-305. A discussion of what Nozick's minimal state might be like if it existed. Suggests that such a state may well be inefficient and generate considerable social disadvantages.

1232. Naverson, J. *The Libertarian Idea*. Philadelphia: Temple Univ. Pr., 1989. A sympathetic exposition of libertarianism written from a contractarian perspective. Discusses moral theory and theories of private property rights in some depth.

1233. Neumann, M. "Entitlements: A Sheep in Wolf's Clothing." *Journal of Value Inquiry* 14,2 (Summer 1980): 149-56. Argues that Nozick's critique of a utilitarian based morality, confuses a general theory of entitlements with his own specific theory. Thus, his critique does not provide sufficient grounds for rejecting the utilitarian approach.

1234. Nielsen, K. "Nozick's Critique of Egalitarianism." *Indian Political Science Review* 18,1 (Jan. 1984): 73-80. Attacks Nozick's implicit claim that people in inferior jobs are inferior people by pointing out that such a view ignores the socialization process.

1235. Norton, D. "Individualism and Productive Justice." *Ethics* 87,2 (Jan. 1977): 113-25. Argues that Nozick's normative conception of the individual is the result of an unacceptable separation of political and moral philosophy. As such it undermines the validity of any arguments based on individualism.

1236. Obler, J. "Fear, Prohibition and Liberty." *Political Theory* 9,1 (Feb. 1981): 65-80. Nozick's theory of the minimal state rests on a dilemma. Either liberty is tenuous or the minimal state must be built on a violation of the rights of some at least.

1237. O'Connor, F. W. "Minimalist Presumptivism: A Response." *Personalist* 59,4 (Oct. 1978): 420-3. Part of a symposium on the minimal state. See 1139, 1149, 1177, 1182., 1196, 1222, 1228.

1238. O'Neill, O. "Nozick's Entitlements." *Inquiry* 19,4 (Winter 1976): 468-81. Criticizes Nozick for failing to show adequately how entitlement arises over previously unsecured resources.

1239. O'Neill, P. "The Inadequacy of Contract Theory in Robert Nozick's *Anarchy, State and Utopia.*" *Personalist* 60,4 (Oct. 1979): 429-32. An analysis of the method used by Nozick to establish the claim that only the minimal state can be justified.

1240. Paul, E. F. "The Just Takings Issue." *Environmental Ethics: An Interdisciplinary Journal dedicated to the Philosophical Aspects of Environmental Problems* 3,4 (Winter 1981): 309-28. Notes that legal judgements of the takings issue rarely exhibit a foundational theory of justice regarding property rights. Evaluates the theories of Rawls and Nozick in terms of their suitability for real world issues.

1241. Paul, J. "Nozick, Anarchism and Procedural Rights." *Journal of Libertarian Studies* 1,4 (Fall 1977): 337-40. Denies Nozick's claim that private agencies or associations can be used to defend procedural rights because they are, in some sense, pre-legal. Nozick is wrong to assume the burden of proof rests with the pro-governmental party.

1242. Paul, J., ed. *Reading Nozick: Essays on Anarchy, State and Utopia.* Totowa, N. J.: Rowan & Littlefield, 1981. An excellent collection of articles devoted to the critical assessment of the positions put forward by Robert Nozick. A good introduction is provided by the editor. Contributors include Robert Paul Wolff, Bernard Williams, Peter Singer, Thomas Nagel, David Lyons, Thomas Scanlon, and Judith Jarvis Thomson.

1243. Paul, J. "The Withering of Nozick's Minimal State." *Philosophy Research Archives* (A Bilingual Microfilm Journal of Philosophy). Fiche 4. 5,1347 (1979): 275-85. Argues that Nozick's justification for the minimal state violates his own principles of entitlement. Consequently the attempt to legitimize the transformation of the "dominant agency" into a nightwatchman state fails.

1244. Perelli-Minetti, C. R. "Nozick on Sen: A Misunderstanding." *Theory and Decision* 8,4 (Oct. 1977): 387-93. Argues that Nozick's principle of distributive justice requires the very aspects of Sen's approach that Nozick claims to have avoided. See entries 1154, 1270.

1245. Pettit, P. "Rights, Constraints, and Trumps." *Analysis* 47,1 (Jan. 1987): 8-14. An analysis of the respective positions of Nozick and Dworkin on rights. Pettit argues that the two positions are analytically equivalent.

1246. Pettit, P. "Robert Nozick, *Anarchy, State and Utopia*." *Theory and Decision* 8,4 (Oct. 1977): 399-411. A review of Nozick which focuses on the extent to which he has made the case for a legitimate and optimal form of political association.

1247. Phillips, D. L. "The Equality Debate: What Does Justice Require?" *Theory and Society* 4,2 (Summer 1977): 247-72. A comparison of Nozick's and Rawls' respective theories of justice focussing on their implications for economic equality.

1248. Philmore, J. "The Libertarian Case for Slavery: A Note on Nozick." *Philosophical Forum* 14,1 (Fall 1982): 43-8. In the light of Nozick's libertarian argument for voluntary contractual slavery, it is argued that, since liberal arguments must include the employment contract of the free enterprise system, they must also include the logical possibility of contractual slavery.

1249. Plattner, M. F. "The New Political Theory." *Public Interest* 40 (Summer 1975): 119-28. A critical though sympathetic review of Nozick, which, noting his reduction of humans to "economic man," argues that his grasp of the wider tradition of political theory is somewhat limited.

1250. Postema, G. J. "Nozick on Liberty, Compensation and the Individual's Right to Punish." *Social Theory and Practice* 6,3 (Fall 1980): 310-37. Focussing on Nozick's analysis of the justification for punishment, Postema argues that, since Nozick's position entails a greater degree of coercion than he admits, his conception of individual liberty is weakened.

1251. Quest, E. "Whatever Arises from a Just Distribution by Just Steps is Itself Just." *Analysis* 37,4 (June 1977): 204-8. Suggests that there are inherent faults in a logic that argues that a series of individual actions based on good decisions will necessarily have a cumulative effect that is also desirable. See entry 1213.

1252. Reiman, J. H. "The Fallacy of Libertarian Capitalism." *Ethics* 92,1 (Oct. 1981): 85-95. Argues that "libertarian capitalism" is a contradiction in terms because of its supporters uncritical and over-simplified assumptions about the nature of property rights and their acquisition.

1253. Replogle, R. "Natural Rights and Distributive Justice: Nozick and Classical Contractarians." *Canadian Journal of Political Science* 17,1 (March 1984): 65-86. Contrasts Nozick's arguments with the classical tradition of natural rights arguments and concludes that the latter are better able to resolve political dilemmas.

1254. Roemer, E. K. "Nozick, Rawls, and Equal Athletic Opportunity in Education." *Philosophy of Education: Society Proceedings* 36 (1980): 322-31. A comparison of Nozick's and Rawls' respective theories as appropriate frameworks for guiding decisions about equal opportunities in school sport.

1255. Roemer, J. E. "A Challenge to Neo-Lockeanism." *Canadian Journal of Philosophy* 18,4 (Dec. 1988): 697-710. Challenges Nozick's claim that allegedly self-evident property rights can justify, even with the Lockean proviso, inequalities in the distribution of income.

1256. Rollins, M. "Distributive Justice." *Kinesis* 14 (Spring 1985): 79-105. A comparison of Nozick's and Rawls' views on distributive justice.

1257. Rothbard, M. N. *The Ethics of Liberty.* New York: Atlantic Highlands Humanities Pr., 1982. An often perceptive critique of various theories of liberty, including Nozick's, leading to Rothbard's own libertarian proposals.

1258. Rothbard, M. N. "Robert Nozick and the Immaculate Conception of the State." *Journal of Libertarian Studies* 1,1 (Winter 1977): 45-57. An extended critique concluding that Nozick has not justified either the state or individual rights.

1259. Russell, P. "Nozick, Need and Charity." *Journal of Applied Philosophy* 4 (Oct. 1987): 205-16. A four part argument which first, provides an analysis of Nozick's theory of entitlement, second, demonstrates that "need" is an appropriate basis for distribution, third, argues that this does not necessarily violate individuals' rights, and finally draws out the general significance of this analysis.

1260. Ryan, C. C. "Yours, Mine, Ours: Property Rights and Individual Liberty." *Ethics* 87,2 (Jan. 1977): 126-41. Criticizes Nozick for treating the link between private property and freedom as self-evident and for failing to address conceptions of justice which reject that premise.

1261. Sampson, G. "Liberalism and Nozick's 'Minimal State'." *Mind* 87,2 (Jan. 1978): 93-7. Argues that the premises on which Nozick bases his defense of liberalism are flawed and therefore counter-productive. See entry 1164.

1262. Sandel, M. J. *Liberalism and the Limits of Justice.* New York: Cambridge Univ. Pr., 1982. An analysis of the conceptual limits of liberalism in its approach to justice. Chapter 2 provides an extended discussion of Nozick and Rawls and their contrasting views.

1263. Sanders, J. T. *The Ethical Argument against Government.* Washington D.C.: Univ. Pr. of America, 1980. A critique of ethical arguments for government written from a perspective sympathetic to, but critical of, Nozick's ideas.

1264. Sanders, J. T. "The Free Market Model versus Government: A Reply to Nozick." *Journal of Libertarian Studies* 1,1 (Winter 1977): 35-44. Asserts that Nozick's claims concerning the rationale for statehood are assertions lacking adequate analytic support, and argues for the free market model of social organization.

1265. Sarkar, H. "The Lockean Proviso." *Canadian Journal of Philosophy* 12,1 (March 1982): 47-59. Asserts that Nozick's claim that the Lockean proviso is not an end-state principle can be shown to be false. Thus the Lockean proviso can lead to interference with individual liberty.

1266. Sayward, C. "Should Persons Be Sacrificed for the General Welfare?" *Journal of Value Inquiry* 16,3 (1982): 149-52. Suggests that the basis for Nozick's theory of the inviolability of the individual lacks substance.

1267. Sayward, C. and Wasserman, W. "Has Nozick Justified the State?" *Pacific Philosophical Quarterly* 62,4 (Oct. 1981): 411-15. Argues that neither of Nozick's two claims regarding the state, namely that it emerges in a morally permissible way and that this therefore justifies its existence, stands up to close scrutiny from an anarchist perspective.

1268. Scanlon, T. "Nozick on Rights, Liberty, and Property." *Philosophy and Public Affairs* 6,1 (Fall 1976): 1-25. Argues that Nozick's particular framework of property rights does not provide an adequate basis for economic liberty.

1269. Schaeffer, D. "Libertarianism and Political Philosophy: A Critique of Robert Nozick's *Anarchy, State and Utopia*." *Interpretation* 12,2-3 (May-Sept. 1984): 301-34. A detailed critical analysis arguing for the weakness of Nozick's conception of justice. Claims that separating the study of politics from morals, as both Nozick and Rawls seek to do, cannot be supported.

1270. Sen, A. "Rights and Agency." *Philosophy and Public Affairs* 11,1 (Winter 1982): 3-39. Examines three key problem areas; rights and moral theory, agent-relative values and the nature of moral evaluation. See entries 1154, 1244.

1271. Shapiro, I. *The Evolution of Rights in Liberal Theory.* Cambridge: Cambridge Univ. Pr., 1986. A comparative analysis of contemporary liberal rights theorists. Argues that normative questions must also take note of empirical debates. The implication of this are drawn out and applied to contemporary debates.

1272. Simmons, J. A. *Moral Principles and Political Obligations.* Princeton: Princeton Univ. Pr., 1980. A broad-ranging discussion of political obligation and consent theory within the liberal tradition with specific consideration of "Nozick's Arguments," pages 118-36.

1273. Simmons, J. A. "The Principle of Fair Play." *Philosophy and Public Affairs* 8,4 (Summer 1979): 148-74. Principally a defense of Nozick's interpretation of the principle of fair play as against the arguments expounded by Rawls and Hart. A revised and shortened version of Chapter 5 in Simmons, *Moral Principles and Political Obligations,* op.cit., entry 1272.

1274. Smith, A. A. "Robert Nozick's Critique of Marxian Economics." *Social Theory and Practice* 8,2 (Summer 1982): 165-88. Nozick's criticisms of Marx cover three areas: the concept of exploitation, the notion of risk, and the question of value. Smith examines each area and concludes that Nozick has not refuted Marx's position.

1275. Sonstegaard, M. "Nozick on Sen: A Reply to Perelli-Minetti." *Theory and Decision* 22,2 (May 1987): 203-7. A response to the specific claims made by Perelli-Minetti. See entry 1244.

1276. Sorensen, R. A. "Nozick's Justice and the Sorites." *Analysis* 46,2 (March 1986): 102-6. Notes that a key aspect of Nozick's entitlement theory is the view that whatsoever arises from an already just situation by just steps is itself just. Following Quest, Sorensen argues that Nozick's position remains prone to the sorites objection. See entry 1251.

1277. Steiner, H. "Justice and Entitlement." *Ethics* 87,3 (Jan. 1977): 150-2. A brief look at the question of entitlement and inheritance.

1278. Steiner, H. "Nozick on Hart on the Right to Enforce." *Analysis* 41,1 (Jan. 1981): 50. A brief statement concluding that Nozick's argument is self-contradictory.

1279. Steiner, H. "Slavery, Socialism, and Private Property." In *Property,* edited by Roland J. Pennock, 244-65. New York: New York Univ. Pr., 1980. (*Nomos,* 22). Demonstrates that a categorical condemnation of slavery is justified only on the basis of a principle entitling each person to equal liberty. Proprietary rights are justified on similar grounds but extend only to non-human objects since the principle of liberty implies that humans can veto any initial assignment of holdings.

1280. Steiner, H. "Vanishing Powers; a Reply to Miller and Wilson." *Analysis* 42,2 (March 1982): 97-8. A brief response in which it is pointed out that Nozick's position entails both the admissibility and the non-admissibility of the same enforcing action. See 1227 and 1291.

1281. Sterba, J. P. *The Demands of Justice.* Notre Dame: Univ. of Notre Dame Pr., 1980. A critical analysis of what Sterba sees as the appropriate foundations of justice. Nozick is discussed in Chapter four, and is also mentioned in the discussion on neo-libertarianism and the "nightwatchman state."

1282. Sterba, J. P. "In Defence of Rawls against Arrow and Nozick." *Philosophia (Israel)* 7,2 (June 1978): 293-303. Argues that Nozick's objections to Rawls' position can be rejected since it can be demonstrated that Rawls' two principles of justice involve an historical process perspective.

1283. Sterba, J. P. "Recent Work on Alternative Conceptions of Justice." *American Philosophical Quarterly* 23,1 (Jan. 1986): 1-22. A critical evaluation of libertarian, welfare socialist, and perfectionist theories of justice.

1284. Swanton, C. "Outline of an Intuitionist Response to Nozick." *Politics* 18,2 (1983): 68-75. Addresses arguments that Nozick has no basis for his theory of property rights and outlines an intuitionist response to his views.

1285. Teitleman, M. *"Anarchy, State and Utopia* by Robert Nozick." *Columbia Law Review* 77,3 (April 1977): 495-509. Compares Nozick's arguments to those of Rawls in *A Theory on Justice* and examines their contrasting conclusions.

1286. Thigpen, R. B. "Two Approaches to the Principles of Justice in Recent American Political Philosophy: A Review Essay." *Journal of Thought* 21 (Winter 1986): 118-26. Argues that recent American discussions of justice exhibit two major approaches. Rawls, Nozick and Ackerman use a hypothetical procedure, while others such as Unger proceed from principles based on conceptions of human nature.

1287. Tucker, D. "Nozick's Individualism." *Politics* 14,1 (May 1979): 709-21. While noting that Nozick's claims about justice rely on his particular assumptions about economic activity, it is argued that it may still be possible for Nozick to develop a theory of justice organized around an egalitarian notion of fairness.

1288. Ullmann-Margalit, E. "Invisible-Hand Explanations." *Synthese* 39,2 (Oct. 1978): 263-92. A comparison of the relative merits of intentional design versus invisible-hand type explanations, with a focus on Nozick.

1289. Van der Veen, R. J. and Van Parijo, P. "Entitlement Theories of Justice: From Nozick to Roemer and Beyond." *Economics and Philosophy* 1,1 (April 1985): 69-81.

1290. Von Magnus, E. "Risk, State and Nozick." *Midwest Studies in Philosophy* 7 (1982): 121-32. A critical analysis of Nozick's views on risk in the context of his wider philosophy.

1291. Wilson, P. "Steiner on Nozick on the Right to Enforce." *Analysis* 41,4 (Oct. 1981): 219-22. Argues that Steiner's argument, entry 1278, is incorrect. See also 1280.

1292. Wolff, J. *Robert Nozick, Property, Justice and the Minimal State.* Oxford: Polity/Blackwells, 1991. Nozick, it is argued, disappoints expectations, since a commitment to liberty leads not to equality and community but to private enterprise and inequality. It is contended that Nozick does not demonstrate that any important inconsistency exists between liberty and equality, and that his views have much in common with any defense of *laissez-faire* capitalism. Sections deal with Libertarianism, rights, the minimal state, the entitlement theory of justice and Nozick as a political philosopher.

1293. Wood, D. "Nozick's Justification of the Minimal State." *Ethics* 88,3 (April 1978): 260-62. Points out that the argument for protection in the minimal state can be made just as strongly for other vital needs such as education. In which case, there is the foundation of an argument for the welfare state.

1294. Yanal, R. J. "Notes on the Foundation of Nozick's Theory of Rights." *Personalist* 60,4 (Oct. 1979): 349-59. Noting the moral principles which provide the basis for Nozick's theory of natural rights, Yanal defends the latter's theory of entitlement, but argues that the Lockean proviso can only be justified on utilitarian grounds.

1295. Young, F. C. "Nozick and the Individualist Anarchists." *Journal of Libertarian Studies* 8,1 (Winter 1986): 43-9. It is argued that, despite Nozick's arguments, his defense of the state would not satisfy the moral reservations of an individualist anarchist.

1296. Yuan-King, S. "Nozick on Marx's Labor Theory of Value and Exploitation." *Philosophical Forum* 11 (Spring 1980): 244-9. Argues that Nozick's criticism of Marx is based on a misunderstanding of the labor theory of value.

1297. Zimmerman, D. "Coercive Wage Offers." *Philosophy and Public Affairs* 10,2 (Spring 1981): 121-45. Attempts to overcome what he perceives to be the weaknesses in Nozick's view that capitalist wage contracts are not coercive.

General Theory and History

1298. Ames, R. T. "Is Political Taoism Anarchism?" *Journal of Chinese Philosophy* 10 (March 1983): 27-48. A comparative study of anarchism and Taoism.

1299. Anderson, T. and Hill, P. J. "An American Experiment in Anarcho-Capitalism: The Not So Wild West." *Journal of Libertarian Studies* 3,1 (Spring 1979): 9-29. Using 19th century frontier America as a case study, Anderson examines the claims that an absence of government does not lead to disorder because the free market effectively provides necessary services for justice and protection. He concludes that the absence of government in frontier society did not produce chaos. Rights were protected and competitive market organizations offering services such as protection and justice existed without becoming monopolies.

1300. Anthony, P. *The Ideology of Work.* London: Tavistock, 1977. Traces ideologies of work since classical times with particular attention to the post Reformation era. Concludes that the modern world is dominated by an ideology of work arising from the need of controllers to exact maximum effort from workers.

1301. Apter, D. "The Old Anarchism and the New - Some Comments." *Government and Opposition* 5,4 (1970): 397-409. Summarizes the key concerns of traditional anarchism, contrasting them with the anarchism espoused by various spokespersons of the youth culture of the late 1960s. Apter notes the shift from the inter-generational appeal of the old anarchism to a more exclusively youth oriented philosophy.

1302. Apter, D. E. and Joll, J., ed. *Anarchism Today.* Garden City, N.Y: Doubleday, 1971. Collection of essays originally published in the journal *Government and Opposition*, plus three supplementary essays. Provides an overview of anarchist theory and practice with an emphasis on the latter. See entries 1301, 1423, 1590, 1635, 1658, 1677, 1689, 1776, 1815 and 1835.

1303. Avrich, P. *Anarchist Portraits.* Princeton, N.J.: Princeton Univ. Pr., 1988. An anarchist history consisting mainly of biographies with sections on Russia, America, Europe and the World. There are some useful discussions of anarchists such as Ricardo Magón, Mollie Steimer and the Australian theorist J. W. Fleming, as well as anarchist subjects, such as, Jewish anarchism in America and Brazilian anarchism, not often covered.

1304. Avrich, P. "Conrad's Anarchist Professor: An Undiscovered Source." *Labor History* 18,3 (1977): 397-402. A short piece of detective work naming Professor Mezzeroff as the likely character upon whom the bomb-carrying Professor in Conrad's *The Secret Agent* is modelled.

1305. Baldelli, G. *Social Anarchism.* Harmondsworth: Penguin, 1972. An attempt to sketch an anarchist approach to society. Shows strong affinities with Proudhon's ethics and seeks to distance itself from the libertarianism of Bakunin.

1306. Bankowski, Z. "Anarchy Rules: O.K.?" *Archiv für Rechts-und Sozialphilosphie* 63 (1977): 327-38. Argues against the view that anarchy is defined by the principle of individualism and suggests that anarchism is an attempt to organize society in a non-authoritarian manner.

1307. Barber, B. R. *Superman and Common Men: Freedom, Anarchy, and the Revolution.* New York: Praeger, 1971. A negative assessment of the potentialities of anarchism. Chapter 2, "Poetry and Revolution: The Anarchist as Revolutionary", raises questions about anarchism's viability as a philosophy of revolution, arguing that it is a utopian doctrine that has attracted no first class minds and has a disdain for the common people it seeks to liberate.

1308. Barclay, H. *People without Government.* Sanday, Orkney: Cienfuegos Pr., 1982. Examines the primitive anarchy of acephalous tribal societies, then looks at anarchist experiments and possible future anarchist communities. Concludes that all human societies are engaged in a continual struggle between freedom and authority.

1309. Barker, J. H. *Individualism and Community: The State in Marx and Early Anarchism.* New York: Greenwood Pr., 1986. Examines the origins of Marx's views of the state and evaluates the conflicts between these views and those of Proudhon. Concludes that the two views of the state are fundamentally incompatible.

1310. Barker, J. H. "Sartre's Dialectical Anarchism: Institution, Sovereignty and the State." *Cogito* 2 (June 1984). Argues that Sartre's *Critique of*

Dialectical Reason provides an account of a social anarchism organized around the praxis of the individual.

1311. Barlas, J. E. *Holy of Holies: Confessions of an Anarchist.* Chelmsford, U.K.: J. H. Clarke, 1887. A short collection of poems on anarchist themes.

1312. Barrett, G. *The Anarchist Revolution.* London: Freedom Pr., 1920. A pamphlet making a general statement of the anarchist position with discussions of direct action and the new society that will result.

1313. Barrett, G. *Objections to Anarchism.* London: Freedom Pr., 1921. An interesting catechism, in pamphlet form, in which the usual objections to an anarchist society - What about incentives? How do you regulate the traffic? What about crime? etc. - are considered and answers essayed.

1314. Bell, T. H. *Edward Carpenter: The English Tolstoi.* Los Angeles: The Libertarian Group, 1932. An obituary pamphlet recording the death of an English anarchist, in June 1929, whose aristocratic origins, anarchist beliefs and mysticism prompted a comparison with Tolstoy. Although opposed to violent revolution, he was not, however, a pacifist.

1315. Benello, G. C. "Anarchism and Marxism: A Confrontation of Traditions." *Our Generation* 10,1 (Spring 1974): 52-69. Explores areas where anarchist thought confronts the tenets of Marxism.

1316. Bennett, D. C. "Anarchy as Utopia." *Studies (Ireland)* 63 (1974). Discusses the debate on the relevance of anarchism to technologically advanced societies with references to books like Reich's *The Greening of America*, entry 1504, and Ward's *Anarchy in Action*, entry 946.

1317. Berlin, I. *Russian Thinkers.* Harmondsworth: Penguin, 1979. Originally the first of four volumes of collected writings and lectures portraying the intellectual ferment of Russia in the nineteenth century. Includes the famous study of Tolstoy, "The Hedgehog and The Fox." See entry 884.

1318. Berman, P. "Philip Levine: The Poetry of Anarchism." *Marxist Perspectives* 2,2 (1979): 29-34. Discusses the link between poetry and anarchism in America with the work of Levine as a starting point. Two of Levine's poems are also reprinted.

1319. Berman, P. *Quotations from the Anarchists.* Harmondsworth: Penguin, 1976. Also published New York: Praeger, 1972. A representative selection of brief excerpts from the writings, letters and speeches of the major anarchist thinkers.

1320. Blatt, M. H. *Free Love and Anarchism.* Urbana & Chicago: Univ. of Illinois Pr., 1989. A biography of the anarchist Ezra Heywood, 1829-1893, an advocate of free love, women's rights and birth control. Includes photographs and bibliography.

1321. Blau, J. L. "Unfettered Freedom." *Transactions of the Charles S. Peirce Society* 7 (Fall 1977): 243-58. A discussion of individualist anarchism (Warren, Andrews and Spooner) in the context of the American debate about liberty in the eighteenth and nineteenth centuries.

1322. Bloom, S. F. "The 'Withering Away' of the State." *Journal of the History of Ideas* 7,1 (Jan. 1946): 112-24. Addresses the question of whether Marx's ideas on a stateless, communist society make him an anarchist. Concludes that, insofar as his ideas suggest the persistence of a minimal state, he is, in fact, considerably closer to the liberal tradition.

1323. Bluestein, A., ed. *Fighters for Anarchism: Mollie Steimer and Sanya Fleshin*. Minneapolis: Soil of Liberty, 1983. London: Refract Pubns., 1983. A collection of writings by Mollie Steimer, 1897-1980, and Simon (Senya) Fleshin, 1894-1981, with an account of their lives by Paul Avrich.

1324. Bonanno, A. M. Introduction. *Strange Victories: The Anti-Nuclear Movement in the US and Europe, Midnight Notes*. London: Elephant Bks., 1985. A discussion of the tactics of the anti-nuclear movement with comments on the role of anarchism.

1325. Bonnano, A. M. *Workers Autonomy*. Port Glasgow: Bratach Dubh Pubns., 1978. A collection of short essays on the themes of workers' councils, self-management and local organization.

1326. Bonnano, A. M. *Anarchism and the National Liberation Struggle*. Port Glasgow: Bratach Dubh Pubns., 1976. A pamphlet that makes an anarchist response to national liberation in the context of a Sicilian separatist struggle supported by the political right.

1327. Bonnano, A. M. *Critique of Syndicalist Methods: Trade Unions to Anarcho-Syndicalism*. Translated J. Weir. Port Glasgow: Bratach Dubh Pubs., 1977. Based on Italian and Spanish examples this is a discussion of the potential and the limitations of revolutionary syndicalism, which, it is argued, even in its anarchist form, can still be the embryonic form of post-revolutionary state organization.

1328. Bool, H. "Henry Bool's Apology for His Jeffersonian Anarchism". In *Individual Anarchist Pamphlets*. New York: Arno Pr., 1972. Part of a collection of pamphlets reprinted in their original form. Published by Bool, Ithica: 1901, this pamphlet comprises a series of letters Bool wrote to the *Ithica Journal* which that journal declined to print. Bool defines his individualist anarchism, associating himself with Proudhon, Spooner, Warren and Tucker, and disassociating himself from the anarchism of Leon Czolgosz, assassin of President McKinley.

1329. Borgatta, E. F. "Anarchy and Utopia." *International Social Science Review* 61 (Autumn 1986): 147-54. Suggests that, because social scientists have largely ignored anarchism as a political philosophy, they have failed to take advantage of the radical perspectives and frameworks it can provide when considering future models of social organization.

1330. Bose, A. *A History of Anarchism.* Calcutta: World Pr., 1977. Suggests that anarchist doctrine is the oldest and most persistent in human history. Argues that it originated in the east and traces its evolution and decline in the West. Concludes that having come a full circle, it is time for it to be reborn in the East. Includes bibliography and index.

1331. Brock, P. *Twentieth Century Pacifism.* London: Van Nostrand, 1970. International in scope, it offers a comprehensive account of the radical peace movement in an historical context.

1332. Brown, C. W. "Thucydides, Hobbes and the Derivation of Anarchy." *History of Political Thought* 8,1 (Spring 1987): 33-62. Assesses the debt of Hobbes to Thucydides and, in particular, their shared beliefs about the nature of conflict. Anarchy in this instance is taken to mean not merely the absence of centralized authority, but a war of all against all.

1333. Brown, L. S. "Anarchism, Existentialism, Feminism and Ambiguity." *Our Generation* 19,2 (Spring/Summer 1988): 1-18. Argues for a strong link between anarchism and existentialism and investigates the connections with feminism.

1334. Brown, L. S. "Beyond Feminism: Anarchism and Human Freedom." *Our Generation* 21,1 (Fall 1989): 201-11. Argues that anarchism must be feminist to remain self-consistent, while, in its basic opposition to all hierachy and domination, anarchism goes beyond feminism.

1335. Buber, M. *Paths in Utopia.* London: Routledge & Kegan Paul, 1949. Distrustful of "systems", especially Marxist ones, Buber looks instead to the anarchists, examining the theories of leading thinkers. He also examines the Israeli agricultural commune as a model for an ideal social structure.

1336. Burns, W. J. *The Masked War.* New York: George H. Doran, 1913. An exposé by a labor union infiltrator who brought anarchists to trial for alleged conspiracies involving dynamite.

1337. Bush, W. C. and Mayer, L. S. "Some Implications of Anarchy for the Distribution of Property." *Journal of Economic Theory* 8,4 (Aug. 1974): 401-12. An attempt to provide a mathematical model of anarchy based on the idea of a natural equilibrium. Not a model of co-operation.

1338. Bush, W. C. *Essays on Unorthodox Economic Strategies: Anarchy, Politics and Population.* Blacksburg, Va.: Univ. Pubns., 1976. A memorial volume in honor of Winston C. Bush. This is a collection of 15 essays by Bush and others, which, among other matters, discuss his use of mathematical models of anarchy.

1339. Carr, E. H. *The Romantic Exiles: A Nineteenth Century Portrait Gallery.* Harmondsworth: Penguin, 1968. A chronicle of the personal relations and circumstances of several Russian exiles, most notably Alexander Herzen and Michael Bakunin.

1340. Carter, A. *Direct Action and Liberal Democracy.* London: Routledge & Kegan Paul, 1973. An analysis of the tradition of direct action, primarily in the context of the events of the 1960s, and the liberal arguments against it.

1341. Carter, A. *The Political Theory of Anarchism.* London: Routledge & Kegan Paul, 1971. An analysis of the anarchist critique of state, society, bureaucracy and democracy, evaluating anarchist claims against those of orthodox political theory.

1342. Christie, S., ed. *The Anarchist Encyclopaedia.* Monograph 1 Cambridge: Cambridge Free Pr., 1985. Designed as a cross-reference source book on current research and thinking in the fields of anarchist thought and practice and social criticism. This edition contains a piece by Graham Kelsey, "Civil War and Civil Peace: Libertarian Aragon 1936-37."

1343. Christie, S. and Meltzer, A. *The Floodgates of Anarchy.* London: Kahn and Averill, 1970. A series of reflections on various aspects of society by two politically active anarchists who eschew the intellectual tradition in anarchist thought.

1344. Clark, J. *The Anarchist Moment: Reflections on Culture, Nature and Power.* Montréal: Black Rose Bks., 1984. A critique of radical theory from an anarchist standpoint. Beginning with a discussion of Marx, Bakunin, liberation and historical materialism, it proceeds to a consideration of the definition of anarchy involving discussion of theorists from Lao Tzu to Bookchin.

1345. Cohn-Bendit, D. and Cohn-Bendit G. *Obsolete Communism: The Left-Wing Alternative.* New York: McGraw-Hill, 1968. A first-hand description of the revolutionary protests of May-June 1968 in France, providing the basis for a critical analysis of the strategy and nature of political parties, trade unions, the student movement and the State in a capitalist society. Argues the case for the necessity and viability of left radicalism.

1346. Coker, F. W. *Recent Political Thought.* New York & London: D. Appleton-Century Co., 1934. Chaper 7, "The Anarchists," examines the ideas of Bakunin, Kropotkin and Tolstoy and discusses "anarchism by the deed." A brief historical discussion seeks to relate the American experience to the European tradition on pages 192-202.

1347. Cole, G. D. H. *Socialist Thought: Marxism and Anarchism: 1850-90.* Vol. 2. London: Macmillan, 1954. A critical summary of socialist literature with emphasis on the movements such as the First International and the Paris Commune. There are excellent critical interpretations of the crucial debates between Marxism and the anarchists.

1348. Comfort, A. *Authority and Delinquency in the Modern State.* London: Routledge & Kegan Paul, 1950. An influential attack on centralized state authority and the corruption of power in the name of modern psychology and sociology. It is argued that the libertarian anarchist conception of social change is more appropriate to the modern era than the totalitarian/institutional approach.

1349. Comfort, A. "Latter-day Anarchism." *Center Magazine* 6,5 (1973): 4-8. Recalls the ideas of many respected figures in American history who were individualist anarchists seeking to defend the rights of individuals and minorities. Suggests that human survival depends on a resurrection of these values.

1350 Costantini, F. *The Art of Anarchy* 43 plates. Sanday, Orkney: Cienfuegos Pr., 1975. A collection of Costantini's dramatic illustrations of significant events and characters in anarchist history.

1351. Coy, P. E. B. "Social Anarchism: An Atavistic Ideology of the Peasant." *Journal of Inter-American Studies and World Affairs* 14,2 (May 1972): 133-49. Begins with an abbreviated history of anarchist thought and looks briefly at Spain. Concludes, using the example of Mexico, that anarchism is a philosophy best applied in small scale rural situations, and that the Mexican Revolution was an interaction of ancient values and modern solutions.

1352. Crosby, P. "The Utopia of Competition." *Personalist* 52,2 (Spring 1971): 379-85. Part of a symposium "Is Government Necessary?" Suggests that the major premises, which lead to the anarchist conclusion that all government is an unnecessary evil, are fundamentally flawed. See entries 1379, 1512, 1578.

1353. Cuzán, A. G. "Do We Ever Really Get Out of Anarchy?" *Journal of Libertarian Studies* 3,2 (Summer 1979): 151-8. An argument that, since we always live in anarchy, the choice is between market anarchy or non-market (political) anarchy.

1354. Damico, L. H. *The Anarchist Dimension of Liberation Theology.* New York: P. Lang, 1987. Examines anarchist themes in the work of some of the leading Latin American theologians, concluding that only the radical solutions of an anarchist perspective can fully meet the needs of the people. Bibliography.

1355. Dauenhauer, B. P. "Does Anarchy make Political Sense: A Response to Schurmann's 'Questioning the Foundation of Practical Philosophy'." *Human Studies* 1, (Oct. 1978). Analyzes certain flaws in Shurmann's argument, op.cit., entry 1527.

1356. De Leon, D. *Socialism versus Anarchism: An Address.* Expanded edition. Brooklyn, New York: Labor News, 1962. The text of an address delivered in 1901 by De Leon, considered in his day the leading American exponent of Marxism, following the assassination of President McKinley by the anarchist Léon Czolgosz. De Leon seeks to disassociate socialism from the deed while providing a class analysis of the situation. Anarchism is criticized and rejected. Also contains an essay by Paul Lafargue, "The Police and the Anarchists," which argues, from a Marxist point of view, that the capitalists and their police use anarchists as a weapon against socialism.

1357. DeLeon, D. *The American as Anarchist: Reflections on Indigenous Radicalism.* Baltimore and London: The John Hopkins Univ. Pr., 1978. An examination of anarchism in America, covering both its individualist and communistic forms. Good bibliography.

1358. Dillon, M. R. "The Perennial Appeal of Anarchism." *Polity* 7,2 (1974): 234-47. Surveys a number of works on anarchism published in the early 1970s, arguing that the anarchist search for autonomy is of little use to political philosophy.

1359. Dolgoff, S. *Fragments: A Memoir.* London: Refract Pubns., 1986. An autobiography by an anarchist author best known for his work on Bakunin.

1360. Dolgoff, S. "The Relevance of Anarchism to Modern Society." In *Contemporary Anarchism*, 37-50. Op.cit., entry 1495. An argument for the continuing relevance of anarchism that attacks Woodcock, Joll and others who, in Dolgoff's view, construct anarchism as history rather than activity.

1361. Drake-Brockman, T. D. "Anarchism: On the Scrap Heap of History." *Australian National University History Journal* 8 (Nov. 1971) 10-18. Argues that anarchism, while often seen as more appropriate to underdeveloped societies, also has potential in a world of modern technology. Thus, it may again be an important force.

1362. Dubois, F. *The Anarchist Peril.* Enlarged with a supplementary chapter by Ralph Derechef. London: T. Fisher Unwin, 1894. A survey of anarchism which is not as unsympathetic or ill-informed as the title suggests. There is a focus on acts of violence which are held responsible for the end of tolerance towards anarchist doctrines.

1363. Durant, W. *Socialism and Anarchism.* New York: Albert & Charles Boni, 1914.

1364. Ehrlich, H. J., ed. *Reinventing Anarchy: What Are Anarchists Thinking These Days.* London: Routledge & Kegan Paul, 1979. A very useful collection of contemporary essays, with coverage of a range of topics including the state and social organization, the liberation of self, anarcho-feminism and anarchist tactics.

1365. Eltzbacher, P. *Anarchism: Exponents of the Anarchist Philosophy.* Translated by Steven T. Byington. With an appended essay on anarcho-syndicalism by Rudolf Rocker. Edited James J. Martin. Freeport, New York: Books for Libraries Pr., 1972. First published in Berlin in 1900, and in London in 1908, this comprehensive work was commended by Kropotkin, although the author was not himself an anarchist. Includes the author's original bibliography and source notes. Consists largely of quotations from the seven major thinkers covered, namely Godwin, Proudhon Stirner, Bakunin, Tolstoy, Tucker and Kropotkin.

1366. Engel, B. A. and Rosenthal, C., ed. *Five Sisters: Women Against the Tsar.* Boston and London: Allen & Unwin, 1987. Originally published London: Weidenfeld & Nicholson, 1976. A collection of memoirs from five women involved in populist revolutionary movements in nineteenth century Russia; Vera Figner, Vera Zasulich, Praskovia Ivanovskaia, Olga Liubatovich, Elizaveta Kovalskaia. The influence of Bakunin and Nechayev on their ideas in particular, and Russian populism in general, is noted.

1367. Fabbri, L. *Bourgeois Influences on Anarchism.* Translated by Chaz Bufe. Introduction by Chantel Cortes. San Francisco: Acrata Pr., 1987. Also London: Refract Pubns., 1984. A re-issue of Fabbri's work with a biographical note by Sam Dolgoff.

1368. Ferguson, K. "Towards a New Anarchism." *Contemporary Crises* 7,1 (Jan. 1983): 39-57. Provides an existentialist reformulation of anarchist principles in which the concept of self embraces process, natural law assumptions are rejected, and politics is defined as the public process by which life is ordered.

1369. Feyerabend, P. "Academic Ratiofascism." *Philosophy of the Social Sciences* 12,2 (June 1982): 191-5. A response to Arne Naess, op.cit., entry 1474. See also entry 1445.

1370. Feyerabend, P. *Against Method: Outline of an Anarchistic Theory of Knowledge.* London: New Left Bks., 1975. A long critique directed against the privileged status of the "scientific method" in modern society, arguing that science is essentially an anarchistic enterprise that cannot be reduced to one single method. Science, having achieved a status similar to religious institutions can no longer be permitted to be so closely bound to the state. Note that Feyerabend attempts to distance himself from political anarchism by describing himself as a Da-da-ist.

1371. Feyerabend, P. "'Science': The Myth and Its Role in Society." *Inquiry* 18,2 (Summer 1975): 167-82. Argues against the privileged status of science and suggests that its close connections with the State be severed. A summary version of the basic argument presented in *Against Method,* op.cit., entry 1370.

1372. Feyerabend, P. *Science in a Free Society.* London: New Left Bks., 1978. A continuation of the arguments Feyerabend developed in *Against Method.* Also includes some extended replies to critics, with a chapter analyzing the rise of a new type of intellectual in the contemporary era.

1373. First of May Group, International Revolutionary Solidarity Movement. *Towards a Citizen's Militia: Anarchist Alternatives to NATO*

and the Warsaw Pact. Sanday, Orkney: Cienfuegos Pr., 1980. A pamphlet
which sets out the basis of armed resistance to state authority, detailing the
methods and tactics of guerrilla warfare.

1374. Fischer, G. "The State Begins to Wither Away...Notes on the
Interpretation of the Paris Commune by Bakunin, Marx, Engels and Lenin."
Australian Journal of Politics and History 25,1 (1979): 29-38. Argues that
Bakunin's views on smashing the State apparatus are closer to those of
Marx and Engels than to those of Lenin. The writings of Marx and Engels on
the Paris Commune form the basis of the argument.

1375. Fleming, M. "Propaganda by the Deed: Terrorism and Anarchist
Theory in Late Nineteenth Century Europe." *Terrorism* 4,1-4 (1980): 1-23.
Argues that propaganda by deed became a key element of anarchist theory,
providing the philosophical justification for acts of individual terror.

1376. Forman, J. D. *Anarchism: Political Innocence or Social Violence.* New
York: F. Watts, 1975. A sympathetic treatment of the principles of
anarchism. Nevertheless, it suggests that, although currently popular as a
result of people's alienation from the political system, anarchism is
unlikely to lead to revolution.

1377. Fowler, R. B. "The Anarchist Tradition of Political Thought." *Western
Political Quarterly* 25,4 (Dec. 1972): 738-52. Examines common themes and
perspectives in the works of seven major theorists; Bakunin, Godwin,
Herzen, Kropotkin, Proudhon, Stirner and Tolstoy.

1378. Fox, J. *Trade Unionism and Anarchism.* Chicago: Social Science Pr.,
1908. A pamphlet arguing for the relevance of anarchism to trade unions
and making a case for the General Strike.

1379. Franzen, D. "Reply to Peter Crosby's 'Utopia of Competition'."
Personalist 52,2 (Spring 1971) 385-93. Argues the case for free market
anarchism and suggests a number of analytical weaknesses in Crosby's
thesis, op.cit., entry 1352. See also entries 1512, 1578.

1380. *Freedom Centenary Edition: October 1886-October 1986.* London:
Freedom Pr., 1986. A collection of essays, on the occasion of the centenary of
the magazine *Freedom*, containing material published during the period in
question plus new articles reflecting on the anarchist tradition. *Freedom* is,
as the book proudly notes, the oldest surviving anarchist magazine.

1381. Friedrich, C. J. "The Anarchist Controversy over Violence." *Zeitschrift
für Politik* 19,3 (1972): 167-77. Examines the relationship between anarchism
and violence. Concludes that violence is more a feature of the thought and
activities of particular anarchists than an inherent characteristic of anarchist
thought in general.

1382. Friedrich, C. J. "Opposition and Government by Violence." *Government and Opposition* 7,1 (1972): 3-19. Explores violence as an expression of political power and of opposition to government.

1383. Gaucher, R. *The Terrorists, from Tsarist Russia to the O.A.S.* Translated from the French by Paul Spurlin. London: Secker & Warburg, 1968. Assesses the efficacy of terrorism past and present, concluding that it can be socially constructive.

1384. Gibson, T. *Youth for Freedom*. London: Freedom Pr.,1952.

1385. Goodway, D., ed. *For Anarchism: History, Theory and Practice.* London: Routledge, 1989. A collection of essays that covers the history of anarchism, with a discussion of anarchism in Italy and Spain, theory and contemporary practice, including co-operatives and the environment.

1386. Goodwin, B. "The Political Philosophy of Money." *History of Political Thought* 7,3 (Winter 1986): 537-68. Contrasts two schools of thought on the role of money, the liberal and the socialist/anarchist. The role of money is further considered in relation to social justice.

1387. Gordin, A. *Communism Unmasked*. New York: I. N. Hord, 1940. A criticism by a Jewish anarchist of Communism as simply another form of exploitation of the proletariat by a new class of masters.

1388. Graham, G. *Politics in its Place: A Study of Six Ideologies*. Oxford: Clarendon Pr., 1986. A philosophical assessment of six political ideologies - liberalism, socialism, nationalism, fascism, conservatism and anarchism.

1389. Graham, M., ed. *Man!: An Anthology of Anarchist Ideas, Essays, Poetry and Commentaries*. London: Cienfuegos Pr., 1974. A comprehensive anthology of articles and essays published between January 1933 and April 1940 in the monthly anarchist journal *Man!* covering many diverse interpretations of anarchism and anarchist ideas. Includes excerpts from the writings of leading thinkers like Bakunin, Proudhon, Kropotkin and Malatesta, pieces by less published theorists, such as Labadie, Voltairine de Cleyre and William C. Owen, and useful items on Marxism, crime, religion, art, drama and literature.

1390. Graham, M. *Marxists and a Free Society. An Anarchist Reply to Isaac Deutscher's Address on 'Socialist Man."* Sanday, Orkney: Simian Pubns., 1976. An anarchist response to Deutscher, making reference to the minutes of the First International and the sabotaging of the Hague Congress by the Marx clique. The author was the former editor of the American anarchist journal *Man!*, closed down by the American government in 1940. At the time of his response Graham was 84.

1391. Greeley, A. M. *No Bigger than Necessary: An Alternative to Socialism, Capitalism and Anarchism*. New York: New American Lib., 1977. An argument against the "doctrine of bigness" by a leading American Catholic thinker. An alternative system is suggested based on the family and the neighborhood. There is a sympathetic discussion of anarchism in chapter five.

1392. Green, G. *The New Radicalism: Anarchist or Marxist?* New York: International Pubs. 1971. A critique of the New Left as represented by theorists like Marcuse. Of interest for analyses of contemporary Marxist and anarchist theory.

1393. Guillet de Monthoux, P. *Action and Existence: Anarchism for Business Administration*. Chichester, West Sussex & New York: J. Wiley, 1983. Examines the place of the individual within the institutions of industrial democratic capitalism. Includes a bibliography and an index.

1394. Hall, D. L. *Eros and Irony: A Prelude to Philosophical Anarchism*. Albany: Suny Pr., 1982. A re-evaluation of the cultural role of philosophy that asserts first, that in modern culture the conception of rational and moral interests has been so constructed as to undervalue aesthetic and religious sensibilities, and, second, that philosophy must be understood as a contradiction between a desire for complete knowledge and the failure to achieve it.

1395. Hall, D. L. "Process and Anarchy: A Taoist Vision of Creativity." *Philosophy East and West* 28 (July 1978): 271-85. Examines different perceptions of anarchy, highlighting a dread in the West of chaos. Suggests a new perspective on anarchy as part of the process of Being.

1396. Hamon, A. F. *The Psychology of the Anarchist*. A translation of *Psychologie de l'anarchiste socialiste*. Paris: 1895 by Jean-Paul Cortane. Vancouver: Pulp Pr., 197? Claiming to be scientifically objective, this study of anarchist character traits concludes that an anarchist is a revolutionary libertarian, an individualist, and an altruist who is sensitive, sensible, concerned for justice, logical, curious and anxious to proselytize.

1397. Hannay, A. "Politics and Feyerabend's Anarchist." In *Knowledge and Politics*, edited by M. Dascal, 241-63. Boulder, Col.: Westview Pr., 1990. Argues that an epistemological anarchism that guaranteed the individual's right to make scientific choices would not necessarily promote rather than hinder discovery.

1398. Harding, M. *The Armchair Anarchist's Almanac*. Illustrated Bill Tidy. London: Arrow, 1982. Originally published London: Robson, 1981. Depicted in the familiar black garb, plus bomb and moustache, anarchists are portrayed as cheerful nihilists who voluntarily adhere to Murphy's Law.

1399. Harper, C. *Anarchy: A Graphic Guide*. London: Camden Pr., 1987. An introduction to anarchism with material drawn from sources like Woodcock's *Anarchism*; liberally illustrated, as the title suggests, with powerful black and white block prints.

1400. Harrigan, A. "Conflict and Nihilism." *Quarterly Review* 363,643 (1965): 26-32. Argues that historically war has often had a noble purpose, but that the impact of Marxist ideologies has had a brutalizing effect on what is called "the conflict impulse" allowing for the triumph of nihilism. Governments are urged to recognize the threat.

1401. Harrison, F. J. *The Modern State: An Anarchist Analysis.* Montréal: Black Rose Bks., 1983. An examination of both capitalist and communist states from an anarchist perspective. Includes an overview of the main anarchist and liberal arguments regarding the state, as well as a rehearsal of the Marx/Bakunin debate and a discussion of subsequent socialist state theory. Also discusses the 1980-82 developments in Poland.

1402. Havel, H. *What's Anarchism?* Chicago: Issued by the International Relations Committee of America, Chicago; Free Society Group of Chicago; International Group of Detroit, 1932. A work setting out the principles of anarchist communism and extolling liberty and equality while denouncing private property and capitalism. Anarchist-communism is hailed as the antidote to Bolshevik state socialism and of direct relevance to the labor movement in America

1403. Hedman, C. G. "An Anarchist Reply to Skinner on 'Weak' Methods of Control." *Inquiry* 17,1 (1974): 105-11. Asserts that Skinner bases his thesis on the unargued assumption of highly centralized forms of social organization. Using anarchist political theory Hedman suggests that radical decentralization would give new potential to the so-called "weak" methods of control.

1404. Henry, E. *Stop Terrorism!.* Translated from the Russian by Gulhammid Sobratee. Edited by Peter Tempest. Moscow: Novosti Pr. Agency, 1982. A study of terrorist organizations in capitalist countries. "Left-extremists" are associated with Nechayev and criticized, on the authority of Lenin, as contrary to working class interests.

1405. Herve, G., *et al. European Socialism and the Problem of War and Militarism.* Translated and abridged by A. M. Thompson. Edited by M. Weitz. New York: Garland, 1972. Contains essays by Herve, Bakunin and Jaures.

1406. Hewitt, M. and Roussopoulos, D. I., ed. *1984 and After.* Montréal: Black Rose Bks., 1984. A collection of essays which provides current perspectives on authority and anarchist alternatives.

1407. Hiskes, R. P. *Community without Coercion.* Newark: Univ. of Delaware Pr., 1982. Concentrates on the idea of community in anarchist thought, arguing that even extremely individualist anarchists such as Benjamin Tucker define it as a key goal. Redefines the notion of self-interest in an attempt to develop a new, more adequate definition of community.

1408. Hobsbawm, E. J. *Revolutionaries: Contemporary Essays*. London: Weidenfeld & Nicolson, 1973. The work of a Marxist historian critically reviewing the political life of his own time while showing little sympathy for the New Left.

1409. Hoffman, A. *Steal This Book*. Co-conspirator Izack Haber. New York: Pirate Functions, distributed by Grove Pr., 1971. Accessories after the fact: Tom Forcade [and] Bert Cohen. Under headings such as "Survive," "Fight," "Liberate" this manual for survival in America offers practical advice on how to rip off the system. Contains appendices on where to get shelter, advice and support, as well as suggestions for further reading. Provides insights into the radical, angry American counter-culture of the late sixties and early seventies.

1410. Hoffman, A. *The "Steal Yourself Rich" Book*. East Orange, N.J.: Timely Pr., 1971. Special edition. Large portions of this book were published under the title *Steal This Book*.

1411. Hoffman, R. L. "Anti-Military Complex: Anarchist Responses to Contemporary Militarism." *Journal of International Affairs* 26,1 (1972):1-28. Suggests that an anarchist perspective on military theory allows for the development of new insights.

1412. Hoffman, R. L. *Anarchism*. New York: Atherton Pr., 1970. A collection of essays arguing for and against the claims of anarchism.

1413. Holterman, T. and Van Maarseveen, H. ed. *Law and Anarchism*. Montréal: Black Rose Bks., 1984. A series of essays on the anarchist theory of law, including discussions of rights, natural law, rules, direct action, social order without the state, Proudhon and Kropotkin.

1414. Hong, N. *The Anarchist Beast: The Anti-Anarchist Crusade in Periodical Literature, 1884-1966*. Minneapolis: Soil of Liberty, 1972?

1415. Horowitz, I. L. ed. *The Anarchists*. New York: Dell, 1964. A very useful anthology, containing excerpts from a wide range of anarchist and libertarian thinkers and revolutionary activists. Includes a good introduction by the editor.

1416. Hueglin, T. O. "Yet the Age of Anarchism?" *Publius: Journal of Federalism* 15,2 (1985): 101-12. Argues that anarchism must be understood first as a critique of modern statism, and, second, as providing a viable system of interest mediation. Contrasts anarchist principles with neo-conservative interpretations of laissez-faire liberalism.

1417. Hulse, J. J. *Revolutionists in London: A Study of Five Unorthodox Socialists*. Oxford: Clarendon Pr., 1970. This study includes chapters on Peter Kropotkin and William Morris.

1418. *International Anarchist Congress. Amsterdam. August 26-31, 1907.* London: Freedom Office, 1907. A pamphlet bringing together reports that appeared in *Freedom* between September and December 1907. The report details the Congress discussions on Anarchism and Organization and Anarchism and Syndicalism.

1419. Ishill, J., ed. *Free Vistas: An Anthology of Life and Letters.* Berkeley Hts., N.J.: Oriole Pr., 1933. A beautifully presented collection from Ishill's private press of poems, extracts and illustrations. There are striking woodcuts by John Buckland Wright and pieces by, or extracts from, Reclus, Godwin, Shelley, Goldman and many others.

1420. Ishill, J., ed. *The Oriole Press: A Bibliography.* Berkeley Hts., N.J.: Oriole Pr., 1953. A collection of book reviews, essays, reprints, bibliographic notes and previously unpublished letters, plus translations from Spanish, Italian, French, German and Romanian. All are beautifully presented by Ishill's Oriole Press with woodcuts, drawings or photographs of Ishill himself, Rudolf Rocker, Eliseé and Elie Reclus, Peter Kropotkin, Emma Goldman, Errico Malatesta and Benjamin Tucker.

1421. Ivansky, Z. "Individual Terror: Concept and Typology." *Journal of Contemporary History* 12,1 (Jan. 1977): 43-63. Argues that revolutionary terrorism in the modern era is different from that of the nineteenth century. Includes a discussion of anarchist 'terror' and populism in Russia.

1422. Jensen, R. B. "The International Anti-Anarchist Conference of 1898 and the Origins of Interpol." *Journal of Contemporary History* 16,2 (1981): 323-47. Discusses the Rome Conference of 1989 which initiated a 25 year anti-anarchist campaign waged to a greater or lesser extent by all European governments. This effort became the basis of a pooling of information between European police forces culminating in the anti-anarchist protocol signed in St Petersburg in 1904. These activities laid the foundation of Interpol and also produced new definitions of political criminals.

1423. Joll, J. "Anarchism - a Living Tradition." *Government and Opposition* 5,4 (1970): 541-54. Summarizes three different ways of looking at the anarchist tradition, explaining its appeal as having "something for everybody." Argues that its international resurgence in the 1960s demonstrates the vitality of the tradition.

1424. Joll, J. *The Anarchists.* London: Methuen, 1979. One of the best surveys of anarchist ideas, anarchist movements and key anarchist thinkers, which situates the development of anarchist thought within the historical context of the radical movements of the nineteenth century.

1425. Kaufmann, W. A. *Existentialism, Religion and Death: 13 Essays.* New York: New American. Lib., 1976. Almost all of the essays in this book have appeared before in other books by Kaufmann. He attacks established wisdom, urging a re-examination of all philosophical positions.

1426. Kavka, G. S. "Nuclear Weapons and World Government." *Monist* 70,3 (July 1987): 298-315. Looks at arguments for centralized authority and world government as a solution to the nuclear threat in the light of arguments by Hobbes and others against anarchy.

1427. Kedward, R. *The Anarchists.* New York: American Heritage, 1971. A short, illustrated work. Deals with anarchism in Europe and America from 1880-1914. Attention is focussed on communal experimentation and the *propagande par le fait* movement. Rather brief, even as a survey, but there are some excellent photographs and illustrations.

1428. Keohane, N. O. "The Radical Humanism of Etienne de la Boétie." *Journal of the History of Ideas* 38,1 (Jan-March 1977): 119-30. An assessment of de la Boétie's *Discourse on Voluntary Servitude* with some comparative remarks concerning Montaigne's views. Concludes that de la Boétie's conclusions regarding human change are pessimistic despite his anarchist premises.

1429. Kipp, D. "Existentialism in Sartre's *Nausea.*" *Indian Philosophical Quarterly* 14 (Jan.-March 1987): 27-57. Focuses on the early anarchist/individualist phases of Sartre's existentialism.

1430. Klassen, W. "The Limits of Political Authority as Seen by Pilgrim Marpeck." *Mennonite Quarterly Review* 56,4 (1982): 342-64. Assessing the life and work of Pilgrim Marpeck, it argues against the view that Anabaptists can be understood as anarchists.

1431. Kline, G. L. *Religious and Anti-Religious Thought in Russia.* London: Unwin, 1968. A chronological examination of ten thinkers, some of them anarchist, seen as representative of the remarkable breadth of religious and political thought in Russia. A final chapter surveys developments since 1917.

1432. Konrad, R. A. "Violence and the Philosopher." *Journal of Value Inquiry* 8,1 (Spring 1974): 37-45. Concludes that it is misleading to attempt to justify violence as a category separate from normal, moral reasoning.

1433. Kornegger, P. "Anarchism: The Feminist Connection." *The Second Wave* 4,1 (1975): 26-37. Argues that radical feminism is anarchism in its purest form. Only when the two positions are fully synthesized can the revolution be considered complete.

1434. Kornegger, P., *et al. Quiet Rumors: an Anarchist Feminist Anthology.* New York: Revisionist Pr., 1984.

1435. Krimerman, L. I. "Anarchism Reconsidered: Past Fallacies and Unorthodox Remedies." *Social Anarchism (Baltimore)* 1,2 (1980). An examination of the claim made by some anarchists that to enter into political alliances with non-anarchists, especially in the parliamentary arena, is self-defeating.

1436. Krimerman, L. I. and Perry, L., ed. *Patterns of Anarchy: A Collection of Writings on the Anarchist Tradition*. New York: Anchor Bks., 1966. A comprehensive and well organized collection of writings in and about the anarchist tradition, with sections on anarchist philosophy, the anarchist critique of the existing order, alternative communities, anarchist criminology and anarchists on education. There is a concluding overview by the editors and a good bibliography.

1437. Lampert, E. *Studies in Rebellion: Belinsky, Bakunin and Herzen*. London: Routledge & Kegan Paul, 1958. Discusses the Russian revolutionary tradition from the time of Nicholas I. There is a detailed study of each of the three thinkers.

1438. Laurin-Frenette, N. "On the Women's Movement, Anarchism and the State." *Our Generation* 15,2 (Summer 1982): 27-40. A discussion of changes in domestic production and the relations of subordination between this sphere and the sphere of non-domestic production, focussing on the role of the state in turning family functions into political ones and creating a state controlled family. Argues that this restructuring of social control has been done partly in the name of feminist principles and that anarchism is necessary to the realization of the subversive potential of feminism.

1439. Law, L. *Bigger Cages, Longer Chairs*. London: Spectacular Times, 1987. As in other Spectacular Times productions images, excerpts, quotes, clippings, cartoons etc. are used to deliver an anarchist message.

1440. Law, L., ed. *Buffo! A Short Anthology of Political Pranks and Anarchic Buffoonery*. New edition 1984, completely revised and updated. London: Spectacular Times, 1982. A series of diverse items, such as excerpts, photographs, clippings, graffiti etc., the purpose of which is summed up by a piece of Rome graffiti from 1978, quoted on page one, "Fantasy will destroy power. Laughter will bury you."

1441. Law, L. *Cities of Illusion*. London: Spectacular Times, 1984. A series of statements, quotes, excerpts and cartoons aimed at building a social relationship between the 'readers' mediated by images.

1442. Law, L. *The Spectacle: The Skeleton Keys*. London: Spectacular Times, 1984. A communications exercise in anarchist ideas using collage, subediting techniques etc. to "flash" messages.

1443. Lerner, M. "Anarchism and the American Counter-Culture." *Government and Opposition* 5,4 (1970): 430-55. Examines the influence of anarchist ideas on the counterculture of the 1960s, especially in relation to violence and the critique of technology. Suggests that anarchist values may well be of more relevance for the future of American society than has previously been suspected.

1444. Lowy, M. "Revolution Against Progress: Walter Benjamin's Romantic Anarchism." *New Left Review* 152 July-Aug. 1985): 42-59. Locates

Benjamin's ideas in the cultural atmosphere of the turn of the century and suggests they represent an association of messianic and anarcho-utopian elements set against a neo-Romantic criticism of progress.

1445. Machan, T. R. "Anarchosurrealism Revisited." *Philosophy of the Social Sciences* 12 (June 1982): 197-9. A response to a response. Machan reacts to Feyerabend's answer to his review essay of *Science in a Free Society*. See entries 1372, 1446.

1446. Machan, T. R. "The Politics of Medicinal Anarchism." *Philosophy of the Social Sciences* 12 (June 1982): 183-9. A review essay of Paul Feyerabend, *Science in a Free Society*, London: New Left Bks., 1978, in which Feyerabend's conception of a free society, his ideas on democratic councils and his belief in the equal value of different traditions of knowledge are critically discussed.

1447. Machan, T. R., ed. *The Libertarian Alternative: Essays in Social and Political Philosophy.* Chicago: Nelson Hall, 1974. Essays in the modern libertarian tradition of market based individualism. Contains some material on anarcho-capitalism.

1448. Maciel, A. S., Enckell, M. and Santin, F. *Another Venice: Ciao, Anarchici-Images from an International Rendez-Vous.* Montréal: Black Rose Bks., 1986. International co-edition; text in English and Spanish. Contains commentaries, and 250 photographs, about a meeting, in Venice in 1984, of anarchists from over 30 countries.

1449. Maloney, P. "Anarchism and Bolshevism in the Works of Boris Pilnyak." *Russian Review* 32,1 (1973): 42-53. Suggests that Pilnyak saw in the early Bolshevik movement a genuinely Russian and essentially anarchistic alternative to the existing order. Communism he saw as a foreign influence which led to the extinction of these values.

1450. Manicas, P. T. "John Dewey: Anarchism and the Political State." *Transactions. Charles S. Peirce Society* 18 (Spring 1982): 133-58. Argues that although Dewey was not an anarchist, his most characteristic ideas have more in common with anarchist political theory than any other tradition, particularly after the shock of World War I radicalized his thought.

1451. Manuel, F. E., ed. *Utopias and Utopian Thought: A Timely Appraisal.* Boston: Houghton Mifflin, 1966. A collection of essays by various authors dealing critically with the question of Utopia and related issues. Although not strictly a work on anarchist thought, it deals with numerous issues and questions of concern to the anarchist tradition. Indeed a large portion of utopian literature is relevant to anarchism and its themes. But it presents a body of sources that is too extensive to cite. Frank Manuel, himself, has, with Fritzie Manuel, also produced *French Utopias*, New York: Free Pr.,1966 and *Utopian Thought in the Western World.* Oxford: Blackwell, 1979. The above entry is presented, then, only as a means of introducing this literature. For further details see entry 2242.

1452. Marsh, M. S. *Anarchist Women, 1870-1920*. Philadelphia: Temple Univ. Pr., 1981. A social and intellectual history of American women anarchists. Their backgrounds are treated as the key to understanding their attitudes and work.

1453. Marx, K., Engels, F. and Lenin, V. I. *Anarchism and Anarcho-Syndicalism*. New York: International Pubs., 1972. A collection of letters and pamphlets critical of anarchist theory and tactics.

1454. Matejko, A. "The Self-Management Theory of Jan Wolski." *International Journal of Contemporary Sociology* 10,1 (1973): 66-87. A tribute to Wolski who is a friend of the author and is described as a "romantic of work." Wolski's aim is not to abolish the state but to abolish wage-earning by transforming labor into a cooperative partnership.

1455. Maximoff (Maksimov), G. P. *Constructive Anarchism*. Foreword by George Woodcock. Chicago: Maximoff Memorial Pubn. Committee, 1952. Originally published in 1933. A discussion of the virtues and values of anarchism by the former editor of *Golas Truda*. Maximoff looks at both the positive and the negative aspects of anarchism, addressing issues that had arisen from discussions among Russian anarchists in exile. The theory of anarchism, its vision of an alternative society and the problems of the political movement are addressed. In the second half of the book Maximoff endorses anarcho-syndicalism as the most productive form of struggle. Also included in this volume is *My Credo*, originally published in 1927, in which Maximoff gives a concise statement of his philosophy. Woodcock's foreword provides useful biographical details.

1456. McDonald, R. J. *Syndicalism: A Critical Examination*. London: Constable, 1912. An attempt to educate the English about syndicalism by clarifying its French origins and links with the British Labor Party. Emphasizes that labor must organize and, through organization, be responsible for the rights and needs of all workers.

1457. McElroy, W. "The Culture of Individualist Anarchism in Late Nineteenth Century America." *Journal of Libertarian Studies* 5,3 (Summer 1981): 291-304. Drawing on material published in Tucker's journal *Liberty*, McElroy examines the assumptions and views of various anarchists, emphasizing internationalism, social reform, and hostility to formal politics.

1458. McElroy, W., ed. *Freedom, Feminism and the State: An Overview of Individualist Feminism*. Washington: Cato Institute, 1982. Anthology of various feminist writings from the 19th and 20th centuries, covering issues such as liberty, sex, marriage, birth control, religion, voting, war, etc.. Written mainly from an individualist feminist perspective.

1459. McKercher, W. R. *Freedom and Anarchy*. Montréal: Black Rose Bks., 1989. A discussion of liberty and individualism focussing on J. S. Mill,

William Morris, and, in Chapter 3, anarchist/libertarian thought and propaganda in England.

1460. McMahon, C. "Autonomy and Authority." *Philosophy and Public Affairs* 16,4 (Fall 1987): 303-28. Suggests the possibility that the acceptance of the authority of another can be the act of an autonomous agent, and, as such, constitutes an argument which might be used as a justification of political society to anarchists.

1461. Melnyk, G. *The Search for Community.* Montréal: Black Rose Bks., 1985. A social history of communes and co-operatives which, it is argued, suggest realistic solutions to modern social and economic problems.

1462. Meltzer, A. *Anarchism: Arguments For and Against.* Sanday, Orkney: Cienfuegos Pr., 1981. A popular, illustrated introduction to anarchism, setting out the tradition's opposition to authority and clearly distinguishing its tenets from those of Marxism.

1463. Meltzer, A., ed. *The 'Black Flag' Anarcho-Quiz Book.* Illustrated Phil Ruff, with other contributions. Sanday, Orkney: Simian Pubs., 1976. A quiz book if not for the converted, certainly for the *cognoscenti.* Answers provided.

1464. Meltzer, A., ed. *The International Revolutionary Solidarity Movement: A Study of the Origins and Development of the Revolutionary Anarchist Movement in Europe 1945-73 with Particular Reference to the First of May Group.* Sanday, Orkney: Cienfuegos Pr., 1976. Includes a brief historical background to the movement, a selection of articles released by them and a useful chronology.

1465. Miller, D. *Anarchism.* London: J.M. Dent & Sons, 1984. A general study of theory, practice and potential in the anarchist tradition.

1466. Molnar, T. "On Legitimacy." *Diogenes* 134 (Summer 1986): 60-77. Examines a shift in attitude regarding the concept of popular sovereignty which indicates a tendency to anarchism.

1467. Momey, R. W. "Two Ways of Justifying Civil Disobedience." *Philosophy Research Archives* 5,1353 (1979): 356-67. Compares the respective arguments used by anarchists and upholders of legal systems to justify civil disobedience. While there are some similarities, there are major differences in their approaches to the issue of punishment.

1468. Morawski, S. "The Ideology of Anarchism - A Tentative Analysis." *Polish Sociological Bulletin* 37 (1977): 31-47. The origins of anarchism are, it is argued, to be found in the 19th century. Anarchism's key principles are asserted as spontaneity, social instinct, direct action, free association, freedom as an absolute, and the critique of capitalism.

1469. Morley, L. *The Progressive Anarchist.* Wakefield: Onex Pubns., 1971. An unusual book from an "anti-expert" which aims to provoke and to challenge irrational beliefs. Argues that authority can be defeated by reason.

1470. Morris, J. "Thoreau, America's Gentle Anarchist." *Religious Humanism* 3 (Spring 1969): 62-5. Argues that Thoreau was one of America's most out-spoken Idealists who exercised considerable influence over some of America's indigenous anarchist thinkers. Suggests that while not completely opposed to government, he was strongly individualist in his philosophical outlook.

1471. Morris, T. "From Liblice to Kafka." *Telos* 24 (Summer 1975): 163-70. Argues that, contrary to the views of many critics, Kafka's central concern was the exploration of authority relations rather than class or metaphysical relations. Kafka's outlook, therefore, is closer to the anarchist tradition than has previously been appreciated.

1472. Muñoz, V. *Anarchists: A Biographical Encyclopaedia.* Translated from the Spanish by Scott Johnson. New York: Gordon Pr., 1981. A series of cryptic biographies in note form covering a number of leading anarchists, and detailing both their major work and activities. Useful for its coverage of a number of anarchists not frequently mentioned, such as Joseph Ishill, Luigi Fabbri, Ricardo Magon, Alberto Ghiraldo, Gustav Landauer, Johann Most and Ramòn de la Sagra.

1473. Muñoz, V. *Max Nettlau: Historian of Anarchism.* Translated by Lucy Ross. New York: Revisionist Pr., 1977. A biography of Nettlau, the foremost historian of anarchism and anarchist thinkers.

1474. Naess, A. "Why Not Science for Anarchists Too? A Reply to Feyerabend." *Inquiry* 18,2 (Summer 1975): 183-94. Defends science in general against the specific claims made by Feyerabend in "'Science': The Myth And Its Role In Society," op.cit., entry 1371. Suggests that the issues worrying Feyerabend are not representative of all science but only of some trends in industrial societies.

1475. Nedava, J. "Abba Gordin: A Portrait of a Jewish Anarchist." *Soviet Jewish Affairs* 4,2 (1974): 73-9. A biographical sketch of Gordin, 1887-1964, a Russian Jew who participated in the Russian Revolution and the foundation of modern Israel.

1476. Nettlau, M. *Anarchy through the Times.* Translated from the Spanish by Scott Johnson. New York: Gordon Pr., 1979. A very good history of anarchist thought and deed by one of the foremost anarchist historians.

1477. Newton, L. "Dimensions of a Right of Revolution." *Journal of Value Inquiry* 71,1 (Spring 1973): 17-28. Analyzes various anarchist views concerning the right to revolution compared to that advocated by John Locke in his *Second Treatise on Government.*

1478. Nicholas, J. P. *Assassinations throughout History*. Chicago: Adams Pr., 1969. Intensely critical of the anarchist position on authority, the author details many famous assassinations, with an emphasis on those committed by self proclaimed anarchists, to demonstrate that anarchists are destructive and irresponsible.

1479. Nomad, M. *Apostles of Revolution*. New York: Collier Bks., 1961. A revised and expanded version of the original 1933 edition with a new introduction by the author. Examines five revolutionary activists including Bakunin, Nechayev, and Johann Most.

1480. Nomad, M. *Dreamers, Dynamiters and Demagogues*. New York: Waldon Pr., 1964. A somewhat eccentric series of reminiscences about his life in the anarchist movement with personal accounts of Kropotkin, Malatesta, Nettlau *et al*.

1481. Nomad, M. *Political Heretics: From Plato to Mao Tse Tung*. Michigan: Ann Arbor Paperbacks, 1968. Studies of various radical thinkers and their ideas.

1482. Nomad, M. *Rebels and Renegades*. Freeport, N.Y.: Books for Libraries Pr., 1968. Looks at the problems associated with the cooperation of workers and intellectuals in the pursuit of power. Intellectuals, it is suggested, often assume control while promising workers power after a notional transition period. Examines a variety of thinkers, such as Malatesta, Ramsay MacDonald, Trotsky and Mussolini.

1483. Novack, D. "The Place of Anarchism in the History of Political Thought." *Review of Politics* 20,3 (1958): 307-29. Surveys a range of anarchist theorists, and treats anarchism as predominantly a 19th century tradition. Concludes that anarchism is now a minor political force but, nevertheless, its importance as a libertarian philosophy should not be underrated.

1484. Novak, D. "Anarchism and Individual Terrorism." *Canadian Journal of Economic & Political Studies* 20,2 (1954): 176-84. A brief discussion of the views of a number of anarchists on violence which tends to repeat many of the old myths.

1485. Okuguchi, K. "Natural Equilibrium in the Bush-Mayer Model of Anarchy: A Dynamic Analysis." *Public Choice* 26 (Summer 1976): 129-35. Stability in the Bush-Mayer (mathematical) model of anarchy is shown to be dependent upon the properties of the individual's utility functions and the number of persons.

1486. Osterfeld, D. "Anarchism and the Public Goods Issue: Law Courts and the Police." *Journal of Libertarian Studies* 9,1 (Winter 1989): 47-68. Argues that government is not necessary to ensure the provision of public goods. Laws, courts, police etc. can all be provided by the free market.

1487. Osterfeld, D. *Freedom Society and the State.* Lanham: Univ. Pr. of America, 1983. Classifies proposals for alternative social structures and economic institutions regarded by anarchists as suitable replacements for the State. The book is primarily concerned with the proposals of individualist anarchism in the form of "anarcho-capitalism." Concludes that while the desirability of anarchism is difficult to assess, because of the intrusion of personal value judgements, the case for the removal of government remains convincing.

1488. Ostergaard, G. "G.B.S. - Anarchist." *The New Statesman and Nation* 5,46 (21 Nov. 1953): 628. Discusses briefly Shaw's little known attachment to individualist anarchism in his early years, a time when he was an admirer of Benjamin Tucker.

1489. Ostergaard, G. *Resisting the Nation State: The Pacifist and Anarchist Tradition.* Studies in Nonviolence No.11. London: Peace Pledge Union, 1982. A comparative analysis of the approach to the state of the anarchist and pacifist traditions with particular attention paid to Christian anarchism and Gandhism.

1490. Overy, B. "Approaches to Non-Violent Revolution." *Gandhi Marg* 17 (2): 1973; pp. 141-149. Expresses concern that the popular image of non-violent revolution might obscure an awareness of attendant difficulties.

1491. Pataud, É. and Pouget, É. *How Shall We Bring About the Revolution: Syndicalism and the Co-operative Commonwealth.* Translated from the French by Charlotte and Frederic Charles. Preface by Peter Kropotkin. New introduction by Geoff Brown. London and Winchester, Mass.: Pluto Pr., 1990. Originally published Oxford: New International Pubg., 1913. A classic statement of the anarcho-syndicalist position by two revolutionary French syndicalists of the nineteenth century. They espouse the idea of a general strike which, by overthrowing both capitalism and the state, will usher in the dawn of a new society of equality and freedom.

1492. Pennock, J. R. and Chapman, J. W., ed. *Anarchism. (Nomos* 19 1978). New York: New York Univ. Pr., 1978. Anarchism was the topic chosen for the 1974 annual meeting of the American Society for Political and Legal Philosophy. Nine papers presented at that meetings plus nine others make up this volume. Because the papers refer to each other some useful dialogue is produced. There are particularly valuable discussions on authority and anarchism and forms of social control in the absence of government. In assessing the common roots of liberals and anarchists their common concern for liberty and equality is stressed. Includes a good bibliography and index.

1493. Peperzak, A. T. "Freedom." *International Philosophical Quarterly* 11 (Sept. 1971): 341-61. Attempts to develop an analysis that, in ruling out the egocentric/individualist approach, makes sociability possible. Provides a justification for the state, while posing the question of what can be learnt from anarchism.

1494. Perkins, R. and Perkins, E. *Precondition for Peace and Prosperity: Rational Anarchy.* St. Thomas, Ont.: The Authors, 140 Talbot St., 1971. Discusses why governments can never facilitate social harmony and, in fact, threaten the very existence of humanity. Sets out to prove that peace can only come about within a rational social structure based on natural moral law, that is anarchism.

1495. Perlin, T. M., ed. *Contemporary Anarchism.* Brunswick, N.J.: Transaction Bks., 1979. A collection of writings by well known participants in the contemporary movement, with an introductory essay that looks at the revival of anarchism in its social and historical context.

1496. Perry, L. *Radical Abolitionism: Anarchy and the Government of God in Antislavery Thought.* Ithaca, N.Y.: Cornell Univ. Pr., 1973. Traces the emergence of various American radical movements from their roots in the anti-slavery arguments of the 1840s and 50s. Annotated bibliography.

1497. Peterson, S. A. "Moral Development and Critiques of Anarchism." *Journal of Libertarian Studies* 3,2 (Summer 1987): 237-45. Argues that the feasibility of mutual aid associations coping with function like education and health care depends on the level of moral development. Progress in the latter may make such associations seem more practical in the future.

1498. Pike, D. A. *Anarcho-Pacifism: Questions and Answers. A Personal View of Anarchism.* Glastonbury, U.K.: D. A. Pike, 1987. A general discussion of anarcho-pacifism that seeks to describe the rules of an ideal society as well as to answer the difficult questions always faced by pacifists about their reaction to potential violence against loved ones.

1499. Plamenatz, J. *Democracy and Illusion.* London: Longman, 1973. Looks at the problems associated with establishing a valid and useful definition of democracy by examining the theories of both its champions and its critics. Includes some discussion of anarchism.

1500. Plechanoff (Plekhanov), G. *Anarchism and Socialism.* Westport, Conn.: Hyperion Reprint Ed. 1981. Translated by Eleanor Max Aveling. Introduction by Robert Rives La Monte. Written in 1885, just before the 1886 meeting of the International in London, it seeks to discredit anarchism through attacks on Proudhon, Kropotkin and other anarchists as simplistic, confused, utopian thinkers and, in their dedication to violence, productive of reaction.

1501. Powell, W. *The Anarchist Cookbook.* With a prefatory note on anarchism today by P. M. Bergman. New York: L. Stuart, 1971. Generally condemned as irresponsible, dangerous and a disgrace to the publishers. A comic book approach to civil violence which gives instructions for concocting a variety of drugs and bombs.

1502. Ramm, H. "Che Guevara: Leninist or Anarchist?" *Social Praxis* 3,3-4 (1975): 261-72. Examines the revolutionary theory and practice of Che

Guevara, arguing that the conception of history implicit in his revolutionary model is idealist and anarchist.Excerpted from Ramm's book *Between Lenin And Guevara: The Marxism of Regis Debray*, Kansas: Regents Pr., 1974.

1503. "Ravachol." *Commonweal* 7,322-323 (16 July - 23 July 1892). A statement by Ravachol of his motives and a justification for his conduct that he was not allowed to read in court.

1504. Reich, C. A. *The Greening of America*. Harmondsworth: Penguin, 1970. A *pièce d'occasion* of the counterculture of the 1960's. Argues a case for the relevance of community as a form of political and social organization.

1505. Reichert, W. O. "Toward a New Understanding of Anarchism." *Western Political Quarterly* 20,4 (1967): 856-65. Argues that the tendency of some theorists to use the advocacy or acceptance of violence as a basis for categorizing anarchist thought is not adequate.

1506. Reichert, W. O. "Anarchism, Freedom and Power." *Ethics* 79,2 (Jan. 1969): 139-49. This is a defense of anarchist approaches to power, pointing up the anarchist distinction between social and political power, as elaborated in the works of Kropotkin and Proudhon, and the rejection of authoritarian principles.

1507. Reichert, W. O. "The Anarchist as Elitist." *Our Generation* 18,1 (Fall-Winter 1986): 63-86. A discussion of anarchist individualism as elitism with reference to the work of Benjamin Barber and Isaac Kramnick, op.cit., entries 302 and 1307.

1508. Reszler, A. "An Essay on Political Myths: Anarchist Myths of Revolt." *Diogenes* 94 (Summer 1976): 34-52. Attempts to link the idea of political revolt as espoused by anarchists to the role of myths in political theory, seeking connections with primordial gestures of revolt and the destructive imagery often used in the quest for human liberation.

1509. Ritter, A. "Anarchism and Liberal Theory in the Nineteenth Century." *Bucknell Review* 19,2 (1971): 37-66. Compares and contrasts the two theories, concluding that the essential differences between them are rooted in conflicting concepts of community.

1510. Ritter, A. *Anarchism: A Theoretical Analysis*. Cambridge & New York: Cambridge Univ. Pr., 1980. Drawing primarily on the works of Godwin, Proudhon, Kropotkin and Bakunin, Ritter aims to demonstrate the need for anarchists to be taken seriously within political theory debates.

1511. Robinson, J. *Anarchism and Modern Society*. Pamphlet. London: S. E. Parker, 1967. A pamphlet that discusses various forms of anarchism, with the aim of establishing which is the most relevant to modern society.

1512. Rollins, L. A. "Reply to C.J. Wheeler." *Personalist* 52,2 (Spring 1971): 400-11. See entry 1578 in particular. Also entries 1352, 1379. Sets out to demonstrate that free market anarchism is logically consistent and that it is Wheeler's argument for limited government which entails a contradiction.

1513. Rooum, D. *Wildcat: Anarchist Comics*. London: Freedom Pr., 1985. A collection of anarchist cartoons based on an anarchist feline character called Wildcat. The strip has appeared in a number of anarchist publications including *Freedom*.

1514. Roussopoulos, D. I., ed. *The Anarchist Papers*. Montréal: Black Rose Bks., 1986. A collection of anarchist essays, including pieces by Murray Bookchin, George Woodcock, Noam Chomsky and Paul Goodman. Also contains material on Goldman and feminism.

1515. Roussopoulos, D. I., ed. *The Anarchist Papers 2*. Montréal: Black Rose Bks., 1989. Another useful collection of anarchist essays, with interesting contributions on feminism, green politics, ecofeminism and deep ecology, plus a long critique of Mill's concept of liberty.

1516. Roussopoulos, D. I., ed. *The Anarchist Papers 3*. Montréal: Black Rose Bks., 1989. Draws together wide-ranging commentaries on anarchist thought from the French Revolution to the modern green movement.

1517. Routley, R. and Routley, V. "The Irrefutability of Anarchism." *Social Alternatives* 2,3 (1982): 23-9. An argument designed to show that the state is undesirable, since it is costly in both moral and material terms, and unnecessary, since it can be replaced by alternative social arrangements.

1518. Rubel, M. and Crump, J., ed. *Non-Market Socialism in the Nineteenth and Twentieth Centuries*. New York: St. Martins Pr., 1987. Claims that nineteenth century socialists were generally agreed that socialism meant a moneyless, classless, stateless society. Proceeds to examine the development of these ideas in the twentieth century, challenging many assumptions along the way.

1519. Runkle, G. *Anarchism, Old and New*. New York: Delacorte Pr. 1972. The work traces linkages between old anarchism, the New Left and the Radical Right and looks at the American individualist tradition.

1520. Russell, B. *Principles of Social Reconstruction*. London: Unwin Bks. 1971. Originally published as a series of lectures in 1915. Russell sets out a philosophy of politics in which he argues that political institutions should be refashioned to promote the creative impulses of human beings. He suggests that the existence of the state, war, and property ensure that creativity is suppressed.

1521. Russell, B. *Roads to Freedom: Socialism, Anarchism and Syndicalism*. London: George Allen & Unwin, 1920. Provides an historical and critical analysis of socialist, anarchist and syndicalist thought. Concludes that each has something positive to offer, but none can be accepted as a whole.

1522. Sampson, R. V. *The Anarchist Basis of Pacifism.* London: Stuart Morris Memorial Fund, Peace Pledge Union, 1970. Published as *Society without the State.* London: Peace Pledge Union, 1980. Aims to show that "the anarchist's concern with the problem of power is logically inherent in the pacifist's insistence on the sanctity of human life." Argues that to end war people must not only refuse to fight but must live in a manner conducive to peace.

1523. Sampson, R. V. *The Psychology of Power.* London: Pantheon Bks., 1965. Rests on the premise that what is morally right cannot be pragmatically wrong or invalidated on the grounds of futility. Power involves the neglect of this moral imperative in the pursuit of political goals. Tolstoyan in inspiration.

1524. Sargent, L. T. "Social Decision Making in Anarchism and Minimalism." *Personalist* 59,4 (Oct. 1978): 358-69. Seeks to explain the basis of social decision making in anarchism and minimalism. It also attempts to arrive at clear definitions of anarchism and libertarianism by showing how anarchist and libertarian theories treat the issue of social decision making.

1525. Schecter, S. *The Politics of Urban Liberation.* Montréal: Black Rose Bks., 1978. A libertarian evaluation of political economy and the significance of the urban context.

1526. Schiller, M. "Anarchism and Autonomy." *Bucknell Review* 21,2-3 (1973): 47-59. Argues that the logical conclusion of political anarchism, since all political authority is unacceptable and illegal, must make direct democracy the only acceptable decision-making system.

1527. Schumann, R. "Questioning the Foundation of Practical Philosophy." *Human Studies* 1 (Oct. 1978) See Dauenhauer, op.cit., entry 1355 for reply. Examines the implications for anarchist philosophy of Heidegger's "question of being."

1528. Schurmann, R. "On Constituting Oneself an Anarchistic Subject." *Praxis International* 6 (Oct. 1986): 294-310. Examines Foucault's suggestion that practical anarchism is a likely mode of self-constitution.

1529. Schwarz, F. C. *The Three Faces of Revolution.* Washington: Capitol Hill Pr., 1972. Having identified the three elements of modern revolution as Communism, Anarchy and Sensualism, it is argued that one must first know the "enemy" before one can mount a counter attack.

1530. Scott, I. "Nineteenth Century Anarchism and Marxism." *Social Science* 47,4 (1972): 212-18. Treats the difference between anarchism and Marxism as corresponding to the divergence between the libertarian and authoritarian approaches to socialism. Notes the contribution of non-

European intellectuals to the development and growth of anarchist philosophy.

1531. Senor, T. D. "What If There Are No Political Obligations: A Reply to Simmons." *Philosophy and Public Affairs* 16,3 (Summer 1987): 260-8. Argues that Simmons is mistaken about the consequences of the conclusion he reaches in his book *Moral Principles and Political Obligations,* entry 1538. See also entries 1207 and 1537.

1532. Serge, V. *Memoirs of a Revolutionary, 1901-1941.* Translated from the French by Peter Sedgwick. London: Oxford Univ. Pr. 1963. A personal account by a participant in the Russian Revolution. It seeks to analyze how and why it went wrong.

1533. Shapiro, J. S. *Movements of Social Dissent in Modern Europe.* Princeton, N.J.: Van Nostrand, 1962. The first half is an assessment of radical ideas of the period 1815-1914, and the second comprises a collection of selected writings of some of the major thinkers. It includes Godwin, Proudhon, Bakunin and Kropotkin but, surprisingly, it does not deal with Marxism.

1534. Shatz, M. S., ed. *The Essential Works of Anarchism.* New York: Quadrangle Bks., 1972. An introductory anthology containing excerpts from important anarchist writings. It includes a thoughtful introductory essay by the editor.

1535. Shaw, G. B. "The Impossibilities of Anarchism." In *The Socialism of Shaw,* edited and introduced by James Fuchs, 109-44. New York: Vanguard Pr., 1926. Not the categorical rejection that the title suggests, but rather a rejection of individualist anarchism while expressing a qualified sympathy for anarcho-communism.

1536. Shipka, T. A. "A Critique of Anarchism." *Studies in Soviet Thought* 27,3 (1984): 247-61. Argues that authority and autonomy must be seen as compatible. The disappearance of government inevitably leads to the appearance of quasi-political structures that perpetuate authority.

1537. Simmons, J. A. "The Anarchist Position: A Reply to Klasko and Senor's Comments on *Moral Principles and Political Obligations."* *Philosophy and Public Affairs* 16,3 (Summer 1987): 269-79. Highlights the differences in philosophical and practical anarchism and argues that the integrity of his position requires a shift in the citizen-state relationship. See entries 1207 and 1531.

1538. Simmons, J. A. *Moral Principles and Political Obligations.* Princeton, N.J.: Princeton Univ. Pr., 1979. Deals with the relationship between political and moral obligations concluding that political obligations should not override moral principles.

1539. Simon, T. W. "Democratizing Eutopia: Environmentalism, Anarchism, Feminism." *Our Generation* 17,1 (Fall-Winter 1985-6): 123-50. Considers three novels, *Ecotopia* (1975) by Ernest Callenbach, *Woman on the Edge of Time* (1976) by Marge Piercy, and *The Dispossessed* (1974) by Ursula Le Guin, in an exploration of the continuities between environmentalism, feminism and anarchism.

1540. Smith, J. B. *Direct Action versus Legislation.* London: Freedom Office, 1909. Pamphlet first published Glasgow: Free Action Anarchist Group, 1899. An appeal to circumvent Parliament, referendums and party government by direct mass action.

1541. Smith, M. P. *The Libertarians and Education.* London: Allen & Unwin, 1983. Brings together the views of educational libertarians from Godwin to A.S. Neill and Paul Goodman. Includes discussions on Fourier, Proudhon, Tolstoy and Ferrer.

1542. Sneed, J. D. "Order without Law: Where Will Anarchists Keep the Madmen?" *Journal of Libertarian Studies* 1,2 (Spring 1977): 117-24. Explores the problem of the provision of prison, court and police services in an anarchist society. Evaluates the possibility of competing private agencies providing them.

1543. Solneman, K. H. Z. *The Manifesto of Peace and Freedom: The Alternative to the Communist Manifesto.* Translated from the German by Doris Pfaff and John Zube. Edited by Edward Mornin. New York: Mackay Society, 1983. A discussion of anarchism as a realistic social alternative to the existing order. Marxism is rejected and an egalitarian, classless, stateless anarchist society described and promoted.

1544. South London Anarchist Group. Compiled. *Anarchist Songbook: To Tunes You Know.* London: The Group, 1981? A collection of topical lyrics to popular tunes on themes of anarchism, feminism, peace, anti-authority etc.

1545. Spring, J. *A Primer of Libertarian Education.* Montréal: Black Rose Bks., 1975. Also New York: Free Life Edns., 1975. An analysis of the libertarian critique of institutionalized education ranging from Rousseau and Godwin to A. S. Neill and Paulo Freire. Some mention is also made of the relevance of the ideas of Max Stirner, Francisco Ferrer, Wilhelm Reich and Leo Tolstoy.

1546. Stalin, J. *Anarchism or Socialism?* Moscow: Foreign Languages Pubg. Hse., 1952. Stalin's critique of anarchism.

1547. Stenstad, G. "Anarchic Thinking." *Hypatia* 3 (Summer 1988): 87-100. Explores the potential of anarchic thinking which denies the limitations of a single reality and therefore opens up a whole range of possibilities for theory and action.

1548. Sturber, D. L. *The Anarchist Constitution*. San Francisco: The Radical Pubg. Co., 1903. Dedicated to the prostitutes of America, as the greatest victims of injustice, the work sets out the main articles of a constitution for an anarchist society.

1549. Suskind, R. *By Bullet, Bomb, and Dagger: The Story of Anarchism*. New York: Macmillan, 1971. Looks at the history and philosophical roots of anarchism concentrating on its violent manifestations in France, Spain, Italy and the United States. Includes a detailed treatment of the Haymarket Affair.

1550. Tao, R. H. S. "Anarchy versus Authority: Towards a Democratic Theory of Law." *Archiv für Rechts und Sozialphilosphie* 63,3 (1977): 305-26. Points to the autocratic bias of traditional legal theory and its inability to provide an adequate theory of democracy. Argues, drawing on Hegel and Kelsen, that anarchism, with its vital affirmation of human freedom, presupposes a society organized along radically democratic lines.

1551. Tassi, A. "Anarchism, Autonomy and the Concept of the Common Good." *International Philosophical Quarterly* 17 (Summer 1977): 273-83. Suggests that the concept of autonomy has a necessary connection with the 'common good', but that the latter must be distinguished from the liberal concept of 'public good' with which autonomy has a different connection.

1552. Taylor, M. *Anarchy and Co-operation*. London: Wiley, 1976. Discusses the anarchist critique of state authority using mathematical models. Challenges the idea that the state is necessary and argues that its existence inhibits voluntary co-operation. See entry 1554.

1553. Taylor, M. *Community, Anarchy and Liberty*. Cambridge & New York: Cambridge Univ. Pr., 1982. An analysis of the political philosophy of anarchist approaches to liberty and equality. Discusses a stateless social order and its possible regulatory mechanisms including the market, using mathematical models. Concludes that communitarian ideals are not necessarily incompatible with individual liberty.

1554. Taylor, M. *The Possibility of Co-operation*. Cambridge & New York: Cambridge Univ. Pr., 1987. Revised edition of Taylor's *Anarchy and Co-operation*. A critique of the liberal theory of the state using game theory and mathematical models. More time is devoted to theories of collective action than in the earlier version. See entry 1552.

1555. Taylor, R. *Freedom, Anarchy and the Law*. Buffalo: Prometheus Bks., 1982. Intended as a text for undergraduate law and political philosophy students, it explores, from a libertarian perspective, the rationale for governments as coercive institutions.

1556. Tcherkesoff (Cherkezov), V. *Pages of Socialist History: Teaching and Acts of Social Democracy*. New York: C. B. Cooper, 1902. Part published as *Concentration of Capital: A Marxian Fallacy*, London: Freedom Pr., 1911. A collection of pieces, written originally for *Les Temps Nouveaux* and *Freedom*, making up a critical discussion of Marxism from an anarchist standpoint.

1557. Thackrah, J. R. *Encyclopedia of Terrorism and Political Violence.* London & New York: Routledge & Kegan Paul, 1987. References relate to ideas, theories and terms, as well as leading figures and victims. Only partially linked to anarchist theory and practice. Includes an index and select bibliography.

1558. Thomas, P. *Karl Marx and the Anarchists.* London & Boston: Routledge & Kegan Paul, 1980. A reasonably comprehensive analysis of Marx's disputes with the anarchists, focussing on Stirner, Proudhon and Bakunin. Key issues of disagreement are canvassed, and Marx's importance as a theoretician and revolutionary activist assessed.

1559. Tullock, G., ed. *Further Explorations in the Theory of Anarchy.* Blacksburg, Va.: Univ. Pubs., 1974. Contains four papers reflecting a range of attitudes towards contemporary anarchism, from mathematical approaches to sympathetic skepticism.

1560. Uyl, D. D. "Freedom and Virtue." *Reason Papers* (Winter 1979). Argues that coercion is incompatible with moral virtue, highlighting the political factors favouring a libertarian approach to human interaction.

1561. Uyl, D. D. "Government and Governed." *Reason Papers* (Fall 1975). Attempts to spell out what forms the organization of public power would take within a libertarian social structure.

1562. Vagts, A. "Intelligensia versus Reason of State." *Political Science Quarterly* 84,1 (1969): 80-105. Discusses the thought, and activities, of thinkers like Voltaire and Proudhon, as well as lesser known members of the European intelligentsia, who share a condemnation of the state as irrational and unethical.

1563. Van Dun, F. "Collective Action, Human Nature and the Possibility of Anarchy." *Philosophica* 21 (1978): 33-53. Essentially a critique of Michael Taylor's *Anarchy And Cooperation,* op. cit., entry 1552, making use of game theory to test the logic of collective action. Concludes that the argument against anarchy retains its force.

1564. Van Duyn, R. *Mesage of a Wise Kabouter.* Translated Hubert Hoskins. Foreword by Charles Bloomberg. London: Gerald Duckworth & Co., 1972. See entry 598.

1565. Venturi, F. *Roots of Revolution.* New York: Knopf, 1960. An account of the conspiracies and struggles associated with populism in nineteenth century Russia. Deals with the period 1848-81. Includes bibliographic notes and a chronological table.

1566. Vizetelly, E. A. *The Anarchists.* Reprint of 1911 edition. New York: Kraus Reprint, 1972. Chronicles 40 years of anarchist violence generally condemning it as perverted individualism. There is an attempt, however, to understand the social context of terrorist activities and thus the motivations underlying them.

1567. W. H. C. (sic) *Confessions of an Anarchist.* London: Grant Richards, 1911. A "confession" by a professed anarchist who claims to have seen the error of his ways. Claiming that anarchism is immoral and violent the author calls for the suppression of anarchist publications.

1568. Wakeman, J. *Anarchism and Democracy.* London: Freedom Pr., 1920. A polemical defense of anarchism that is stronger on rhetoric than argument.

1569. Walker, E. C. "Communism and Conscience." In *Individual Anarchist Pamphlets.* New York: Arno Pr., 1972. Originally published by Walker himself, New York: 1904, this pamphlet discusses the idea of equal rights and the responsibilities they imply. The more liberty one has, Walker argues, then the more responsibility. Communists and socialists are criticized for seeing problems in social rather than individual terms.

1570. Walter, N. *About Anarchism.* Reprinted Melbourne: Brickburner Pr., 1977, with a couple of very minor additions to the text. Originally published London: Freedom Pr., 1969. An introduction to the basic ideas, aims, and methods espoused by anarchists.

1571. Warner, C. "The Proprietary Theory of Justice in the Libertarian Tradition." *Journal of Libertarian Studies* 6, 3-4 (Summer-Fall 1982): 289-316. On the assumption that the proprietary theory of justice is the key to libertarian analysis, Warner sketches the theory and its roots in early doctrines of natural law, evaluating the contributions of Grotius, Locke, and Pufendorf, and tracing the possible implications of the theory for anarchism.

1572. Warner, S. D. "Anarchical Snares: A Reading of Locke's *Second Treatise.*" *Reason Papers* 14 (Spring 1989): 1-24. Noting that Locke argues on occasion that the doctrine of natural rights can lead to anarchism, Warner seeks to show that the theory of natural rights can co-exist with a case for the existence of government.

1573. Warriner, G. *Confessions of an Anarchist Disguised as a Poet.* Cirencester, U.K.: Warriner, 1987. A collection of poems published by the poet himself.

1574. Watner, C. "'Oh, Ye Are For Anarchy!' Consent Theory in the Radical Libertarian Tradition." *Journal of Libertarian Studies* 8,1 (1986): 111-37. An historical perspective on the anarchy versus limited government debate.

1575. Webster, N. H. *World Revolution: The Plot against Civilization.* 6th Edition. Revised, edited and brought up-to-date by Anthony Gittens. Devon: Britons Pub. Co., 1971. Traces and links the historical developments of socialism and anarchism, concluding with an exhortation to Britain to save herself and Christian civilization from the menace they represent.

1576. Weisbord, A. *The Conquest of Power: Liberalism, Anarchism, Syndicalism, Socialism, Fascism, and Communism.* 2 vols. London: Secker & Warburg, 1938. Presents, from a Marxist perspective, an exposition and critique of major political traditions. The section on anarchism, in the first volume, depicts it as negative and futile.

1577. Weiss, T. G. "The Tradition of Philosophical Anarchism and Future Directions in World Policy." *Journal of Peace Research* 12,1 (1975): 1-17. Surveys the literature of philosophical anarchism and argues that it has heuristic value, both for the clarification of global values and for the resolution of global problems.

1578. Wheeler, C. J. "Justice and Anarchy." *Personalist* 52,2 (Spring 1971): 393-400. Sets out the weaknesses in the concept of free market anarchism. See entries 1352, 1379, 1512.

1579. White, J. R. *The Meaning of Anarchism.* Introduction by Albert Meltzer. Sanday, Orkney: Cienfuegos Pr., 1980. A very brief pamphlet which looks at the anarchist position on political power with particular reference to the Spanish situation.

1580. White, J. D. "Despotism and Anarchy: The Sociological Thought of L.I. Mechnikov." *Slavonic and East European Review* 54,3 (1976): 395-411. Locates Mechnikov, a little studied social theorist, within the tradition of nineteenth century Russian political thought. There are similarities with Kropotkin in his ideas regarding the importance of collective action.

1581. Wilde, O. *The Soul of Man under Socialism.* Preface by Robert Ross. London: A. L. Humphreys, 1912. Criticizes the institutions of government and private property from an individualist anarchist perspective. Condemns altruism for perpetuating rather than eliminating poverty, and proposes a solution in the form of libertarian, as opposed to authoritarian, socialism.

1582. Winterer, L. *The Social Danger: Or, Two Years of Socialism in Europe and America.* Translation of *Le Socialisme Contemporain,* Paris: 1894, by Rev. J. P. Roles. Chicago & New York: Belford, Clarke & Co, 1886. A study that looks at the history and theory of anarchism and the character of anarchist movements in European countries, Russia and America. The negative approach is characterized by L'Abbé Winterer's assertion that just as Christian literature endorses virtue, so anarchist literature endorses crime.

1583. Wittfogel, K. A. "Marxism, Anarchism and the New Left." *Modern Age* 14,2 (Spring 1970): 114-28. Concludes that the efforts of the New Left to discredit Western liberal democracies benefit the authoritarian communist regimes of which they are supposed to be equally critical.

1584. Woodcock, G., ed. *The Anarchist Reader*. London: Fontana, 1977. A useful collection of readings covering a wide range of anarchist thought. Includes pieces by Read, Faure, Bookchin, Ward and Goodman, as well as contributions from the classic thinkers.

1585. Woodcock, G. "Anarchist Phases and Personalities." *Queen's Quarterly* 87,1 (1980): 82-96. A review of ten of the books on anarchism which appeared during the late seventies.

1586. Wooden Shoe. *Anarchy in the Film*. London: The Wooden Shoe, 1967. Originally published as the sixth edition of the journal *Anarchy*, this is a collection of short essays on anarchism and the cinema.

1587. Woodworth, F. *Anarchism*. Tucson, Ariz.: The Match! Pamphlet Series, 1974. A discussion of the meaning of anarchism and of the workings of a stateless society in the form of a catechism. The essay first appeared in *The Match!* a monthly anarchist journal edited by Woodworth, 9-11 (Sept.-Nov. 1973).

1588. Yarros, V. *Anarchism: Its Aims and Methods*. Boston: Benjamin R. Tucker, 1887. Argues that, while the final goal is the abolition of the state, the policy of anarchists must be to win the confidence of people and persuade them, through education, to reject state authority. Thus, anarchism does not necessarily mean violence.

1589. Zerzan, J. and Carnes, A. *Questioning Technology: A Critical Anthology*. London: Freedom Pr., 1988. Argues that those who reject the tyranny of persons often overlook the dominating potential of technology because it is viewed as objective and value-free. Concludes that human judgement must be used to control technology and decide on its appropriate use in pursuit of human liberty.

The Anarchist Experience

ARGENTINA

1590. Bayer, O. *Anarchism and Violence: Severino Di Giovanni in Argentina, 1923-1931.* Introduction by Alfredo M. Bonnano and Jean Weir. Translated Paul Sharkey. Catania: Elephant Eds., 1986. An attempt to reconstruct the violent revolutionary activities of the Italian anarchist Severino Di Giovanni in Argentina in the 1920s.

1591. Colombo, E. "Anarchism in Argentina and Uruguay," in *Anarchism Today,* 181-211. Op.cit., entry 1302. An overview of the origins and development of the anarchist movements in Argentina and Uruguay.

1592. Jordan, D. C. "Authoritarianism and Anarchy in Argentina." *Current History* 68,401 (1975): 1-4. Offers an analysis of the Peronist legacy in Argentina and concludes that, as extreme left wing activities will inevitably provoke right wing extremists to repressive actions, moderation is the key to a politically stable future.

1593. Molneux, M. "No God, No Boss, No Husband: Anarchist Feminism in Nineteenth Century Argentina." *Latin American Perspectives* 13,1 (1986): 119-45. Based on an analysis of the Argentinean anarchist-feminist journal *La Voz de la Mujer* published during the period 1896-97.

1594. Quesada, F. *Argentine Anarchism and "La Protesta."* Translated by Scott Johnson. New York: Gordon Pr., 1978. Documents the thirty five most vital years of the long running newspaper *La Protesta*, which began in 1897 and has remained the representative newspaper of the anarchist community.

1595. Thompson, R. "The Limitations of Ideology in the Early Argentine Labor Movement: Anarchism in the Trade Unions, 1890-1920." *Journal of Latin American Studies* 16,1 (1984). Argues that strikes and other industrial action arose in the course of improving working conditions rather than for ideological reasons. Anarchist strength varied from region to region and anarchists were not always true to their theories. The importance of anarchist ideology for the Argentine labor movement has been greatly exaggerated by historians.

AUSTRALIA

1596. Anderson, J. *Art and Reality: John Anderson on Literature and Aesthetics.* Edited Janet Anderson, Graham Cullum and Kimon Lycos. Sydney: Hale & Iremonger, 1982. A representative collection of Anderson's writings on art and culture.

1597. Anderson, J. *Studies in Empirical Philosophy.* Sydney: Angus & Robertson, 1962. A commemorative collection of philosophical essays by Australia's foremost exponent of libertarian ideas.

1598. Andrews, J. A. *The Handbook of Anarchy.* Edited Bob James. Melbourne: Libertarian Resources, 1986. A collection of writings by a nineteenth century anarchist, 1865-1903.

1599. Baker, A. J. *Anderson's Social Philosophy: The Social and Political Life of Professor John Anderson.* Sydney: Angus & Robertson, 1979. A short biographical study of libertarian philosopher John Anderson and his ideas and influence on intellectual affairs.

1600. Baker, A. J., ed. *The Sydney Line: A Selection of Comments and Criticisms by Sydney Libertarians.* Sydney: L. R. Hiatt, 1963. A selection of articles from the late 1950's and early 1960's reprinted from the Libertarian Society's Broadsheet. A brief introduction outlines the historical background.

1601. Burgmann, V. "One Hundred Years of Anarchism." *Arena* 74 (1986): 104-14. Surveys the formative years of the Melbourne Anarchist Club and discusses the role of three of its leading protagonists, J. W. Fleming, J. A. Andrews, and David Andrade.

1602. Cresciani, G. "The Proletarian Migrants: Fascism and Italian Anarchists in Australia." *Australian Quarterly* 51,1 (1979): 4-19. Argues that although the anarchist movement was numerically very small, it was historically significant. Offers an assessment of their motives, activities and influence.

1603. James, B. "John William Fleming." In *Australian Dictionary of Biography.* Vol. 8, edited by B. Nairn and G. Serle, 521-22. Melbourne: Melbourne Univ. Pr., 1966-86. Gives a brief summary of the life of this Irish immigrant bootmaker who became an anarchist agitator, a member of the Melbourne Anarchist Club and a friend of J. A. Andrews. Includes short bibliography.

1604. James, B. "Latter-Day Witches. Anarchists in Australia." *The Raven* 1,1 (1986): 69-76. Discusses the formation of the Melbourne Anarchist Club three days before the Haymarket incident in 1886, and the stigma thereafter attached to the movement.

1605. James, B., ed. *A Reader of Australian Anarchism, 1886-1896*. A.C.T.: Pialligo, 1979. A collection of writings by nineteenth century Australian anarchists including D. A. Andrade, W. R. Winspear and J. A. Andrews, with an introductory essay and brief biographical comments on each of the contributors by the editor.

1606. James, B., ed. *What Is Communism? And other Anarchist Essays by J. A. Andrews*. Prahran, Vic.: Backyard Pr., 1985. Collection of writings and speeches of the nineteenth century anarchist J. A. Andrews.

1607. Libertarian Socialist Organization, Queensland. *You Can't Blow Up a Social Relationship: The Anarchist Case against Terrorism*. Brisbane, Qld.: Libertarian Socialist Organization, 1978? This pamphlet cites numerous Australian and international examples which demonstrate that terrorist activities are more generally carried out by the right than the left. Exploring the idea of state terrorism and police frame-ups, it concludes by condemning violence as an authoritarian threat to humanism.

1608. Nursey-Bray, P. F. "Francesco Fantin: Internment and Anti-Fascism in Australia." *Studi Emigrazione (Rome)* 26,94 (June 1989): 195-220. An account of the internment of an anarchist labor organizer in 1942, his death at the hands of fascists in the internment camp, and the subsequent investigation, trial and scandal.

1609. Reeves, A. "David and Charles Andrade." In *Australian Dictionary of Biography*. Vol. 7, 64-5. Op.cit., entry 1603. A brief summary of the lives of these two brothers who were anarchists and booksellers. David Andrade was instrumental in the formation of the Melbourne Anarchist Club. Includes a short but useful bibliography.

1610. Reeves, A. "J. A. Andrews." In *Australian Dictionary of Biography*. Vol. 7, 69-70. Op.cit., entry 1603. A brief summary of the Australian anarchist journalist and theoretician whose ideas were mainly derived from Kropotkin. Includes a very short but useful bibliography.

BRAZIL

1611. Dulles, J. W. F. *Anarchists and Communists in Brazil, 1900-1935*. Austin: Univ. of Texas Pr., 1973. A thorough-going examination of the formation and activities of the Brazilian Left in relation to national politics and the emerging labor movement. Includes glossary, index and appendices on prices, wages and strikes.

1612. Maram, S. L. "Labor and the Left in Brazil, 1890-1921: A Movement Aborted." *Hispanic American Historical Review* 57,2 (1977): 254-73. Suggests that the failure of the anarchist movement in Brazil stemmed more from its lack of internal organization and discord than from the repressive measures taken against anarchists. Assesses the role of immigrants in the formation of the labor movement.

CHINA

1613. Ames, R. T. "Is Political Taoism Anarchism?" *Journal of Chinese Philosophy* 10 (March 1983): 27-48. A comparative study of anarchism and Taoism.

1614. Bernal, M. "The Triumph of Anarchism over Marxism." In *China in Revolution*, edited M. C. Wright, 97-142. Stanford, Calif.: Stanford Univ. Pr., 1968. Discusses the origins of radical social movements in China focussing on the way in which the socialist movement was converted to anarchism.

1615. Clark, J. P. "On Taoism and Politics." *Journal of Chinese Philosophy* 10 (March 1983): 65-88. Argues that Taoist thought is one of the earliest expressions of an organic, ecological anarchism in which a society based on co-operative self realization is the aim.

1616. Clifford, P. "The *New Century (Xinshiji*) Magazine and the Introduction of Anarchism to China." *Wiener Bietrage zur Gesch. Der Neuzeit (Austria)* 7 (1980): 174-90. Looks at the history of the *Xinshiji* and its influence on political life in early Republican China.

1617. Dirlik, A. "The New Culture Movement Revisited: Anarchism and the Idea of Social Revolution in New Culture Thinking." *Modern China* 11,3 (1985): 251-301. Considers an area of anarchist influence largely neglected by historians. Concludes that the most significant impact made by the anarchists in China was the radicalization of the discourse on social alternatives and objectives.

1618. Dirlik, A. and Krebs, E. S. "Socialism and Anarchism in Early Republican China." *Modern China* 7,2 (1981): 117-53. A careful analysis of the differences between socialism and anarchism in early Republican China, which suggests that anarchist ideas dominated revolutionary thought before 1919.

1619. Dirlik, A. *The Origins of Chinese Communism.* Oxford: Oxford Univ. Pr., 1989. Argues that the anarchist influence on the revolutionary movement in China was strong before 1920, forming a point of resistance to the idea of centralized party rule. Marxist-Leninism, it is suggested, gained

strength largely as a response to immediate organizational neec
than because it was ideologically dominant.

1620. Dirlik, A. "The Path Not Taken: The Anarchist Alternative in Chinese
Socialism, 1921-1927." *International Review of Social History* 34,1 (1989): 1-
41. Discusses the Chinese anarchist movement, its criticism of Bolshevism
and the strategy and activities of the anarchist movement in the period in
question.

1621. Dirlik, A. "The Revolution that Never Was: Anarchism in the
Guomindang." *Modern China* 15,4 (1989): 419-62. Argues that the
controversial participation of anarchist leaders in Chiang Kai-shek's
Nationalist Party in 1927-8 weakened the movement and made its
suppression in 1929 that much easier.

1622. Dirlik, A. "Vision and Revolution: Anarchism in Chinese
Revolutionary Thought on the Eve of the 1911 Revolution." *Modern China*
12,2 (1986): 123-65. Describes the contribution of two Chinese anarchist
societies - one in Paris and one in Tokyo - in the reorientation of
revolutionary goals from the political to the cultural.

1623. Gaaster, M. "The Anarchists." In *Chinese Intellectuals and the
Revolution of 1911*. Washington: Univ. of Washington Pr., 1969. A
discussion of the ideas of Chang Ping-lin, Wu Chih-hui and Liu Shih-p'ei.

1624. Hall, D. L. "The Metaphysics of Anarchism." *Journal of Chinese
Philosophy* 10 (March 1983): 49-64. Argues for an important philosophical
link between Taoism and anarchism.

1625. "Internationalist." *The Origins of the Anarchist Movement in China*.
Foreword by Stuart Christie. London: Coptic Pr., 1968. A pioneer work,
much of its content drawn from contacts with Chinese workers and sailors.
Lacking in historical details, it conveys successfully the spirit of the
anarchist movement.

1626. Lang, O. *Pa Chin and His Writings*. Harvard: Harvard Univ. Pr., 1967.
A political and literary biography of the anarchist novelist who came under
attack during the Cultural Revolution.

1627. Muñoz, V. *Li Pei Kan and Chinese Anarchism*. New York: Revisionist
Pr., 1976.

1628. Pickowicz, P. G. "The Chinese Anarchist Critique of Marxist-
Leninism." *Modern China* 16,4 (Oct. 1990): 450-67. A favorable review of
Dirlik's *The Origins of Chinese Communism*, op.cit., entry 1613. The book
was written and released before the events of June 1989, while the review
was written in the aftermath. The review reflects on the incisiveness of
Dirlik's analysis, and on the anarchist critique of Marxism and the state in
general, both of which are seen as vindicated by the Tienmin Square
massacre.

1629. Scalapino, R. A. and Yu, G. T. *The Chinese Anarchist Movement.* Westport, Conn.: Greenwood Pr., 1980. Credits anarchism with important contributions to the Chinese communist movement, concluding that it was both its "antithesis and its logical predecessor."

1630. Zarrow, P. *Anarchism and Chinese Political Culture.* New York: Columbia Univ. Pr., 1990. Concentrating on anarchist influences in the twentieth century, there is a detailed discussion of anarchism and Chinese political culture including the anarchist influences on the Chinese Revolution and on women's liberation. Includes a select bibliography.

1631. Zhelokhovtsev, A. "Ba Jin: Writer and Patriot." *Far Eastern Affairs* 1 (1984): 120-32. Biographical sketch of a Chinese novelist and translator who was much influenced by the ideas of Bakunin and Kropotkin. Ba Jin is a pseudonym comprising the first syllable of Bakunin and the last of Kropotkin.

CUBA

1632. Dolgoff, S. *The Cuban Revolution: A Critical Perspective.* Montréal: Black Rose Bks., 1977. Examines Castro's regime from an anarchist perspective, detailing the close connection between the Cuban labor and socialist movements and Spanish anarcho-syndicalism.

1633. Ramm, H. "Che Guevara: Leninist or Anarchist." *Social Praxis* 3,3-4 (1975): 261-72. See entry 1502.

FRANCE

1634. Carr, R. P. *Anarchism in France: The Case of Octave Mirbeau.* Montréal: McGill-Queens Univ. Pr., 1977. Examines, in the context of nineteenth century France, the connections between anarchism and literature.

1635. Gombin, R. "The Ideology and Practice of Contestation Seen through Recent Events in France." *Government and Opposition* 5,4 (1970): 410-29. Examines the libertarian trend in the events of May 1968. Reprinted in *Anarchism Today*, 14-33. Op.cit., entry 1302.

1636. Halperin, J. U. *Félix Fénéon: Aesthete and Anarchist in Fin de Siècle Paris.* New Haven, Conn.: Yale Univ. Pr., 1988. A life of Félix Fénéon, who, from the mid-1880s, was intimately involved in three great movements for artistic and social change: symbolist literature, post-impressionist art and anarchist agitation for workers' rights. The study treats the three fields under separate headings.

1637. Longoni, J. C. *Four Patients of Dr. Deibler: A Study in Anarchy.* London: Lawrence & Wishart, 1970. Details the lives and deaths of four anarchists who were executed in France for terrorist activities between 1892 and 1894. Uses primary sources and contemporary reports.

1638. Miller, O. J. "Anarchism and French Catholicism in *Ésprit.*" *Journal of the History of Ideas* 37,1 (1976): 163-74. Considers anarchist ideas in relation to the Catholic orientation of the journal, arguing that the anarchist element has been much underrated in the past. Credits *Ésprit* with a readiness to facilitate dialogue between ideas.

1639. Parry, R. *The Bonnot Gang.* London: Rebel Pr., 1987. An account of a group of anarchists, who, inspired by Stirner, took to "illegalism" as a form of protest in the years before 1914. The so-called Bonnot Gang, named after Jules Bonnot, was responsible for an armed robbery from the *Société Genérale*, the largest of the Parisian banks.

1640. Sonn, R. D. *Anarchism and Cultural Politics in Fin de Siècle France.* Lincoln, Neb. & London: Univ. of Nebraska Pr., 1989. A discussion of anarchist politics and culture in France, in particular Paris, in the 1890s, looking not just at the politics of violence, but also at the anarchist press, libraries, schools, and even the anarchist cabaret.

1641. Sonn, R. D. "Language, Crime and Class: The Popular Culture of French Anarchism in the 1890s." *Historical Reflections* 11,3 (1984): 351-72. Looks at the influence of the argot of marginalized groups in France, for instance criminals, on anarchist language usage.

1642. Stafford, D. *From Anarchism to Reformism: A Study of the Political Activities of Paul Brousse within the First International and the French Socialist Movement.* London: Weidenfeld & Nicolson, 1971. Aims to redress the alleged bias of Marxist historiography which has led to an unjustifiable neglect of Brousse's political career. Argues that Brousse's "possibilism" suggests one direction in which anarchism today might develop, advocating, as it does, the abandoning of utopian intransigence and direct action, but the retention of practical and constructive theories of local community organization. Bibliography and index.

GERMANY

1643. Aust, S. *The Baader-Meinhof Group: The Inside Story of a Phenomenon.* London: Bodley Head, 1987. A detailed history of the activities of the Baader-Meinhof group, later called the Red Army Faction. Illustrations, portraits and plates.

1644. Becker, J. *Hitler's Children: The Story of the Baader-Meinhof Terrorist Gang.* Philadelphia: Lippincott, c. 1977. A journalistic account of the Baader-Meinhoff group and their activities as urban guerillas. Attempts to show a direct link between Nazi ideology and the ideas informing the actions of the Baader-Meinhoff, and by implication, other left-wing groups.

1645. Carlson, A. R. *Anarchism in Germany*. Metuchen, N.J.: Scarecrow Pr., 1972. The first in a proposed two volume set aimed at covering the period 1830-1933. This volume covers 1830-1889 with special emphasis on the later period. Suggests that the prime significance of anarchism in this period was in the repressive measures it provoked. Includes bibliography and index.

1646. Horchem, H. J. *West Germany's Red Army Anarchists*. London: Institute for the Study of Conflict, 1974. Details the activities of the Baader-Meinhof Gang from the point of view of Germany's Security Service. Equates anarchism with terrorism and concludes that violent anarchism will not die out while people are still prepared to accept ideological solutions to social conflicts.

1647. Sun, R. "Misguided Martyrdom: German Social Democratic Response to the Haymarket Incident, 1886-87." *International Labor and Working-Class History* 29 (1986): 56-67. Discusses the way in which the German Social Democrats, while expressing solidarity with the Chicago anarchists and condemning the official handling of the incident, did not extend their support to the anarchist movement as a whole.

INDIA

Only a representative selection of work on Gandhi is given.

1648. Bandyopadhyaya, J. *The Social and Political Thought of Gandhi*. Bombay: Allied Pubs., 1969. A general discussion of the social and political aspects of *Satyagraha*. Chapter VI, "State and Government," examines the relationship of his thought to anarchism.

1649. Bondurant, J. V. *Conquest of Violence: The Gandhian Philosophy of Conflict*. Princeton, N.J.: Princeton Univ. Pr., 1958. A classic study of Gandhi's political philosophy of *Satyagraha*. A comprehensive work with a useful bibliography.

1650. Doctor, A. H. *Anarchist Thought in India*. Bombay: Asia Publishing Hse, 1964. Seeks to locate modern anarchist thought within Indian philosophy and concludes that an anarchist element was introduced by Gandhi's ideas. Suggests that Gandhian anarchism would, in fact, achieve the opposite of its aims.

1651. Fischer, L. *The Life of Mahatma Gandhi*. London: Jonathan Cape, 1951. A biographical study with some discussion of Gandhi's important ideas.

1652. Gandhi, M. K. *An Autobiography or the Story of My Experiments with Truth*. Harmondsworth: Penguin, 1982. A work describing the practical application of his beliefs which would lead, Gandhi believed, to a loose federation of village republics.

1653. Gandhi, M. K. *The Constructive Programme: Its Meaning and Place.* Ahmedabad: Navajiva, 1945. A discussion of the programme for the reconstruction of the Indian social order as one of free decentralized village communities. It details 18 items of social activity, including the building of communal unity, the development of village industries, adoption of craft-based education, outlawing of untouchability, and the improvement of the condition of women. All of this was to be achieved on the basis of Truth and Non-Violence.

1654. Gandhi, M. K. *The Essential Gandhi.* Edited Louis Fischer. New York: Vintage Bks., 1973. Extracts from a wide range of Gandhi's writings, arranged chronologically, which covers his basic principles and methodology and some of the principal political struggles.

1655. Gandhi, M. K. *Selected Writings.* Edited Ronald Duncan. A selection which attempts to show the development of Gandhi's philosophy, especially of those ideas which are relevant to Western philosophy.

1656. Green, M. *Tolstoy and Gandhi.* New York: Basic Bks., 1983. A comparative study of the lives and ideas of the two men that uses a direct juxtaposition of the key stages of their lives as the basis for discussion.

1657. Joll, J. "Anarchism in Action". *Government and Opposition* 8,1 (1973): 115-23. A review of Geoffrey Ostergaard and Melville Currell, *The Gentle Anarchists: A Study of the Leaders of the Sarvodaya Movement for Non-Violent Revolution in India,* op. cit., entry 1658.

1658. Ostergaard, G. C. *The Gentle Anarchists: A Study of the Leaders of the Sarvodaya, a Movement for Non-Violent Revolution in India.* Oxford: Clarendon Pr., 1971. An account of the history, ideology and activities of the Sarvodaya movement, Sarvodaya meaning a social commitment to the welfare of all. Drawing inspiration from Gandhi's Constructive Programme of the 1930s, the Sarvodaya movement of the 1960s shared many common features with anarchism; a belief in direct action, in the need to build from below, from the people; a belief in the need for decentralization, especially economic; a belief in the need to remove the state and create a free society. It remained, of course, committed to non-violent methods. Part of the early chapters published in *Anarchism Today,* 145-63. Op.cit., entry 1302.

1659. Ostergaard, G. "Indian Anarchism: The Curious Case of Vinoba Bhave." In *For Anarchism: History, Theory and Practice,* 201-16. Op.cit., entry 1385. Looks at the Indian anarchism in the shape of the Sarvodaya movement. Inspired by Gandhi and carried on by Vinoba Bhave and Jayaprkash Naraya until their deaths respectively in 1982 and 1979.

1660. Richards, G. *The Philosophy of Gandhi: A Study of His Basic Ideas.* London: Curzon Pr., 1982. An examination of Gandhi's philosophy, arguing that Hindu beliefs provide its foundation. The work examines Gandhi's concept of truth, explores the moral, social and economic consequences of

Gandhi's teaching and offers some brief comparisons with the ideas of Paul Tillich and E. F. Schumacher.

1661. Tahtinen, U. *The Core of Gandhi's Philosophy.* New Delhi: Havzlchas, 1979. Provides an interpretation of Gandhi's ideas in terms of Western moral philosophy with some attention being paid to the issue of violence versus non-violence.

ISRAEL

1662. Cohen, J. E. *Anarchism and Libertarian Socialism in Israel: A Study of Anti-Statist Movements.* New York: Buber Pr., 1975.

ITALY

1663. Bayer, O. *Anarchism and Violence: Severino Di Giovanni in Argentina 1923-31.* Introduction by Alfred M. Bonnano and Jean Weir. Translated Paul Sharkey. Catania: Elephant Eds., 1986. See entry 1595.

1664. Bertrand, C. L. "The Bienno-Russo: Anarchists and Revolutionary Syndicalists in Italy 1919-1920." *Historical Reflections* 9,2 (1982): pp. 382-402. Argues that infighting between anarchists and reformists led to the eventual defeat of the Italian workers in 1921.

1665. Bertrand, C. L. "Italian Revolutionary Syndicalism and the Crisis of Intervention: Aug.-Dec. 1914." *Canadian Journal of History* 10,3 (1975): 349-67. Highlights the paradox wherein heightened class consciousness at the time of the Intervention Crisis could not be effectively mobilized because of severe ideological divisions within the Unione Sindacale Italiana.

1666. Levy, C. "Italian Anarchism, 1970-1926." In *For Anarchism: History, Theory and Practice* 25-78. Op.cit., entry 1385. A broad discussion of Italian anarchism during its formative period.

1667. Pick, D. "The Faces of Anarchy: Lombrosa and the Politics of Criminal Science in Post-Unification Italy." *History Workshop Journal* 21 (Spring 1986): 60-81. Argues that Lombrosa's work successfully integrated numerous factors in the production of a coherent theory explaining the position of Italy in the latter part of the nineteenth century.

1668. Ravindranathan, T. R. *Bakunin and the Italians.* Kingston/Montréal: McGill-Queen's Univ. Pr., 1988. A detailed historical discussion of the important influence of Bakunin, focussing on the development of Italian anarchism in the 1860s and 1870s.

1669. Valpreda, P. *The Valpreda Papers.* Translated from the Italian by Cormac O Cuillean; with an introduction by Gaia Servadio. London: Gollancz, 1975. Written while the author was detained without trial for over two years, this is the diary of an Italian anarchist ballet dancer who was charged over a bombing incident despite inadequate evidence. A very useful introduction puts this infamous case in its political context and draws parallels with the Dreyfus affair in France

JAPAN

1670. Badinoff, B. and Ozeki, H. "Anarchism in Japan." *Anarchy* 1,5 (1972): 2-7/24-30. The first part provides a detailed coverage of the pre-war labor movement, including the struggle with the communists; the second surveys contemporary attitudes and activities of anarchist groups.

1671. Bernal, M. "The Triumph of Anarchism over Marxism, 1906 - 1907." In *China in Revolution*, edited M. C. Wright, 97-142. Stanford, Calif.: Stanford Univ. Pr., 1968. Although the main focus is on the Chinese anarchist movement, there is some discussion of the activities of Chinese anarchists in Japan and the relationship between the Japanese and Chinese movements.

1672. Billingsley, P. *The Japanese Anarchists*. Brighton: Smoothie Pubns., 1974. Produced by the Leeds Anarchist Group as Direct Action Pamphlet No. 4 in the late sixties. A very brief pamphlet outlining the progress of anarchism and syndicalism in Japan with references to Kotoku Shusui and Osugi Sakae.

1673. Large, S. S. "The Romance of Revolution in Japanese Anarchism and Communism during the Taisho Period." *Modern Asian Studies* 11,3 (1977): 441-67. Examines the tradition of the Left through two of the leading figures of the period, Osugi Sakae (1895-1923) and Watenabe Masanosuke (1859-1928), focussing on the establishment of links between individualism and collectivism.

1674. Notehelfer, F. G. *Kotoku Shusui: Portrait of a Japanese Radical*. Cambridge: Cambridge Univ. Pr., 1971. An opponent of militarism and nationalism Kotoku Shusui was executed for high treason in 1911. He was a leader of the early Japanese Socialist movement and became a symbol of protest. The work argues that anarchism in Japan developed through a cultural transformation of the samurai ethic under the pressure of the political changes post 1868. Includes bibliography, glossary and index.

1675. Stanley, T. A. *Osugi Sakae, Anarchist in Taish-0 Japan: The Creativity of the Ego*. Cambridge, Mass.: Council of East Asian Studies, Harvard University. Distributed by Harvard Univ. Pr., 1981. Primarily a biography of Japan's most important anarchist, which concentrates on psychological motivations rather than Sakae's political ideas. Some attention is paid, however, to his influence within the growing anarchist-socialist tradition in Japan.

1676. Taurumi, E. P. "Feminism and Anarchism in Japan: Takamure Itsue 1894-1964." *Bulletin of Concerned Asian Scholars* 17,2 (1985): 2-19. Argues that the only political philosophy which fully accommodates the needs of women is anarchism.

1677. Tsuzuki, C. "Anarchism in Japan." *Government and Opposition* 5,4 (1970): 501-22. Looks at anarchism predominantly as an intellectual movement, examining its influence on the student upheavals in Japan in the 1960s. Concludes that it was not anarchism as such but the emotional appeal of nihilism which sustained the student radicals. Reprinted in *Anarchism Today*, 105-26. Op.cit., entry 1302.

1678. Tsuzuki, C. "Kotoko, Osugi and Japanese Anarchism." *Hototsubashi Journal of Social Studies* (March 1966). Discusses the lives and ideas of Kotoko and Osugi in the context of the history of the anarchist movement. Argues that anarchism in Japan grew out of traditional Eastern nihilism.

KOREA

1679. Chong-sik Lee. *The Politics of Korean Nationalism*. Los Angeles: Univ. of Calif. Pr., 1963. There is a limited discussion of Korean anarchism, in chapters 9-11, in the context of the anti-Japanese struggle from the late 19th century to 1945.

1680. Ha Ki-Rak. *A History of the Korean Anarchist Movement*. Taegu, Kor.: Anarchist Pubs. 1986. A history of anarchism in Korea focussing on its origins and its role during the Japanese occupation and in the immediate post war period.

1681. Nym Wales and Kim San. *Song of Ariran, A Korean Communist in the Chinese Revolution*. New York: Ramparts Pr., 1972. A first-hand account of the career of a Korean revolutionary with some discussion of his terrorist anarchist phase.

1682. Scalapino, R. and Chong-sik Lee. *Communism in Korea*. 2 vols. Los Angeles: Univ. of Calif. Pr., 1972. A very detailed study of the origin of radical movements in Korea that contains some information on anarchism dispersed through the whole. Useful for background information.

MEXICO

1683. Avrich, P. "Prison Letters of Ricardo Flores Magon to Lilly Sarnoff." *International Review of Social History* 22,3 (1977): 279-422. While in Leavenworth prison, between 1920 and 1922, Magon wrote 42 letters to Sarnoff in which he described the horrors of prison life and discussed some of the major issues of the day, such as the Russian Revolution.

1684. Coy, P. E. B. "Social Anarchism: An Atavistic Ideology of the Peasant." *Journal of Inter-American Studies and World Affairs* 14,2 (1972): 133-49. See entry 1351.

1685. Hart, J. M. *Anarchism and the Mexican Working Class, 1860-1931.* Austin: Univ. of Texas Pr., 1978. Assesses the role of anarchism and its impact on both urban and rural movements in Mexico in the period 1860-1931. Discusses its eventual decline. Includes index and bibliography.

1686. MacLachlan, C. M. *Anarchism and the Mexican Revolution: The Political Trials of Ricardo Flores Magon in the United States.* Berkeley: Univ.of California Pr., 1991.

1687. Magon, R. F. *Mexico: Land and Liberty.* Montréal: Black Rose Bks., 1977. Essays by the famous activist and theorist of the Mexican Revolution.

1688. Poole, D. Compiled and introduced. *Land and Liberty: Anarchist Influences in the Mexican Revolution.* Montréal: Black Rose Bks., 1977. A collection of articles first published in the journal *Regeneration* by Ricardo Flores Magon, William C. Owen and Antonio de P. Aranjo. Includes a detailed introductory essay on Magon and an historical outline of the revolution. Chronology and annotated bibliography.

NETHERLANDS

1689. De Jong, R. "Provos and Kabouters," in *Anarchism Today*, 164-80. Op.cit., 1302. London: Macmillan, 1971. A discussion of contemporary Dutch anarchism.

1690. Van Duyn, R. *Message of a Wise Kabouter.* Translated by Hubert Hoskins. Foreword by Charles Bloomberg. London: Gerald Duckworth & Co., 1972. See entry 598.

RUSSIA

1691. Arshinov, P. *History of the Makhnovist Movement, 1918-1921.* Preface by Nicolas Walter. London: Freedom Pr., 1987. Translation of Arshinov's history of the anarchist army in the Ukraine, including a discussion of politics, military tactics and key figures.

1692. Avrich, P. "Anarchism and Anti-Intellectualism in Russia." *Journal of the History of Ideas* 27,3 (July-Sept. 1966): 381-90. Describes a deep seated distrust of intellectuals in Russian anarchism in the early twentieth century which is ascribed to the influences of Bakunin, Marxism and French syndicalism.

1693. Avrich, P., ed. *The Anarchists in the Russian Revolution.* With 44 illustrations. London: Thames and Hudson, 1973. A selection of speeches, manifestos, letters, posters, songs etc. of the anarchists with introductory and linking commentaries by the editor. It is a very useful compilation of primary source documents.

1694. Avrich, P. *Kronstadt 1921*. Princeton, N.J.: Princeton Univ. Pr., 1970. Regarded by many as one of the best studies of the Kronstadt revolt. Provides a detailed picture of the Kronstadt programme, the involvement of the anarchists and the relationship of events to general discontent within the Bolshevik party. Includes annotated bibliography and index.

1695. Avrich, P. *The Russian Anarchists*. New York: Norton, 1978. Well researched history of the ideas, programmes and contributions of the anarchist movement in the Russian Revolution, tracing its emergence at the end of the 19th century to its demise post 1917.

1696. Brinton, M. *The Bolsheviks and Workers' Control 1917-1921: The State and Counter-revolution*. London: Solidarity, 1970. An analysis of the fate of the Russian Revolution intended as a yardstick for the evaluation of contemporary debates over workers' control and self-management.

1697. Ciliga, A. *The Kronstadt Revolt*. London: Freedom Pr., 1942. Discusses the Kronstadt Revolt to point up the ways in which the mechanism of social revolution can be distorted and fall prey to counter-revolution.

1698. Ciliga, A. *The Russian Enigma*. Translated F. C. Renier & A. Cliff. A critical but balanced appreciation of the Russian experience, based on extensive travel in the country over a period of ten years, plus a stay in a Russian prison. Commended by anarchists as giving an accurate picture.

1699. D'Agostino, A. *Marxism and the Russian Anarchists*. San Francisco: Germinal Pr., 1977. An analysis of the serious disagreements between Marxism and anarchism which goes on to suggest that the Bolshevik Revolution presented anarchists with an insoluble dilemma: to accept the need for an organized seizure of power and therefore cease to be anarchists, or to reject the demand and remain impotent.

1700. Daniels, R. V. "The Kronstadt Revolt of 1921: A Study in the Dynamics of Revolution." *American Slavic and East European Review* 10 (Dec. 1951): 239-54. Suggests that an analysis of the Kronstadt revolt sheds valuable light both on the conditions which facilitated the emergence of Stalin, and on trends within the contemporary Soviet regime.

1701. Durant, W. *The Lesson of Russia*. London: G. P. Putnam & Sons, 1933. Records the disillusionment of a radical individualist who journeyed to Russia with high hopes and returned bitterly denouncing the despotism and authoritarian destruction of freedom that he had witnessed.

1702. Footman, D. *Civil War in Russia*. London: Faber & Faber, 1961. Includes a chapter on Makhno.

1703. Footman, D. "Nestor Makhno and the Russian Civil War." *History Today* 6,12 (1956): 811-20. Emphasizes the importance of the role of Makhno as an individual in his fight against both White and Red Russians. Notes the importance of his attempt to put anarchist principles into practice when others, such as the Moscow Anarchists, had been cowed into mere rhetoric.

1704. Harrison, F. "The Soviet Response To Anarchism." *Our Generation* 13,1 (1979): 35-50. Looks at the Marxist-Leninist response to the perceived threat of anarchism and offers a critique of the Soviet position from an anarchist viewpoint.

1705. Kathov, G. "The Kronstadt Rising." *Soviet Affairs* 2 (1959). Suggests that the perpetuation of lies about the Kronstadt rising, 30 years after the event, demonstrates its enormous political significance. Claims it was the manifestation of the struggle between the government and the revolutionary masses. Includes a bibliographical note.

1706 Malet, M. *Nestor Makhno in the Russian Civil War*. London: Macmillan, 1982. A sympathetic and extremely thorough investigation of the life, activities and ideas of Makhno, which is useful for details particularly of Makhno's military organization and campaigns. However, the narrative struggles a little to emerge from the plethora of dates and places.

1707. Malia, M. *Alexander Herzen and the Birth of Russian Socialism, 1812-1855*. Cambridge, Mass.: Harvard Univ. Pr., 1961. An examination of the forces which shaped Herzen's life and thought before he developed his theory of Russian socialism based on the peasant commune. Does not cover the later part of his life. Includes index and bibliography.

1708. Maloney, P. "Anarchism and Bolshevism in the Works of Boris Pilnyak." *Russian Review* 32,1 (1973): 42-53. Suggests that Pilnyak saw in the early Bolshevik movement a genuinely Russian and essentially anarchistic alternative to the existing order. Communism was a foreign influence which led to the extinction of these values.

1709. Maximoff (Maksimov) G. P. *Bolshevism: Promises and Reality*. Glasgow: The Anarchist Fedn., 1940. First published in 1935 this is a first hand assessment of Bolshevism by the former co-editor of *Golas Truda*. He laments the death of the Russian Revolution but looks forward to a genuine revolution based on free soviets and communes with democratic, communal production.

1710. Maximoff (Maksimov), G. P. *The Guillotine at Work*. Sanday, Orkney: Cienfuegos Pr., 1978. An indictment of the suppression of the anarchists in the Russian Revolution.

1711. Mett, I. *The Kronstadt Uprising*. With an introduction by Murray Bookchin. Montréal: Black Rose Bks., 1971. First published in the 1930s. Takes as its focus the people involved in the uprising rather than the leaders and manifestoes; also contains hitherto unavailable documents and a good bibliography.

1712. Naimark, N. M. *Terrorists and Social Democrats: The Russian Revolutionary Movement under Alexander III.* Cambridge, Mass.: Harvard Univ. Pr., 1983. Provides a record of the activities of various radical groups which were active during the 1880s in Russia. Includes index and bibliography.

1713. Naimark, N. M. "The Workers' Section and the Challenge of the 'Young' Narodnaia Volia, 1881-1884." *Russian Review* 37,3 (1978): 273-97. Suggests that the Narodnaia Volia continued to dominate the revolutionary movement after the assassination of Alexander II.

1714. Palij, M. *The Anarchism of Nestor Makhno.* Seattle: Univ. of Washington Pr., 1976. A detailed critique of Makhno's activities and strategies in the Ukrainian peasant movement and Russian Revolution with strong emphasis on the political, cultural and socio-economic heritage of the country. Extensive use of primary sources. Bibliography and index.

1715. Rosenthal, B. G. "The Transmutation of the Symbolist Ethos: Mystical Anarchism and the Revolution of 1905." *Slavic Review* 36,4 (1977): 608-27. Examines the emergence of the mystical anarchism of Georgii Chulkov and Viacheslav Ivanov as a short-lived response to the 1905 Revolution.

1716. Voline. (Vselod Mikhailovich Eichenbaum. 1882-1945). *The Unknown Revolution, 1917-1921.* Montréal: Black Rose Bks., 1975. Also New York: Free Life Edns., 1975. Detroit: Black & Red, 1974. A detailed social history of the Russian revolution written by a Russian anarchist who was on the editorial board of *Golos Truda.* Contains substantial discussions of "Bolshevism and Anarchism," 173-436, "Kronstadt (1921)," 441-510, and "Ukraine. 1918-1921," 541-712, and a good introduction by Rudolph Rocker.

1717. Walicki, A. *A History of Russian Thought: From the Enlightenment to Marxism.* Stanford: Stanford Univ. Pr., 1979. Analyzes key writers and thinkers of the nineteenth century Russian revolutionary tradition, including anarchists, from a Marxist-Leninist perspective.

1718. Yaroslavsky, E. *The History of Anarchism in Russia.* London: Lawrence & Wishart, 1940? A critical review of anarchism in Russia before, during and after the Revolution, written from a Marxist standpoint.

1719. Yelensky, B. *In the Struggle for Equality.* Chicago: A. Berkman Aid Fund, 1958. A discussion by a Russian born anarchist of the Russian revolutions of 1905 and 1917 and of the role played by the American anarchist movement in helping refugees.

SPAIN

1720. Abad, D. S. *After the Revolution.* New York: Greenberg Pubs., 1937. A theoretical work, focussing on the future directions of the post revolutionary society. A useful work on social reconstruction written for the Sargossa Congress of 1936.

1721. Ackelsburg, M. A. *Free Women of Spain: Anarchism and the Struggle for the Emancipation of Women.* Bloomington, Ind.: Indiana Univ. Pr., 1991.

1722. Ackelsberg, M. A. "'Separate and Equal?' *Mujeres Libres* and Anarchist Strategy for Women's Emancipation." *Feminist Studies* 11,1 (1985): 63-83. Examines the revolutionary role of *Mujeres Libres* during the Spanish Civil War, noting their efforts to ensure that, as part of the liberation struggle, the anarchist movement empowered women.

1723. Amsden, J. "Industrial Collectivization under Workers' Control: Catalonia, 1936-1939." *Antipode* 10-11, 3-1 (1979): 99-113. Draws parallels with problems experienced in the U.S.S.R., concluding that the ultimate barrier to success was political.

1724. Amsden, J. "Spanish Anarchism and the Stages Theory of History." *Radical History Review* 18 (Fall 1978): 66-75. Condemns the use by Carr and Hobsbawm of a theory that suggests history proceeds in stages and is critical of Kaplan for being insufficiently critical of Hobsbawm's approach. Recommends instead the theory of combined and uneven development. See entry 1762.

1725. Bar, A. *Syndicalism and Revolution in Spain: The Ideology and the Syndical Practice of the CNT in the period 1915-1919.* New York: Gordon Pr., 1981. A detailed and exhaustive study of the changing ideas and tactics of the CNT during a crucial and formative period in its history.

1726. Bolloten, B. *The Spanish Revolution: The Left and the Struggle for Power during the Civil War.* Chapel Hill: Univ. of Nth. Carolina Pr., 1979. A general study of the struggles within the Left during the Civil War with special attention to the "Friends of Durruti" group and the role of the Communists. A revised and updated version of the author's *The Grand Camouflage*, 1962.

1727. Bookchin, M. "Looking Back at Spain." *Our Generation* 17,2 (Spring-Summer 1986): 53-96. Fifty years after Franco launched his attack on the elected government in Spain, Bookchin reflects on the revolutionary nature of the struggle against the Fascists and the reasons why its real social and economic dimensions continue to be so effectively obscured.

1728. Bookchin, M. *The Spanish Anarchists: The Heroic Years, 1868-1936.* New York: Free Life Eds., 1977. See entry 171.

1729. Borkenau, F. *The Spanish Cockpit*. Ann Arbor: Univ. of Michigan Pr., 1963. Provides a detailed and sympathetic account of the anarchists' contribution to the social revolution. Originally published in 1938.

1730. Boyd, C. "The Anarchists and Education in Spain, 1868-1909." *Journal of Modern History* 48,4 (Dec. 1976). Available on microfiche from Univ. Microfilms, 300 North Zeeb Rd., Ann Arbor, Michigan 48106. A discussion of the anarchist education programme in Spain, noting its transition from revolutionary to evolutionary goals, and arguing that collaboration with Francisco Ferrer from 1900-1906 isolated anarchists from working class needs.

1731. Brademas, S. J. "A Note on the Anarcho-Syndicalists and the Spanish Civil War." *Occidente* 11,2 (1955): 121-35. Argues that the Spanish were making war and revolution at the same time, and stresses that, to understand this situation, a strong focus on the key forces for revolutionary change, the working class movements, is necessary.

1732. Breitbart, M. M. "Anarchist Decentralism in Rural Spain 1936-1939." *Antipode* 10-11,3-1 (1979): 83-98. Describes some of the changes brought about by the implementation of anarchist forms of economic and social organization in rural Spain. Argues that even in defeat they made a valid contribution that can inform latter-day movements.

1733. Breitbart, M. M. "The Integration of Community and Environment: Anarchist Decentralisation in Rural Spain, 1936-39." In *The Human Experience of Space and Place*, edited by A. Buttimer and D. Seamon, 86-119. London: Croom Helm, 1980. This article is basically a combination of her two articles, entries 1732 and 1733, and concludes that the root of personal freedom is social action.

1734. Breitbart, M. M. "Spanish Anarchism: An Introductory Essay." *Antipode* 10-11,3-1 (1979): 60-70. This article introduces four others on the theme of Spanish anarchism in a special issue of *Antipode*, and looks at how collectivization created new social relations of production.

1735. Brenan, G. *The Spanish Labyrinth*. 2nd edition, 1950. Cambridge: Cambridge Univ. Pr., 1971. While only half the book actually deals with Spanish anarchism, the work as a whole gives a good account of the Spanish struggle and the anarchists' part in it. Chapters 6 and 7 deal specifically with the historical background of Spanish anarchism.

1736. Brome, V. *The International Brigades: Spain 1936-1937*. London: Mayflower-Dell, 1967. An account of the background and motivations of those who went to Spain to support the Republicans. Though not strictly concerned with Spanish anarchism, it contains some useful information on the revolution itself.

1737. Broué, P. and Témime, E. *Revolution and the Civil War in Spain,*. London: Faber & Faber, 1972. An analysis of the origins, events and consequences of the war, covering political, economic, diplomatic and military factors. Includes bibliography and index.

1738. Carr, R. *Modern Spain, 1875-1980*. Oxford: Oxford Univ. Pr., 1981. Interprets the Spanish situation as a contradiction between imposed liberalism and entrenched traditional values. Includes glossary, chronology, annotated bibliography, index.

1739. Carr, R. *The Republic and the Civil War in Spain*. London: Macmillan, 1971. A collection of contributions by specialists. Includes a chapter on anarchist agrarian collectives by Hugh Thomas. Annotated chapter bibliographies, chronology, glossary, index.

1740. Carr, R. *Spain 1808-1939*. Oxford: Clarendon Pr., 1968. This volume in the Oxford History of Modern Europe series examines the question of why Spanish liberalism failed to provide stability. Includes bibliographical essay, chronological table, index.

1741. Carr, R. *The Spanish Tragedy*. London: Weidenfeld & Nicholson, 1977. Blames the defeat of the Republic on a lack of international support and factionalism within the Popular Front. Includes select bibliography, index, glossary of political terms.

1742. Casas, J. G. *Anarchist Organization: The History of the FAI*. Translated by Abe Bluestein. Montréal: Black Rose Bks., 1986. Casas, who served as a general secretary of the CNT, traces the development, suppression and revival of this organization of anarchist militants.

1743. Casey, J. "The Spanish Anarchist Peasant: How Primitive a Rebel?" *Journal of European Studies* 8,1 (1978): 34-43. A review article suggested by Kaplan's *Anarchists Of Andalusia*, op.cit., entry 1762, in which it is argued that anarchism could have emerged only under the specific conditions which prevailed in Spain.

1744. CNT-FAI. *Buenventura Durruti*. Barcelona: Official Propaganda Services, CNT-FAI, 1936? Contains tributes to the anarchist Buenventura Durruti who was killed in battle at Madrid 20 November, 1936.

1745. Coser, L. "Remembering the Spanish Revolution." *Dissent* 33 (Winter 1986): 53-8. A memoir of the events of 1936.

1746. Diez, G. *Spain's Struggle against Anarchism and Communism*. New York: Paulist Pr., 1938? A pamphlet written to decry anarchism and communism and their ruthless excesses while defending the Spanish church and clergy against charges of wealth and privilege.

1747. Dolgoff, S. *The Anarchist Collectives: Workers' Self-Management in the Spanish Revolution, 1936-1939*. Introductory essay by Murray Bookchin. Montréal: Black Rose Bks., 1974. An important collection of first hand reports and writings concerning the actual workings of self-management initiatives during the revolution.

1748. Eisenwein, G. R. *Anarchist Ideology and the Working Class Movement in Spain, 1868-1898.* Berkeley, Los Angeles & Oxford: Univ. of California Pr., 1989. Eisenwein repudiates millenarian explanations of Spanish anarchism which depict it as a primitive and undeveloped political theory. Viewing anarchism as a mixture of Proudhonian federalism and Bakuninist collectivism, he argues for its role in providing a working class ideology and identity in the political struggle.

1749. Engels, F. *The Bakuninists at Work: Review of the Uprising in Spain in the Summer of 1873.* Moscow: Progress Pubs., 1971. Engel's analysis of the Spanish revolt in 1873 in which he attempts to show the revolutionary bankruptcy of anarchist methods and strategies.

1750. Fraser, R. *Blood of Spain: An Oral History of the Spanish Civil War.* New York: Harper & Row, 1978. Generally reviewed as an excellent oral history which gives an overview of the war. Includes chronology, glossary, bibliography, name index, general index.

1751. Friends of Durruti Group (Barcelona). *Towards a Fresh Revolution.* Barcelona 1938. Translated by Paul Sharkey. Sanday, Orkney: Cienfuegos Pr., 1978. Written as a message of hope in the face of defeat, this pamphlet analyzes the situation and makes proposals for the future. Contains a preface, written forty years later, which includes further reflections and a call to mobilize.

1752. Garcia-Ramon, D. "The Shaping of the Rural Landscape: Contributions of Spanish Anarchist Theory." *Antipode* 10-11,3-1 (1979): 71-82. Sets out to explain the vast transformations which occurred, under anarchist influence, in the use of rural space in Spain.

1753. George, G. "Social Alternatives and the State: Some Lessons of the Spanish Revolution." *Social Alternatives* 2,3 (1982): 30-44. A discussion of the relevance of the Spanish experience to contemporary social movements.

1754. Gilmore, D. "Letters of Blood and Fire." *Radical History Review* 18 (1978): 60-5. A review of Kaplan's *Anarchists of Andalusia*, op.cit., entry 1762, which basically endorses her conclusions.

1755. Golden, L. "The Libertarian Movement in Contemporary Spanish Politics." *Antipode* 10-11,3-1 (1979): 114-18. Describes the largely unpublicized resurgence of the anarcho-syndicalist National Confederation of Labor which was reconstituted in 1976.

1756. Gregory, W., Morris, D. and Peters, D. *The Shallow Grave: A Memoir of the Spanish Civil War.* London: Gollancz, 1986. A detailed memoir by

Walter Gregory which gives a sympathetic account of the anarchists' role in the revolution.

1757. Hobsbawm, E. J. *Primitive Rebels: Studies in Archaic Forms of Social Movement in the 19th and 20th Centuries*. Manchester: Manchester Univ. Pr., 1971. Although this covers a broad range of social movements, "The Andalusian Anarchists," which forms chapter five, is a key contribution that is a point of reference for numerous other pieces.

1758. Hobsbawm, E. J. "The Spanish Background." *New Left Review* 40 (Nov.-Dec. 1966): 85-90. Argues that the blame for the failure to achieve stability in modern Spain lies squarely with the anarchists. Particular reference to Raymond Carr's book on the period 1808-1939. See entry 1740.

1759. Jackson, G. *A Concise History of the Spanish Civil War*. New York: The John Day Co., 1974. An illustrated introduction to the Spanish Civil war that sets out clearly, and in an attractive way, the main lines of the conflict, both political and military.

1760. Jackson, G. *The Spanish Republic and the Civil War 1931-1939*. Princeton, N.J.: Princeton Univ. Pr., 1965. A liberal account of the revolution which is not very sympathetic to the anarchist contribution.

1761. Jackson, G. "The Spanish Popular Front, 1934-7." *Journal of Contemporary History* 5,3 (1970): 21-35. Refutes any contention that the Popular Front electoral victory was fraudulent, but says internal conflict prevented them from governing effectively. However, despite problems, their period of rule has become significant as a symbol.

1762. Kaplan, T. *Anarchists of Andalusia, 1868-1903*. Princeton, N.J.: Princeton Univ. Pr., 1977. Reconstructs this movement from archival material with an emphasis on its social and economic context that argues against the view that it was a spontaneous millenarian movement.

1763. Kaplan, T. "Other Scenarios: Women and Spanish Anarchism." In *Becoming Visible: Women in European History*, edited by R. Bridenthal and C. Koonz, 400-21. Boston: Houghton Mifflin, 1977. Argues that even within anarchism women continued to be cast in passive roles. Suggests that women were more radical in their behavior and goals when they formed separate associations on the basis of gender.

1764. Kaplan, T. "The Social Base of Nineteenth-Century Andalusian Anarchism in Jerez de la Frontera." *Journal of Interdisciplinary History* 6,1 (1975): 47-70. Emphasizes the role of petty producers in revolutionary activities and asserts the utility of anarchist strategies in the solution of social problems.

1765. Kaplan, T. "Spanish Anarchism and Women's Liberation." *Journal of Contemporary History* 6,2 (1971): 101-10. An analysis of the role of women in the revolution. Concludes that, despite anarchist ideology, the role of women did not change substantially.

1766. Kelsey, G. *Anarchosyndicalism, Libertarian Communism and the State: The CNT in Zaragoza and Aragon, 1930-37.* Boston: Kluwer, 1989.

1767. Kelsey, G. "Civil War and Civil Peace: Libertarian Aragon 1936-37." In *The Anarchist Encyclopaedia,* edited by S. Christie. Cambridge: Cambridge Free Pr., 1985. A piece written for Christie's collection of information regarding current research on anarchist thought and practice. The anarchist movement in Aragon is given close attention.

1768. Kern, R. "Anarchist Principles and Spanish Reality: Emma Goldman as a Participant in the Civil War 1936-39." *Journal of Contemporary History* 11,2-3 (1976): 237-59. A negative assessment of Goldman's analysis of the revolutionary struggle.

1769. Kern, R. *Red Years Black Years: A Political History of Spanish Anarchism, 1911-1937.* Philadelphia: Institute for the Study of Human Issues, 1978. A study of Spanish anarchism covering the period 1911-1937 with ample notes and a comprehensive bibliography. It concludes that, as a social movement, anarchism died out with the consolidation of Franco's dictatorship.

1770. Leval, G. *Collectives in Spain.* London: Freedom Pr., 1945. A pamphlet containing a brief discussion of collectivization in Spain.

1771. Leval, G. *Collectives in the Spanish Revolution.* Translated from the French by Vernon Richards. London: Freedom Pr., 1975. A detailed study of a number of representative anarchist collectives, both urban and rural, aimed at presenting an analysis of the social dimensions of the revolutionary struggle. Includes informative bibliographic notes.

1772. Leval, G. *Social Reconstruction in Spain.* London: Spain and the World, 1938. An early account of the Spanish social revolution with accounts of the formation of industrial and agrarian collectives, education, the family wage system, new cultivation methods etc.

1773. Linehan, F. A. "Right, Left and Centre: The Second Spanish Republic." *History Journal* 15,1 (1972). A review article of three books: Stanley G. Payne, *The Spanish Revolution,* 1970; Edward E. Malefakis, *Agrarian Reform and Peasant Revolution in Spain* 1970; and Richard A. H. Robinson, *The Origins Of Franco's Spain. The Right, The Republic and the Revolution,* 1970. See entries 1786, 1775.

1774. MacDougall, I. *Voices from the Spanish Civil War.* Edinburgh: Polygon Bks., 1986. These oral recollections of twenty survivors who left Scotland to fight in Spain illuminate the struggle from the point of view of ordinary working class people.

1775. Malefakis, E. *Agrarian Reform and Peasant Revolution in Spain: Origins of the Civil War.* New Haven: Yale Univ. Pr., 1970. Uses statistics and an historical perspective to show that land reform has been undermined by a lack of concern for agrarian matters among republican leaders.

1776. Maura, J. R. "The Spanish Case." *Government and Opposition* 5,4 (1970): 456-79. Attempts to explain how and why Spanish anarchism succeeded in developing such a strong mass organization. Reprinted in *Anarchism Today,* 60-83. Op.cit., entry 1302.

1777. Maura, J. R. "Terrorism in Barcelona and Its Impact on Spanish Politics 1904-1909." *Past and Present* 41 (1968): 130-83. Argues that the violence of the confrontation in Barcelona between terrorism and official repression meant that terrorism became a legislative issue by 1908.

1778. Meaker, H. H. *The Revolutionary Left in Spain, 1914-1923.* Stanford, Calif.: Stanford Univ. Pr., 1974. A detailed account of anarchist and socialist, activities in Spain between World War I and the Primo dictatorship. Though not sympathetic to the anarchists, nevertheless it is a well-researched study containing much useful information.

1779. Meltzer, A., ed. *The International Revolutionary Solidarity Movement: 1st of May Group,.* Sanday, Orkney: Cienfuegos Pr., 1976. Deals with one aspect of the guerilla movement in Spain in the post-1960 era.

1780. Meltzer, A., ed. *Miguel Garcia's Story.* London: BLM Refrac., 1982. A collection of autobiographical fragments by Garcia, a Spanish anarchist who, on being released after 20 years in jail, continued his political opposition to Franco from London.

1781. Meltzer, A., ed. *A New World in Our Hearts: The Faces of Spanish Anarchism.* Sanday, Orkney: Cienfuegos Pr., 1978. A collection of essays on anarchism in Spain that concentrates on the labor movement, the CNT and the issues pertinent to the emerging democracy in the Spain of the 1970s.

1782. Minta, J. R. *The Anarchists of Casas Viejas.* Chicago: Univ. of Chicago Pr., 1982. Focuses on anarchist activity in one region during the early 1930s.

1783. Montseny, F. *Militant Anarchism and the Reality in Spain.* Glasgow: Anti-Parliamentary Communist Federation, 1937. A statement from the front, pledging unity with anti-Fascist forces and looking forward confidently to an anarchist future.

1784. Morrow, F. *Revolution and Counter-Revolution in Spain.* Including "The Civil War in Spain." New York: Pathfinder Pr., 1974. Originally published in 1938, it remains one of the best Marxist analyses of the revolution. The opening chapter, "The Civil War in Spain," was originally a pamphlet published in 1936 and offers an overview of the history of the Spanish Republic from 1931 to 1936.

1785. Orwell, G. *Homage to Catalonia*. Harmondsworth: Penguin Bks., 1980. Originally published in 1938, it is an excellent and insightful first-hand account of the nature of the revolution. This edition also contains the essay "Looking Back on the Spanish War" written in 1943.

1786. Payne, S. *The Spanish Revolution*. New York: 1970. Well-researched and informative, it is nevertheless not sympathetic to the anarchists' struggle.

1787. Paz, A. *Durruti: The People Armed*. Translated Nancy Macdonald. Montréal: Black Rose Bks., 1977. Published in U.K., Nottingham: Spokesman Bks., 1976. A thorough biography of the Spanish revolutionary Buenaventura Durruti and his contributions to the anarchist cause during the Spanish Civil War. Two thirds of the biography covers the period 1931-36. Includes, as an appendix, Durruti's interview with the *Toronto Daily Star* 5/8/36. Contains numerous footnotes and detailed bibliography.

1788. Peirats, J. *Anarchists in the Spanish Revolution*. Toronto: Solidarity Bks., 1977. One of the best detailed histories on the background to the revolution, and one that discusses the social forces involved.

1789. Preston, P. *The Spanish Civil War 1936-39*. London: Weidenfeld, 1986. An illustrated history of the Spanish struggle.

1790. Prevost, G. "The Anarchist Critique of the State: Theory and Practice of the Spanish CNT." *Our Generation* 18,1 (Fall/Winter 1986): 87-102. Discusses the ambivalence of the CNT towards state power, co-operating and, on occasion, participating in its exercise. The post 1977 position of the CNT is reviewed. A response is made by a CNT activist in the same issue. See Juan Gómez Casas, "Ambivalence Towards the State: A Comment," pages 103-8.

1791. Ralle, M. "The Spanish Regional Federation of the International Workingmen's Association: An Enduring Legacy." *Cahiers d'Histoire de l'Institut de Récherches Marxistes* 37 (1989): 85-106. Discusses the Spanish regional federation of the 1st International as the basis for the development of Spanish anarchism despite the legal ban of 1974.

1792. Richards, V. "July 19, 1936: Republic or Revolution?" *Anarchy* 5 (July 1961): 129-36. Argues that in concentrating on winning the war the anarchist and syndicalist leaders sacrificed the revolution, and, in doing so, lost the war.

1793. Richards, V. *Lessons of the Spanish Revolution*. London: Freedom Pr., 1972. A considerably expanded version of the original 1953 edition which focuses on why the revolution was defeated. Less concerned with Franco's actual military victory, it concentrates on the forces at work within the revolutionary movement, both within and beyond Spain.

1794. Rider, N. "The Practice of Direct Action: The Barcelona Rent Strike of 1931." In *For Anarchism: History, Theory and Practice*, 79-108. Op. cit, entry 1385. A discussion of the evolving tactics of the CNT in relation to working class political needs which focuses on housing and the Barcelona rent strike of 1931.

1795. Rocker, R. *The Truth about Spain*. New York: Freie Arbeiter Stimme, 1936 and *The Tragedy of Spain*. New York: Freie Arbeiter Stimme, 1937. Two short pamphlets setting out for an American audience the issues of the Spanish Civil War. *The Truth about Spain* provides a survey of Spanish history preceding the Civil War, emphasizing the positive role of the CNT and its broad level of social support. The reactionary role of the Church in Spanish politics is discussed and its alliance with Fascism noted. The CNT, the FAI and the Spanish people are not, it is stressed, allied to Bolshevism, but are fighting against Fascism for the values of civilization. For *The Tragedy of Spain* see entry 816.

1796. Seidman, M. "Work and Revolution: Workers' Control in Barcelona in the Spanish Civil War, 1936-38." *Journal of Contemporary History* 17,3 (July 1982): 409-34. An analysis of the economic and social development in Barcelona as part of the social revolution.

1797. Stein, L. *Beyond Death and Exile: The Spanish Republicians in France 1939-1955*. Cambridge, Mass.: Harvard Univ. Pr., 1980. An account of the generally disgraceful treatment of Spanish refugees in France. Based on interviews and local archival material.

1798. Tellez, A. *Sabate: Guerilla Extraordinary*. Introduction Alfredo Bonnano. London: Elephant, 1985. Originally published London: Davis Pr., 1974. A biography of a Spanish anarchist guerilla fighter and leader of the CNT, known as *El Quico*, who continued his armed resistance to the Franco regime until his death at the hands of the militia in 1960.

1799. Thomas, H. "Anarchist Agrarian Collectives in the Spanish Civil War." In *A Century of Conflict, 1850-1950*. Essays for A. J. P. Taylor, edited by Martin Gilbert, 247-63. New York: Atheneum Publishers, 1967. An attempt to assess the data relating to agrarian collectives during the revolution, concluding that they were probably a success.

1800. Thomas, H. *The Spanish Civil War*. New York: Harper & Row, 1961. Often regarded by non-anarchists as the definitive account of the civil war. Takes a somewhat superficial approach to the underlying social forces involved. It concentrates mainly on the military struggles. A new edition has been published London: Hamish Hamilton, 1986.

UNITED KINGDOM

1801. Aldred, G. A. *Pioneers of Anti-Parliamentarism*. Glasgow: Strickland Pr., 1940. See entry 3.

1802. *The Angry Brigade: 1967-1984.* Documents-Chronology. London: Elephant, 1985. Introduction by Jean Weir. Originally published Port Glasgow: Bratach Dubh Pubns., 1978. A collection of statements issued by the Angry Brigade. Weir's introduction seeks to situate the group in relation to anarchism and revolutionary struggle.

1803. Becker, H. "Johann Most." *The Raven* 1,4 (March 1988): 291-321. An autobiography by Most first published in *Freiheit* 4, (15 May 1881).

1804. Carr, G. *The Angry Brigade: The Cause and the Case.* London, Gollancz, 1975. A study of the Angry Brigade based on information collected by Gordon Carr for a BBC television news documentary written and produced in 1973. Illustrations.

1805. Christie, S. *The Christie File.* Sanday, Orkney: Cienfuegos Pr., 1980. A personal account of the activities of one of Britain's foremost anarchists during the 1960s and 1970s, that discusses, in particular, the massive conspiracy trial of the Angry Brigade in 1971.

1806. Meltzer, A. *The Anarchists in London, 1935-1955.* Sanday, Orkney: Cienfuegos Pr., 1976. Forward by Stuart Christie. Offers an account of this largely neglected, or misrepresented, period from one who was an active participant at the time.

1807. Nomad, M. "Johann Most, Terrorist of the Word." In *Apostles of Revolution*, 257-99. New York: Collier Bks., 1961. A study of the revolutionary activities of Most and his career in Germany, London and New York, looking at *Freiheit* and his relationships with various anarchist groups.

1808. Oliver, H. *The International Anarchist Movement in Late Victorian London.* New York: St. Martin's Pr., 1983. A succinct study of late 19th century anarchists with some attention given to biographical details and the prevailing intellectual climate. A useful source work about little known anarchists.

1809. Porter, B. "The *Freiheit* Prosecutions, 1881-1882." *History Journal* 23,4 (1980): 833-50. An analysis of the prosecution of Johann Most, publisher of *Die Freiheit*, for the publication of an editorial celebrating the assassination of Tsar Alexander II. After his imprisonment the journal proceeded to identify itself with the Irish rebels who assassinated Lord Cavendish in Phoenix Park and was suppressed. It resumed publication, under Most, in New York. See 1854.

1810. Quail, J. *The Slow Burning Fuse: The Lost History of the British Anarchists.* London & New York: Paladin, 1978. A description of the British anarchist movement from its origins in the 1880s to about 1930, by which time it had suffered a near total eclipse. Argues that, although never a mass movement, nonetheless, at moments of maximum strength, it was of equal importance to Marxist groups. Includes index and bibliography.

1811. Rogers, C. *The Battle of Stepney: The Sidney Street Siege: Its Causes and Consequences*. London: R. Hale, 1981. A detailed study of the Sidney Street Seige, in which the association between immigrants from Eastern Europe and the alleged anarchist character of the siege is discussed. There is also discussion of the press uproar over foreign immigrants who were presumed to be responsible for the importation of violent 'foreign' doctrines like anarchism.

1812. Seymour, H. "The Genesis of Anarchism in England." In *Free Vistas*. Volume Two. Op.cit., 1419. A discussion of the origins of the British movement.

1813. Shelley, D. "Anarchists and the Committee of 100." *Anarchy* 50 (April 1965). Discusses the relationship between anarchism and pacificism within the Campaign for Nuclear Disarmament.

1814. Shipley, P. *Revolutionaries in Modern Britain*. London: Bodley Head, 1976. A compilation of programmes, goals and strategies of the radical left organizations in Britain based on an analysis of the publications of each group.

1815. Stafford, D. "Anarchists in Britain Today." *Government and Opposition* 5,4 (1970): 480-500. Examines the resurgence of British anarchism in the light of the appearance of the "New Left" in the early 1960s. Suggests that anarchism has only a minority appeal. Reprinted in, *Anarchism Today*, 84-104. Op.cit, entry 1302.

UNITED STATES

Note that only a selection of the material on Sacco and Vanzetti is presented.

1816. Adamic, L. *Dynamite: The Story of Class Violence in America*. New York: The Viking Pr., 1931. Argues that the roots of crime and terrorism in America lie deep in American history, especially the history of the labor movement; "the inevitable result of the brutalizing conditions in American industry."

1817. Adelman, W. J. *Haymarket Revisited: A Tour Guide of Labor History Sites and Ethnic Neighborhoods Connected with the Haymarket Affair*. Chicago: Illinois Labor History Society, 1976. The book takes the reader on an imaginary tour of the remains of those parts of Chicago where working class radicals, mainly of German origin, congregated.

1818. Aldred, G. A. *The Chicago Martyrs*. With Portraits of the Comrades Who Were Tried. London: Freedom Pr., 1912. See entry 2.

1819. Anderson, T. and Hill. P.J. "An American Experiment in Anarcho-Capitalism." *Journal of Libertarian Studies* 3,1 (Spring 1979): 9-29. Using

19th century frontier America as a case study, Anderson examines the claims that an absence of government does not lead to disorder because the free market effectively provides necessary services for justice and protection. He concludes that the absence of government in frontier society did not produce chaos. Rights were protected and competitive market organizations offering services such as protection and justice existed without becoming monopolies.

1820. Avrich, P. *The Haymarket Tragedy*. Princeton: Princeton Univ. Pr., 1984. A detailed study of the Haymarket affair in the framework of an analysis of the origins and development of the anarchist tradition in the United States. Acknowledges the European roots of anarchism, whilst discussing the contributions of Albert and Lucy Parsons, and other radical workers and unionists, to American anarchism.

1821. Avrich, P. *The Modern School Movement: Anarchism and Education in the United States*. Princeton, N.J.: Princeton Univ. Pr., 1980. Covers the period 1910-60, examining the successes and eventual collapse of the schools based on Ferrer's model. Argues that education has always been an important concern for radicals and discusses the politics and philosophy of radical educationalists.

1822. Avrich, P. *Sacco and Vanzetti: the Anarchist Background*. Princeton, N.J.: Princeton Univ. Pr., 1991.

1823. Brissenden, P. F. *The I.W.W.: A Study of American Syndicalism*. New York: Columbia Univ. Pr., 1957. A descriptive and historical sketch of what the author describes as the drift from parliamentary to industrial socialism, as epitomized by the history of the Industrial Workers of the World in the United States. Written in 1918, when the I.W.W. was just 13 years old, it attempts to address popular misconceptions about the movement.

1824. David, H. *The History of the Haymarket Affair; a Study in the American Social Revolutionary and Labor Movements*. New York: Russell & Russell, 1958. A comprehensive history of the incident which the author suggests produced the first "red-scare" in American history.

1825. DeLeon, D. *The American as Anarchist: Reflections on Indigenous Radicalism*. Baltimore: John Hopkins Univ. Pr., 1978. Attempts to argue the case that a species of anarchist thought is indigenous to the American experience, with its roots in religious dissent and the development of American capitalism. Excellent bibliography.

1826. Eyges, T. B. *Beyond the Horizon: The Story of a Radical Emigrant*. Boston, Mass.: Group Free Society, 1944. Written as a biographical sketch of his experiences during fifty years of activity in the Socialist and Labor Movement. Includes brief episodes such as meetings with Kropotkin, Trotsky and Most.

1827. Felix, D. *Protest: Sacco and Vanzetti and the Intellectuals.* Bloomington: Indiana Univ. Pr., 1965. Argues in favor of the guilt of Sacco and Vanzetti and seeks an explanation as to why the case, like that of Dreyfus, produced such an enraged reaction from intellectuals.

1828. Foner, P. S., ed. *The Autobiographies of the Haymarket Martyrs.* New York: Monad Pr., 1977. These autobiographies were first solicited by the Chicago labor journal *Knights of Labor* while the eight men convicted were awaiting trial. Foner has brought them together in one volume with an editorial essay in which he calls them "America's first labor-revolutionary martyrs."

1829. Gallagher, D. *All the Right Enemies: The Life and Murder of Carlo Tresca.* New Brunswick & London: Rutgers Univ. Pr., 1988. A biography of Carlo Tresca, 1879-1943, who, born in the Abruzzi, emigrated to the United States in 1904 and played a significant part in the American anarchist movement until his murder in 1943, allegedly at the instigation of Mussolini.

1830. Ganz, M. *Rebels: Into Anarchy-And Out Again.* In collaboration with Nat. J. Ferber. With illustrations by M. Leone Bracker. Millwood, N.Y.: Kraus Reprint Co., 1976. An autobiography which describes the poverty of immigrant families in America at the turn of the century, Ganz's association with radical activists like Goldman and Berkman, and her eventual conversion to American patriotism in the war against Germany.

1831. Hunter, R. *Violence and the Labor Movement.* New York: Arno Pr., 1969. Outlines the debate about political as against direct action, characterizing it as social democracy versus anarchism. While conceding that not all anarchists are terrorists, it is argued that terrorism is the dominant tendency. Concludes that propaganda by deed is destructive for society and the labor movement.

1832. Jacker, C. *The Black Flag of Anarchy: Antistatism in the United States.* New York: Scribner, 1968. Focuses primarily on individualist anarchism, discussing Josiah Warren and Benjamin Tucker.

1833. Kebabian, J. S. *The Haymarket Affair and the Trial of the Chicago Anarchists 1886.* New York: H. P. Kraus, 1970. A useful collection of original manuscripts, letters, articles and printed material of the anarchists which are otherwise very difficult to obtain.

1834. Larkin, O. "The Trial of Sacco and Vanzetti." In Robert S. Brumbaugh, ed. *Six Trials,* 92-106. New York: Thomas Y. Cromwell, 1969. A discussion of the trial of Sacco and Vanzetti as one of political note, in a collection that includes the trials of Socrates, Galileo and Dreyfus.

1835. Lerner, M. "Anarchism and the American Counter-Culture." *Government and Opposition* 5,4 (1970): 430-55. Also in *Anarchism Today,* 32-59. Op.cit., entry 1302. See entries 1443 and 1849.

1836. Lum, D. D. *The Great Trial of the Chicago Anarchists*. New York: Arno Pr., 1969. This contemporary version of the Haymarket incident is condensed from the official records.

1837. Lyons, E. *Life and Death of Sacco and Vanzetti*. New York, Da Capo., 1970. Originally published in 1927 this represents a contemporary account of Sacco and Vanzetti.

1838. Madison, C. "Anarchism in the United States." *Journal of the History of Ideas* 6,1 (Jan. 1945): 46-66. Contrasts the historical contexts of European and American anarchist movements, suggesting that individualist anarchism was a natural expression of the American pioneer experience while communist anarchism was a foreign importation.

1839. Martin, J. J. *Men Against the State: The Expositors of Individualist Anarchism in America, 1827-1908*. Colorado Springs: Ralph Myles, 1970. Originally published DeKalb, Ill.: Adrian Allen, 1953. A thorough study of the antecedents and development of individualist anarchism, and libertarian thought generally, in the United States. There are chapters on Warren, Spooner and Tucker with discussion of Ezra Heywood, William B. Greene, J. K. Ingalls and Stephen Pearl Andrews. A bibliographic essay and appendices provide useful information on individualist anarchism. Includes detailed bibliography.

1840. McClean, G. N. *The Rise and Fall of Anarchy in America*. New York: Haskell Hse. Pubns., 1972. Originally published Philadelphia: R.G. Badoux, 1890. Deals primarily with the Haymarket affair, May 4th 1886, and includes biographies and speeches of the anarchists involved. Gives a good feel for attitudes of the period, anarchism being treated unsympathetically as a conspiracy against law and order.

1841. Montgomery, R. H. *Sacco-Vanzetti: The Murder and the Myth*. New York: Devin-Adair Co., 1960. A discussion of the trial, which lasted from 1920 to 1927, for robbery and murder, of Bartolomeo, Vanzetti and Nicola Sacco. The trial became a *cause celèbre* because of the defendents anarchist allegiance and their alleged role in the distribution of anarchist literature. Many believed that it was their radical politics, in the midst of a red scare, that was the key factor determining their prosecution and execution. This study is unsympathetic to their position. Indeed, it was the first to try to prove that the defendents were fairly convicted.

1842. Nelson, B. C. *Beyond the Martyrs: A Social History of Chicago's Anarchists, 1870-1900*. New Brunswick: Rutgers Univ. Pr., 1988. The Haymarket bomb, the riot and its aftermath are analyzed as events within a complex process of industrialization, immigration and class formation. Includes select bibliography.

1843. Newfield, J. *A Prophetic Minority*. N.Y.: New American Library, 1966. Argues that anarchism was an important influence within the New Left and radical thought in the 1960s.

1844. Nomad, M. "Johann Most, Terrorist of the Word." In *Apostles of Revolution*, 257-99. New York: Collier Bks., 1961. See entry 1807.

1845. Perrier, H., Collomp, C., Cordillot, M. and Debouzy, M. "The 'Social Revolution' in America? European Reactions to the 'Great Upheaval' and to the Haymarket Affair." *International Labor and Working Class History* 29 (1986): 38-52. The treatment meted out to those caught up in the Haymarket Affair exposed, European radicals believed, the superficiality of the much vaunted freedom and democracy of the United States.

1846. Porter, K. A. *The Never-Ending Wrong*. London: Secker and Warburg, 1977. A short personal reflection on memories of the Sacco-Vanzetti trial by the author of *Ship of Fools*. It includes comments on anarchism and a record of a meeting with Emma Goldman.

1847. Reichert, W. O. *Partisans of Freedom: A Study in American Anarchism*. Bowling Green, Ohio: Bowling Green Univ. Popular Pr., 1976. An attempt to present an objective account of the history of anarchist thought in America. Includes sketches of many little known anarchists as well as some who might be surprised to find themselves called anarchists.

1848. Roediger, D. and Rosemont, F., ed. *Haymarket Scrapbook*. Chicago: Charles H. Kerr Pubg. Co., 1986. An extensive compilation of documentation, illustration and commentary relating to the Haymarket affair. Includes bibliography.

1849. Roszak, T. *The Making of a Counter-Culture*. London: Faber & Faber, 1970. Discusses anarchism, specifically the anarchist beliefs of Paul Goodman, in the context of the counter-culture movement of the 1960s.

1850. Russell, F. *Tragedy in Dedham : The Story of the Sacco-Vanzetti Case*. London: Longmans, 1963. A comprehensive history of the trial and conviction of Sacco and Vanzetti that is sympathetic to their position.

1851. Schaak, M. *Anarchy and Anarchists*. New York: Arno Pr., 1977. Written in 1899 this comprises a lengthy discussion of the background to the Haymarket incident, covering communism, socialism and nihilism, with a detailed account of the trial and execution of the anarchists. Written from a law and order point of view, but surprisingly free of polemic, given that Schaak was the Captain of Police in charge of the investigation that led to the conviction of Spies, Parsons etc.

1852. Schuster, E. M. *Native American Anarchism: A Study of Left-Wing American Individualism*. Department of History of Smith College, Northampton, Mass. New York: AMS Pr., 1970. Attempts a delineation of the character of American anarchism and the conditions which fostered its growth. Assesses its significance in American history, emphasizing individualist anarchism and dealing only cursorily with communist anarchism which is regarded as an import.

1853. Sun, R.C. "Misguided Martyrdom: German Social Democratic Responses to the Haymarket Incident, 1886-87." *International Labor and Working Class History* 29 (1986): 53-67. The German Social Democrats condemned the handling of the incident and expressed solidarity with the Chicago anarchists. However, their support was not extended to anarchism or the anarchist movement in general.

1854. Trautmann, F. *The Voice of Terror: A Biography of Johann Most.* Westport, Conn.: Greenwood Pr., 1980. An attempt to give a balanced view of this man of extremes by allowing him to speak for himself. He was arguably the leading anarchist agitator in late nineteenth century America, after his removal there in 1883, imprisoned time and again, not for what he did, but for what he said. Includes chronology, bibliography, index and a transcript of his "Pittsburg Proclamation." See entry 1809.

1855. Veysey, L. *The Communal Experience: Anarchist Mystical Communities in Twentieth Century America.* Chicago: Univ. of Chicago Pr., 1978. Originally published as *The Communal Experience: Anarchist and Mystical Counter-Cultures in America,* New York: Harper & Row, 1973. A discussion of twentieth century intentional communities in America. There is coverage of anarchist communities in Part 1, Chapters 2 and 3.

1856. Werstein, I. *Strangled Voices: The Story of the Haymarket Affair.* New York: Macmillan, 1970. Details the events of 4 May 1886, discussing the hysteria induced in both press and general population by the vision of an anarchist threat. There is consideration of the social and economic factors underlying the events with a discussion of labor history in America.

Theses

1857. Abbott, M. J. E. 1974. *Anarchy and Anarchism: Santayana on the Nature of Moral and Political Authority.* Vanderbilt University, Ph.D.

1858. Ackelsburg, M. A. 1976. *The Possibility of Anarchism: The Theory and Practice of Non-Authoritarian Organization.* Princeton University, Ph.D.

1859. Arum, P. M. 1971. *Georges Dumoulin: Biography of a Revolutionary Syndicalist.* University of Wisconsin, Ph.D.

1860. Arthur, A. S. 1980. *The Problem of Providing Adequate Grounds for Political Obligation.* Syracuse University, Ph.D.

1861. Backer, T. B. 1978. *The Mutualists : The Heirs of Proudhon in the First International, 1865-1878.* University of Cincinnati, Ph.D.

1862. Barker, J. H. 1983. *The Concept of the State in Marx and Anarchism.* Purdue University, Ph.D.

1863. Baron, L. 1975. *The Eclectic Anarchism of Erich Mühsam.* University of Wisconsin, Madison. Ph.D.

1864. Beebee, P. K. 1975. *Toward an Anarchistic Conceptual Framework of Alternative Learning Experiences.* University of Virginia, Ph.D.

1865. Berman, M. H. 1963. *Marx on Individuality and Freedom.* University of Cambridge, B.Litt

1866. Berry, E. W. 1969. *Rhetoric for the Cause, the Analysis and Criticism of the Persuasive Discourse of Emma Goldman, Anarchist Agitator, 1906-1919.* University of California, Los Angeles, Ph.D.

1867. Blatt, M. H. 1983. *The Anarchism of Ezra Heywood, 1829-1893: Abolition, Labor Reform and Free Love.* Boston University Graduate School, Ph.D.

1868. Boris, E. C. 1981. *Art and Labor: John Ruskin, William Morris, and the Craftsman Ideal in America, 1876-1915.* Brown University, Ph.D.

1869. Brademas, S. J. 1953. *Revolution and Social Revolution: A Contribution to the History of the Anarcho-Syndicalist Movement in Spain, 1930-1937.* University of Oxford, D.Phil. See entry 1731.

1870. Breitbart, M. M. 1978. *The Theory and Practice of Anarchist Decentralism in Spain, 1936-1939.* Clark University, Ph.D. See entries 1732, 1733 and 1734.

1871. Brooks, F. H. 1988. *Anarchism, Revolution and Labor in the Thought of Dyer D. Lum: "Events Are the True Schoolmasters."* Cornell University, Ph.D.

1872. Brown, F. K. 1921. *A Life of William Godwin.* University of Oxford, D.Phil. See entry 284.

1873. Bucci, J. A. 1974. *Philosophical Anarchism and Education.* Boston University School of Education, Ed.D.

1874. Butler, J. 1960. *Fernand Pelloutier and the Emergence of the French Syndicalist Movement.* Ohio State University, Ph.D.

1875. Cahm, J. 1984. *Peter Kropotkin and Revolutionary Action: A Study of the Development of His Approach in the Context of the Development of the Anarchist Movement in Western Europe, 1872-1886.* University of London, University College, Ph.D. See entry 550.

1876. Carlson, A. R. 1970. *Anarchism in Germany: The Early Movement.* Michigan State University, Ph.D.

1877. Carnochan, P. J. 1981. *The Role of the Intelligensia in the Political Thought of the Revolutionary Narodnik Strategists: Bakunin, Lavróv and Tchachev.* University of Birmingham, M.Soc.Sc.

1878. Carr, B. C. L. 1976. *Variations on the Anarchist: Politics Reflected in Fiction.* Indiana University, Ph.D.

1879. Carroll, J. B. 1972. *A Study of the 'Anarcho-psychological' Critique of Major Alternative Models of Social and Economic Morality and Behaviour.* University of Cambridge, Ph.D. See entry 840.

1880. Chalwin, R. D. A. 1985. *Philosophy of Science in the Anarchism of Peter Kropotkin.* University of Wales, Swansea, M.A.

1881. Chan, P. A. W. 1979. *Liu Shifu (1884-1915): A Chinese Anarchist and the Radicalization of Chinese Thought.* University of California, Berkeley, Ph.D.

1882. Claasen, P. J. 1985. *Anarchist Movements and the Ideas of Bakunin.* University of Pretoria, M.A. Afrikaans text.

1883. Clark, J. 1974. *The Social and Political Philosophy of William Godwin.* Tulane University, Ph.D. See entry 288.

1884. Clarke, M. 1928. *French Syndicalism, 1910-1927.* University of California, Berkeley, Ph.D.

1885. Cochran, C. 1970. *The Politics of Interest. The Eclipse of Community in Contemporary American Political Theory.* Duke University, Ph.D.

1886. Collits, P. G. 1983. *The Individual and the Political Order in the Thought of F. A. Hayek and Robert Nozick: A Critical Examination.* Australian National University, M.A.

1887. Coon, D. J. 1988. *Courtship with Anarchy: The Sociopolitical Foundations of William James's Pragmatism.* Harvard University, Ph.D.

1888. Crampton, D. N. 1973. *Shelley's Political Optimism: "The Mask of Anarchy" to "Hellas."* University of Wisconsin, Madison, Ph.D.

1889. Crowder, G. E. 1987. *The Idea of Freedom in Nineteenth Century Anarchism.* University of Oxford, Ph.D.

1890. D'Agostino, A. W. 1971. *Marxism and the Russian Anarchists.* University of California, Los Angeles, Ph.D. See entry 1699.

1891. Damico, L. H. 1985. *The Anarchist Dimension of Liberation Theology.* Florida State University, Ph.D. See entry 1354.

1892. Danley, J. R. 1976. *An Examination of Process Arguments in Robert Nozick's "Anarchy, State and Utopia."* University of Rochester, Ph.D.

1893. Del Giudice, M. N. 1982. *The Young Bakunin and Left Hegelianism: Origins of Russian Radicalism and the Theory of Praxis, 1814-1842.* McGill University, Ph.D.

1894. DeLucia, M. 1965. *The Remaking of French Syndicalism, 1911-1918.* Brown University, Ph.D.

1895. Downer, W. M. 1977. *Freedom, Community and Anarchism: The Political Thought of Paul Goodman.* University of Kansas, Ph.D.

1896. Dubin, B. H. 1973. *A Critical Review of the Social and Educational Theories of Josiah Warren and his Individualist School of Anarchism.* University of Illinois, Urbana-Champaign, Ph.D.

1897. Ebner, D. 1968. *Benjamin R. Tucker: The Ideology of the Individualist Anarchist in America.* New York University, Ph.D.

1898. Eichrodt, J. B. 1975. *Anarchy and Culture: Dmitri Merezhkovsky and the 'Kairos'.* Columbia University, Ph.D.

1899. Eisenwein, G. R. 1987. *Anarchist Ideology and the Working Class Movement in Spain, 1868-1900, with Special Reference to the Ideas of Richard Mella.* University of London, London School of Economics, Ph.D. See entry 1748.

1900. Espers, T. 1961. *The Anarchism of George Landauer.* University of Chicago, M.A.

1901. Estey, J. 1911. *Revolutionary Syndicalism: An Exposition and a Critique.* University of Wisconsin, Ph.D.

1902. Ferrandino, M. M. 1977. *Patriarchy and Biological Necessity: A Feminist and Anarchist Critique.* State University of New York, Buffalo, Ph.D.

1903. Fishman, S. 1960. *Prophets, Poets and Priests: A Study of Men and Ideas that Made the Munich Revolution.* University of Wisconsin, Ph.D.

1904. Fitzgerald, E. P. 1973. *Emile Pouget, the Anarchist Movement, and the Origins of Trade-Unionism in France, 1880-1901.* Yale University, Ph.D.

1905. Fitzpatrick, M. C. 1980. *Justice and Labour: A Consideration of Proudhon's Notion of Justice, with Reference to His Mutual Credit Scheme.* University of Kent, Ph.D.

1906. Fleishman, A. H. 1963. *Conrad's Politics: Community and Anarchy in the Fiction of Joseph Conrad.* John Hopkins University, Ph.D.

1907. Fleming, M. A. 1976. *The Theoretical Works and the Political Activities of Elisée Reclus: A Study in the Development of Anarcho-communism.* University of London, London School of Economics, Ph.D. See entry 801.

1908. Fowler, M. C. 1978. *Essays on Nozick's Libertarianism.* Princeton University, Ph.D. See entries 1178 and 1179.

1909. Fredricks, S. F. 1972. *Social and Political Thought of Federica Montseny, Spanish Anarchist, 1923-1937.* University of New Mexico, Ph.D.

1910. Freeman, D. A. 1976. *Anarchy Revisited: Two Schools of Thought.* Claremont Graduate School, Ph.D.

1911. George, W. 1921. *French Political Theory since 1848 with Special Reference to Syndicalism.* Harvard University, Ph.D.

1912. Ghosh-Pastidar, K. 1984. *Conceptions of Individual Autonomy and Self Responsibility.* University of Oxford, D.Phil.

1913. Goldberg, H. J. 1973. *The Anarchists View the Bolshevik Regime, 1918-1922.* University of Wisconsin, Madison, Ph.D.

1914. Goldberger, S. 1985. *Ervin Szabo, Anarcho-Syndicalism and Democratic Revolution in Turn-of-the-Century Hungary.* Columbia University, Ph.D.

1915. Goodman, J. S. 1981. *Anarchy, State and Utopia and the Natural Right of Property.* University of London, University College, M.Phil.

1916. Goodstein, P. H. 1981. *The Theory of the General Strike: From the French Revolution until World War I.* University of Colorado, Boulder, Ph.D.

1917. Gordon, E. A. 1978. *Anarchism in Brazil: Theory and Practice.* Tulane University, Ph.D.

1918. Hagedorn, C. J. 1984. *On the Treatment of Anarchist Educational Theory and Theorists in Selected Histories of Education.* Saint Louis University, Ph.D.

1919. Halbrook, S. 1972. *The Marx-Bakunin Controversy.* Florida State University, Ph.D. See entry 72.

1920. Hall, B. N. I. 1971. *A History and Critique of American Individualist Anarchists' Economic Theories.* Duke University, Ph.D. See entries 12 and 967.

1921. Hamby, J. L. 1974. *Gentle Anarchist: The Political and Social Thought of Paul Goodman.* University of Missouri, Columbia, Ph.D.

1922. Harmon, C. C. 1984. *The Red and the Black: Collusion between Leftist and Rightist Terrorists in Europe.* Claremont Graduate School, Ph.D.

1923. Hart, J. M. 1970. *Anarchist Thought in Nineteenth-Century Mexico.* University of California, Los Angeles, Ph.D. See entry 1685.

1924. Hartog, S. R. 1962. *The State of Anarchy: The Political Philosophy of Prince Peter Kropotkin.* University of London, London School of Economics, M.Sc.

1925. Hewitt, G. W. 1977. *Revolution, Tradition and Order: The Nineteenth Century Anarchist Experience.* State University of New York, Binghamton, Ph.D.

1926. Hinely, S. D. 1987. *Charlotte Wilson: Anarchist, Fabian and Feminist.* Stanford University, Ph.D.

1927. Hiskes, R. P. 1978. *Community and Freedom: The Political Theory of Cooperative Individualism.* University of Indiana, Ph.D. See entry 1199.

1928. Hoffman, R. 1967. *The Social and Political Theory of P.-J. Proudhon.* Brandeis University, Ph.D. See entry 720.

1929. Holmes, P. H. 1978. *Leo Tolstoi as a Theorist of Non-violent Social Revolution and His Relationship with Mahatma Gandhi.* University of Missouri, Columbia, Ph.D.

1930. Hudon, P. 1972. *The Concept of Revolutionary Class among French Socialists, Babeuf to Proudhon.* Georgetown University, Ph.D.

1931. Hutton, J. G. 1987. *A Blow of the Pick: Science. Anarchism and the Neo-Impressionist Movement.* Northwestern University, Ph.D.

1932. James, R. N. 1985. *Anarchism and Political Violence in Sydney and Melbourne, 1886-1896.* La Trobe University, M.A. See entry 1604.

1933. Jarrell, W. O. 1974. *Some Anarchistic Implications of the Writings of Thomas Paine.* Emory University, Ph.D.

1934. Johns, P. A. 1946. *The Anarchist Movement in the Nineteenth Century: A Social Psychological Study.* University of Wisconsin, Madison, Ph.D.

1935. Johnston, D. A. 1973. *An American Anarchist: An Analysis of the Individualist Anarchism of Benjamin R. Tucker.* University of New Mexico, Ph.D.

1936. Jones, T. D. M. 1987. *Coercion.* (Nozick). University of Glasgow, Ph.D.

1937. Judson, H. H. 1977. *The Concept of Freedom in Anarchist Thought.* University of California, Santa Barbara, Ph.D.

1938. Kingston, H. D. 1932. *The Influence of William Godwin on Shelley.* University of Birmingham, M.A.

1939. Krebs, E. S. 1978. *Liu Shifu and Chinese Anarchism, 1905-1915.* University of Washington, Ph.D.

1940. Land, C. E. L. 1938. *The Novels of William Godwin.* University of Birmingham, M.A.

1941. Lee, S. H. 1978. *Does Moral Freedom Imply Anarchism?* Georgetown University, Ph.D.

1942. Lee, S. 1981. *Goodman's Paradox.* Southern Illinois University, Carbondale, Ph.D

1943. Leeder, E. J. 1985. *The Gentle Warrior: Rose Pesotta, Anarchist and Labor Organizer.* Cornell University, Ph.D.

1944. Leighten, P. D. 1983. *Picasso: Anarchism and Art, 1897-1914.* Rutgers the State University of New Jersey, New Brunswick, Ph.D.

1945. Leon, D. H. 1972. *The American as Anarchist: A Socio-Historical Interpretation.* University of Iowa, Ph.D. See entry 1357.

1946. Levine, L. 1970. *The Labor Movement in France: A Study in Revolutionary Syndicalism.* University of Southern California, Ph.D.

1947. Levitas, I. 1974. *The Unterrified Jeffersonian: Benjamin R. Tucker. A Study of Native American Anarchism as Exemplified in His Life and Times.* New York University, Ph.D.

1948. Lewisohn, D. 1967. *The Political Philosophy of William Godwin.* University of Sussex, M.A.

1949. Lothstein, A. S. 1980. *From Privacy to Praxis: The Case for John Dewey as a Radical Social Philosopher.* New York University, Ph.D.

1950. Luebbering, K. H. 1980. *Learning for Nowhere: Educational Thought in Anarchist Tradition.* University of Missouri, Columbia, Ph.D.

1951. Lund, P. 1976. *The Educational Ideas of Ivan Illich and the Relevance of Them to the British Educational System.* University of Nottingham, M.Phil.

1952. Lynch, H. M. 1976. *Patterns of Anarchy and Order in the Works of John Rechy.* University of Houston, Ph.D.

1953. Mancini, M. J. 1974. *The Covert Themes of American Anarchism, 1881-1908: Time, Space and Consciousness as Anarchist Myth.* Emory University, Ph.D.

1954. Marshall, P. H. 1977. *William Godwin: A Study in the Origins, Development and Influence of His Philosophy.* University of Sussex, D.Phil. See entry 305.

1955. Martin, J. J. 1949. *Individualist Anarchism in the United States ; a Survey of Native Anti-Statist Thought and Action, 1827-1908.* University of Michigan, Ph.D. See entry 1839.

1956. Mayor, J. L. 1984. *Property and Welfare in Liberal Political Philosophy.* (Nozick). Middlesex Polytechnic, Ph.D.

1957. Meaker, G. H. 1968. *Spanish Anarcho-Syndicalism and the Russian Revolution, 1917-1922.* University of Southern California, Ph.D.

1958. Morrison, P. J. 1978. *The Communist Party of Australia and the Australian Radical-Socialist Tradition, 1920-1939.* University of Adelaide, M.A.

1959. Morton, K. W. 1986. *Community as Metaphor: Anarchy and Structure in American Culture, 1830-1920.* University of Minnesota, Ph.D.

1960. Muller, V. L. 1980. *The Idea of Perfectability from Condorcet to Gandhi.* University of California, Santa Barbara, Ph.D.

1961. Nelson, B. C. 1986. *Culture and Conspiracy: A Social History of Chicago Anarchism, 1870-1900.* Northern Illinois University, Ph.D.

1962. Newbrough, M. G. 1975. *Individualist Anarchism in American Political Thought.* University of California, Santa Barbara, Ph.D.

1963. Newman, S. L. 1983. *Liberalism at Wit's End: The Libertarian Revolt against the Modern State.* Cornell University, Ph.D.

1964. Nowlin, W. G. 1980. *The Political Thought of Alexander Berkman.* Tufts University, Ph.D.

1965. Osgood, H. L. 1889. *Socialism and Anarchism.* Columbia University, Ph.D.

1966. Osterfeld, D. E. 1977. *Anarcho-Capitalism: The Development of an Alternative to Government.* University of Cincinnati, Ph.D. See entry 1487.

1967. Palij, M. 1971. *The Peasant Partisan Movement of the Anarchist Nestor Makhno, 1918-1921.* University of Kansas, Ph.D. See entry 1714.

1968. Parrish, T. C. 1985. *Agrarian Politics and Regional Class Formation in La Rioja, Spain, 1868-1975.* New School for Social Research, Ph.D.

1969. Paterson, R. W. K. 1961. *Max Stirner's Philosophy of Education.* University of St. Andrews, B.Phil. See entry 849.

1970. Patsouras, L. 1966. *Jean Grave, French Intellectual and Anarchist, 1854-1939.* Ohio State University, Ph.D. See entry 456.

1971. Perez, J. A. 1986. *Anarchism in the Works of Pio Baroja.* New York University, Ph.D. Spanish text.

1972. Perez-Adan, J. 1986. *Reformist Anarchism, 1800-1936.* Macquarie University, Ph.D.

1973. Perlin, T. M. 1970. *Anarchist-Communism in America, 1890-1914.* Brandeis University, Ph.D. See entry 1495.

1974. Pernicone, N. 1971. *The Italian Anarchist Movement: The Years of Crisis, Decline, and Transformation, 1879-1894.* University of Rochester, Ph.D.

1975. Perry, L. C. 1967. *Antislavery and Anarchy: A Study of the Ideas of Abolitionism Before the Civil War.* Cornell University, Ph.D.

1976. Peterson, C. J. 1960. *Philosophical Anarchism: A Comparative Study of American and European Theory.* University of California, Berkeley, Ph.D.

1977. Philp, M. F. E. 1980. *William Godwin's Political Justice, 1791-1796.* University of Oxford, M.Phil.

1978. Pickles, W. 1928. *Pierre-Joseph Proudhon and Karl Marx.* University of Leeds, M.A. See entry 736.

1979. Presiot, H. K. 1931. *The Economic and Political Theory of William Godwin and His Debt to French Thinkers.* University of Oxford, D.Phil.

1980. Prevost, G. F. 1977. *Marxism and Anarchism - Some Problems in the Controversy.* University of Minnesota, Ph.D.

1981. Price, S. M. 1936. *The Reception and Influence of the Works of Leo Tolstoy in England, 1870-1910.* University of Manchester, M.A.

1982. Protic, M. 1987. *The Ideology of the Serbian Radical Movement, 1881-1903: Sources, Characteristics, Developments.* University of California, Santa Barbara, Ph.D.

1983. Rabinowitz, J. T. 1978. *Emergent Problems and Optimal Solutions: A Critique of Robert Nozick's "Anarchy, State and Utopia."* Massachusetts Institute of Technology, Ph.D.

1984. Riley, T. A. 1946. *John Henry Mackay, Germany's Anarchist Poet: A Study in Individualism.* Harvard University, Ph.D.

1985. Ritter, A. I. 1965. *Proudhon: Realist, Radical Moralist.* Harvard University, Ph.D. See entry 744.

1986. Robinson, P. 1971. *Psychological Ethics in William Godwin's Political Justice, 1798.* University of North Staffordshire, Keele. M.A.

1987. Rogers, J. A. 1957. *Prince Peter Kropotkin, Scientist and Anarchist: A Biographical Study of Science and Politics in Russian History.* Harvard University, Ph.D.

1988. Rogers, L. E. 1975. *Anarchism and Libertarian Education.* University of Nebraska, Lincoln, Ph.D.

1989. Rosen, F. 1964. *Progress and Democracy in William Godwin's Contribution to Political Philosophy.* University of London, London School of Economics, Ph.D. See entry 320.

1990. Roslak, R. S. 1987. *Scientific Aesthetics and the Aetheticized Earth: The Parallel Vision of the Neo-Impressionist Landscape and Anarcho-Communist Social Theory.* University of California, Los Angeles, Ph.D.

1991. Salerno, S. 1986. *The Early Labor Radicalism of the Industrial Workers of the World: A Socio-Cultural Critique.* Brandeis University, Ph.D.

1992. Sarracino, C. T. 1974. *Henry Miller, Spiritual Anarchist.* University of Michigan, Ph.D.

1993. Schultz, K. D. 1984. *Revolutionary versus Evolutionary Anarchism: An Intra-Theory Comparative Analysis.* Florida State University, Ph.D.

1994. Sciabarra, C. M. 1988. *Toward a Radical Critique of Utopianism: Dialectics and Dualism in the Works of Friedrich Hayek, Murray Rothbard and Karl Marx.* New York University, Ph.D.

1995. Shuford, R. W. 1974. *Anarchism and Social Action in America: A Case Study of an Alternative Health Care Facility.* Northwestern University, Ph.D.

1996. Silberman, M. 1979. *Tolstoy and America: A Study in Reciprocal Influence.* County University of New York, Ph.D

1997. Silverman, W. Z. 1988. *Gyp: Right Wing Anarchist at the Fin de Siècle.* New York University, Ph.D.

1998. Sonn, R. D. 1981. *French Anarchism as Cultural Politics in the 1890's.* University of California, Berkeley, Ph.D. See entry 1640.

1999. Stanley, T. A. 1978. *Osugi Sakae: A Japanese Anarchist.* University of Arizona, Ph.D. See entry 1675.

2000. Steakley, J. D. 1986. *Anarchism and Culture: The Political and Cultural Theories of Erich Mühsam.* Cornell University, Ph.D.

2001. Steinke, G. E. 1955. *The Anarchistic, Expressionistic and Dadaistic Phases in the Life and Work of Hugo Ball.* Stanford University, Ph.D.

2002. Stevenson, B. J. H. 1972. *The Ideology of American Anarchism, 1880-1910*. University of Iowa, Ph.D.

2003. Straus, R. 1973. *The Anarchist Argument: An Analysis of Three Justifications of Anarchism*. Columbia University, Ph.D.

2004. Suits, D. B. 1977. *The Political Theory of Lysander Spooner*. University of Waterloo, Ph.D.

2005. Sykes, T. 1974. *The Practice of Revolutionary Syndicalism in Italy, 1905-1910*. Columbia University, Ph.D.

2006. Tager, F. M. S. 1979. *A Radical Approach to Education: Anarchist Schooling-The Modern School of New York and Stelton*. Ohio State University, Ph.D.

2007. Taylor, A. 1980. *Liberty and Equality in the Social Order, with Special Reference to the Views of John Rawls and Robert Nozick*. The Catholic University of America, Ph.D.

2008. Taylor, M. J. 1975. *Anarchy and Co-operation*. University of Essex, Ph.D. See entry 1552.

2009. Thomas, D. P. 1973. *Karl Marx's Disputes with the Anarchists*. Harvard University, Ph.D. See entry 1558.

2010. Thomas, J. A. 1964. *The Philosophical Anarchism of William Godwin: His Philosophy of Man, State and Society*. University of Southern California, Ph.D.

2011. Varias, A. 1986. *Anarchists in Fin-de-Siècle Paris*. New York University, Ph.D.

2012. Vaughan, W. H. I. 1970. *Toward an Anarchistic Theory of Education: A Systematic Examination of the Educational Thought of Paul Goodman*. University of Kentucky, Ph.D.

2013. Vincent, K. S. 1981. *Pierre-Joseph Proudhon and the Rise of French Socialism*. University of California, Berkeley, Ph.D. See entry 753.

2014. Waggoner, G. A. 1983. *The Black Hand: Agrarian Anarchism in Southern Spain, 1881-1883*. Columbia University, Ph.D.

2015. Wake, W. E. 1977. *Anarchism and Education: Development of a Framework for Non-authoritarian Education*. University of Maryland College Park, Ph.D.

2016. Waters, K. B. 1981. *The Demands of Libertarianism: Is Robert Nozick's Minimal State Justified?* University of Connecticut, Ph.D.

2017. Weaver, C. E. 1982. *Anarchy, Planning and Regional Development: The Regional Question in Historical Perspective.* University of California, Los Angeles, Ph.D.

2018. Wesely, R. J. 1981. *The Triumph of the System: Alexander Berkman, Anarchism, and America.* Saint Louis University, Ph.D.

2019. White, M. K. 1921. *William Godwin: His Life, Work and Influences.* University of Sheffield, M.A.

2020. Williams, D. 1974. *William Godwin's Struggle for Autonomy, 1791-1797.* University of Kentucky, Ph.D. See entry 327.

2021. Williams, M. R. 1923. *William Godwin: Philosopher and Man of Letters.* University of Bristol, M.A.

2022. Williams, M. G. 1974. *Politics without Love: Anarchism in Turgenev, Dostoevsky and James.* University of Michigan, Ph.D.

2023. Winter, P. 1984. *Politics and Society in Marx and Proudhon.* University of Manchester, Ph.D.

2024. Yates, S. A. 1983. *The Significance of Feyerabend's "Anarchism" for Contemporary Philosophy of Science.* University of Georgia, Ph.D.

2025. Yoast, R. A. 1974. *The Development of Argentine Anarchism: A Socio-Ideological Analysis.* University of Wisconsin, Madison, Ph.D.

2026. Zarrow, P. G. 1987. *Chinese Anarchists: Ideals and the Revolution of 1911.* University of California, Berkeley, Ph.D. See entry 1630.

Journals

JOURNALS OF HISTORICAL SIGNIFICANCE

2027. *L'Agitazione*. Ancona. Edited by Errico Malatesta 1897-1898. Malatesta published, in the journal, articles which discussed some of the views put forward by Kropotkin in *The Conquest of Bread*.

2028. *L'Anarchie*. Paris. April 1905-July 1914. Articles reprinted as *Libertad*. Edited Roger Langlais. Paris: Editions Galilée, 1976.

2029. *The Anarchist*. London. March 1885-August 1888. Edited by Henry Seymour, a follower of Benjamin Tucker, this was a journal associated with neo-Proudhonian and individualist anarchist views.

2030. *Arbeiter Zeitung*. Berne. July 1876-October 1877. A German-language newspaper set up in Berne by Paul Brousse; first published on 15th July, 1876, it ceased publication with the issue of 13 October, 1877.

2031. *L'Associazione*. Nice/London. 1889-1890. Edited by Errico Malatesta it was published with the intention "to constitute an international socialist-anarchist-revolutionary party with a common platform." (Max Nettlau, *Errico Malatesta*, 42. Op.cit., entry 639).

2032. *L'Avant-Garde*. La Chaux-de-Fonds. June 1877-December 1878. Started by Paul Brousse in La Chaux-de-Fonds on 2 June 1877, it closed with the issue of 2 December 1878. Brousse was arrested by the Swiss government and sentenced to two months in gaol. *L'Avant-Garde* was designated the successor journal to *Bulletin De La Fédération Jurassienne*, by the editor of that journal, James Guillaume, after its closure in March 1878. However *L'Avant-Garde* was more aggressive - "un journal d'attaque" (Kropotkin) - than its predecessor.

2033. *Blast.* San Francisco. January 1916-June 1917. A journal edited by Alexander Berkman. Reproduced New York: Greenwood Reprint, 1970.

2034. *Bulletin de la Fédération Jurassienne.* La Chaux-de-Fonds. 1872-March 1878. Edited by James Guillaume, this was very much a Bakuninist journal. Kropotkin contributed significantly to it during its final year of publication.

2035. *The Commonweal.* London. February 1885-May 1894. The paper of Morris's Socialist League, which, when the anarchist faction was in the ascendency, took on a decidedly anarchist character. The anarchists won a majority on the executive council in 1889 and deprived Morris of the editorship. In December 1890 *Commonweal* appeared as a monthly with the subhead "A Journal of Revolutionary Socialism." It resumed weekly publication in May 1892 with the subhead, "A Revolutionary Journal of Anarchist Communism."

2036. *Le Droit Social.* Lyon. 12th February 1882-23rd July 1882. The first of a series of periodicals published in Lyon in this period. As each was suppressed by the authorities, it was replaced by a successor. They reflect Lyon's importance as a center for the dissemination of anarchism in the 1880s.

2037. *Fanal.* Berlin. October 1926-July 1931. Edited by the anarchist intellectual Erich Mühsam, who, with Gustav Landauer, was one of the leaders of the Bavarian Soviet in 1919. Mühsam had previously published and edited the journal *Kain*, Munich: 1911-14/1918-19. He hanged himself while in the "protective custody" of the Nazis.

2038. *Freedom.* London. October 1886-November/December 1927. May 1930-July/September 1936. August 1945-. The anarchist journal with the longest existence. Founded by Kropotkin, Charlotte Wilson and others it has been a vehicle for anarchist ideas and programmes for over a century, after surviving a troubled period during the 1930s. It was absorbed by *Fighting Call* in October 1936, a paper published by the Freedom Group, London, and the Anti-Parliamentary Communist Federation, Glasgow. *Fighting Call* ceased publication in February 1937. *Spain and the World*, December 1936-December 1938, and *Revolt*, February 1939-June 1939, provided, in succession, a forum for anarchist ideas until *War Commentary*, incorporating *Freedom*, appeared in November 1939. *War Commentary* ran until August 1945, when *Freedom* reappeared as *Freedom Through Anarchism*. This title was maintained up to and including the issue of 14 December 1946. On 4 January 1947 the title *Freedom* was resumed with Vol.8, No.1.

2039. *Freiheit.* London. January 1879-December 1882. New York. 1883-August 1910. Founded by Johann Most this was the first anarchist paper published in England. Most was jailed in 1881 for celebrating the assassination of Tsar Alexander II, and the paper was suppressed in 1882 for its support of Irish assassins. A few issues were produced in Geneva but, following the release of Most, the base was moved to New York in 1883, from where Most's fiery journalism provided a backdrop to the Haymarket Affair of 1886.

2040. *Le Journal du Peuple*. Paris. 22 January-August 1899. Established by Sébastien Faure as daily form of *Le Libertaire*, it failed after a short period, and Faure reverted to the weekly format.

2041. *Le Libertaire*. Paris. November 1895-June 1914/1919- 1958? Established by Sébastien Faure, this proved to be the longest lasting of French anarchist periodicals distributed on a national level. Normally a weekly, it was published on a daily basis as *Le Journal du Peuple* in 1899, and on a daily basis as *Le Libertaire* from December to March 1923.

2042. *Liberty*. New York. 1881-April 1908. Suspended from December 1900 to December 1902. Periodical founded and edited by Benjamin Tucker and expressing in its columns his individualist anarchist views. George Bernard Shaw, among others, was impressed.

2043. *Man!* San Francisco. January 1933-April/May 1940. An anarchist journal of prose, poetry and comment, edited by Marcus Graham. Material for the May 1940 issue was turned over to the U. S. Federal Attorney who advised the printer to cease printing further issues or face prosecution by the Government. It was the ninth printer in seven and a half years of existence. The journal folded in the face of this pressure. A collection of articles, extracts etc. from the journal is published as *Man!*, op.cit., entry 1389.

2044. *Mother Earth*. New York. March 1906-August 1917. The periodical founded by Emma Goldman and Alexander Berkman, containing not only their writings but those of other eminent American anarchists of the period, including Voltairine de Cleyre and Hippolyte Havel.

2045. *Pensiero e Volontà*. Rome. January 1924-October 1926. Due to censorship, only 16 numbers appeared in 1925 and the bi-monthly journal suspended publication in 1926. It was edited during this period by Errico Malatesta, who also wrote some important pieces for the journal.

2046. *Le Père Peinard*. Paris. February 1889-January 1894. October/November 1896-1902?. A journal founded and edited by Émile Pouget, it sought to propagate anarchist ideas in a popular form, especially anarcho-syndicalist views. Like *La Révolte* it fell foul of the laws against anarchist propaganda promulgated in 1894.

2047. *Le Peuple*. Paris. November 1848-13th June 1849. 15th June-13th October 1850. As Proudhon's second periodical this was the successor to *Le Représenant du Peuple*. After support for an insurrection against Louis-Napoleon it was closed down and its premises wrecked. It reappeared for a short period in 1850 as a successor to *La Voix du Peuple*.

2048. *La Questione Sociale*. Firenze. Edited by Malatesta 1884-85. Published some important pieces of the young Malatesta.

2049. *Le Représentant du Peuple*. Paris. February 1848-September 1848. First Issue 7 February 1848. Proudhon's first periodical, in which he set out his views on property and mutuality. At its height the circulation reputedly reached an amazing 40,000 copies. It was suppressed in September 1848.

2050. *Revolt*. London. Feb.-June 1939. The successor journal to *Spain and the World*.

2051. *La Révolte*. Paris. September 1887-March 1894. First edition 17 September 1887. *La Révolté* was the successor to *Le Révolté*, edited by Jean Grave. It received the support of Elisée Reclus. It was highly regarded in anarchist circles as it continued and maintained the standards of its predecessor. However, in 1894, *La Révolte* collapsed as a result of new laws against anarchistic propaganda. Kropotkin contributed many articles to this journal, some of which were later published as *La Conquête du Pain*. *La Révolte* was succeeded by *Les Temps Nouveaux*.

2052. *Le Révolté*. Geneva. February 1878-March 1885/Paris. April 1885-September 1887. A journal, founded by Peter Kropotkin, and published from 1879 to 1887, that received moral and financial support from Elisée Reclus. It was a journal of considerable significance to the anarchist movement with serious and well-written articles that set out the principles of anarchist communism. Many of Kropotkin's articles in this journal were later published in *Paroles d'un Révolté*, op.cit. entry, 514. Designed as a successor to the banned *L'Avant-Garde*, the journal was first published in Geneva in February, 1879, by Kropotkin and two friends - described by Kropotkin as "the half-literate" François Dumartheray and "the novice" Georg Herzig. The journal had a wider circulation (some two thousand copies) than either the *Bulletin* or *L'Avant-Garde*. During Kropotkin's imprisonment at Clairvaux, Herzig and Dumartheray continued to publish the paper. Jean Grave, at the request of Reclus, and with Kropotkin's consent, took over the editorship of the paper at the end of 1883. Early in 1885, following increasing official harassment from the Swiss authorities, Grave moved the operations of the paper from Geneva to Paris. By 1 January, 1887, its circulation had grown to 8,000. Later that year Grave changed the name of the paper to *La Révolte* in a effort to deflect official attention.

2053. *Spain and the World*. London. December 1936-December 1938. A fortnightly journal published by Freedom Press from 1936-39; included articles by Emma Goldman, Camillo Berneri and Herbert Read. In 1939 it was incorporated in *Revolt*.

2054. *Les Temps Nouveaux*. Paris. May 1895-August 1914. 1916-June 1919. July 1919-June/July 1921. Edited by Jean Grave with the help of Kropotkin, the latter writing many articles for the journal. It was the successor to *La Révolte*.

2055. *Umanità Nova.* Daily. Milan. Rome. Edited by Malatesta, 1920-22. At its peak it had a daily circulation of 50,000.

2056. *La Voix du Peuple.* Paris. 1 October 1849-14 May 1850. Proudhon's third periodical, financed by Alexander Herzen. Even more popular than its predecessors it was suppressed in May 1850. It was preceded and succeeded by *Le Peuple.*

2057. *Volontà.* Ancona. Edited by Malatesta from its inception, in June 1913, until June 1914. In this journal Malatesta developed his anti-war position and criticized those anarchists, such as Kropotkin, who had adopted a pro-war stance.

CONTEMPORARY JOURNALS

The great majority of the journals cited below are drawn from lists produced by *The Anarchist Age*, P. O. Box 29, Parkville, Victoria 3052, Australia, and are reprinted with the permission of the editors of that journal. They invite enquires or correspondence.

Argentina :

2058. *32 Gremios Democráticos.* José Grunfeld, Moreno 1702-1°,1093 Buenos Aires. An anarchist broadsheet that has been produced for the past 22 years.

2059. *Democráticos.* Casilla de Correo 1138, Correo Central, 1000 Buenos Aires. Anarchist newsletter.

2060. *Ideaacción.* Grupo Impulso, Sarmiento 4694, Rosario. An anarchist journal produced in Rosario.

2061. *El Libertario.* Carlos N. Farino, Brasil 1551, (1154), Buenos Aires. A broadsheet produced by the Federación Libertaria Argentina.

Australia :

2062. *Activate.* P.O Box 509, Port Melbourne, Victoria 3207. A publication by a group of anarchists in Port Melbourne.

2063. *The Anarchist Age.* P.O. Box 20, Parkville, Victoria 3052. Formerly the *Libertarian Workers Monthly*, this six-monthly journal is produced by the Melbourne based Libertarian Workers for a Self-Managed Society.

2064. *Black and Blue.* P.O. Box 25, Collingwood, Victoria 3066. A production of the Anarchist Black Cross in Melbourne.

2065. *Black Star.* Box 92, Students Council, Macquarie University, N.S.W. 2109. The journal produced by the Anarchist Students Union.

2066. *Circle A.* Propaganda Collective, Box 92, Students Union, Macquarie University, N.S.W. 2109. The paper of the Anarchist Students' Union.

2067. *Ecstasy.* Ecstasy Productions, G.P.O. Box 4644TT, Melbourne, Victoria 3001. Anarchist poems and other writing.

2068. *The Future Now.* Box 482, Wooloongabba, Queensland 4102. Produced in Brisbane, this is an anarchist publication featuring poetry and montage.

2069. *Mutual Aid.* P.O. Box 187, West End 4101, Queensland. A publication by a libertarian Catholic Group.

2070. *Rebel Worker.* P.O. Box 92, Broadway, Sydney, N.S.W. 2007. The monthly publication of the Anarcho-Syndicalist Federation.

2071. *Red and Black.* P.O. Box 115, Enmore, N.S.W. 2042. Published twice yearly, this is a journal of essays and articles on various aspects of anarchist thought.

2072. *Sparks.* P.O. Box 1066, Nth. Richmond, Victoria, 3121/P.O. Box 259, Darlinghurst, N.S.W. 2010. Publication of the Transport Workers Association, an anarcho-syndicalist organization based on the public transport systems of Victoria and New South Wales.

2073. *Squat It.* 301, St Georges Road, North Fitzroy, Victoria 3065.

2074. *Stand Up and Squat.* P.O.Box 332, North Quay, Queensland 4002. A publication of the West End Anarchists.

2075. *Unity.* P.O. Box 214, Broadway, N.S.W. 2007. The journal of the anarcho-syndicalist postal workers.

2076. *Vacant Lot.* Freedom Collective, P.O.Box 203, Fremantle, W.A. 6160. A broadsheet produced in Western Australia.

Belgium :

2077. *Alternative Libertaire.* 2 Rue de l'Inquisition, 1040 Bruxelles. A monthly French language anarchist publication.

2078. *De Nar.* Bunderneef 2, 1710 Dilbeek. A Flemish language journal that sometimes contains anarchist material.

Canada:

2079. *Anarchist Black Cross.* P.O. Box 6326 Sth. A, Toronto, Ontario M5W 1P7. Regular newsletter providing world-wide information on anarchist and other anti-authoritarian prisoners.

2080. *Anytime Now.* Affinity Place, Argenta, B.C. VOG 1BO. Libertarian discussion journal.

2081. *Demolition Derby.* C.P. 1554, Succ. B, Montréal, Quebec. Journal of revolutionary theory and analysis.

2082. *Ecomedia Bulletin.* P.O. Box 915, Station F, Toronto, Ontario M4Y 2N9. Bi-weekly covering local and international issues from an anarchist viewpoint.

2083. *Endless Struggle.* P.O. Box 69601, Stn. K, Vancouver, B.C. V5K 4W7. Anarchist journal.

2084. *Kick It Over.* P.O. Box 5811, Station A, Toronto, Ontario. Anarcho-feminist journal.

2085. *Open Road.* Box 6135, Station G, Vancouver, B.C. V6R 4G5. Anarchist journal.

2086. *Our Generation.* 3981 Boulevard St-Laurent, Montréal, Quebec H2W 1Y5. A semi-annual journal of articles and reviews devoted to the theory and practice of contemporary anarchism and libertarian socialism with material on anarchist history. Originally a peace journal entitled *Our Generation Against Nuclear War* which began with the Fall 1961 issue.

2087. *Reality Now.* P.O. Box 6326, Station A, Toronto, Ontario M5W 1P7. An informative anarchist journal.

Chile:

2088. *Accioni Directa.* Casilla 52.330, Santiago-1. An anarchist journal produced by the Santiago Anarchist Collective.

Cuba:

2089. *Guangara Libertaria.* P.O.Box 1516, Riverside Station, Miami, Florida, 33135-1516. Quarterly journal published in Spanish by Cuban anarchists in exile.

Eastern Europe:

2090. *Iztok.* B.P. 70, 75663 Paris Cedex 12. Published in French this details anarchist activity in Eastern Europe.

Esperanto:

2091. *Liberecana Ligilo.* P. Persson, Svartvilisv 14, S-123 52 Farsta, Sweden (Svedio). Produced by the Anarchist/Libertarian wing of the world Esperanto movement. See also entry 2142.

France :

2092. *L'Anarchie.* Marcel Renoulet, B.P. 205, 42005 Saint Étienne, Cedex. Publication of the *Alliance Ouvriée Anarchiste.*

2093. *Bulletin C.R.I.R.A.* Secretariet de la Crira, 145 Rue Amelot 75011, Paris. Bulletin of international anarchist news produced by the French Anarchist Federation.

2094. *Cercle Études.* Documentation Anarchiste, B.P. 28, 33031 Bordeaux, Cedex. Newsletter of the Bordeaux based Circle of Anarchist Studies.

2095. *Chroniques Libertaires.* B.P. 266, 75624 Paris, Cedex 13/or Centre de Propagande et de Culture Anarchiste, B.P. 21, 94190 Villeneuve-Saint-Georges. An anarchist journal which reviews the local and international anarchist press.

2096. *Femmes Libres.* 61 Rue Pauly, 33130 Beglés. Newsletter of Libertarian Free Women. They organize regular international meetings, the last being in Bordeaux in August 1990.

2097. *Feuille Anarchiste.* 122 Ave. de Choisy, Paris (13e). Anarchist journal.

2098. *L'Homme Libre.* B.P. 205, 42005 Saint Étienne. A quarterly journal.

2099. *Humeurs Noirs.* B.P. 79, 59370, Mons en Baroeue. Publication of the Anarchist Federation.

2100. *I.F.A. Bulletin.* 145 Rue Amelot, 75011 Paris. Bulletin of the *Internationale des Féderations Anarchistes.*

2101. *Interrogations.* B.P. 243, 75564 Paris, Cedex 12. An anarchist journal focussing on environmental issues.

2102. *Le Libertaire.* 25 Rue Dune d'Aplemont, 76600 Le Havre. Monthly journal.

2103. *Lutter!* B.P. 602, 75530 Paris. A publication of the French Libertarian Communists.

2104. *Le Monde Libertaire.* 145 Rue Amelot, 75011 Paris. The weekly newspaper of the French Anarchist Federation.

2105. *L'Unisme.* B.P. 105, 94402 Vitry, Cedex. Anarchist journal.

2106. *Volonté Anarchiste.* 145 Rue Amelot, 75011 Paris. Anarchist journal produced by the Groupe Fregnes-Antony.

Germany :

2107. *A.I.T Press Releases.* I.A.A., Postfach 101223, 5000 Köln 1. Press releases from the International Workers Association regarding anarchist struggles across the world.

2108. *Schwarzer Faden.* Postfach 1159, D-7031 Grafenau-1. Excellently produced anarchist journal.

2109. *Subversion.* Postlagerkarte 002263B, D-1000 Berlin 12. A journal of "modern revolutionary thought."

2110. *Trafik.* Verlag und Versand Internationaler Libertarer Medien, Peter Peterson, Edvardstrasse 40, 4330 Mulheim/Ruhr 1. A journal of libertarian culture and politics.

Greece :

2111. *Anarchia.* T.O. 26050, 1022 Athens. Produced monthly by anarchist activists.

2112. *Anarchist Covenant.* T.O. 30658, 1033 Athens. Monthly journal containing pieces on Marxism and anarchism.

2113. *Antieeoysia.* Aohna Kasaph, T.O. 31421, 100 35, Athens 47. Well-produced anarchist journal.

2114. *Dokimh.* T.O. 26050, 10022, Athens 5. A monthly anarchist journal of news and comment.

2115. *Enantia.* Filipou 46, T.O. 65403, Kavala. Bi-monthly journal with pieces on Marxism and anarchism.

Hungary :

2116. *Anarcho-Info.* Autonomia, c/- Eonos Klub, Karolyi M.ut. 9, H-1053 Budapest. Small publication, in English, outlining anarchist activities in Hungary.

Ireland :

2117. *Ainriail.* c/o 7 Winetaven Street, Belfast 1. A journal produced by Belfast anarchists that focuses on issues in Northern Ireland.

Israel :

2118. *Problemen.* 203 Ben Jehuda, Tel Aviv 63502. Anarchist journal published in Hebrew.

Italy:

2119. *Anarchismo.* A.M. Bonnano, C.P. 61, 95100 Catania. A well-produced journal that examines contemporary issues from an anarchist viewpoint.

2120. *L'Agitatore Anarchico.* G. Ruzza, Via C. Mercuri No. 9/0-13045, Gattinara. A journal from the *Gruppo Anarchico in Gattinara.*

2121. *Anarres.* Via S. Pietro 5, 54033 Carrara (MS). Anarchist journal of news and comment.

2122. *A Rivista Anarchica.* Editrice A, C.P. 17120, 20170 Milano. Well-produced monthly journal covering events and ideas in the anarchist movement on a global basis.

2123. *Autonomen.* Edizioni Sapere Collettivo, Via Finuli 29, 20092 Cinisello Bàlsamo, Milano. A journal of the Italian autonomist movement.

2124. *Bolletino di Collegamento Nazionale.* Vincenzo Italiano, C.P. 391-80100, Napoli. Bulletin of Italian anarchist news.

2125. *Centro di Documentazione Pistoia.* Co-operativa CDP, C.P. 347, Via degli Orati 29, 51100 Pistoia. A bi-monthly anarchist bulletin produced by the anarchist library and documentation center in Pistoia.

2126. *Collegamenti Wobbly.* c/- Comitato Cabral, Via Massena 31, Torino. Well-produced journal.

2127. *Comidad.* Vincenzo Italiano, C.P. 391, 80100 Napoli. Anarchist bulletin for the Collegamento Nazionale in Naples. Appearing bi-monthly it looks at contemporary issues and reprints excerpts from the Italian anarchist media.

2128. *Communismo Libertario.* C.P. 558, 57100 Livorno. The journal of the Italian Libertarian and Anarchist Communists.

2129. *CRAN.* C.P. 264, 41100, Modena. The periodical of the Italian Christian Anarchist Movement.

2130. *Dintorni.* Centrostudi CDM, C.P. 259, Via Rainusso 130, 41100 Modena. Newsletter produced by the Anarchist Study Center, Modena.

2131. *Germinal.* Via Mazzini II, 32124 Trieste. Anarchist journal of news and comment regularly produced in Trieste.

2132. *Homo Sapiens.* C.P. 705, 70121 Bari. Well-produced left-libertarian journal.

2133. *Operai Contro.* C.P. 17168, 20170 Milano, Leoncavallo. A journal produced every two months.

2134. *Pantagruel.* Edizioni Anarchismo, C.P. 61, 95100 Catania. A journal of anarchist social, political and philosophical analysis. Supplement to *Anarchismo.*

2135. *Provocazione.* C.P. 61, 95100 Catania. Anarchist journal.

2136. *Seme Anarchico.* C.P. 217, 25154 Brescia. Monthly anarchist journal produced for the last ten years by Brescia anarchists.

2137. *Senzapatria.* C.P. 72, Calolziocorte, (BG). An anti-military and anti-authoritarian publication.

2138. *Sicilia Libertaria.* Giuseppe Gurrieri, Vico Leonardo Imposa 4, 97100 Ragusa. A monthly Sicilian anarchist journal of news and comment.

2139. *Umanità Nova.* Federazione Anarchica Italiana, Viale Monza 255, 20126 Milano or Via Ernesto Rossi 80, 57100 Livorno. A weekly newspaper produced by the Italian Anarchist Movement.

2140. *Volontá.* Editrice A, Via Rovetta 27, 20127 Milan. Anarchist journal of theory and ideas.

Japan:

2141. *Hiroshima Anarchist Bulletin.* 1539 Ibara, Shiraki Asakijaku, Hiro si Machi, Hiroshima-ken. Bulletin produced by Hiroshima anarchist group.

2142. *Libera Volo.* A.R. Hensulitejo. 103 Senrien 1-6-39, Tojonaka Osaka, 56 Japan. The monthly journal of the Japanese Anarchist Federation produced in Esperanto.

2143. *Libertaire.* Yachi yodai Kita, 7-4-60, Yachinjo-shi Chiba, 276 Japan. A journal published over the past twenty years by a Tokyo based anarchist group.

Korea:

2144. *Federation of Korean Anarchists-Bulletin.* CIRA, P.O. 1938, Kwanghwamun, Seoul. Bulletin of the Federation of Korean Anarchists.

Mexico:

2145. *Inquietudes.* Eliseo Rojas, A.P. M-10596, Mexico L. A journal published by *Tierra y Libertad.*

2146. *Regeneraçion.* A.P. 9090, Mexico I.D.F. Newsletter of the Mexican Anarchist Organization.

2147. *Tierra y Libertad.* A.P. 10596, Mexico I.D.F. Anarchist journal in production for over fifty years.

Netherlands :

2148. *Buiten de Orde.* Faustlaan 34, Amstelveen. Anarchist journal.

2149. *Nieuwe Strijd.* Volkstraat 22, 2517 RM, Den Haag. Journal produced by the Independent Revolutionary Syndicalist Union.

2150. *Recht Voor Allen.* Fis. P. Calandlaan 50, P.B. 1149, Amsterdam. A journal produced by the Social Anarchists.

2151. *De Raaf.* P.B. 51217, Amsterdam. A journal containing a wide selection of anarchist articles.

2152. *Totalweiger.* p/a Totalweigerspreekuur, AMB, Pontanusstraat 20, Nijmegan. Anarchist journal.

2153 *De Zwarte.* P.B. 1023, Den Haag. Well-produced anarchist journal.

New Zealand :

2154. *Anti-System 12.* c/- Anarchy Organization, P.O. Box 14156, Kilbirnie, Wellington.

2155. *The State Adversary.* P.O. Box 78-104, Greylynn, Auckland. Discussion journal produced by an anarchist publishing house, Lancaster Publishing.

Poland :

2156. *Acapella.* Adam Jagusiak, ul. Grunwaldzka 33/3, Sopot, Poland. Anarchist journal produced by freedom and peace activists.

2157. *Action.* Piotr J. K. Tyminski, A. I. Rewolucji Pazdziernikowej 97/19, 01-424 Warszawa. Information bulletin on anarchism and anarchist activity produced in English.

2158. *Anarcholl.* Dariusz Misiuna, ul. Guliwera 29, 03-610 Warszawa. Anarchist publication with an English summary.

2159. *Atak.* Marcal Mularski, ul. Morska 64/8, 75-234 Koszalin. Anarchist journal.

2160. *Awers.* Jaroslaw Bednarek. ul. Knietskeiego 3B/3, 75-445 Koszalin. Journal of the Polish Alternative Youth Movement.

2161. *Biuletyn Informacyiny FA.* Marek Kurzyniec, ul. Smolemsk 16/8, 31-112 Krakow. Bulletin of the Polish Anarchist Federation.

2162. *Fraternite.* Piotr J.K. Tyminski, A 1. Rewolucji Pazdziernikowej 97/19, 01-424 Warszawa. A journal focussing on the history and theory of anarchism.

2163. *Homek.* Janusz Waluszkio, ul. Stare Domki 6/9, 80-857 Gdansk. Newsletter by the Gdansk Alternative Society Movement.

2164. *Kulturka Press.* Rafal Kasprzak, ul. Bieruta 17/40, 64-920 Pila. Magazine of comment, and musical and literary reviews, all from an anti-statist position.

2165. *Mat Paryadka.* P.O.Box 67, 81-806 Sopot 6. Anarchist journal with articles on a wide variety of topics.

2166. *Rebelianat Poranny.* Stalislaw Gorka, ul. Energetykow 8/9, 41-76 Ruda Slaska. Anarchist journal produced in the Silesia region.

2167. *Rewolta.* Piotr Salwowski, ul. Mieszka I 48, 05-090 Raszyn, Warszawa. Anarchist journal produced by the Alternative Society Movement and the Anarchist Federation.

2168. *Spartakus.* Janusz Waluszko, ul. Stare Domki 6/9, 80-857 Gdansk. A journal of libertarian politics and culture.

2169. *Szajba.* Andrzej Tokarski, ul. Wolnosci 17/1, 67-120 Kozuchow. Contains articles on anarchist themes.

Portugal :

2170. *A Batalha.* Apartada 5085, 1702 Lisboa Codex. An anarchist journal of news and comment founded in 1919. Appears every two months.

2171. *Aideia.* Av. Guerra Janqueiro, 19-5°-E°, 1000 Lisboa. A publication by Portuguese and Brazilian anarchists which reviews anarchist culture and thought.

2172. *Antitese.* Apartado 40, 2801 Almada Codex. A libertarian/anarchist education journal.

2173. *Ekomedia.* C.D. 1 Centelha, Apartado 241, 3003 Coimbra Codex. A bulletin of Portuguese news from a libertarian perspective produced in English.

Spain :

2174. *Cenit.* Cenit-CNT, CCP 15 574 49K, 33 Rue des Vignoles, 75 020 Paris. The organ of the C.N.T. in exile.

2175. *C.N.T..* Apdo. de Correos 282, 48080 Bilbao. Bi-monthly journal of the C.N.T., providing analysis of Spanish and international anarcho-syndicalist activities.

2176. *CNT.* c/- Magdalena 29, 20 Piso, Madrid. Monthly journal of the breakaway C.N.T.

2177. *La Estiba.* c/- del Mar, 97-08003 Barcelona. Monthly journal produced by the Anarcho-Syndicalist Dock Workers for its members.

2178. *La Libertad.* C.A.S.P.A., Apdo. de Correos No. 55-106, 28080 Madrid. A journal of news and comment of a Madrid anarchist group.

2179. *Polémica.* A. Lopez, Administrador, Valencia 465, 4°-3ª, 08013 Barcelona. A monthly journal of criticism and views produced by the Spanish Anarchist Movement.

2180. *Rojo y Negro.* Redacción, Sagunto 15. Anarchist journal.

2181. *Solidaridad Obrera.* Pza. de Medinaceli, 6, Entl., 1A, 08002, Barcelona. A monthly journal produced by the C.N.T. de Cataluña since 1907.

2182. *Tetuan.* Apdo. de Correos 28021, 28080 Madrid. New publication from Madrid.

Sweden:

2183. *Brand.* Box 15015, 5-10465, Stockholm. Previously known as *Total Brand*, the journal has been in existence for some ninety years.

2184. *SAC Newsletter.* Central Organization of Swedish Workers, Sveavagen 98, 11350 Stockholm. SAC is a syndicalist trade union made up of autonomous local branches. The newsletter seeks to inform organizations abroad of their activities.

Turkey:

2185. *Efendisiz.* Ufuk Ozcan, P.K. 953, 34437 Sirkeci, Istanbul. Bi-monthly anarchist journal.

2186. *Kara.* P.K. 1053, 34437 Sirkeci, Istanbul. Anarchist journal.

United Kingdom : England:

2187. *Anarchy.* Box A, 84b, Whitechapel High Street, London E1 7QX. A journal of debate about anarchist theory and history in the 1960s and early 1970s when edited by Colin Ward. It later became a journal of news and comment more directly linked to the activist movement.

2188. *Black Flag.* 121 Railton Rd., London SE 24. A journal of news and comment for anarchist activists.

2189. *Bulletin of Anarchist Research.* T. V. Cahill, Dept. of Politics, University of Lancaster, Lancaster LA 14YL. Anarchist journal for discussion, reviews and exchange of research information.

2190. *Direct Action.* P.O. Box 761, Camberwell SDO, London SE59 JH. Newsletter of the Direct Action Movement, an anarcho-syndicalist organization.

2191. *Endless Struggle.* Hooligan Pr., B.M. Hurricane, London WC1N 3XX. A journal concentrating on anarchist activity, particularly in Europe.

2192. *Freedom.* Freedom Pr., 84b Whitechapel High Street, London E1 7QX. Journal of articles and comment produced for 104 years, though not continuously. See 2033.

2193. *Green Anarchist.* 19 Magdalen Road, Oxford OX41 RP or 34 Cowley Rd, Oxford, OX41 H2. The magazine of the Green Anarchists of the U.K.

2194. *Here and Now.* P.O. Box 109, Leeds LS5 3AA. A journal which presents a radical, libertarian viewpoint on contemporary issues.

2195. *Insurrection.* Elephant Editions, B.M. Elephant, London WC1N 3XX. An anarchist journal of discussion and comment.

2196. *Libertarian Education.* The Cottage, The Green, Leire, Leicestershire. A journal that aims at the liberation of learning.

2197. *Organise.* P.O.Box 263, Sheffield S1 3EX. The journal of the British Anarcho-Communist Federation.

2198. *A Pinch of Salt.* c/- 24 South Road, Hockley, Birmingham B18. A Christian anarchist journal.

2199. *The Raven.* Freedom Pr., 84b Whitechapel High Street, London E1 7QX. An anarchist quarterly containing articles and reviews on anarchist theory and history.

2200. *Solidarity.* c/- 123 Lathom Road, London E6 2EA. A journal of libertarian socialism focussing on an analysis of current issues.

United Kingdom : Scotland :

2201. *Counter Information.* 11 Forth Street, Edinburgh EH1. A journal that keeps activists informed of current disputes and protests. Over 20,000 distributed.

2202. *Pavlovs Dogs.* c/- Boomtown Bks., 167 King Street, Aberdeen AB2 3AE. Anti-authority journal.

United States :

2203. *The Alarm.* 1340 West Irving Park Road, Suite 122, Chicago 60613. Quarterly publication aimed at the provision of local and international news from a libertarian socialist perspective.

2204. *ALF Newsletter.* Association of Libertarian Feminists, 225 Layfayette, No 1212, New York, NY 10012. Anarcho-feminist journal.

2205. *Anarchist Labor Bulletin.* Incendiary Publications, P.O. Box 2100095, San Francisco, LA 94121-0095. An anarcho-syndicalist publication from the Anarchist Labor Network.

2206. *Anarchy: A Journal of Desire Armed.* c/- CAL, P.O. Box 1446, Columbia, MO 65205-1446. Anarchist journal with articles on contemporary issues and an extensive letter section.

2207. *Bayou La Rose.* P.O.Box 2576, San Diego, CA 92112. Anarchist journal featuring material on class, human rights and ecological issues.

2208. *Black Rose.* Box 1075, Boston, MA 02103. Anarchist quarterly.

2209. *Fifth Estate.* P.O.Box 02548, Detroit, MI 48202. A quarterly anarchist journal that has been published for over 18 years.

2210. *Gay Anarchist Circle.* P.O. Box 840, Washington DC, 20044. Gay anarchist journal.

2211. *Green Synthesis.* League for Ecological Democracy, P.O. Box 1858, San Pedro, CA 90733. An ecological magazine in which anarchist viewpoints are often expressed. It is the successor to *Synthesis.*

2212. *Greyzone.* Back Room Anarchist Bks., 2, E.27th Street, Minneapolis, MN 55408. Newsletter of the Twin Cities Anarchists.

2213. *Ideas and Action.* P.O. Box 40400, San Francisco, CA 94140. An anarcho-syndicalist publication produced by the Workers Solidarity Alliance of San Francisco.

2214. *Instead of a Magazine.* P.O. Box 433, Willimantic, CT 06226. Anarchist periodical.

2215. *Libertarian Labor Review.* Box 2824, Champaign, ILL 6/825. A journal of anarcho-syndicalist ideas and discussion.

2216. *Little Free Press.* Rt. 1, Box 102, Cushing, MN 56443. Anarchist periodical produced in Minneapolis.

2217. *Love and Rage.* P.O. Box 3, Prince Street Station, New York, NY 10012. A revolutionary anarchist news monthly written in English and Spanish.

2218. *A New World Rising.* Box 33, 77 Ives Street, Providence, RI 020906. A publication featuring 'alternative' news.

2219. *Non Violent Anarchist Newsletter.* Slough Pr., Box 1385, Austin, TX 78767.

2220. *Overthrow*. P.O. Box 392, Canal Street Station, New York, NY 10013. An anti-authoritarian publication from the Yippie Movement.

2221. *Processed World*. 37 Clementin Street, San Francisco, CA 94105. A libertarian journal produced by the Bay Area Center for Art and Technology, San Francisco.

2222. *The Seditionist*. Incendiary Publications, P.O. Box 210095, San Francisco, CA 94121-0095. Monthly anarchist journal.

2223. *Social Anarchism*. Atlantic Center for Research and Education, 2743 Maryland Ave., Baltimore, MD 21218. A semi-annual journal containing essays and articles on anarchist theory and practice.

Uruguay :

2224. *Comunidad*. Box 15128, S-10465 Stockholm, Sweden. A Spanish language anarchist journal produced by Uruguayans living in exile in Sweden.

USSR :

2225. USSR. *Yepitoe Ehamr*. A,R. 188, Neruryrag, 198303 Ukraine. Newsletter produced by Ukrainian anarchists.

Bibliographies and Other Sources of Information

2226. *100 Anos de Anarquismo em Portugal, 1887-1987*. Lisboa: Biblioteca National, 1988. A bibliography of material produced by the Portuguese anarchist movement in the last century.

2227. *AK Distribution Catalogue*. A catalogue of anarchist literature available from Anarchist Book Service, 3 Balmoral Place, Stirling, Scotland IK8 2RD.

2228. *The Anarchist Press In Britain. Part I: The Publications Of Freedom Press (1928-1976)*. London: Harvester Pr., 1979.

2229. Avakumovic, I. "Books on Anarchism and Anarchists." *Russian Review* 33,1 (1974).

2230. *CDP - Notiziario*. Pistoia: Centro di Documentazione di Pistoia, 1986. A listing of groups and journals held by the Center, dealing with anarchism, anti-nuclear movements and ecological issues. See C.D.P., C.P. 347, Via degli Orati 29, 51100 Pistoia, Italy.

2231. *Centre International de Récherches sur l'Anarchisme*. C.P. 214, CH - 1211 Geneva 13, Switzerland. A center with perhaps the most comprehensive anarchist library in the world. Issues an annual catalogue of new acquisitions.

2232. *Centro de Documentació Historico-Social Ateneu Enciclopedic Popular*. Montalegre 5, Barcelona 1, Spain. An anarchist documentation center and library.

2233. *Centrolibro*. Catania: Centrolibro, 1983. A catalogue of anarchist and libertarian publications held by Centrolibro, Vico Rao 8, 95124, Catania, Italy.

2234. Chilcote, R. H. *Brazil and Its Radical Left: An Annotated Bibliography on the Communist Movement and the Rise of Marxism, 1922-1972.* Millwood, N.Y.: Kraus International Publications, 1980.

2235. *Cultural Libertaria.* Vitoria: 1987. A catalogue of current and past anarchist literature produced as a bulletin. Available from Apto. 1687, 01080 Vitoria, Spain.

2236. Goehlert, R. "Anarchism: A Bibliography of Articles, 1900-1975." *Political Theory* 4,1 (Feb. 1976): 113-27.

2237. Laird, R. *Ad-Lib Reading Guide to Anarchism.* Collingwood, Vic.: Strawberry Pr., 1973.

2238. Lakos, A. *International Terrorism: A Bibliography.* Boulder, Colorado: Westview Pr., 1986.

2239. *Left Bank Distribution.* Seattle: 1989. An extensive directory of anarchist titles held by LBD. Apply 5241- University Way NE, Seattle, WA 98105, U.S.A.

2240. *Left Index.* Reference and Research Services 511, Lincoln St., Santa Cruz, CA 95060. Edited Joan Nordquist. A quarterly index to periodicals of the left. Back issues available.

2241. Maitron, J. "Bulletin Anarchiste 1970-1972." *Mouvement Social* 83 (1973).

2242. Lewis, A. O.. *Utopian Literature in the Pennsylvania State Universities Libraries: A Selected Bibliography.* University Park, Pa.: Pennsylvania State Universities Libraries, 1984.

2243. McElroy, W. *Liberty, 1881-1908: A Comprehensive Index.* St Paul, Minn.: M. E. Coughlin, c1982.

2244. Mickolus, E. F. *The Literature of Terrorism: A Selectively Annotated Bibliography.* Westport, Conn. & London: Greenwood Pr., 1980.

2245. Mickolus, E. F. and Flemming, P. *Terrorism 1980-1987: A Selectively Annotated Bibliography.* Westport, Conn.: Greenwood Pr., 1988.

2246. Muñoz, V. *Anarchists, a Biographical Encyclopaedia.* New York: Gordon Pr., 1980.

2247. *Nautilus.* A book list of contemporary anarchist titles produced by a Turin anarchist group. Apply to C.P. 1311, Torino 10100, Italy.

2248. Nederman, C. J. "Recent Books in Political Theory: 1977-1979." *Political Theory* 9,1 (Feb. 1981): 121-92.

2249. Nettlau, M. *Bibliographie de L'Anarchie.* Préface d'Elisée Reclus. New York: Burt Franklin, 1968. Originally published Bruxelles: 1887, subtitled "Brief History of Anarchism". Published Imola: P.Galeati, 1964 and in New York: 1968 as No. 219 in the Burt Franklin bibliography and reference series.

2250. Sherington, N. *A Handlist of Anarchist Material in the Library of the University of Stirling.* Brighton: Smoothie Pubns, 1976.

2251. Walter, N. "Anarchism in Print: Yesterday and Today. A Bibliographical Note." In *Anarchism Today*, 127-44. Op.cit., entry 1302. Reprinted from *Government and Opposition* 5,4 (1970): 523-40.

Authors, Thinkers
and Activists Index

The numbers below refer to entry numbers, not page numbers

Subject Index

The numbers below refer to entry numbers, not page numbers

About the Compiler and Editor

PAUL NURSEY-BRAY is a Senior Lecturer in Politics at the University of Adelaide, Australia. He is the editor of *Aspects of Africa's Identity* (1973) and has contributed articles to *Current Affairs Bulletin*, *Arena*, *African Affairs*, *Australian Left Review*, and the *Journal of the Historical Society of South Australia*.